# 外贸英文制单

# FOREIGN TRADE DOCUMENTATION

## （第四版）

主　编 ◎ 张爱玲

首都经济贸易大学出版社

Capital University of Economics and Business Press

· 北 京 ·

**图书在版编目（CIP）数据**

外贸英文制单 / 张爱玲主编. -- 4 版. -- 北京 ：
首都经济贸易大学出版社，2024. 6. -- ISBN 978-7
-5638-3702-1

Ⅰ. F740.44

中国国家版本馆 CIP 数据核字第 20248MF562 号

**外贸英文制单（第四版）**

张爱玲　主编

**WAIMAO YINGWEN ZHIDAN**

| | |
|---|---|
| 责任编辑 | 田玉春 |
| 封面设计 |  TEL: 010-65976003 |
| 出版发行 | 首都经济贸易大学出版社 |
| 地　　址 | 北京市朝阳区红庙（邮编 100026） |
| 电　　话 | (010)65976483　65065761　65071505(传真) |
| 网　　址 | http://www.sjmcb.com |
| E - mail | publish@cueb.edu.cn |
| 经　　销 | 全国新华书店 |
| 照　　排 | 北京砚祥志远激光照排技术有限公司 |
| 印　　刷 | 北京市泰锐印刷有限责任公司 |
| 成本尺寸 | 170 毫米×240 毫米　1/16 |
| 字　　数 | 517 千字 |
| 印　　张 | 23 |
| 版　　次 | 2010 年 1 月第 1 版　2013 年 10 月第 2 版<br>2018 年 1 月第 3 版　**2024 年 6 月第 4 版**<br>2024 年 6 月总第 7 次印刷 |
| 书　　号 | ISBN 978-7-5638-3702-1 |
| 定　　价 | 48.00 元 |

# Contents

# 目　录

# Chapter 1　Overview

【本章提要】

鉴于对外贸易的国际性和复杂性,外贸单证的作用至关重要。了解外贸单证的常见种类、基本内容,以及有关国际惯例,无论是对进出口商、贸易促进机构还是政府相关部门,都显得十分必要和重要。

在对外贸易实践中,外贸单证通常用作履约证明、物权证明、结算与融资工具等,极大促进了国际贸易的顺利、有效进行,甚至被称为对外贸易的发动机。

外贸单证贯穿于对外贸易的各个阶段。基于不同视角,外贸单证可分为进口单证/出口单证,基本单证/附加单证,金融单证/商业单证,贸易商单证/专业机构单证/官方单证,交货/运输/保险/支付/官方手续单证。

要做好外贸单证,需谨记三个 C(完整、正确、简明)和一个 T(及时)。

According to the statistics of OECD, an average overseas transaction needs 35 kinds of documents with a total of 360 copies. Trade documentation and related procedures are an important component of international trade transactions and international trade facilitation system.

One key reason is that overseas trades are international. Sellers and buyers are typically located across borders, and hence they need something to evidence the performance of their main obligations—the complying delivery of the contracted goods and the duly payment at the agreed price. Particularly in the cases of sales under FOB, CFR and CIF trade terms, the international trade is performed by symbolic delivery and documentary payment, i. e. the sellers tender the trade documents in exchange for payment from the buyers[1].

Another important reason is that overseas trades are complex. The smooth going of international trade usually demands close cooperation and effective coordination among many supporting sectors, which all demand a specific kind of document. For instance, the carrier or the freight forwarder needs a document to witness the receipt of goods, the carriage contract and the title of goods (if necessary). The insurance company needs a certificate to prove their contractual relationship with the insured. The inspection organization needs a document to certify the results of inspection. The customs authority needs a customs invoice and other related documents to clear the customs procedures. The bank, particularly under a letter of credit, needs to

---

[1]　UNCTAD secretariat. The Use of Transport Documents in International Trade. UNCTAD/SDTE/TLB,2003(03).

determine whether the documents presented by the beneficiary constitute a complying presentation and decides to honor/negotiate it or not.

Consequently, it is of great necessity for dealers to get familiar with international trade documentation, including essentials, facts, documentation techniques and tendencies, and for government agencies and international trade facilitation organizations to improve trade documents by simplification, standardization, harmonization and automation.

Although there is no substitute for practical experience, this book will provide the reader with a solid foundation on which to build further knowledge of the documentary requirements of international trade.

## 1.1　Definition

The word document originated from the Latin word documentum. It can be used as a noun, which means a piece of paper that provides an official record of something. It can also be used as a verb, which means to support (a claim) with evidence[1].

Professionally, "documents" means financial documents and/or commercial documents, where "financial documents" include bills of exchange, promissory notes, cheques, or other similar instruments used for obtaining the payment of money, and "commercial documents" include invoices, transport documents, documents of title or other similar documents, or any other documents whatsoever, not being financial documents[2].

International trade documents here refers to the generally used documents in international trade transaction, in paper or digital form. No matter what kind of payment technique is used, the delivery of the goods and the payment of the contract value are usually based on the documents relating to the transaction. They are even more important in the case of L/C payment. This book is to discuss the documents relating to letter of credit transactions, from the perspective of businessmen and banks respectively.

## 1.2　Functions

Generally, trade documents play important roles in international trade payment. Under any letter of credit, banks deal with documents but not goods, services or performance to which the

---

[1]　Collins Essential English Dictionary. 2nd Edition. HarperCollins Publishers 2004, 2006.

[2]　URC 522 (Uniform Rules for Documentary Collections, ICC Publication No. 522) Article 2. ICC (International Chamber of Commerce) is a non-profit, private international organization that works to promote and support global trade and globalization. It serves as an advocate of some world businesses in the global economy, in the interests of economic growth, job creation, and prosperity. As a global business organization, made up of member states, it helps the development of global outlooks on business matters. ICC has direct access to national governments worldwide through its national committees among others.

documents may relate[1], and the beneficiary can obtain the proceeds of goods from the bank only when the stipulated documents are duly presented to the nominated bank, to the confirming bank, or to the issuing bank and they constitute a complying presentation[2]. The significance of documents in L/C based international trade can never be overstated. Similarly, the "collection" means the handling of documents (commercial documents and financial documents)[3]. However, documents may have the following important functions in fields other than the payment.

### 1.2.1 Evidencing the Fulfillment of Obligations

Documents serve as the evidence that the exporter has fulfilled its obligations under a sales contract. The importer effects payment against the documents submitted by the exporter, for the documents describe the details of the transaction.

For example, commercial invoice, the seller's bill of sale for the goods sold, specifies type of goods, quantity and price of each type and terms of sale[4]. From the contents of commercial invoice, the buyer can determine whether the goods purchased apparently comply with the sales contract. A clean, shipped on board bill of lading implies that the seller has delivered the contracted goods on board the vessel at the port of shipment on the date or within the agreed period and in sound condition. And a certificate of origin certifies the country of origin of the merchandise required by certain foreign countries for tariff and other non-tariff purposes. Therefore, providing necessary documents are usually one of the most important obligations of the seller.

Taking CFR for instance, according to Incoterms® 2020[5], in addition to providing the goods in conformity with the contract of sale, the seller must provide the commercial invoice, the usual transport document for the agreed port of destination, export license or other official authorization, and any other evidence required by the contract. Where the seller and the buyer have agreed to communicate electronically, the document mentioned above may be replaced by an equivalent electronic data interchange (EDI) message[6].

### 1.2.2 Representing the Title to the Ownership of the Goods

As for the buyer/consignee, a document of title needs to be presented in order to obtain delivery of the goods from the carrier. This type of document provides exclusive control over the goods, that is, controlling the documents means controlling the goods. If the document is made out in negotiable form, the rights inherent in the document may be transferred by delivery of the

---

[1]  UCP 600 (Uniform Customs and Practices for Documentary Credits, ICC Publication No. 600) Article 5.
[2]  UCP 600 Article 7 and 8.
[3]  URC 522 Article 2a.
[4]  http://www.lectlaw.com/def/c062.htm.
[5]  International Rules for Interpretation of Trade Terms, ICC Publication No. 715. It took effect in the year 2020.
[6]  Incoterms® 2020, CFR: A1, A2, A4, A8, A10.

document, with any necessary endorsement[1]. In this case, the seller delivers the goods by releasing the documents, transfer the title to the goods by delivering the documents.

This role that documents play makes it possible for the seller to sell the goods in transit, for the carrier to deliver the goods to the bona fide owner of the goods; and for the banks to get involved in international trade.

### 1.2.3 Instrument of Financing

Trade documents represent the title to the ownership of the goods, and thus they allow for the trade finance in international trade practice. For example, in the case of L/C, the beneficiary may discount/negotiate the trade documents with the negotiating bank before the time of payment is due; in the case of documentary collection on D/P after sight basis, the importer may borrow the documents with a "trust receipt" from the collecting bank and improve their liquidity; in the case of open account transaction, the exporter may sell his trade documents to a factor or forfeiter without recourse, and obtain proceeds of goods sold in advance.

### 1.2.4 Facilitating International Trade

Trade documents can help identify the import and export items in terms of description, value and ownership for trade and control purposes. They allow for the tracking of cargo so that the importers and exporters know where their shipments are and when they will arrive at the final destination. Trade documents are also important evidence of goods clearance. They can be used for trade finance and payment for the goods in the case of L/C[2].

While trade documents are an integral and necessary part of international trade, trade documentation and related procedures are an important component of the trade facilitation system. Efforts have been made to simplify and improve trade documentation to facilitate international trade.

Accordingly, documents are the engine of international trade. Errorless documents, to a great extent, can facilitate the movement of goods, the transfer of goods title, the processing of payment, the customs clearance, and the healthy development of international trade.

## 1.3 Types

Using different criterion, trade documents can be categorized into different types.

### 1.3.1 Importation/Exportation Documents

According to the direction of goods movements, trade documents can be grouped into

---

[1] UNCTAD secretariat. The Use of Transport Documents in International Trade. UNCTAD/SDTE/TLB,2003(03).

[2] http://www.unescap.org/tid/publication/chap4_2224.pdf.

importation documents and exportation documents. The former includes import permit/license (if necessary), letter of credit under L/C based transaction, import customs declaration under trade terms other than DDP, etc. The latter includes export permit/license (if necessary), certificate of inspection, export customs declaration under trade terms other than EXW, commercial invoice, packing list, certificate of origin (if necessary), insurance policy under CIF and CIP trade terms, bill of exchange, etc.

### 1.3.2 Basic/Additional Documents

According to the roles that documents play in international trade, trade documents can be divided into basic documents and additional ones. Basic documents are usually required in every typical trade transaction, for instance, under CIF trade term, commercial invoices, bills of lading, insurance policies are the basic documents provided by the exporter. While additional documents are not necessarily required in every trade transaction, such as customs invoices, consular invoices, certificates of origin, certificates of inspection, etc.

### 1.3.3 Financial/Commercial Documents

According to the nature and function of documents in international trade, trade documents can be classified into financial documents and commercial documents. Financial documents refer to negotiable documents of unconditional order or unconditional promise to pay, including drafts, promissory notes, cheques, or other similar instruments in international payment. Commercial documents are usually called shipping documents, including commercial invoices, transportation documents, or other non-financial documents.

### 1.3.4 Trader/Professional Organization/Official Documents

According to the issuer of documents, trade documents can be categorized into trader's documents, professional organizations' documents, and official documents. Drafts, commercial invoices and packing lists are usually made and issued by the exporter under a sales contract. Bills of lading are usually prepared by the exporter and signed by the carrier. Insurance policies/certificates are issued by insurance company. While customs invoices, consular invoices, import/export licenses, certificates of origin, and certificates of inspection are issued by governmental institutions or NGOs.

### 1.3.5 Delivery/Transportation/ Insurance/Payment/Formality Documents

According to the international trade procedures to which the documents may relate, trade documents may be sorted into delivery documents, transportation documents, insurance documents, payment documents, and formality documents.

Specifically, delivery documents are closely related to the goods delivery, including commercial invoice, packing list, and weight list. Transportation documents evidence goods receipts, carriage contract, and title of goods sold, consisting of negotiable bill of lading, non-negotiable bill of lading, other transport documents and their electronic alternatives. Insurance documents are issued by the insurer to the insured, covering insurance policy, insurance certificate, and a declaration under an open cover. Payment documents are drafts, promissory notes and checks. Formality documents are required for the sake of formality, such as import and export permits/license, certificate of origin, certificate of inspection, customs invoice, and consular invoice.

Moreover, according to the relationship of trade documents and their status in international trade, trade documents may be labeled as original documents and derivative documents. For instance, sales contract is usually the original and underlying document of many derivative documents, including commercial invoice, and L/C.

Due to its high frequency of practical use, letter of credit itself is often regarded as one of the international trade documents.

To sum up, a document may belong to more than two types of trade documents. For example, an original clean on board bill of lading is a basic exportation document, signed by carrier as a transportation document and goods title, and it is a kind of commercial document. Hereinafter, this book will present the trade documents in detail according to the international trade procedure.

## 1.4 Quality Requirements

Trade documents with good quality are the key to effective and efficient international trade and payment. Generally, verification of the documents includes checking the following: completeness, correctness, timeliness, and conciseness.

### 1.4.1 Completeness

Completeness here has three meanings.

(1) The types of trade documents must be complete. The type requirement of trade documents depends on the specific trade term, payment term, statutory requirements, and international usual customs and practices. In addition to the basic documents, some additional documents (if necessary) must be presented completely and duly. For example, in the case of an L/C based transaction under CIF trade term, the complete set of trade documents usually include commercial invoice, bill of lading, certificate of inspection, insurance policy, bill of exchange, packing list, general certificate of origin, manufacturer's certificate, shipping advice, beneficiary's statement, GSP(generalized system of preference) certificate of origin, and certificate of shipping company.

(2) The number of documents required must be complete. Transport document must

indicate the number of originals that has been issued, "be the sole original transport document or, if issued in more than one original, be the full set as indicated on the transport document" [①]. For instance, an L/C term as "full set of 3/3 original Bill of Lading" implies that the number of the full set of original B/L is three, and the beneficiary is required to submit the original B/L in triplicate. Omitted or redundant number of documents must be avoided.

(3) The contents of trade documents must be complete. As for the financial documents, all rights and obligations of negotiable instruments must be literally determined, and thus they must be in the form of a document containing certain requisite items. For instance, a bill of exchange (B/E) must be in writing, signed by the maker or drawer, be an unconditional order to pay, state a fixed amount of money, not require any undertaking in addition to the payment of money, be payable on demand or at a definite time, and be payable to order or to bearer [②]. A B/E with one of the above-mentioned items omitted will be null. As for the commercial documents, all rights and obligations of parties concerned must subject to the contents of relevant document. For example, commercial invoice usually include the word "invoice", the invoice number, date, beneficiary's name and address, consignee's name and address, shipping mark, article number, specification, quantity, packing, unit price, total value, and the required signature. Incomplete documents will be void and not be accepted by banks.

### 1.4.2 Correctness

Correctness is the most important quality requirement for trade documentation and trade payment settlement. Correct documents are the basis of complying presentation and duly payment from the bank or the buyer. The so called correctness here has seven meanings:

- Conformity with all the terms and conditions of the sales contract.
- Conformity with all the terms and conditions of the Letter of Credit.
- Consistency of the documents.
- Consistency of the goods delivered.
- Compliance with the International Chamber of Commerce (ICC) Uniform Customs and Practice for Documentary Credits, ICC Publication No. 600 (UCP 600) and subsequent revisions.
- Compliance with the International Standard Banking Practice [e. g. International Standard Banking Practices for Documents Examinations, ICC Publication No. 821(ISBP 821) and subsequent revisions].
- Compliance with the trade rules, statutory requirements and administrative regulations of the importing/exporting countries.

---

① UCP 600 Article 19.

② UCC (Uniform Commercial Code) 3 - 104(a).

### 1.4.3 Timeliness

Timeliness of trade documents is the basic requirement of trade documentation and important guarantee of timely payment. For instance, an L/C usually stipulates time of shipment, validity of L/C, validity for presentation and negotiation. Tardy documentation may prevent from the smooth going of shipment, inspection, customs declaration, loading, shipment and payment. As for the timeliness of trade documents, there are two aspects.

(1) The documents must be dated logically. For instance, a document may be dated prior to the issuance date of the letter of credit, but must not be dated later than its date of presentation[1]; the date of commercial invoice can not be later than that of B/L and insurance policy; the date of B/L can not be earlier than the L/C stipulated earliest date of shipment, and not be later than the L/C stipulated latest time of shipment; the date of insurance policy/certificate can not be later than the date of B/L; the date of packing list should be later than the date of commercial invoice and earlier than the date of B/L; the date of certificate of origin can not be earlier than the date of commercial invoice, but not later than the date of B/L; the date of shipping advice cannot be earlier than the date of B/L.

(2) The documents must be presented to the related party in due time. A presentation including one or more original transport documents must be made by or on behalf of the beneficiary no later than 21 calendar days after the date of shipment as described in these rules, but in any event not later than the expiry date of the credit[2]. Later presentation of documents will constitute stale documents, which will not be accepted by banks, and thus payment cannot be obtained duly.

### 1.4.4 Conciseness

Conciseness of trade documents refers to simplified and clear content, standard and reasonable format, and tidy appearance. All these requirements aim at avoiding unnecessary errors and omissions, improving the quality of trade documents and thus increasing their operation efficiency.

(1) Contents simplification. For instance, the description of the goods, services or performance in a commercial invoice must correspond with that appear in the credit[3], while the description of the goods, services or performance, if stated, in documents other than the commercial invoice, may be in general terms not conflicting with their description in the credit[4].

(2) Format standardization. In order to avoid the complexities and cumbersomeness for

---

① UCP 600 Article 19.
② UCP 600 Article 14.
③ UCP 600 Article 18 (c).
④ UCP 600 Article 14(e).

traders to complete and for authorities to verify the trade documents, some standardized and harmonized document layouts are strongly recommended by some international or governmental organizations and NGOs, including the SWIFT (Society for Worldwide Inter-bank Financial Telecommunication), the ISO (International Organization for Standardization), the UN/CEFACT (United Nations Centre for the Trade Facilitation and Electronic Business), the UNTD-ED (United Nations Trade Data Elements Directory), the UN/EDIFACT (United Nations Electronic Data Interchange for Administration, Commerce and Transport), and the SITPRO of U. K. , etc. [1]Moreover, some international usual customs and practices as UCP 600, ISBP 821 for UCP 600, URC 522, Incoterms® 2020 and the like may provide useful governance for trade documents completion and verification.

(3) Appearance tidiness. A tidy-looking document may indicate the precise working style of the document makers, the professional image and high efficiency of the company. In order to guarantee the tidiness of the documents, some international standards mentioned above should be adopted. Furthermore, some unnecessary corrections and alterations must be precluded. However, you can make some necessary corrections and alterations with authentication. For instance, if there are any corrections and alterations need to be made on a draft, they must have been authenticated by the drawer. It is worthy of noting that, in some countries a draft showing corrections or alterations will not be acceptable even with the drawer's authentication. Issuing banks in such countries should make a statement in the credit to the effect that no correction or alteration should appear in the draft[2]. Similarly, corrections and alterations on a bill of lading must be authenticated. Such authentication should be made by the carrier, master (captain) or any of their agents (if different from the agent issued/signed it), provided that they are identified as an agent of the carrier or the master (captain). Non-negotiable copies of bills of lading do not need to include any signature or authentication when there is alteration or correction made on the original[3].

## 1.5   Key Documents and Procedures Involved in International Trade

### 1.5.1   Registration

In most countries, the company engaged in imports and exports is required to register[4]

---

[1]   UNCTAD Trust Fund for Trade Facilitation Negotiations Technical Note No. 13, Simplification of Trade Documentation using International Standards.

[2]   ISBP 821 for UCP 600 Article 55-56.

[3]   ISBP 821 for UCP 600 Article 109-110.

[4]   There are professional agency specializing the registration for charging commissions.

with a government authority such as the Ministry of Commerce or the Registry of Companies[1].

Generally the registration has three important functions: to identify the importing and exporting companies; to collect their trade statistics; and to exercise some control over their activities. In order to reduce the costs of starting an import/export business and facilitate trade, most countries including China have been making efforts to simplify the procedure of the registration.

A digital or paper application form of registration is firstly required to complete by the company. The application form typically require the following information: name and address of company; date of incorporation; authorized and paid up capital; particulars of shareholders and shareholding; business activity of company; name and address of auditors; names of key officers.

In China, the last two items, name and address of auditors and names of key officers, are usually not required. However, the name and address of company must be filled bilingually, both in Chinese and English; the authorized and paid up capital should be in terms of both Chinese Yuan (CNY) and United States Dollar (USD); and the number of the effective identification certificate of the company's representative is required.

After registration, each company will obtain a personal and unique registration number from the authority agency. This unique number is for all its future transactions with various government agencies for trade documentation purposes.

In practice, a company may misuse the registration number of another company for its trade documents such as customs permits, import and export permits, licenses and certificates of origin. However, a company should always keep the following points in mind.

● The registration number is not transferable. A company should not use the registration number of another for its own import and export purpose.

● Duly notification of information change is required. When there is any change in the particulars of the application form, such as the change of address and directors, the company should inform the agency issuing registration number in due time.

● A bank guarantee may be provided. Where the registration number is to be used to import dutiable goods, the Customs and Excise Department may require a bank guarantee to be lodged before it allows the registration number to be used to import and export goods.

● Penalties will be imposed on those who misused the registration number.

## 1.5.2 Import and Export Permits

As their names implied, export/import permits are permits to export/import issued by an authority permit officer. In some cases, export/import permits are interchangeably used with such terminologies as customs declaration, bills of export/import or shipping bills[2].

---

[1]  http://iecms. ec. com. cn/iecms/index. jsp.

[2]  http://www. unescap. org/tid/publication/chap4_2224. pdf, improving trade documentation.

The major functions of export/import permits are listed as below:

• To ensure that an individual or organization intending to export/import goods conform to the export/import specifications and compliance with the provisions of international agreements[1].

• To serve as an instrument of control by the governmental agencies. Specifically, they can be used to help customs and other relevant authorities to identify and clear the goods, and to control the outflow/inflow of goods of strategic nature or of smuggled and stolen goods. Hence, effective import and export permits should allow quick and accurate identification[2] of the goods.

• To enforce the health, safety, security and other environmental requirements. For example, food imported must be tested by the relevant Ministry to ensure that they are fit for human consumption. Again, trade with certain countries may be banned because of political or security reasons.

• To help the Department of Statistics and the relevant agencies to compile trade statistics[3]. It can not only provide data on the trade flows to the government and the private sector, but also inform trade and customs enforcement units of the pattern of its bilateral trade. By collecting and analyzing the reliable and efficient trade data, enforcement officers can monitor trade flows, detect any irregularities in trade patterns, and develop a risk management system to determine non-compliance of trade laws.

In practice, the export/import permits usually involve the following key documents, procedures, parties and agencies:

• With the export permit, the freight forwarder will exchange for the shipping order and be able to lodge the goods with the shipping agency for export.

• When the goods are loaded on board the vessel, the ship's captain will issue a mate's receipt.

• The freight forwarder will exchange the mate's receipt with the shipping agency for the bill of lading as evidence that the goods have been shipped, and the title of goods.

• With the bill of lading, the exporter will be able to negotiate with the bank for payment of the goods against the letter of credit.

---

① For instance, export and import of endangered wild animals, plants and their products.

② Identification should be based on the HS codes and should distinguish between dutiable and non-dutiable goods and controlled and non-controlled goods.

③ For instances, in Hong Kong, China, the Import and Export (Registration) Regulations, Chapter 60, require traders to lodge with the Hong Kong, China, Customs and Excise Department an import/export declaration within 14 days after the importation/exportation of the goods. To ensure accurate collection of trade statistics, the Commissioner of Customs and Excise Department authorizes specific officers of the Census and Statistics Department to enforce the regulations relating to the lodgment of accurate and complete import/export declarations.

- With the import permit, the freight forwarder will exchange with the shipping agencies for the delivery order.

- With the delivery order, the freight forwarder will be able to obtain the release of the goods from the port authority for delivery to the importer.

The flow of application process of the import and export permits usually involves several parties and agencies. Specifically, the importer, exporter or freight forwarder (the declarant) prepare and submit his inward or outward declarations application to the relevant agency such as the Customs and Excise Department[1], Ministry of Health or the Ministry of Environment for processing and approval.

In general, for non-dutiable and non-controlled goods, the processing and approval of the import and export permits is quite simple. However, for dutiable or controlled goods, additional steps are required. The same applies to goods subject to quota control, such as textiles and garments exported to the quota countries.

A simple schema on the flow of import and export permits is shown in figure 1. 1[2].

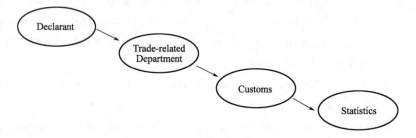

**Figure 1. 1   Import and export permits flow (simplified)**

### 1.5.3   Certificate of Origin

(1) Rules of origin. Given today's growing trade in raw material and intermediate inputs, it is a more complex task to determine the origin status of a finished product. Appropriate Rules of Origin (ROs) are thus required.

Usually, the ROs are the rules of determining the origin of the product. The ROs may be based on the percentage criterion or the process criterion, and vary according to the importing country's scheme of preference. They can be classified into Non-preferential Rules of Origin and Preferential Rules of Origin. Non-preferential rules of origin are merely used to determine the origin status of the goods. It does not confer any tariff benefits for the goods, but applies in

---

① If duty is payable for imports, the Customs and Excise Department will require that payment be made before the permit is approved.

② http://www. unescap. org/tid/publication/chap4_2224. pdf, improving trade documentation.

the cases of tariffs for quota control, anti-dumping measures and satisfies the needs of the buyer for an originating product. And preferential rules of origin are used to determine which goods enter a country under preferential treatment, i. e. they are used to establish whether the goods are eligible for special treatment under a trading arrangement between two or more economies. Preferential tariffs at zero or reduced rates of duty are applied to goods that are the products or manufacture of a preference or recipient country. The principal objective of preferential rules of origin is to ensure that benefits of the donor country are restricted to only those selected trading partners that qualify.

(2) Certificate of origin and related procedures. A certificate of origin (CO) certifies that the products being exported originate and are manufactured in the country of the seller. It is an essential document in international trade required for duty and import control purposes.

With the CO, the importer is assured that the products being purchased indeed originate and are manufactured in the country of the exporter. Importing countries consider the origin of imported goods when determining the duty assessed on the goods imported and their original status. Some imports are given preferential access. Other considerations are whether the goods imported are subject to quota and whether the goods come from an embargoed nation. In this case, the goods will not be allowed entry.

The CO issuing unit will register the manufacturers and set up a system to ensure that the manufacturers comply with the ROs. The unit will inspect and verify that the manufacturer has the necessary machinery and manpower to make the products and that it maintains proper records as stipulated under CO issuing regulations. For textiles and garments, the unit will also verify that the manufacturer's products meet the processing criteria of quota countries. Before a CO can be issued, a manufacturer is required to submit a Manufacturing Cost Statement for each product. This is to confirm that product complies with the ROs.

To facilitate trade and for effective administration of the COs system, the relevant ministry may authorize organizations such as the Chambers of Commerce or Trade Associations (or authorized organizations) to issue non-preferential certificates of origin. In this way, the exporters may choose the organizations to obtain the COs for their convenience. In issuing the COs, the authorized organizations are subject to the same Regulations and are required to exercise due diligence to ensure the COs is properly issued.

### 1.5.4 Procedures and documents flow of typical transaction

To summarize, the documents required and procedures involved in international trade depend on the terms and conditions of sales contract, letter of credit, statutory regulations of importing/exporting country, and usual customs and practices. Besides some key steps and procedures in import/export preparation, business negotiation, Figure 1.2 and 1.3 show us a general picture of

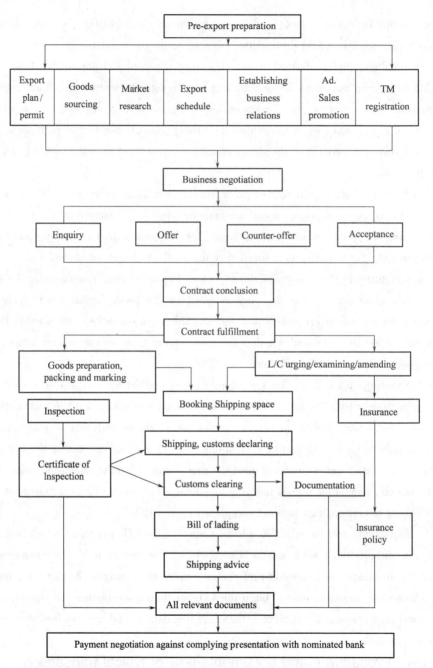

**Figure 1. 2   Flow of documents and procedures of a typical L/C based exporting under CIF**

procedures and documents flow of typical export (L/C based trade under CIF trade term and seaway transportation) and import transaction (L/C based trade under FOB trade term and seaway transportation) respectively.

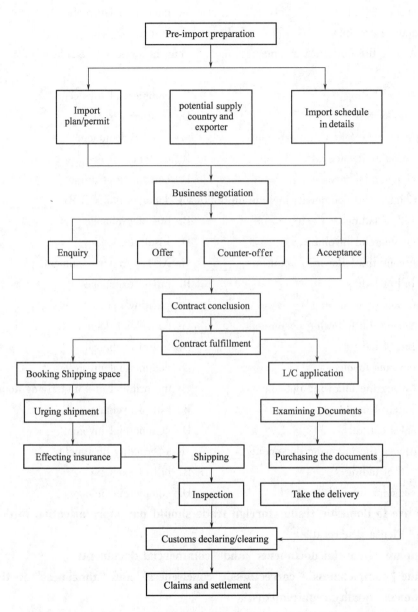

**Figure 1.3　Flow of documents and procedures of a typical L/C based importing under FOB**

## Questions and Problems

### I . Choose the best answer to fill in the blank.

1. Among the following documents, the buyer can determine from_____whether the goods purchased apparently comply with the purchase contract.

A. bill of lading                B. commercial invoice

C. letter of credit                D. insurance policy

2. Among the following documents,_____ can be used as the title to the ownership of the goods sold.

A. bill of lading                B. commercial invoice

C. seaway bill                 D. insurance policy

3. Among the following documents,_____ is a basic document.

A. consular invoice            B. customs invoice

C. commercial invoice         D. certificate of origin

4. Commercial documents include the following documents EXCEPT_____.

A. bill of lading                B. bill of exchange

C. commercial invoice         D. insurance policy

5. Among the following documents,_____ is NOT a trader document.

A. bill of lading                B. bill of exchange

C. commercial invoice         D. packing list

6. Among the following documents,_____ is an official document.

A. bill of lading                B. bill of exchange

C. customs invoice            D. commercial invoice

7. Among the following documents,_____ is the original and underlying document.

A. letter of credit                B. bill of exchange

C. sales contract               D. commercial invoice

8. Among the following documents,_____ is a formality document.

A. bill of lading                B. bill of exchange

C. consular invoice            D. commercial invoice

II. **Relative to domestic trade, foreign trade should pay more attention to documentation. Please discuss it.**

III. **Compare "financial documents" and "commercial documents".**

IV. **Define "completeness" "correctness" "conciseness" and "timeliness" in the case of documents quality requirements.**

# Chapter 2　International Contract of Sale

## 【本章提要】

相比较国内贸易,对外贸易伙伴之间的商业文化、习俗和语言差异显著,因此,买卖双方签订一份正式的载明双方一致意思的详尽的书面合同,显得更为必要和重要。

基于不同视角,外贸合同可分为进口/出口合同,明示/默示合同,格式合同,双边/单边合同,装运/到达合同等。

合同成立必须经过要约和接受两个阶段,必要时还会经过要约邀请和反要约。因此,买卖双方必须理解要约邀请和要约的区别,能根据要约的生效、撤回与撤销条件,及要约的变更等来判断要约的效力,能根据有效接受的构成条件判定双方契约关系的成立等。只有正确理解贸易伙伴的真实意图,才能有效促进交易的达成和合同的顺利履行。

合同履行中一旦出现一方违约,另一方可根据适用法律和国际惯例、合同条款和违约程度,主张适当的损害赔偿权利。由于国与国之间有关合同的法律和惯例各有不同,进出口双方需要在合同中明确规定适用的法律和国际惯例。

合同内容事关买卖双方切身利益,合同条款要在遵循适用法律和国际惯例的前提下,尽可能做到完整、准确,做到合同条款之间不矛盾、不冲突。一项有效的国际货物销售合同一般应包括:品质条款、价格条款、支付条款、数量条款、包装条款、违约条款、不可抗力条款等。

另外,随着电子商务的日益流行,贸易双方有必要及时了解有关电子商务的法律和国际惯例。

Different countries have different business cultures and even languages. In order to minimize the risk of misunderstandings, it is advisable for the importer and the exporter to have a clear written formal understanding, that is, an international contract of sale in writing.

This chapter covers the essentials of contracts in international transactions, containing the definition, the types, the formation and creation, the contents, the breach of contract and remedies, and the relevant governing laws and usual practices.

## 2.1　Definitions

A contract is an exchange of promises between two or more parties to do or refrain from doing an act which is enforceable in a court of law[1].

According to legal scholar Sir John William Salmond, a contract is "an agreement creating and defining the obligations between two or more parties".

A sales contract is a formal contract by which a seller agrees to sell and a buyer agrees to buy, under certain terms and conditions spelled out in writing in the document signed by both parties. It can also be called agreement of sale, contract for sale, sale agreement, or sale contract[2]. When the buyer and the seller are located across borders, the sales contract becomes an international contract of sale.

The significance of sales contract lies in many aspects.

Firstly, it identifies what is being sold to whom and for how much, and thus defines the most important obligations of both the seller and the buyer.

Secondly, it takes into account the specific terms and conditions of sale (such as delivery dates, currency and payment terms), and constitutes the most important underlying and original document for the derivative documents (such as letter of credit, commercial invoice, transportation document). Consequently, sales contract acts as the cornerstone for both the international trade transaction and this particular book titled "Foreign Trade Documentation".

Finally, it stipulates the country under whose law the contract is governed. This is particularly important for international trade contracts.

## 2.2 Governing Laws and Usual Practices

There are quite a lot of laws and usual practices governing international contract of sale.

### 2.2.1 UNCISG (1980)

The UNCISG[3] was established in 1980 and recognizes the rules for commercial contracts. It establishes uniform-rules for drafting international sales contracts, and sets the legal rights and obligations of the seller and the buyer under such contracts. the UNCISG rules apply automatically to the sales contracts between the countries having ratified the convention.

The majority of international trade contracts are governed by the UNCISG. As of July 2008, the UNCISG had been ratified by 71 countries that account for a significant proportion of world trade, making it one of the most successful international uniform laws[4]. Unless they specify that UNCISG rules do not apply, exporters and importers from signatory countries are

---

① http://en. wikipedia. org/wiki/Contract.

② http://www. businessdictionary. com/definition/contract-of-sale. html.

③ The United Nations Commission on International Trade Law (UNCITRAL) Convention on Contracts for the International Sale of Goods (1980).

④ Outlined in 2. 4-2. 7 are some of the very basic principles of international contract law, which will provide a useful foundation for further reading.

bound by the Convention's terms.

## 2.2.2 ICC Incoterms

The contract should set out where the goods is to be delivered, who arranges transport, who is responsible for insuring the goods, who pays for insurance, who handles customs procedures, and who pays any duties and taxes. To avoid confusion and transaction cost, ICC Incoterms® 2020 should be used.

ICC Incoterms (International Rules for the Interpretation of Trade Terms by International Chamber of Commerce) is internationally agreed standard trade terms. Since 1936, Incoterms has been revised eight times (1953, 1967, 1976, 1980, 1990, 2000, 2010, and 2020). The latest edition, Incoterms® 2020, contains 4 groups, 11 trade terms in total, features an in-depth introduction to help users select the appropriate Incoterms rule for their sale transaction.

Incoterms® 2020 incorporates expanded explanatory notes for users at the start of each Incoterms® rule and assist users with accurately interpreting the latest edition of the Incoterms rules to avoid costly misinterpretations or misapplications. On the release of Incoterms® 2020, ICC Secretary General John W. H. Denton AO said: "Incoterms® 2020 rules make business work for everyone by facilitating trillions of dollars in global trade annually. Because they help importers and exporters around the world to understand their responsibilities and avoid costly misunderstandings, the rules form the language of international sales transactions, and help build confidence in our valuable global trading system." ①

To be noted, various versions of Incoterms are parallel. However, the later edition usually has more detailed agreements and explanations than the earlier one. It is thus recommended to use the new edition of Incoterms, and to include the edition number when signing the contract so as to avoid any disagreements or misinterpretation.

## 2.2.3 Others

In addition to the UNCISG 1980 and ICC Incoterms® 2020, the following laws and related international trade usual customs and practices may be applicable to the import/export contracts with China:

● The Contract Law of the People's Republic of China, March 15, 1999 (Chapter 1 to Chapter 9, Chapter 18 Technology Contract).

● The Uniform Commercial Code (UCC) (Article 2) in most United States and Canadian jurisdictions.

● Sale of Goods Act (1979) and English contract law in England, Wales, and other

---

① https://iccwbo.org/news-publications/news/icc-releases-incoterms-2020/.

countries across the Commonwealth.

- ICC Uniform Customs and Practice for Documentary Credit, 2006 Revision, in force on July 1, 2007 (UCP 600).
- Institute Cargo Clauses (ICC) by U. K.
- China Insurance Clauses (CIC) by PICC.
- Uniform Rules for Collection by ICC (URC 522), etc.

## 2.3 Types

There are various kinds of sales contract (S/C). Different type of S/C implies different obligations to different parties concerned, applies to different contract laws, involves different procedures of operation, determines different modes of payment, and requires different kinds of trade documents. It is thus important for the involved parties to understand the frequently used types of S/C.

### 2.3.1 Import/Export Contract

According to the flow direction of the contracted subject goods, S/C may be grouped into import contract and export contract. The former is also called purchase contract, while the latter is often called sales contract. They are actually of the same contents and formats, but of different perspectives.

### 2.3.2 Verbal/Non-verbal Contract

According to the formality of contract conclusion and evidence, S/C may be classified into verbal contract and non-verbal contract.

Any contract that uses words, spoken or written, is a verbal contract. Thus, all oral contracts and written contracts are verbal contracts. This is in contrast to a "non-verbal contract", also known as "a contract implied by the acts of the parties", which can be either implied in fact or implied in law.

According to the UNCISG article 11, a contract of sale need not necessarily be concluded in or evidenced by writing and is not subject to any other requirement as to form. It may be proved by any means, including witnesses.

However, as one of the contracting parties of the UNCISG, China insisted that all the contracts concluded with China be in written form and that they be applicable to only the contracts concluded between the parties of the different signatories in their places of operation. The terminology "writing" here includes letter, fax, e-mail, telegram, telex, and EDI.

### 2.3.3 Standard form Contract

A standard form contract (sometimes referred to as an adhesion contract or boilerplate contract) is a contract between two parties that does not allow for negotiation, i. e. take it or leave it[1]. It is often a contract concluded between unequal bargaining partners.

In international trade, difficulties may arise when both the exporter and the importer have standard form contract and try to gain the upper hand. This is often referred to as the "battle of the forms" and the two parties must negotiate to agree on common ground and the exact terms that will constitute the contract.

As international contracts of sale tend to rely on the exchange of a lot of paperwork and most of these documentations are prepared by the seller, the exporter is advised to prepare some standard terms and conditions of sale that can be incorporated into the documentation in addition to the specific terms of the contract. The exporter is recommended to set out clearly the standard terms and conditions and attach them to all documentation sent out to the importer, and to ask the importer to sign and return a copy of the terms and conditions to acknowledge them and agree to their incorporation in the contract. Once the terms and conditions have been agreed, the contract can be formed and signed.

### 2.3.4 Bilateral/Unilateral Contract

Contracts may be bilateral or unilateral. A bilateral contract, the more common of the two, is an agreement in which each of the parties to the contract makes a promise or promises to the other party. International contract of sale is a typical bilateral contract, including the exporter and the importer.

A unilateral contract is an agreement in which one party to the contract makes a promise or promises to another party. The most common type of unilateral contract is the insurance contract, in which the insurance company promises to pay the insured a stated amount of money if a covered event occurs for which the insured paid premiums.

### 2.3.5 Shipment/Arrival Contract

According to the delivery terms used and the nature of the sales contract, S/C can be divided into shipment contract and arrival contract. Shipment contract is usually based on such trade terms as FAS, FOB, FCA,CFR, CIF, CPT and CIP, while arrival contract is based on such trade terms as DAP,DAT,DDU, DDP.

Under shipment contract, the seller is bound to pay the normal transport cost for the carriage of the goods by a usual route and in a customary manner to the agreed place, while the buyer is responsible for the risk of loss of or damage to the goods and additional costs resulting from events occurring subsequent to shipment and dispatch.

Under arrival contracts, the seller would bear all risks and costs until the goods have actually arrived at the agreed point.

---

[1] http://en. wikipedia. org/wiki/Standard_form_contract.

Moreover, in practice of international trade, S/C may take the form of informal contract, including sales confirmation, sales agreement, memorandum, order from the buyer, or intent from the agent of the buyer. If material terms and conditions of potential transaction are stated in the informal contracts, unconditionally agreed upon by the seller and the buyer, and counter-signed by them, the informal contracts are of same legal effects as formal contracts.

In international trade, the most commonly used type of S/C is bilateral shipment contract in writing, with standard terms and conditions incorporated.

## 2.4　Formation of Contract

Formation of a contract may contain several steps. Every sales contract contains an offer, and an acceptance. Some sales contract contains an invitation to make offers[1], and a counter-offer.

### 2.4.1　Invitation to Make Offers

In the UNCISG (article 14), a proposal which is not addressed to one or more specific persons is to be considered merely as an invitation to make offers, unless the contrary is clearly indicated by the person making the proposal.

An invitation to make offers is an action by one party which may appear to be a contractual offer but which is actually inviting others to make an offer of their own. It may be regarded as a request for expressions of interest.

For instance, promotional brochures and other forms of advertising where goods are marketed to potential buyers are usually considered an "invitation to make offers". That is to say, the promotional materials are designed to generate enquiries from which an offer may subsequently be made and consequently they cannot be used as the basis of a contract.

### 2.4.2　Offer

Offer is required by every sales contract. In the UNCISG (article 14), a proposal for concluding a contract addressed to one or more specific persons constitutes an offer if it is sufficiently definite and indicates the intention of the offeror to be bound in case of acceptance.

(1) Sufficiently definite contents. A proposal is sufficiently definite if it indicates the goods and expressly or implicitly fixes or makes provision for determining the quantity and the price.

Specifically, an offer sets out clearly the nature of the goods to be sold and the monetary value that the seller expects to receive for them. The offer must contain details of the type, quantity and quality of the goods to be sold, and may also include a description to the

---

[1]　It is called invitation to treat in the U. K. , and invitation to bargain in the U. S.

component parts to demonstrate "origin" or to comply with the buyer's specific requirements.

When stating the price of the goods in the offer, the exporter should explain how the price has been reached and in which currency it is listed, as well as setting out the invoicing and payment terms. Reference to the Incoterm① to be used in the contract should also be made at this stage in order to clarify which party will be responsible for the shipping, insurance and other costs.

Ideally, the offer should also contain details of the method of transportation, the ports of shipment and destination and the delivery dates at each location. It must be stated clearly as well which party is to bear the responsibility for organizing the carriers.

In summary, the offer should contain every conceivable detail of the transaction in an unambiguous way so that the terms are instantly understandable to the buyer.

(2) Reaching rule. Contrary to the Mail Box Rule in the common law of contracts, the UNCISG insists on the Reaching Rule. That is, an offer becomes effective when it reaches the offeree. Here "reaches" means the offer reaches the addressee when it is made orally to the offeree or delivered by any other means to him personally, to his place of business or mailing address or, if he does not have a place of business or mailing address, to his habitual residence (UNCISG article 15, 24).

(3) Withdrawal, revocation and termination. Even if it is irrevocable, an offer may be withdrawn if the withdrawal reaches the offeree before or at the same time as the offer. However, the e-commerce makes it impossible and constitutes a challenge for the traditional contract law.

Until a contract is concluded an offer may be revoked if the revocation reaches the offeree before he has dispatched an acceptance. However, an offer cannot be revoked: (a) if it indicates, whether by stating a fixed time for acceptance or otherwise, that it is irrevocable; (b) if it was reasonable for the offeree to rely on the offer as being irrevocable and the offeree has acted in reliance on the offer.

An offer, even if it is irrevocable, is terminated when a rejection reaches the offeror, or when the stated validity in the offer is overdue.

(4) Defining irrevocable. Despite of the fact that the UNCISG use the term "irrevocable" in several cases, it does not define it in detail. Alternatively, the UCC ( § 2-205) states the requirements for a firm and irrevocable offer as follows:

- It is an offer to buy or sell goods.
- It is made by a merchant.
- It is a signed writing ("authenticated record" instead in the new version of UCC).

①   See appendix, sales contract specimen 1, A3.

● It states a no-longer-than-three-months period of irrevocability.

### 2.4.3 Counter-offer

Once the offer is made by the seller to the buyer, one of three scenarios may occur: (a) the offer may be accepted and the contract agreed[①]; (b) the offer may be rejected for whatever reasons the buyer may have; or (c) the offer may be agreed in principle but modified with further terms, conditions or qualifying statements by the buyer. The third scenario is considered to be a counter-offer of the original offer.

In the common law of contracts, the Mirror Image Rule states that an offer must be accepted exactly without modifications. An attempt to accept the offer on different terms instead creates a counter-offer, and this constitutes a rejection of the original offer[②].

In the UNCISG (article 19), a reply to an offer which purports to be an acceptance but contains additions, limitations or other modifications is a rejection of the offer and constitutes a counter-offer. However, only material alterations to the original offer constitute a counter-offer. Among other things, additional or different terms relating to the price, payment, quality and quantity of the goods, place and time of delivery, extent of one party's liability to the other or the settlement of disputes are considered to alter the terms of the offer materially.

A counter-offer can be considered a new offer. Responsibility is then passed back to the exporter, who must decide whether or not to accept the counter-offer or to insist that the original offer is the only one under consideration. The battle of the forms then begins, with both sides negotiating the exact terms and conditions of the contract.

Alternatively, the exporter may decide to accept the counter-offer but should do so only when wholly aware of all the financial and legal obligations contained in the new offer.

### 2.4.4 Acceptance

Every S/C has an acceptance. An effective acceptance of the offer commits both the seller and the buyer to the specific terms of the sale and forms a legally binding contract that cannot be amended unless the two parties agree in writing.

(1) Effective acceptance. An effective acceptance has some characteristics:

● An effective acceptance should be made by the person (the offeree) to whom the offer was made.

● An effective acceptance should refer to the terms of the offer and indicate assent to the offer by a statement or by other conduct. Since silence or inactivity does not in itself amount to acceptance (UNCISG article 18, 23).

However, if, by virtue of the offer or as a result of practices which the parties have estab-

---

① See 2.4.4 for details.
② Source: Wikipedia, the free encyclopedia.

lished between themselves or of usage, the offeree may indicate assent by performing an act, such as one relating to the dispatch of the goods or payment of the price, without notice to the offeror, the acceptance is effective at the moment the act is performed, provided that the act is performed within the stated or reasonable period of time. This does not apply in China.

- An effective acceptance should reach the offeror within the stated time or within a reasonable time.

An acceptance of an offer becomes effective at the moment the indication of assent reaches the offeror. Same as the case of an offer, the declaration of acceptance must "reach" the addressee when it is made orally to the offeror or delivered by any other means to him personally, to his place of business or mailing address or, if he does not have a place of business or mailing address, to his habitual residence.

An acceptance is not effective if the indication of assent does not reach the offeror within the time he has fixed or, if no time is fixed, within a reasonable time, due account being taken of the circumstances of the transaction, including the rapidity of the means of communication employed by the offeror. An oral offer must be accepted immediately unless the circumstances indicate otherwise.

(2) Validity for acceptance. A period of time for acceptance may be fixed by the offeror in a telegram or a letter. Here the validity for acceptance begins to run from the moment the telegram is handed in for dispatch or from the date shown on the letter or, if no such date is shown, from the date shown on the envelope.

A period of time for acceptance may also be fixed by the offeror by telephone, telex or other means of instantaneous communication. And the validity for acceptance begins to run from the moment that the offer reaches the offeree.

Official holidays or non-business days occurring during the period for acceptance are included in calculating the period. However, if a notice of acceptance cannot be delivered at the address of the offeror on the last day of the period because that day falls on an official holiday or a non-business day at the place of business of the offeror, the period is extended until the first business day which follows (UNCISG article 20).

(3) Conditional acceptance. A reply to an offer which purports to be an acceptance but contains additional or different terms which do not materially alter the terms of the offer constitutes an acceptance, unless the offeror, without undue delay, objects orally to the discrepancy or dispatches a notice to that effect. If he does not so object, the terms of the contract are the terms of the offer with the modifications contained in the acceptance (UNCISG article 19).

(4) Late acceptance. A late acceptance is nevertheless effective as an acceptance if without delay the offeror orally so informs the offeree or dispatches a notice to that effect.

If a letter or other writing containing a late acceptance shows that it has been sent in such circumstances that if its transmission had been normal it would have reached the offeror in due time, the late acceptance is effective as an acceptance unless, without delay, the offeror orally informs the offeree that he considers his offer as having lapsed or dispatches a notice to that effect ( UNCISG article 21).

(5) Withdrawal of acceptance. An acceptance may be withdrawn if the withdrawal reaches the offeror before or at the same time as the acceptance would have become effective ( UNCISG article 22). However, the e-commerce makes it more difficult and constitutes a challenge for the traditional contract law.

Although offers can be accepted verbally, orally or in writing, the acceptance should be made in writing to provide both the buyer and seller with the security of having documented proof of the contract.

A contract is concluded at the moment when an acceptance of an offer becomes effective, even though a formal contract in writing is not yet signed.

## 2.5  Breach of Contract

As acceptance of the offer creates a legally binding contract, the agreed terms and conditions must be fulfilled if the contract is not to be breached.

Breach of contract is a legal concept in which a binding agreement or bargained-for exchange is not honored by one or more of the parties to the contract by non-performance or interference with the other party's performance[1].

Different laws of contract define breach of contract into different types. According to the U. S. law of contracts, breach of contract may be minor breach or material breach. According to the U. K. common law of contracts, breach of contract may be breach of warranty and breach of condition. According to the UNCISG, breach of contract may be non-fundamental breach of contract and fundamental breach of contract.

Breach of contract occurs either unintentionally or deliberately. If it is apparent that one of the parties to the contract has no intention of meeting their obligations, this is seen as a deliberate breach of contract and may be considered theft or fraud, which will go beyond the control of contract law. If it occurs unintentionally, the injured party may claim different remedies based on different circumstances.

### 2.5.1  Circumstances

As for the seller and the buyer, a contract may be breached under different circumstances.

---

① http://en. wikipedia. org/wiki/Breach_of_contract.

(1) Seller's breach of contract. The seller must deliver the goods, hand over any related documents and transfer the property in the goods, as required by the contract and the UNCISG. However, the seller may fail to perform any of his obligations under the circumstances listed below:

- Non-delivery of goods.
- Late delivery of goods.
- Non-complying delivery of goods (in quality, quantity, packing, or a third party related industrial property or other intellectual property).
- Non-complying delivery of documents.
- Non-performance of shipment liability when the contract requires (e. g. under group C trade terms).
- Non-performance of insurance liability when the contract requires (e. g. under CIF or CIP trade terms).

(2) Buyer's breach of contract. The buyer must pay the price for the goods and take delivery of them as required by the contract and the UNCISG. However, the buyer may fail to perform any of his obligations under the following circumstances:

- Reject to pick up goods.
- Reject to make payment.
- Non-performance of relevant liabilities under specified terms of delivery (e. g. shipment arrangement under FOB).
- Non-performance of relevant liabilities under specified mode of payment (e. g. duly establishment of L/C).

## 2.5.2 Remedies

As regards the remedies, there are different legal recourses for different parties in different situations.

(1) Remedies for breach of contract by the seller. According to the UNCISG①, in the case of the seller's breach of contract, the buyer may claim remedies as listed below:

- Require specific performance by the seller of his obligations.
- Require delivery of substitute goods only if the lack of conformity constitutes a fundamental breach of contract.
- Require the seller to remedy the lack of conformity by repair.
- Claim liquidated damages of a specific percentage of the price of such goods or a specific amount.

---

① See article 45-52 for details.

• Reduce the price when the goods do not conform to the contract, and no other remedies are made by the seller.

• Declare the contract avoided if the failure to make delivery completely or in conformity with the contract amounts to a fundamental breach of the contract. A breach of contract committed by one of the parties is fundamental if it results in such detriment to the other party as to deprive him substantially of what he is entitled to expect under the contract, unless the party in breach did not foresee and a reasonable person of the same kind in the same circumstances would not have foreseen such a result (UNCISG article 29).

(2) Remedies for breach of contract by the buyer. According to the UNCISG[1], in the case of the buyer's breach of contract, the seller may claim the following remedies:

• Require the buyer to pay the price, take delivery or perform his other obligations, unless the seller has resorted to a remedy which is inconsistent with this requirement.

• Claim damages for delay in performance.

• Declare the contract avoided if the failure by the buyer to perform any of his obligations amounts to a fundamental breach of contract, or if the buyer does not perform his obligation to pay the price or take delivery of the goods within the additional period of time fixed by the seller, or if he declares that he will not do so within the period so fixed. Usually, in cases where the buyer has paid the price, the seller loses the right to declare the contract avoided.

To avoid the above-mentioned potential breach of contract and subsequent troubles and difficulties, both the seller and the buyer thus strongly demand a complete and very detailed sales contract in written form, stipulating their specific obligations, binding their performances, and providing contingent alternatives for the potential breach of contract.

## 2.6　Contents

Despite of the varied models and different wordings of sales contract, their contents are quite similar. Several commonly used specimens of sales contract are introduced in this section.

### 2.6.1　ICC Model International Sales Contract

ICC Model International Sales Contract (Manufactured Goods for Resale) is a flexible and clear model contract providing directions to sellers and buyers of manufactured goods. It allows users either to incorporate only the general conditions or to include the specific conditions, which set out standard terms common to all contracts with the ICC General Conditions of Sale.

---

① See article 61-65 for details.

ICC Model International Sales Contract consists of two parts, specific conditions (Part A) and general conditions (Part B).

(1)Part A. Specific Conditions. These specific conditions have been prepared in order to permit the parties to agree with the particular terms of their sales contract by completing the spaces left open or choosing (as the case may be) between the alternatives provided in this document. It is quite easy-to-use for first-time traders.

In addition to the detailed information of the contract itself (name and address of the seller and the buyer; contract number, date and place of signing contract), there are 16 specific conditions (A1~A16):

A1    Goods sold: description of the goods.

A2    Contract price: including currency, amount in numbers and amount in letters.

A3    Delivery terms: 11 terms (according to Incoterms® 2020) are recommended, and carrier related information.

A4    Time of delivery: the date or period (e. g. week or month) on which or within which the seller must perform his delivery obligations according to clause A4 of the respective Incoterm.

A5    Inspection of the goods by buyer: time and place.

A6    Retention of title.

A7    Payment conditions: four alternatives provided, covering payment on open account, payment in advance, documentary collection, and irrevocable documentary credit. In the case of open account, the most risky mode of payment for the seller, it recommends the seller to back open account by demand guarantee or standby letter of credit. In the case of irrevocable documentary credit, the very commonly used mode of payment in international trade practice, it recommends the seller and the buyer to make sure of the type of credit (confirmed or unconfirmed), the place of issue and confirmation (if applicable), the method of availability (by payment at sight, by deferred payment, by acceptance of a time draft, and by negotiation), and the allowance of partial shipments and transshipment.

A8    Documents: indicate documents to be provided by seller. Parties are advised to check the Incoterm they have selected under A3 of these specific conditions, alternative documents listed here are: transport documents (indicate type of transport document required), commercial invoice, certificate of origin, packing list, certificate of inspection, insurance document, and etc.

A9    Cancellation date.

A10   Liability for delay.

A11   Limitation of liability for lack of conformity.

A12   Limitation of liability where non-conforming goods are retained by the buyer.

29

A13  Time-bar.

A14  Applicable law.

A15  Resolution of disputes.

A16  Other: this indicates that the ICC Model does not prevent the parties from agreeing on other terms.

(2) Part B. General Conditions. These general conditions have been prepared in order to provide the legal protection demanded by traders, including both first-time trader and experienced practitioners.

There are 14 articles in total. In addition to the explanation of general principles, these articles cover aspects as characteristics of the goods, inspections of the goods before shipment, price, payment conditions, interests in case of delayed payment, retention of title, contractual term of delivery, documents, late-delivery, non-delivery and remedies therefore, non-conformity of the goods, cooperation between the parties, force majeure, and resolutions of disputes.

These complete and complementary general conditions do provide legal protections to parties to the contract. Obviously, all these legal protections come from the terms and conditions agreed by the buyer and the seller to the contract, the UNCISG, the law of exporting country, the ICC Incoterms® 2020, and the like.

In view of its easy-to-use and high degree of legal protection for all traders, the ICC Model International Contract of Sale is strongly recommended to prospective and established traders.

For its detailed contents, please refer to sales contract specimen 1 in the appendix of this chapter.

### 2.6.2　China's Export Contract Model

Typically, a written sales contract in China contains three parts of contents: preamble/heading, body, and witness.

(1) Preamble/Heading. The heading part of a contract mainly introduces essentials of the contract itself, covering:

- Name of contract.
- Reference number of contract.
- Place of contract being signed.
- Date of contract being signed.
- Name and address of the seller and its contact person (if any).
- Name and address of the buyer and its contact person (if any).

(2) Body. The body is the most important part of a contract, usually contains the following terms and conditions:

- Name of the commodity/goods descriptions.
- Quantity.
- Price or trade term.
- Quality of goods.
- Packing.
- Payment.
- Shipment.
- Commodity inspection.
- Insurance.
- Claim.
- Dispute settlement/breach clause.
- Force majeure.

According to the UNCISG, price, quality and quantity of goods, time and place of delivery, and payment are essential or indispensable for a contract to take force.

(3) Witness. The witness, constituting the ending part of a contract, usually states languages used in the contract and their effects, number of the original contract and copies, the enclosures and their legal force seal and/or signatures of legal representative or agent.

For the detailed contents, please refer to sales contract specimen 2 and specimen 3 in the appendix of this chapter.

Specimen 2 and specimen 3 are both exporting contract frequently used in China. Specimen 2 uses English as its contract language, whereas specimen 3 is bilingual, both in Chinese and in English. The readers are strongly recommended to read them with care, compare the similarities and dissimilarities, and understand the practical meaning and legal implication of each term and condition setting forth in them.

## 2.7 Online Trading Related Model Laws

With the development of information technology and internet, every company with a website has the potential to generate international enquiries through the global nature of the World Wide Web (www). Admittedly, the proportion of business-to-business trading (B2B), including importing and exporting, is not as great as the amount of trade from business-to-consumer (B2C). However, more and more business is being conducted online, and businesses must be aware of the legal and contractual implications of buying and selling via the internet.

However, there are no real issues on online offers and counter-offers as their communication differs only in format. The main issue regarding contracts agreed over the internet is that of acceptance. The traditional written acceptance of the offer provides both buyer and seller with documented proof of the contract, but this does little to clarify the position with e-commerce. In particular, how can the seller determine when the contract has been accepted and how the buyer's signature is obtained?

In order to promote the electronic commerce, the UNCITRAL① has successively published three key Model Laws that are of relevance to online trading since 1996.

### 2.7.1 UNMLEC 1996

UNMLEC 1996 (UNCITRAL Model Law on Electronic Commerce) was adopted by the UNCITRAL on 12 June 1996. The Model Law is intended to facilitate the use of modern means of communications and storage of information. It is based on the establishment of a functional equivalent in electronic media of paper-based concepts such as "writing", "signature" and "original". By providing standards by which the legal value of electronic messages can be assessed, the Model Law should play a significant role in enhancing the use of paperless communication. The Model Law also contains rules for electronic commerce in specific areas, such as carriage of goods②.

### 2.7.2 UNMLES 2001

UNMLES 2001 (UNCITRAL Model Law on Electronic Signatures) was adopted by the UNCITRAL on 5 July 2001. The Model Law aims at bringing additional legal certainty to the use of electronic signatures. Building on the flexible principle contained in article 7 of the UNCITRAL Model Law on Electronic Commerce, it establishes criteria of technical reliability for the equivalence between electronic and hand-written signatures. The Model Law follows a technology-neutral approach, which avoids favoring the use of any specific technical product. The Model Law further establishes basic rules of conduct that may serve as guidelines for assessing possible responsibilities and liabilities for the signatory, the relying party and trusted third parties intervening in the signature process③.

### 2.7.3 UNCECIC 2005

UNCECIC 2005 (UNCITRAL Convention of Electronic Communication in International Contract) was adopted by the UNCITRAL on 23 November 2005. The Convention aims to en-

---

① United Nations Commission on International Trade Law, core legal body of the United Nations system in the field of international trade law. It is a legal body with universal membership specializing in commercial law reform worldwide for over 40 years. UNCITRAL's business is the modernization and harmonization of rules on international business. These include: conventions, model laws and rules which are acceptable worldwide; legal and legislative guides and recommendations of great practical value; updated information on case law and enactments of uniform commercial law; technical assistance in law reform projects; and regional and national seminars on uniform commercial law.

② http://www.uncitral.org/uncitral/en/uncitral_texts/electronic_commerce/1996Model.html.

③ http://www.uncitral.org/uncitral/en/uncitral_texts/electronic_commerce/2001Model_signatures.html.

hance legal certainty and commercial predictability where electronic communications are used in relation to international contracts. It addresses the determination of a party's location in an electronic environment; the time and place of dispatch and receipt of electronic communications; the use of automated message systems for contract formation; and the criteria to be used for establishing functional equivalence between electronic communications and paper documents—including "original" paper documents—as well as between electronic authentication methods and hand-written signatures[①].

For the purpose of this chapter, the legal implications of contracts agreed via e-mail or website trading will be examined, although exporters and importers should also seek additional legal advice before entering into any form of online international trade agreement.

## Questions and Problems

### I. Choose the best answer to fill in the blank.

1. A message bearing the content as "⋯ have the intention to purchase 1,000 gross 'Black Girl' toothpaste, please quote us the best price and the earliest shipment time" is called_____.

A. an offer
B. an invitation to make offer
C. a counter-offer
D. an acceptance

2. If the CIF price of a product is USD 100/set, freight charge USD 10/set, insurance premium USD 0.01/set, commission rate 2%, the commission payment based on CIF price should be_____.

A. USD 1.6/set
B. USD 1.63/set
C. USD 2.0/set
D. USD 2.04/set

3. Which one of the following exporting prices is correctly expressed?_____.

A. CNY 3.50 CIF Shanghai
B. USD 3.50/piece CIF
C. RMB 3.50/piece CIFC London
D. USD 3.50/piece CIFC2 London

4. According to UNCISG, a contract can be established when_____.

A. an acceptance becomes effective
B. the seller and buyer sign on a written contract
C. the contract is approved by authorities
D. an offer reaches the offeree

5. When the offeree makes modification to the following items other than_____, his reply will be seen as a counter-offer.

A. the price
B. the payment term
C. the packing
D. the quality and quantity

---

① http://www.uncitral.org/uncitral/en/uncitral_texts/electronic_commerce/2005Convention.html.

6. An offer will be terminated when_____ .

A. it is rejected                                  B. it is counter-offered

C. it is legally revoked                      D. all of the above

7. A cabled offer reached the offeree on Dec. 12. However on Dec. 11 the offeror had informed the offeree by fax that the offer had been invalid. This act can be considered as_____ .

A. a withdrawal of an offer               B. an amendment of an offer

C. a new offer                                      D. a revocation of an offer

8. A foreign buyer cabled that "offer dated 10 Aug. accepted, if 5% commission included". This is_____ .

A. an acceptance                               B. a counter-offer

C. an inquiry                                       D. an offer

9. Company A made an offer to Company B. Under which condition can the two parties establish a deal? _____ .

A. Company C which is recognized by Company A accepted the offer within validity period

B. Based on previous experience, Company B indicated acceptance without receiving the offer

C. Company B accepted the offer within validity period, but suggested earlier shipment

D. Within the validity period, Company B accepted the offer completely

10. There are altogether_____ terms defined by the Incoterms® 2020.

A. 6                      B. 9                      C. 13                      D. 11

11. Among all the Incoterms® 2020_____ imposes the minimum obligation and cost to the seller.

A. EXW                      B. CIF                      C. DAP                      D. DDP

12. Among all the Incoterms® 2020_____ imposes the minimum obligation and cost to the buyer.

A. EXW                      B. CIF                      C. DAP                      D. DDP

13. The term CIF should be followed by_____ .

A. named port of shipment                B. named place of destination

C. named place of loading                  D. named port of destination

14. FOB and CFR share one thing that_____ .

A. risk is transferred when the goods shipped on board the carrying vessel

B. they can be used in any mode of transport

C. the seller will be responsible for the unloading at the port of destination

D. none of the above

15. The Incoterms® 2020 requires the buyer to handle the import customs clearance except under_____ .

A. EXW                      B. FCA                      C. DAP                      D. DDP

**Ⅱ. Case analysis.**

1. On Nov. 20th, Lee Co. offered to sell goods to Dee Inc. at USD 500 per case CIF London, "Offer valid if reply here 11/27." On Nov. 22nd Dee cabled back, "Offer accepted if USD 480 per case." As Lee was considering the bid, the market price went over USD 500. On Nov. 25th, Dee cabled an unconditional acceptance of Lee's initial offer. Could Lee reject Dee's acceptance? Why or why not?

2. Company X offered to sell goods to Company Y, "Shipment within 2 months after receipt of L/C, offer valid if reply here 5 days." Two days later, Company Y cabled back, "Accept your offer shipment immediately." Company X didn't reply. Two more days later, Company X received Company Y's L/C requiring immediate shipment. At this time, the market price of the goods went up by 20%. What options did Company X have to deal with Company Y?

**Ⅲ. Fill in the blank form contact in English with the following particulars.**

✓卖方:北京轻工产品进出口公司

✓买方:纽约贸易公司

✓商品名称:永久牌自行车

✓规格:RE110 型

✓数量:1 000 辆

✓单价:CIF 纽约每辆 100 美元

✓包装:木箱装

✓装运期:2024 年 3 月 31 日前自中国港口至纽约,不允许分批装运和转船

✓付款条件:凭不可撤销即期信用证付款,于装运期前一个月开到卖方,并于上述装运期后 15 天内在中国议付有效

✓保险:由卖方根据中国人民保险公司 1981 年 1 月 1 日中国保险条款按发票金额的 110%投保一切险和战争险

✓签约日期和地点:2023 年 10 月 11 日于北京

✓合同号码:AC4789

## CONTRACT No.

**Sellers:**

**Buyers:**

The undersigned Sellers and Buyers have agreed to close the following transaction according to the terms and conditions stipulated below:

**Commodity:**

**Specifications:**

**Quantity:**

**Unit Price:**

**Total Value:**

**Packing:**

**Shipping Mark:**

**Insurance:**

**Time of Shipment:**

**Port of Shipment:**

**Port of Destination:**

**Terms of Payment:**

The sellers                                              The buyers

_____                              _____

Done and signed in Beijing on this____day of_____ , **20**_____.

## IV. Calculations and sales contract drafting.

√Seller：DESHENG TRADING CO. , LTD. 29TH FLOOR KINGSTAR MANSION, 123 JINLIN RD. , SHANGHAI CHINA

√Buyer：NFO GENERAL TRADING CO. , 521 JALAN STREET, TORONTO, CANADA

√Terms of sale：CIF5% TORONTO

√Goods descriptions：CHINESE CERAMIC DINNERWARE

- 542 Sets of DS1511 30-Piece Dinnerware and Tea Set @ USD23. 50/SET
- 800 Sets of DS2201 20-Piece Dinnerware Set @ USD20. 40/SET
- 443 Sets of DS4504 45-Piece Dinnerware Set @ USD23. 20/SET
- 254 Sets of DS5120 95-Piece Dinnerware Set @ USD30. 10/SET

√More or less clause：With 10% more or less of shipment allowed at the sellers' option

√Packing：PACKED IN CARTONS

- DS2201：2 SETS TO A CARTON
- DS1151,DS4504,DS5120：ONE SET TO A CARTON

√Shipping Marks：AT BUYER's OPTION BEFORE GOODS TO BE SHIPPED

√Time of Shipment & Means of Transportation：TO BE SHIPPED IN MAY, 2024, ALLOWING PARTIAL SHIPMENTS AND TRANSSHIPMENT

√Port of Loading & Destination：FROM SHANGHAI TO TORONTO

√Insurance：TO BE EFFECTED BY THE SELLER FOR 110% OF CONTRACTED CIF VALUE, AGAINST WPA, BREAKAGES AND DAMAGES, AND WAR RISKS OF C. I. C DATED 1981-01-01.

√Terms of Payment：IRREVOCABLE LETTER OF CREDIT PAYABLE BY DRAFT AT SIGHT, TO RAECH THE SELLER BEFORE APRIL 5 AND TO REMAIN VALID FOR NEGOTIATION IN CHINA UNTIL 15 DAYS AFTER THE TIME OF SHIPMENT.

√DATE：2024-03-05

√SIGNED IN：SHANGHAI, CHINA

√S/CNO. ：SHDS13007

1. Calculate the total commission to be paid to the middle businessman.

2. Calculate the net CIF-based amount for the seller.

3. Fill in the following blank form sales contract.

**销售合同**

# SALES CONTRACT

| 卖方 SELLER： | 编号 NO.： | |
| | 日期 DATE： | |
| | 地点 SIGNED IN： | |
| 买方 BUYER： | | |

买卖双方同意以下条款达成交易：

    This contract is made by and agreed between the BUYER and SELLER，in accordance with the terms and conditions stipulated below.

| 1.品名及规格<br>Commodity & Specification | 2.数量<br>Quantity | 3.单价及价格条款<br>Unit Price & Trade Terms | 4.金额<br>Amount |
| --- | --- | --- | --- |
| | | | |
| | | | |
| Total | | | |

| 允许<br>With | 溢短装，由卖方决定<br>More or less of shipment allowed at the sellers' option |
| --- | --- |

| 5.总值<br>Total Value | |
| --- | --- |
| 6.包装<br>Packing | |
| 7.唛头<br>Shipping Marks | |
| 8.装运期及运输方式<br>Time of Shipment & Means of Transportation | |

续表

| | |
|---|---|
| 9. 装运港及目的地<br>Port of Loading & Destination | |
| 10. 保险<br>Insurance | |
| 11. 付款方式<br>Terms of Payment | |
| 12. 备注<br>Remarks | |

| The Buyer | The Seller |
|---|---|
| (signature) | (signature) |

# Appendix

## Sales Contract Specimen 1

# International Sale Contract
## (Manufactured Goods Intended for Resale)
### (ICC Model)

### A. Specific Conditions

These specific conditions have been prepared in order to permit the parties to agree the particular terms of their sale contract by completing the spaces left open or choosing (as the case may be) between the alternatives provided in this document. Obviously this does not prevent the parties from agreeing other terms or further details in box A16 or in one or more annexes.

| Seller | Contact Person | Buyer | Contact Person |
|---|---|---|---|
| name and address | name and address | name and address | name and address |
| _____ | _____ | _____ | _____ |
| _____ | _____ | _____ | _____ |
| _____ | _____ | _____ | _____ |

The present contract of sale will be governed by these specific conditions (to the extent that the relevant boxes have been completed) and by the ICC General Conditions of Sale (Manufactured Goods Intended for Resale) which constitute part B of this document.

| Seller | Buyer |
|---|---|
| Signature | signature |
| _____ | _____ |

place: _____ date: _____     place: _____ date: _____

### A1  Goods Sold

Description of the goods

_____

_____

_____

If there is insufficient space parties may use an annex.

### A2  Contract Price (Art. 4)

Currency: _____

amount in numbers:_____ amount in letters:_____

**A3 Delivery Terms**

**Recommended terms** ( according to Incoterms® 2020 )

☐ **EXW** Ex Works                                      named place:_____

☐ **FCA** Free Carrier                                   named place:_____

☐ **CPT** Carriage Paid to                 named place of destination:_____

☐ **CIP** Carriage and Insurance Paid to   named place of destination:_____

☐ **DAP** Delivered at Place                        named place:_____

☐ **DPU** Delivered at Place Unloaded     named place of destination:_____

☐ **DDP** Delivered Duty Paid              named place of destination:_____

**Other terms** ( according to Incoterms® 2020 )

☐ **FAS** Free alongside Ship               named port of shipment:_____

☐ **FOB** Free on Board                      named port of shipment:_____

☐ **CFR** Cost and Freight                 named port of destination:_____

☐ **CIF** Cost Insurance and Freight      named port of destination:_____

**Other delivery terms**

☐ _____

**Carrier** ( where applicable )

Name and Address                        Contact Person

_____          _____

_____          _____

_____          _____

**A4 Time of Delivery**

Indicate here the date or period ( e. g. week or month) at which or within which the Seller must perform his delivery obligations according to clause A4 of the respective Incoterm.

_____

_____

_____

**A5 Inspection of the Goods by Buyer ( Art. 3)**

☐ Before shipment place of inspection:_____

☐ Other:_____

**A6 Retention of Title ( Art. 7)**

☐ Yes        ☐ No

**A7 Payment Conditions ( Art. 5)**

☐ Payment on open account ( Art. 5. 1)

Time for payment ( if different from Art. 5. 1)_____ days from date of invoice.

Other: _____

☐ Open account backed by demand guarantee or standby letter of credit (Art. 5. 5)

☐ Payment in advance (Art. 5. 2)

Date (if different from Art. 5. 2): _____

☐ Total price _____     ☐ _____ % of the price

☐ Documentary collection (Art. 5. 5)

☐ D/P Documents against payment     ☐ D/A Documents against acceptance

☐ Irrevocable documentary credit (Art. 5. 3)

☐ Confirmed     ☐ Unconfirmed

Place of issue (if applicable): _____ Place of confirmation (if applicable): _____

Credit available:     Partial shipments:     Transshipment:

☐ By payment at sight     ☐ Allowed     ☐ Allowed

☐ By deferred payment at: _____ days     ☐ Not allowed     ☐ Not allowed

☐ By acceptance of drafts at: _____ days

☐ By negotiation

Date on which the documentary credit must be notified to seller (if different from Art. 5. 3).

☐ _____ days before date of delivery     ☐ other: _____

Other: _____

(e. g. cheque, bank draft, electronic funds transfer to designated bank account of seller)

**A8  Documents**

Indicate here documents to be provided by Seller. Parties are advised to check the Incoterm they have selected under A3 of these Specific Conditions.

☐ Transport documents: indicate type of transport document required _____

☐ Commercial invoice     ☐ Certificate of origin

☐ Packing list     ☐ Certificate of inspection

☐ Insurance document     ☐ Other: _____

**A9   Cancellation Date**

To be completed only if the parties wish to modify Art. 10. 3.

If the goods are not delivered for any reason whatsoever (including force majeure) by (date) _____ the buyer will be entitled to cancel the contract immediately by notification of the seller.

**A10   Liability for Delay (Art. 10. 1, 10. 4 and 11. 3)**

To be completed only if the parties wish to modify Art 10. 1, 10. 4 or 11. 3.

Liquidated damages for delay in delivery shall be:

☐ _____ % (of price of delayed goods) per week, with a maximum of

_____ % (of price of delayed goods) or:

☐ _____ ( specify amount )

In case of termination for delay, Seller's liability for damages for delay is limited to _____ % of the price of the non-delivered goods.

### A11   Limitation of Liability for Lack of Conformity ( Art. 11. 5 )

To be completed only if the parties wish to modify Art. 11. 5.

**Seller's liability for damages arising from lack of conformity of the goods shall be:**

☐ limited to proven loss ( including consequential loss, loss of profit, etc. ) not exceeding _____ % of the contract price; or:

☐ as follows ( specify ) :

_____

### A12   Limitation of Liability Where Non-conforming Goods Are Retained by the Buyer ( Art. 11. 6 )

To be completed only if the parties wish to modify Art. 11. 6.

**The price abatement for retained non-conforming goods shall not exceed:**

☐ _____ % of the price of such goods or:

☐ _____ ( specify amount )

### A13   Time-bar ( Art. 11. 8 )

To be completed only if the parties wish to modify Art. 11. 8.

Any action for non-conformity of the goods ( as defined in Art. 11. 8 ) must be taken by the buyer not later than _____ from the date of arrival of the goods at destination.

### A14( a ), A14( b ) Applicable Law ( Art. 1. 2 )

To be completed only if the parties wish to submit the sale contract to a national law instead of UNCISG. The solution hereunder is not recommended:

( a ) This sales contract is governed by the domestic law of _____ ( country ).

To be completed only if the parties wish to choose a law other than that of the seller for questions not covered by UNCISG.

( b ) Any questions not covered by UNCISG will be governed by the law of _____ ( country ).

### A15   Resolution of Disputes ( Art. 14 )

The two solutions hereunder ( arbitration or litigation before ordinary courts ) are alternatives: parties cannot choose both of them. If no choice is made, ICC arbitration will apply, according to Art. 14.

☐ Arbitration                    ☐ Litigation ( ordinary courts )

☐ ICC ( according to art. 14. 1 ) in case of dispute the courts of

Place of arbitration _____ ( place )

☐ Other _____ ( specify ) shall have jurisdiction

**A16   Other**

**B. General Conditions**

**Art. 1   General**

**1.1**   These General Conditions are intended to be applied together with the Specific Conditions (part A) of the International Sale Contract (Manufactured Goods Intended for Resale), but they may also be incorporated on their own into any sale contract. Where these General Conditions (Part B) are used independently of the said Specific Conditions (Part A), any reference in Part B to Part A will be interpreted as a reference to any relevant specific conditions agreed by the parties. In case of contradiction between these General Conditions and any specific conditions agreed upon between the parties, the specific conditions shall prevail.

**1.2**   Any questions relating to this Contract which are not expressly or implicitly settled by the provisions contained in the Contract itself (i. e. these General Conditions and any specific conditions agreed upon by the parties) shall be governed:

A. by the United Nations Convention on Contracts for the International Sale of Goods (Vienna Convention of 1980, hereafter referred to as UNCISG), and

B. to the extent that such questions are not covered by UNCISG, by reference to the law of the country where the Seller has his place of business.

**1.3**   Any reference made to trade terms (such as EXW, FCA, etc. ) is deemed to be made to the relevant term of Incoterms published by the International Chamber of Commerce.

**1.4**   Any reference made to a publication of the International Chamber of Commerce is deemed to be made to the version current at the date of conclusion of the Contract.

**1.5**   No modification of the Contract is valid unless agreed or evidenced in writing. However, a party may be precluded by his conduct from asserting this provision to the extent that the other party has relied on that conduct.

**Art. 2   Characteristics of the Goods**

**2.1**   It is agreed that any information relating to the goods and their use, such as weights, dimensions, capacities, prices, colors and other data contained in catalogues, prospectuses, circulars, advertisements, illustrations, price-lists of the Seller, shall not take effect as terms of the Contract unless expressly referred to in the Contract.

**2.2**   Unless otherwise agreed, the Buyer does not acquire any property rights in software, drawings, etc. which may have been made available to him. The Seller also remains the exclusive owner of any intellectual or industrial property rights relating to the goods.

**Art. 3   Inspection of the Goods before Shipment**

If the parties have agreed that the Buyer is entitled to inspect the goods before shipment, the Seller must notify the Buyer within a reasonable time before the shipment that the goods are ready for inspection at the agreed place.

### Art. 4　Price

**4.1**　If no price has been agreed, the Seller's current list price at the time of the conclusion of the Contract shall apply. In the absence of such a current list price, the price generally charged for such goods at the time of the conclusion of the Contract shall apply.

**4.2**　Unless otherwise agreed in writing, the price does not include VAT, and is not subject to price adjustment.

**4.3**　The price indicated under A2 (contract price) includes any costs which are at the Seller's charge according to this Contract. However, should the Seller bear any costs which, according to this Contract, are for the Buyer's account (e.g. for transportation or insurance under EXW or FCA), such sums shall not be considered as having been included in the price under A2 and shall be reimbursed by the Buyer.

### Art. 5　Payment Conditions

**5.1**　Unless otherwise agreed in writing, or implied from a prior course of dealing between the parties, payment of the price and of any other sums due by the Buyer to the Seller shall be on open account and time of payment shall be 30 days from the date of invoice. The amounts due shall be transferred, unless otherwise agreed, by teletransmission to the Seller's bank in the Seller's country for the account of the Seller and the Buyer shall be deemed to have performed his payment obligations when the respective sums due have been received by the Seller's bank in immediately available funds.

**5.2**　If the parties have agreed on payment in advance, without further indication, it will be assumed that such advance payment, unless otherwise agreed, refers to the full price, and that the advance payment must be received by the Seller's bank in immediately available funds at least 30 days before the agreed date of delivery or the earliest date within the agreed delivery period. If advance payment has been agreed only for a part of the contract price, the payment conditions of the remaining amount will be determined according to the rules set forth in this article.

**5.3**　If the parties have agreed on payment by documentary credit, then, unless otherwise agreed, the Buyer must arrange for a documentary credit in favour of the Seller to be issued by a reputable bank, subject to the Uniform Customs and Practice for Documentary Credits published by the International Chamber of Commerce, and to be notified at least 30 days before the agreed date of delivery or at least 30 days before the earliest date within the agreed delivery period. Unless otherwise agreed, the documentary credit shall be payable at sight and allow partial shipments and transshipments.

**5.4**　If the parties have agreed on payment by documentary collection, then, unless otherwise agreed, documents will be tendered against payment (D/P) and the tender will in any case be subject to the Uniform Rules for Collections published by the International Chamber of Commerce.

**5.5**  To the extent that the parties have agreed that payment is to be backed by a bank guarantee, the Buyer is to provide, at least 30 days before the agreed date of delivery or at least 30 days before the earliest date within the agreed delivery period, a first demand bank guarantee subject to the Uniform Rules for Demand Guarantees published by the International Chamber of Commerce, or a standby letter of credit subject either to such Rules or to the Uniform Customs and Practice for Documentary Credits published by the International Chamber of Commerce, in either case issued by a reputable bank.

### Art. 6   Interest in Case of Delayed Payment

**6.1**  If a party does not pay a sum of money when it falls due the other party is entitled to interest upon that sum from the time when payment is due to the time of payment.

**6.2**  Unless otherwise agreed, the rate of interest shall be 2% above the average bank short-term lending rate to prime borrowers prevailing for the currency of payment at the place of payment, or where no such rate exists at that place, then the same rate in the State of the currency of payment. In the absence of such a rate at either place, the rate of interest shall be the appropriate rate fixed by the law of the State of the currency of payment.

### Art. 7   Retention of Title

If the parties have validly agreed on retention of title, the goods shall remain the property of the Seller until the complete payment of the price, or as otherwise agreed.

### Art. 8   Contractual Term of Delivery

Unless otherwise agreed, delivery shall be "Ex Works" (EXW).

### Art. 9   Documents

Unless otherwise agreed, the Seller must provide the documents (if any) indicated in the applicable Incoterm or, if no Incoterm is applicable, according to any previous course of dealing.

### Art. 10   Late-delivery, Non-delivery and Remedies Therefor

**10.1**  When there is delay in delivery of any goods, the Buyer is entitled to claim liquidated damages equal to 0.5% or such other percentage as may be agreed of the price of those goods for each complete week of delay, provided the Buyer notifies the Seller of the delay. Where the Buyer so notifies the Seller within 15 days from the agreed date of delivery, damages will run from the agreed date of delivery or from the last day within the agreed period of delivery. Where the Buyer so notifies the Seller after 15 days of the agreed date of delivery, damages will run from the date of the notice. Liquidated damages for delay shall not exceed 5% of the price of the delayed goods or such other maximum amount as may be agreed.

**10.2**  If the parties have agreed upon a cancellation date in Box A9, the Buyer may terminate the Contract by notification to the Seller as regards goods which have not been delivered by such cancellation date for any reason whatsoever (including a force majeure event).

**10.3** When article 10.2 does not apply and the Seller has not delivered the goods by the date on which the Buyer has become entitled to the maximum amount of liquidated damages under article 10.1, the Buyer may give notice in writing to terminate the Contract as regards such goods, if they have not been delivered to the Buyer within 5 days of receipt of such notice by the Seller.

**10.4** In case of termination of the Contract under article 10.2 or 10.3 then in addition to any amount paid or payable under article 10.1, the Buyer is entitled to claim damages for any additional loss not exceeding 10% of the price of the non-delivered goods.

**10.5** The remedies under this article are exclusive of any other remedy for delay in delivery or non-delivery.

### Art. 11 Non-Conformity of the Goods

**11.1** The Buyer shall examine the goods as soon as possible after their arrival at destination and shall notify the Seller in writing of any lack of conformity of the goods within 15 days from the date when the Buyer discovers or ought to have discovered the lack of conformity. In any case the Buyer shall have no remedy for lack of conformity if he fails to notify the Seller thereof within 12 months from the date of arrival of the goods at the agreed destination.

**11.2** Goods will be deemed to conform to the Contract despite minor discrepancies which are usual in the particular trade or through course of dealing between the parties but the Buyer will be entitled to any abatement of the price usual in the trade or through course of dealing for such discrepancies.

**11.3** Where goods are non-conforming (and provided the Buyer, having given notice of the lack of conformity in compliance with Art. 11.1, does not elect in the notice to retain them), the Seller shall at his option:

(a) Replace the goods with conforming goods, without any additional expense to the Buyer, or

(b) Repair the goods, without any additional expense to the Buyer, or

(c) Reimburse to the Buyer the price paid for the non-conforming goods and thereby terminates the Contract as regards those goods.

The Buyer will be entitled to liquidate damages as quantified under Art. 10.1 for each complete week of delay between the date of notification of the non-conformity according to Art. 11.1 and the supply of substitute goods under Art. 11.3(a) or repair under Art. 11.3(b) above. Such damages may be accumulated with damages (if any) payable under Art. 10.1, but can in no case exceed the aggregate 5% of the price of those goods.

**11.4**  If the Seller has failed to perform his duties under Art. 11.3 by the date on which the Buyer becomes entitled to the maximum amount of liquidated damages according to that article, the Buyer may give notice in writing to terminate the Contract as regards the non-conforming goods unless the supply of replacement goods or the repair is effected within 5 days of receipt of such notice by the Seller.

**11.5**  Where the Contract is terminated under Art. 11.3(c) or Art. 11.4, then in addition to any amount paid or payable under Art. 11.3 as reimbursement of the price and damages for any delay, the Buyer is entitled to damages for any additional loss not exceeding 10% of the price of the non-conforming goods.

**11.6**  Where the Buyer elects to retain non-conforming goods, he shall be entitled to a sum equal to the difference between the value of the goods at the agreed place of destination if they had conformed to the Contract and their value at the same place as delivered, such sum not to exceed 15% of the price of those goods.

**11.7**  Unless otherwise agreed in writing, the remedies under this article 11 are exclusive of any other remedy for non-conformity.

**11.8**  Unless otherwise agreed in writing, no action for lack of conformity can be taken by the Buyer, whether before judicial or arbitral tribunals, after 2 years from the date of arrival of the goods. It is expressly agreed that after the expiry of such term, the Buyer will not plead non-conformity of the goods, or make a counter-claim thereon, in defence to any action taken by the Seller against the Buyer for non-performance of this Contract.

### Art. 12  Cooperation Between The Parties

**12.1**  The Buyer shall promptly inform the Seller of any claim made against the Buyer by his customers or third parties concerning the goods delivered or intellectual property rights related thereto.

**12.2**  The Seller will promptly inform the Buyer of any claim which may involve the product liability of the Buyer.

### Art. 13  Force Majeure

**13.1**  A party is not liable for a failure to perform any of his obligations in so far as he proves:

(a) That the failure was due to an impediment beyond his control, and

(b) That he could not reasonably be expected to have taken into account the impediment and its effects upon his ability to perform at the time of the conclusion of the Contract, and

(c) That he could not reasonably have avoided or overcome it or its effects.

**13.2**  A party seeking relief shall, as soon as practicable after the impediment and its effects upon his ability to perform become known to him, give notice to the other party of such impediment and its effects on his ability to perform. Notice shall also be given when the ground of relief ceases.

Failure to give either notice makes the party thus failing liable in damages for loss which otherwise could have been avoided.

**13. 3** Without prejudice to Art. 10. 2, a ground of relief under this clause relieves the party failing to perform from liability in damages, from penalties and other contractual sanctions, except from the duty to pay interest on money owing as long as and to the extent that the ground subsists.

**13. 4** If the grounds of relief subsist for more than six months, either party shall be entitled to terminate the Contract with notice.

### Art. 14 Resolution of Disputes

**14. 1** Unless otherwise agreed in writing, all disputes arising in connection with the present Contract shall be finally settled under the Rules of Arbitration of the International Chamber of Commerce by one or more arbitrators appointed in accordance with the said Rules.

**14. 2** An arbitration clause does not prevent any party from requesting interim or conservatory measures from the courts.

## Sales Contract Specimen 2

# Sales Contract

No:

Date:

For Account of:

Indent No:

This contract is made by and between the Sellers and the Buyers; Whereby the Sellers agree to sell and the Buyers agree to buy the under-mentioned goods.

According to the terms and conditions stipulated below and overleaf:

(1) Names of commodity(ies) and specification(s):

(2) Quantity:

(3) Unit price:

(4) Amount TOTAL: _____% more or less allowed.

(5) Packing:

(6) Port of loading:

(7) Port of destination:

(8) Shipping marks:

(9) Time of shipment: within _____ days after receipt of L/C, allowing transshipment and partial shipment.

(10) Terms of payment: by 100% Confirmed, Irrevocable and Sight Letter of Credit to remain valid for negotiation in China until the 15th day after shipment.

(11) Insurance:

☐ Covers all risks and war risks only as per the Clauses of the People's Insurance Company of China for 110% of the invoice value.

☐ To be effected by the Buyer.

(12) The buyer shall establish the covering Letter of Credit before _____ _____; failing which, the Seller reserves the right to rescind this Sales Contract without further notice, or to accept whole or any part of this Sales Contract, non-fulfilled by the Buyer, or to lodge claim for direct losses sustained, if any.

(13) Documents: the sellers shall present to the negotiating bank, Clean On Board Bill of Lading, Invoice, Quality Certificate issued by the China Commodity Inspection Bureau or the

Manufacturers, Survey Report on Quantity/Weight issued by the China Commodity Inspection Bureau, and Transferable Insurance Policy or Insurance Certificate when this contract is made on CIF basis.

(14) For this contract signed on CIF basis, the premium should be 110% of invoice value. All risks insured should be included within this contract. If the Buyer asks to increase the insurance premium or scope of risks, he should get the permission of the Seller before time of loading, and all the charges thus incurred should be borne by the Buyer.

(15) Quality/Quantity discrepancy: in case of quality discrepancy, claim should be filed by the Buyer within 30 days after the arrival of the goods at port of destination; while for quantity discrepancy, claim should be filed by the Buyer within 15 days after the arrival of the goods at port of destination. It is understood that the Seller shall not be liable for any discrepancy of the goods shipped due to causes for which the Insurance Company, Shipping Company, other transportation organizations and/or Post Office are liable.

(16) The seller shall not be held liable for failure or delay in delivery of the entire lot or a portion of the goods under this Sales Contract in consequence of any Force Majeure incidents.

(17) Arbitration: all disputes in connection with this contract or the execution thereof shall be settled friendly through negotiations. In case no settlement can be reached, the case may then be submitted for arbitration to China International Economic and Trade Arbitration Commission in accordance with the provisional Rules of Procedures promulgated by the said Arbitration Commission. The arbitration shall take place in Beijing and the decision of the Arbitration Commission shall be final and binding upon both parties; neither party shall seek recourse to a law court or other authorities to appeal for revision of the decision. Arbitration fee shall be borne by the losing party. Or arbitration may be settled in the third country mutually agreed upon by both parties.

(18) The buyer is requested always to quote THE NUMBER OF THE SALES CONTRACT in the Letter of Credit to be opened in favour of the Seller.

(19) Other conditions: our Contract Template Database is complied in accordance with laws of P. R. China.

This English document is translated according to its Chinese version. In case of discrepancy, the original version in Chinese shall prevail.

Sellers                                                                                 Buyers

# Sales Contract Specimen 3

# 销售合同
# Sales Contract

编号(No. ): _____

签约地(Signed at): _____

日期(Date): _____

卖方(Seller): _____

地址(Address): _____

电话(Tel): _____传真(Fax): _____

电子邮箱(E-mail): _____

买方(Buyer): _____

地址(Address): _____

电话(Tel): _____ 传真(Fax): _____

电子邮箱(E-mail): _____

买卖双方经协商同意按下列条款成交:

The undersigned Seller and Buyer have agreed to close the following transactions according to the terms and conditions set forth as below:

1. 货物名称、规格和质量(Name, Specifications and Quality of Commodity):

2. 数量(Quantity):

3. 单价及价格条款(Unit Price and Terms of Delivery):

［除非另有规定,"FOB""CFR""CIF"均应依照国际商会制定的《2020 年国际贸易术语解释通则》(INCOTERMS® 2020)办理。］

［The terms FOB, CFR, or CIF shall be subject to the International Rules for the Interpretation of Trade Terms (INCOTERMS® 2020) provided by International Chamber of Commerce (ICC) unless otherwise stipulated herein. ］

4. 总价 (Total Amount):

5. 允许溢短装(More or Less): _____%。

6. 装运期限(Time of Shipment):

收到可以转船及分批装运之信用证 _____ 天内装运。

Within _____ days after receipt of L/C allowing transshipment and partial shipments.

7. 付款条件(Terms of Payment):

买方须于 _____ 前将保兑的、不可撤销的、可转让的即期付款信用证开到卖方,该信用证的有效期延至装运期后 _____ 天在中国到期,并必须注明允许分批装运和转船。

By Confirmed, Irrevocable, Transferable L/C to be available by sight draft to reach the Seller before _____ and to remain valid for negotiation in China until _____ after the Time of Shipment. The L/C must specify that transshipment and partial shipments are allowed.

买方未在规定的时间内开出信用证,卖方有权发出通知取消本合同,或接受买方对本合同未执行的全部或部分,或对因此遭受的损失提出索赔。

The Buyer shall establish a Letter of Credit before the above-stipulated time, failing which, the Seller shall have the right to rescind this Contract upon the arrival of the notice at Buyer or to accept whole or part of this Contract non fulfilled by the Buyer, or to lodge a claim for the direct losses sustained, if any.

8. 包装(Packing):

9. 保险(Insurance):

按发票金额的 _____ %投保 _____ 险,由 _____ 负责投保。

Covering _____ Risks for _____ % of Invoice Value to be effected by the _____ .

10. 品质/数量异议(Quality/Quantity Discrepancy):

如买方提出索赔,凡属品质异议须于货到目的口岸之日起 30 天内提出,凡属数量异议须于货到目的口岸之日起 15 天内提出,对所装货物所提任何异议于保险公司、轮船公司、其他有关运输机构或邮递机构所负责者,卖方不负任何责任。

In case of quality discrepancy, claim should be filed by the Buyer within 30 days after the arrival of the goods at port of destination, while for quantity discrepancy, claim should be filed by the Buyer within 15 days after the arrival of the goods at port of destination. It is understood that the Seller shall not be liable for any discrepancy of the goods shipped due to causes for which the Insurance Company, Shipping Company, other Transportation Organization/or Post Office are liable.

11. 由于发生人力不可抗拒的原因,致使本合约不能履行,部分或全部商品延误交货,卖方概不负责。本合同所指的不可抗力系指不可干预、不能避免且不能克服的客观情况。

The Seller shall not be held responsible for failure or delay in delivery of the entire lot or a portion of the goods under this Sales Contract in consequence of any Force Majeure incidents which might occur. Force Majeure referred to in this contract means unforeseeable, unavoidable and insurmountable objective conditions.

12. 仲裁(Arbitration)：

因凡本合同引起的或与本合同有关的任何争议,如果协商不能解决,应提交中国国际经济贸易仲裁委员会深圳分会,按照申请仲裁时该会当时施行的仲裁规则进行仲裁。仲裁裁决是终局的,对双方均有约束力。

Any dispute arising from or in connection with the Sales Contract shall be settled through friendly negotiation. In case no settlement can be reached, the dispute shall then be submitted to China International Economic and Trade Arbitration Commission (CIETAC), Shenzhen Commission for arbitration in accordance with its rules in effect at the time of applying for arbitration. The arbitral award is final and binding upon both parties.

13. 通知(Notices)：

所有通知用 _____ 文写成,并按照如下地址用传真/电子邮件/快件送达给各方。如果地址有变更,一方应在变更后 _____ 日内书面通知另一方。

All notice shall be written in _____ and served to both parties by fax/e-mail/courier according to the following addresses. If any changes of the addresses occur, one party shall inform the other party of the change of address within _____ days after the change.

14. 本合同为中英文两种文本,两种文本具有同等效力。本合同一式 _____ 份。自双方签字(盖章)之日起生效。

This Contract is executed in two counterparts each in Chinese and English, each of which shall be deemed equally authentic. This Contract is in _____ copies effective since being signed / sealed by both parties.

The Seller：　　　　　　　　　The Buyer：
卖方签字：　　　　　　　　　　买方签字：

# Chapter 3　Documentary Letter of Credit

## 【本章提要】

国际贸易货款支付方式有:预付货款,跟单信用证,跟单托收,赊销。不同国家和地区习惯和适合采用的付款方式不同。中国的大宗交易多采用跟单信用证方式付款。

按照不同的标准和方法,信用证可分为可撤销/不可撤销信用证,保兑/未保兑信用证,即期付款/延期付款/承兑/议付信用证,信开/电开信用证,可转让/不可转让信用证,跟单/光票信用证,可循环信用证,背对背信用证,备用信用证,等等。信用证的种类不同,信用证的使用方法、相关银行对受益人的责任和义务都不同。

除信用证本身的基本信息(当事人信息、信用证类别、开证日期和到期日、所用货币种类及金额、使用方法)之外,信用证主要涵盖有关货物、运输、汇票及货运单据、银行费用等内容。

信用证交易通常包括买方(开证申请人)申请开证,开证行开证,通知行通知信用证,卖方(受益人)审证或请求改证,卖方按信用证规定交货给承运人、交单给被指定银行(是指被开证行指定的银行,如议付行、保兑行、付款行),被指定银行审单并议付/兑付相符交单,被指定银行将单据寄往偿付行/开证行要求偿付,开证行兑付相符交单并向买方提示单据要求兑付,买方付款赎单后凭运输单据向承运人提货等阶段。

及时开立符合合同规定的信用证是买方的重要义务,也是卖方履行合同的前提和基础。卖方能否安全及时收回货款,则取决于他的交单行为和所交单据是否构成相符交单。

外贸实践中,卖方常常因单证不符而遭银行拒付。因此,卖方在收到信用证后要仔细审核,一旦发现信用证条款与合同不符或难以满足,要及时联系买方修改信用证。卖方交货后则要严格按照信用证规定制作和提交单据,特别要注意及时交单,尽可能做到交单日和信用证到期日之间有足够长的时间间隔,以便修改银行审单发现存在不符点的那些单据。

信用证项下的相关银行只处理单据,仅对相符交单履行兑付或议付承诺。除信用证本身的条款条件之外,银行还根据跟单信用证统一惯例(UCP),以及国际标准银行实务(ISBP)来判定是否构成相符交单。因此为了保证相符交单和安全及时收回货款,卖方在制单和交单过程中对信用证规定、适用的 UCP 条款和 ISBP 要全面理解和准确把握。

In international trade, Cash in Advance, Open Account, Documentary Collection, and

Documentary Credit are four commonly used terms of payment. The first three are customer's credit based terms, where there exist inequity in risk sharing between the buyer and seller. However, Letter of Credit ( L/C) , a document issued by a bank that guarantees the payment of a customer's draft, substitutes the bank's credit for the customer's credit[1], has been the most frequently used terms of payment over the past nine decades[2]. It is thus greatly necessary to master L/C and its related knowledge, containing the definition, concerned parties, procedures, types, specimen and items, checklists for examination and amendment, and usual customs and practices.

## 3.1 Definition

Letter of Credit can be defined into different versions from different perspectives. Here are three typical definitions introduced by the International Chamber of Commerce ( ICC).

(1) A letter of credit is a written undertaking by a bank given to the seller at the request, and on the instruction, of the buyer to pay at sight or at a determinable future date up to a stated sum of money, within a prescribed time limit and against stipulated documents which were complied with the terms and conditions of the credit ( ICC Publication No. 415) .

(2) A letter of credit is an arrangement, however named or described, whereby a bank acting at the request and on the instructions of a customer or on its own behalf,

• To make a payment to the order of a third party, or is to accept and pay bills of exchange; or

• To authorize another bank to effect such payment, or to accept and pay such bills of exchange; or

• To authorize another bank to negotiate against stipulated documents, provided that the terms and conditions of the credit are complied with ( ICC Publication No. 500,UCP 500).

(3) Credit means any arrangement, however named or described, that is irrevocable and thereby constitutes a definite undertaking of the issuing bank to honour a complying presentation.

Where the word "honour" means:

• To pay at sight if the credit is available by sight payment.

• To incur a deferred payment undertaking and pay at maturity if the credit is available by deferred payment.

• To accept a bill of exchange ( "draft" ) drawn by the beneficiary and pay at maturity if the credit is available by acceptance.

The terminology "complying presentation" means a presentation that is in accordance with

---

① http://dictionary. die. net/letter%20of%20credit.

② The formal maturation of the letter of credit was in the 1920s.

the terms and conditions of the credit, the applicable provisions of these rules and international standard banking practice (UCP 600 article 2).

The third definition is strongly recommended for its conciseness and completeness.

## 3.2  Parties Concerned

### 3.2.1  Basic Parties

The basic parties involved in a typical commercial documentary letter of credit transaction are applicant, issuing bank, and beneficiary.

● Applicant means the party on whose request the credit is issued. That is, the importer.

● Issuing bank means the bank that issues a credit at the request of an applicant or on its own behalf. It is also called Opening Bank, and is usually the bank located in the importer's country. By issuing a credit, the bank assumes full responsibility for payment after the proper drafts and documents have been presented[1].

● Beneficiary means the party in whose favour a credit is issued. Accordingly, it is the party who is entitled to receive the payment. That is, the exporter.

The relationship between the applicant and the beneficiary is bound by the sales contract agreed upon by them, that between the applicant and the issuing bank is bound by the application for the L/C, and that between the beneficiary and the issuing bank is bound by the L/C itself.

### 3.2.2  Derivative Parties

However, some derivative parties may be involved in the practice of international trade payment under L/C.

● Advising bank means the bank that advises the credit at the request of the issuing bank. It is usually the bank located in the exporter's country and the correspondent of the issuing bank.

● Confirming bank means the bank (often, but not always the advising bank) that adds its confirmation to a credit upon the issuing bank's authorization or request. Confirmation means a definite undertaking in addition to that of the issuing bank, to honour or negotiate a complying presentation.

● Negotiating bank is the bank (often, but not always the advising bank) that buys an exporter's draft submitted to it under a letter of credit and then forwards the draft and documents to the issuing bank for reimbursement.

● Paying bank is the bank (often, but not always the issuing bank) that makes payment

---

[1]  An issuing bank should not incorporate in a credit administrative conditions such as a requirement for an additional set of copy documents to be presented for the issuing bank's use, or a condition that all documents may not be stapled. If, nevertheless, such conditions are incorporated into a credit but not complied with, this will not constitute a reason for refusal. (ISBP 821 preliminary consideration, ix. )

to the beneficiary against presentation of stipulated documents.

• Accepting bank is the bank (often, but not always the issuing bank) that effects acceptance on the time draft under an acceptance credit.

• Nominated bank means the bank with which the credit is available or any bank in the case of a credit available with any bank (UCP 600 Article 2). It may be a confirming bank, negotiating bank or paying bank acting on its nomination from the issuing bank.

Upon negotiation or honour effected, the nominated bank is entitled to obtain reimbursement from the reimbursing bank (issuing bank). In this case, the nominated bank that claims reimbursement from the reimbursing bank is called the claiming bank.

A claiming bank shall not be required to supply a reimbursing bank with a certificate of compliance with the terms and conditions of the credit (UCP 600 Article 4). If not reimbursed by the reimbursing bank (other than the issuing bank), the claiming bank is entitled to obtain reimbursement from the issuing bank. If there is any loss of interest, it should be assumed by the issuing bank.

• Reimbursing bank is the bank (often, but not always the issuing bank) that serves as a source of funds for payment to the beneficiary of L/C.

• Presenter means a beneficiary, bank or other party that makes a presentation. Where presentation means either the delivery of documents under a credit to the issuing bank or nominated bank or the documents so delivered.

The relationship between the beneficiary and the nominated bank is bound by the L/C itself. The relationship between the nominated bank and the issuing bank is bound by the L/C instruction, uniform customs and practices for documentary credits (UCP 500 or 600, and ISBP).

## 3.3 Procedures

The detailed procedures of a documentary credit operation are summarized as nine steps in figure 3.1.

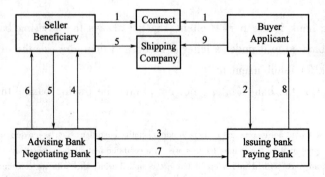

**Figure 3.1 Operation Procedure of a Documentary Credit**

### 3.3.1 Sales Contract Conclusion

The importer and the exporter conclude a sales contract, stipulating that payment will be made by a documentary credit.

According to the UCP 600 article 4, a credit by its nature is a separate transaction from the sale or other contract on which it may be based, banks are in no way concerned with or bound by such contract, even if any reference whatsoever to it is included in the credit.

However, the sales contract is the basis for the buyer to apply for a letter of credit; the contents of the sales contract determine terms and conditions of L/C. In order to avoid any subsequent disputes, both the buyer and the seller should be cautious to the sales contract under L/C terms of payment.

### 3.3.2 L/C Application

First, an importer will request the issuing bank to open L/C along with the following documents.

- An application.
- Indent or proforma invoice[①].
- Import registration certificate (IRC).
- Taxpayer identification number (TIN).
- Insurance cover note with money receipt (when necessary).
- A bank account.

Second, after examining the above-mentioned documents carefully, the issuing bank officer delivers the following forms to be filled up by importer, and bank officer will check:

- Whether the goods to be imported is permissible or not.
- Whether the goods to be imported is demandable or not.

The forms are:

- Import merchandize permit form (if any).
- L/C application form.
- L/C authorization form (if any).

### 3.3.3 L/C Issuance

Issuing bank issues L/C, sending it to the advising bank by airmail or (more commonly) electronic means such as telex or SWIFT.

Upon receipt of the above mentioned forms from the importer, the bank officer prepares L/C. Before preparing L/C, the bank officer scrutinizes the application to make sure that the

---

① The proforma invoice is a legal document between the supplier and the customer to describe the details of a certain commodity. The proforma invoice is needed for all international non document shipments, and is used for the customs in the country of destination to determine the customs value.

terms and conditions of the L/C are complied with the UCP 600 and Exchange Control & Import Trade Regulation of the importing country (if any), and to ensure the eligibility of the goods to be imported.

Then the issuing bank opens L/C in accordance with the terms and conditions of the application form.

After the issuance of L/C, the issuing bank informs its corresponding bank, called "advising bank" or "confirming bank" located in exporter's country to advice and forward the credit to the exporter, and simultaneously the officer makes L/C opening vouchers.

### 3.3.4  L/C Advice

Advising bank establishes apparent authenticity of the letter of credit using signature books or test codes, then informs the seller (beneficiary). Advising bank may confirm L/C, i. e. add its own payment undertaking, and become confirming bank. The confirming bank, regardless of any other consideration, must negotiate or honour a complying presentation without recourse to the seller.

### 3.3.5  L/C Examination and Amendment

The seller should now check that L/C matches sales contract, and that all its terms and conditions can be satisfied (e. g. all documents can be obtained in good time). If there is anything that may cause a problem, an AMENDMENT must be requested.

Then the seller ships the goods, assembles the documents required by the L/C (invoice, transport document, etc.), and presents them to a bank located in his country.

Before presenting the documents to the bank, the seller should check them for discrepancies with the L/C, and correct the documents where necessary.

Moreover, the beneficiary must present the documents to the bank specified in the credit for settlement. In a free negotiation credit, however, the beneficiary can present the documents to any bank for negotiation or honour.

### 3.3.6  Documents Examination and Negotiation

The advising bank checks the documents against the L/C. If the documents are compliant, the bank negotiates or honours the seller.

After the settlement, the advising bank may become a paying bank, an accepting bank, or negotiating bank, depending on the manner in which the credit is available.

### 3.3.7  Forwarding Documents for Reimbursement

The advising bank forwards the documents to the issuing bank for reimbursement. The issuing bank now checks the documents itself. If they are in order, it reimburses the seller's bank immediately.

Before making payment/reimbursement to the claiming bank, the issuing bank must examine the documents, and if there is any discrepancy in the documents, it will refuse to take over the documents and hence refuse to pay. Thus, it is wise for the seller's bank to examine the documents carefully to ensure the compliance of the documents; otherwise the documents will be dishonored.

### 3.3.8 Redeeming the Documents

The issuing bank presents the documents to the buyer for payment or acceptance, and the buyer redeems the documents.

After reimbursing the seller's bank, the issuing bank advises the buyer to redeem the documents. Likewise, the buyer examines the documents to ensure their compliance with the credit before effecting reimbursement to the issuing bank.

If the buyer finds discrepancies in the documents, he may refuse to take over the documents and hence refuse to pay. Thus, it is wise for the issuing bank to examine the documents carefully to ensure the compliance of the documents; otherwise the documents will be dishonored. It is also wise for the issuing bank to make sure that the applicant is reliable and creditworthy before issuing a letter of credit.

Upon buyer's payment of the amount due or acceptance of the draft, the issuing bank debits the buyer and releases the documents (including transport document), so that the buyer can claim the goods from the carrier.

### 3.3.9 Picking up goods from the carrier

The buyer redeems the documents and picks up the goods against the documents from the shipping company.

Up till now, the documentary credit operation comes to an end.

## 3.4 Types

There are various kinds of letter of credit. Different type of L/C constitutes different undertaking of the issuing bank, involves different procedures, requires different kinds of trade documents, and provides different degrees of guarantee to the beneficiary. It is thus important for the concerning parties to understand the types of L/C.

### 3.4.1 Revocable and Irrevocable L/C

Traditionally, L/C was divided into Revocable L/C and Irrevocable L/C.

Revocable L/C, as the name signifies, is one letter of credit which can be cancelled by the issuing bank at any time without any obligation on its part. Since revocable letters of credit are subject to cancellation without notification, they are not usually acceptable to the businessmen. They are, however, used effectively for shipments between affiliated companies and in other instances when there is no doubt concerning creditworthiness and mutual trust between the parties.

Irrevocable documentary L/C constitutes a definite undertaking of the issuing bank, provided that the stipulated documents are presented to the nominated bank or to the issuing bank and that the terms and conditions of the credit are complied with, to pay, accept draft and/or documents presented under the documentary credit (ICC Publication No. 515).

Irrevocable letter of credit cannot be cancelled, rescinded or recalled without agreement of all parties to the credit. This guarantees that a buyer's payment to a seller will be received on time and for the correct amount.

According to the UCP 600, all credits are irrevocable. The detailed articles are given below:

• Credit means any arrangement, however named or described, that is irrevocable and thereby constitutes a definite undertaking of the issuing bank to honour a complying presentation (UCP 600 Article 2).

• A credit is irrevocable even if there is no indication to that effect (UCP 600 Article 3).

• An issuing bank is irrevocably bound to honour as of the time it issues the credit (UCP600 Article 7).

### 3.4.2  Confirmed and Unconfirmed L/C

Confirmed L/C constitutes a definite undertaking of the confirming bank, in addition to that of the issuing bank, to honour or negotiate a complying presentation. Confirming bank is often, but not always, the advising bank located in the exporter's country who adds its confirmation to a credit upon the issuing bank's authorization or request.

When the seller has little confidence in or does not know the financial strength of the foreign issuing bank, he may request the issuing bank to nominate a confirming bank to add confirmation.

If a bank is authorized or requested by the issuing bank to confirm a credit but is not prepared to do so, it must inform the issuing bank without delay and may advise the credit without confirmation (UCP 600 article 8).

The confirming bank is irrevocably bound to honour or negotiate as of the time it adds its confirmation to the credit. As a result, confirmed L/C provides a double assurance of payment to the beneficiary. A confirmed letter of credit also protects against unfavorable exchange regulations and shortages of foreign currency in the importing country. However, confirmations are not necessary for all letters of credit.

Unconfirmed L/C means that the L/C doesn't have any payment guarantee by a bank in the exporter's country in addition to the bank originally issuing the credit. It contains the obligation of the issuing bank only. This type is usually used when the opening bank enjoys an undoubted reputation and financial strength or the transaction is small. In this arrangement, an expensive confirmation commission can be curtailed.

### 3.4.3 Sight Payment / Deferred Payment/Acceptance/Negotiation L/C

A credit must state whether it is available by sight payment, deferred payment, acceptance or negotiation (UCP 600 article 6).

Sight Payment L/C constitutes the definite undertaking of the issuing bank to pay at sight upon complying presentation of documents. It is usually preferred by the exporter for the immediate payment from the issuing bank. Under sight payment L/C, a draft may not be needed.

Deferred Payment L/C constitutes the definite undertaking of the issuing bank to incur a deferred payment undertaking and pay at maturity. The deferred payment is usually to be made a fixed number of days after shipment or presentation of prescribed documents.

Deferred payment credit doesn't call for a time draft drawn on and accepted by the issuing bank. Under this type, a period of credit is agreed by buyer and seller. When documents are presented "in order" by the seller, the bank does not accept a bill of exchange, but instead gives a letter of undertaking to the seller advising him when he will receive his money. However, there being no draft, the beneficiary party's ability to discount or sell his right to payment is restricted[1].

It is used where a buyer and a seller have close working relationship, and the seller is prepared to finance the purchase by allowing the buyer a grace period for payment.

Acceptance L/C constitutes the definite undertaking of the issuing bank to accept a bill of exchange ("draft") drawn by the beneficiary and pay at maturity.

A credit must not be issued available by a draft drawn on the applicant (UCP 600 article 6). This implies that the acceptor of the time draft under acceptance L/C should be the issuing bank, and the acceptance L/C is banker's acceptance L/C.

Banker's acceptance credit calls for time drafts to be drawn on and accepted by the issuing bank. Under this type, the paying bank guarantees to make payment in a specified number of days after its acceptance of the time draft.

Under any banker's acceptance credit and deferred payment credit, the seller is to be paid

---

[1]  http://www. businessdictionary. com/definition/deferred-payment-letter-of-credit-L-C. html.

in a specified number of days after the presentation of the stipulated documents, and that's why they can be called Usance L/C (Time L/C).

Negotiation L/C means a credit allows the beneficiary to negotiate the purchase price from a bank nominated by the issuing bank or any bank. Negotiation means the purchase by the nominated bank of drafts (drawn on a bank other than the nominated bank) and/or documents under a complying presentation, by advancing or agreeing to advance funds to the beneficiary on or before the banking day on which reimbursement is due to be paid by the nominated bank (UCP 600 article 2). Accordingly, negotiation L/C can be divided into restricted negotiation L/C and free negotiation L/C.

### 3.4.4 Mail and Cable L/C

Mail credit refers to letter of credit issued by the issuing bank, transmitted to the advising bank and then to the beneficiary by mail (often airmail). Usually the issuing bank provides the advising bank with the specimen of signature, against which the advising bank can ensure the authenticity of letter of credit. Comparatively, mail credit costs more time but lower expense, and are frequently used in the transactions of small amount and longer time of shipment.

Cable credit refers to letter of credit issued by the issuing bank, transmitted to the advising bank and then to the beneficiary by telegraphic transmission (telex, fax, SWIFT). Usually the issuing bank provides the advising bank with test key, against which the advising bank can ensure the authenticity of letter of credit. Cable credit costs less time but higher expense, and are commonly used nowadays.

As the development of information technology, SWIFT L/C is becoming one of the most commonly used L/C in international trade settlement. See appendix for the SWIFT telex field definition.

### 3.4.5 Transferable and Non-transferable L/C

Transferable L/C means a credit that specifically states it is "transferable" (UCP 600 article 38). It is an irrevocable L/C with two (and only two) successive beneficiaries. In this arrangement, the first beneficiary (an intermediary or importer's foreign representative) can assign part or whole of the L/C amount to a second beneficiary (the supplier or manufacturer)[1].

To be transferable, the L/C must be so marked by the issuing bank on the instructions of the buyer or importer. On the instructions of the first beneficiary the advising bank can transfer it to the second beneficiary but not any further. It is used extensively in China, Japan,

---

[1]  http://www. businessdictionary. com.

Korea, and Singapore among others. When the credit is transferred, all conditions must remain as in the original credit except that the amount of the credit, quantity of goods called for and the unit price may be reduced, or the period of validity and/or shipment may be shortened.

Non-transferable credit is one that can not be transferred. If a letter of credit is not indicated with "transferable", it is a non-transferable credit.

### 3.4.6 Back to Back Credit

Back to back credit is an arrangement in which one irrevocable L/C serves as the collateral for another, the advising bank of the first L/C becomes the issuing bank of the second L/C.

Back to back credit arises in circumstances similar to those of the transferable credit. In this arrangement, the middleman receives a credit in his favor from the buyer and ask his bank (usually the advising bank of the primary credit) to establish a second credit in favor of his supplier against the security of the credit in his own favor. The second credit is similar to the first except that the amount may be lower and it has a shorter validity to allow time for substitution of invoices and other contingencies.

In contrast to a "transferable letter of credit", permission of the ultimate buyer (the applicant or account party of the first L/C) or that of the issuing bank is not required in a back-to-back L/C. It is used mainly by middlemen (intermediaries) to hide the identity of the actual supplier or manufacturer. Also called counter credit or reciprocal letter of credit[1].

Since there are two separate credits instead of one as in the case of a transferable credit, there may appear some problems in the matching of documents and credit terms.

### 3.4.7 Revolving L/C

Revolving L/C means a single L/C that covers multiple-shipments over a long period. Instead of arranging a new L/C for each separate shipment, the buyer establishes an L/C that revolves either in value (a fixed amount is available which is replenished when exhausted) or in time (an amount is available in fixed installments over a period such as week, month, or year)[2]. That is to say, a revolving credit permits repeated drawings by the beneficiary within a specified amount and period.

L/C may be revolved in time in two types: in the cumulative type, the sum unutilized in a period is carried over to be utilized in the next period; whereas in the non-cumulative type, it is not carried over.

---

① http://www.businessdictionary.com.

② http://www.businessdictionary.com.

### 3.4.8  Red Clause Credit

Red clause credit refers to L/C that carries a provision (traditionally written or typed in red ink) which allows a seller to draw up to a fixed sum from the advising bank or paying bank, in advance of the shipment or before presenting the prescribed documents. Red clause credit is also called an anticipatory credit or a packing credit, which allows its beneficiary to borrow against it before fulfilling its all requirements.

In cases where no shipment is made under the letter of credit or when the loan is not repaid by the beneficiary, the issuing bank or the importer is liable for repayment plus interest. In fact, it is the buyer who is extending an unsecured loan to the seller and bears the financial risk. In addition, the importer assumes the currency risk as well, since red clause advances are usually in the local currency.

Due to the high risk to the importer, before permitting red clause advances, the importer must have sufficient confidence in capacity and integrity of the beneficiary. It is used only where the buyer and seller have close working relationship.

### 3.4.9  Standby L/C

Standby L/C refers to L/C which a bank issues on behalf of its customer to serve as a guarantee to the beneficiary of the letter of credit that the bank's customer will perform a specified contract with the beneficiary. If the customer defaults, the beneficiary may draw funds against the letter of credit as penalties or as payments, whichever the terms of the credit provide[1]. It serves as a parallel (collateral) payment source in case the primary source fails to meet its obligations in part or in full.

Standby L/C is primarily a substitute for a performance bond or payment guaranty. It originated in the 1800s in the United States, and underwent a rapid development in the early 1950s in the U.S. and Japan, where banks were legally barred from issuing certain types of guaranties. Till the end of 1998, the outstanding value of Standby L/C was as much as SEVEN times of the value of Commercial Documentary L/C. And this resulted in the introduction of International Standby Practice (ICC Publication No. 590) in 1998.

To sum up, one L/C may belong to different types of credit. Practically, the most frequently used types are confirmed, irrevocable, documentary L/C, which is usually available by draft at sight or after sight, and remain valid for negotiation in the beneficiary's locality within a specific period of time after date of B/L.

---

[1]  http://www. teachmefinance. com/Financial_Terms/standby_letter_of_credit. html.

## 3.5 Contents of a Letter of Credit

The example of a confirmed irrevocable letter of credit in figure 3. 2[1] illustrates the various parts of a typical letter of credit.

---

**INTERNATIONAL BANKING GROUP**      **ORIGINAL**

**Megabank Corporation**

P. O. BOX 1000, ATLANTA, GEORGIA 30302 · 1000

**CABLE ADDRESS: MegaB**

**TELEX NO. 1234567**

**SWIFT NO. MBBABC 72**

OUR ADVICE NUMBER: EA00000091

ADVICE DATE: 24MAR24      * * * * AMOUNT * * * *

ISSUE BANK REF: 3312/HBL/22341     USD * * * * 25 000. 00

EXPIRY DATE: 24JUN24

BENEFICIARY:           APPLICANT:

THE WALTON SUPPLY CO.      HHB HONG KONG

2356 SOUTH N. W. STREET     34 INDUSTRIAL DRIVE

ATLANTA, GEORGIA 30345     CENTRAL, HONG KONG, CHINA

WE HAVE BEEN REQUESTED TO ADVISE TO YOU THE FOLLOWING LETTER OF CREDIT AS ISSUED BY:

THIRD HONG KONG BANK

1 CENTRAL TOWER

HONG KONG, CHINA

PLEASE BE GUIDED BY ITS TERMS AND CONDITIONS AND BY THE FOLLOWING:

CREDIT IS AVAILABLE BY NEGOTIATION OF YOUR DRAFT(S) IN DUPLICATE AT

SIGHT FOR 100 PERCENT OF INVOICE VALUE DRAWN ON US ACCOMPANIED BY THE

FOLLOWING DOCUMENTS:

1. SIGNED COMMERCIAL INVOICE IN 1 ORIGINAL AND 3 COPIES.
2. FULL SET 3/3 OCEAN BILLS OF LADING CONSIGNED TO THE ORDER OF THIRD HONG KONG
   BANK, HONG KONG NOTIFY APPLICANT AND MARKED FREIGHT COLLECT.
3. PACKING LIST IN 2 COPIES.

EVIDENCING SHIPMENT OF: 5 000 PINE LOGS-WHOLE-8 TO 12 FEET

                       FOB SAVANNAH, GEORGIA

SHIPMENT FROM: SAVANNAH, GEORGIA     TO: HONG KONG, CHINA

LATEST SHIPPING DATE: 24JUN24

PARTIAL SHIPMENTS NOT ALLOWED     TRANSSHIPMENT NOT ALLOWED

ALL BANKING CHARGES OUTSIDE HONG KONG ARE FOR BENEFICIARYS ACCOUNT.

DOCUMENTS MUST BE PRESENTED WITHIN 21 DAYS FROM B/L DATE.

AT THE REQUEST OF OUR CORRESPONDENT, WE CONFIRM THIS CREDIT AND ALSO ENGAGE WITH YOU

THAT ALL DRAFTS DRAWN UNDER AND IN COMPLIANCE WITH THE TERMS OF THIS CREDIT WILL BE DULY

HONORED BY US.

PLEASE EXAMINE THIS INSTRUMENT CAREFULLY. IF YOU ARE UNABLE TO COMPLY WITH THE TERMS OR

CONDITIONS, PLEASE COMMUNICATE WITH YOUR BUYER TO ARRANGE FOR AN AMENDMENT.

---

**Figure 3. 2   Specimen of a Confirmed Irrevocable Letter of Credit**

---

[1] http://www.unzco.com/basicguide/figure13.html.

### 3.5.1  Items on the Credit Itself

Items on the credit itself include the issuing bank, the beneficiary, the applicant, the confirming bank, the form of credit, the issuing date, the expiry date and place, the L/C amount and currency, the method of availability, and etc.

In this sample, the detailed information is listed below:

- The issuing bank: The Third Hong Kong Bank, Hong Kong.
- The beneficiary: The Walton Supply Company.
- The applicant: HHB Hong Kong.
- The confirming bank: The Megabank Corporation.
- The form of credit: confirmed, irrevocable, documentary credit.
- The date of issue: March 8, 2024.
- The expiry date and place: June 23, 2024, Atlanta Georgia.
- The L/C amount and currency: USD 25 000.00.
- The method of availability: is available by negotiation of the draft at sight for 100% invoice value drawn on the issuing bank accompanied by commercial documents.

### 3.5.2  Items on Draft

It is the drawn clause of the draft(s), mainly concerns the drawer, the drawee, and the payee, the numbers, etc.

In this sample, the detailed information is as follows:

- The drawer: The Walton Supply Company.
- The drawee: The Third Hong Kong Bank, Hong Kong.
- The payee: The Walton Supply Company.
- The numbers: in duplicate.
- The tenor of payment: at sight.

### 3.5.3  Items on Shipping Documents and Goods

Items on shipping documents are commercial invoices, bills of lading, packing list, etc. In this specimen, they are:

- Signed commercial invoice in 1 original and 3 copies.
- Full set 3/3 ocean bills of lading consigned to the order of the Third Hong Kong Bank, Hong Kong, notify applicant and marked freight collect.
- Packing list in 2 copies.
- Evidencing shipment of: 5 000 pine logs−whole−8 to 12 feet, FOB Savannah, Georgia.

### 3.5.4  Items on Transport

Items on transport cover the port of loading/shipment, the port of discharge or destination, the latest date of shipment, etc. and whether partial shipment or transshipment permitted or not.

In this example, the shipment was transported from Savannah, Georgia to Hong Kong, China on or before June 2, 2024, neither partial shipments nor transshipment was allowed.

### 3.5.5 Items on Charges

Items on charges usually stipulate who will bear all banking charges outside the importing country. In the specimen of figure 3.2, all banking charges outside Hong Kong, China were for the account of the beneficiary.

### 3.5.6 Other Items

Other items, depending on different cases, may include the instructions, the undertaking clauses of the issuing bank and the confirming bank (if any), authorized signatures for the issuing bank, or the test key or SWIFT authentic key, and the notation of the credit subject to the UCP 500/600, etc.

In the specimen of figure 3.2, the latest date for documents presentation, the definite undertaking of both the issuing bank and the confirming bank, and a friendly reminding for necessary L/C amendment were covered in other items.

To elaborate the items of L/C more clearly, the specimen of SWIFT L/C is given below[1].

| ******* AUTH. CORRECT WITH CURRENT KEY ******* | |
|---|---|
| FIN VAK | {F21 INGBCZPPAXXX0243009253} |
| {4: {177: Date and Time (YYMMDDHHMM) | :241117 1352 |
| {451: acceptance/rejection | :0} } |
| { 1: FIN MESSAGE/Session/OSN | F01 INGBCZPPAXXX 0243 009253 |
| {2: Output Message Type | 700 issue of a documentary credit |
| Input Time/MIR | 1452 241117IDBLILITBHAI1320277510 |
| Received from | IDBLILITBHAI |
| | Israel discount bank ltd. |
| | Haifa |
| Output Date/Time | 241117 1353 |
| Priority/Delivery/Obsol | Normal } |

---

① Johan Bergamin. Payment Techniques in Trade Finance. ING BARINGS, April/May 1999.

{4

:27 sequence of total

    1/2

:40A form of documentary credit:

    IRREVOCABLE

:20 documentary credit number:

    070 S3423946/K21

:31C date of issue:

    241117

:31D Date and place of expiry:

    241231 CZECH REP

: 50 applicant:

    KESHET PLADA LTD.

    IND. ZONE

    CARMIEL, 20100, ISRAEL

:59 beneficiary:

    FERROSTAR LTD.

    P. O. BOX 121

    PRAHA, 4, CZECH REP.

:32b currency code amount

    currency code:      USD US Dollar

    amount:         # 78,068.74 #

:39B maximum credit amount:

    MAXIMUM

---

:41a available with/by—swift add:

    INGBCZPPXXX

    ING Bank/Internationale Nederlanden

    Bank

    Prague

    BY PAYMENT

:43P partial shipments:

    NOT PERMITTED

:43 transshipment

    NOT PERMITTED

:44 on board/disp/taking charge:

    EUPROEAN PORT

:44B for transportation to:

    HAIFA PORT ONLY

:45A descr goods and/or services:

14. 747 METERS OF SEAMLESS PIPES QUANLITY ST 44 WITH CUT ENDS IN DOUBLE
   RANDOW LENGTH AS FOLLOWS:
   9,782.5M SIZE 70.0×5.6
   4,965.0M SIZE 88.9×6.0
   ABOVE GOODS CFR HAIFA PORT ONLY

:71B charges:

   ALL BANKING CHARGES OUTSIDE ISRAEL INCLUDING TELEX/SWIFT CHARGES ON BENEFICIA-
   RIES' ACCOUNT

:49 confirmation instructions:

   WITHOUT

:53A reimbursement bank—BIC:

   IDBYUS33

   Israel discount bank of New York

   New York, NY

:78 instructions to pay/accepting bk:

   1. UTILIZATION TO BE ADVISED TO US BY TELEX /SWIFT AND PAYMENT TO BENEFICIARIES TO
   BE CARRIED OUT THREE WORKING DAYS AFTER DATE OF YOUR TELEX/SWIFT ADVICE TO US
   EVIDENCING AMOUNT OF DOUCMENTS INVOLVED AND VALUE DATE

:72 sender to receiver information:

   PLEASE ADKNOWLEDGE RECE PT

{5: {MAC: OECBA175 Authentication Result

   { CHK: 5A86B59CADC7 Checksum Trailer}

| * * * * AUTH. CORRECT WITH CURRENT KEY * * * * | |
| --- | --- |
| FIN VAK | {F21 INGBCZPPAXXX0243009253 } |
| {4: { 177: Date and Time (YYMMDDHHMM) | :241117 1352 |
| {451: acceptance/rejection | :0} } |
| { 1: FIN MESSAGE/Session/OSN | F01　INGBCZPPAXXX 0243 009253 |
| {2: Output Message Type | 700 issue of a documentary credit |
| Input Time/MIR | 1452 241117IDBLILITBHAl1320277510 |
| Received from | IDBLILITBHAI |
| | Israel discount bank ltd. |
| | Haifa |
| Output Date/Time | 241117 1353 |
| Priority/Delivery/Obsol | Normal} |

{4:
:27 sequence of total:
   2//2
:20 documentary credit number:
   070S3423947 / K21
:46b documents required:
   (A) 3/3 ORGINAL CLEAN ON BOARD BILLS OF LADING PLUS NON NEGOTIABLE COPIES MADE
       OUT OR ENDORSED TO THE ORDER OF ISRAEL DISCOUNT BANK LTC. HAIFA MARKED
       070s34423947/K21, NOTIFY: PIPE FITTINGS CARMIEL LTD, IND. ZONE, CARMIEL 20100,
       FREIGHT PREPAID AND DUE TO DANGER OF CONFISCATION WARRANTED VESSEL IS NOT
       TO CALL AT PORTS AND NOT TO ENTER THE TERRITORIAL WATERS OF SYRIA LEBANON
       JORDAN IRAQ SAUDI ARABIA YEMEN SUDAN LIBYA OR OTHER ARAB COUNTRIES EXCEP-
       TING EGYPT PRIOR TO UNLOADING IN ISRAEL UNLESS IN DISTRESS OR SUBJECT TO FORCE
       MAJEURE.
   (B) DETAILED PACKING LIST(s) IN FIVE COPIES.
   (C) BENEFICIARIES ORIGINAL COMMERCIAL INVOICES DULY HAND SIGNED AND STAMPED BY
       THEM IN SIX COPIES STATING THAT:
       1. GOODS ARE OF CZECH. ORIGIN.
       2. GOODS CONFORM TO ORDERER's ORDER AND PROFORMA INVOICE NUMBER 0007/25
          DATED 24/11/25.
       3. GOODS ARE OF FIRST QUALITY.
   (D) MILL TEST CERTIFICATE.
:47B additional conditions
       1. INSURANCE COVERED HERE BY BUYERS.
       2. THIS DOCUMENTARY CREDIT SUBJECT TO UCPDC 2007(ICC600).
       3. KINDLY ALSO ADVISE BENEFCIARIES BY PHONE 02 426969.

   4. VERY IMPORTANT
ALL SHIPPING DOCTS. TO BE ISSUED IN THE NAME OF PIPE FITTINGS CARMIEL LTD. P. O.
       BOX 233 CARMIEL
{5: {MAC: 7DAEOE3E} Authentication Result

## 3.6　Checklists of Documentary Credit

Documentary credit involves so many parties, procedures, and documents that it deserves careful considerations. The following checklists are recommended to different parties at different procedures of L/C operation.

### 3.6.1　Checklist for the Exporter When Negotiating Sales Contract

During the preliminary negotiations stage, the exporter must make sure of the nine points mentioned below:

(1) Irrevocable & Confirmed.

(2) Documentary or clean credit.

(3) Available by sight payment, deferred payment, acceptance, or negotiation.

(4) Where is the credit to be used to make payment?

(5) What currency is to be used?

(6) The detailed arrangements, particularly:

• The correct name of the beneficiary company, its spelling and the address.

• The exact details of the goods; the total value of the letter of credit.

• The date of expiry, which must be extensive enough to permit manufacture, testing, packing and shipping.

• The arrival of the credit; the method of notification (airmail, telex, SWIFT, etc.) must be laid down, and the UCP 500/600 should be specified to control the behavior of the parties to the credit.

• The mode of transport influences the requirements of the letter of credit.

• The types and the numbers of document required, and the particular requirements of the country concerned.

(7) If the cargo must be shipped on deck, it must be permitted "on deck" shipment in the letter of credit and the insurance policy.

(8) If pre-packing inspection or test is required, it is important to make sure the exact names, addresses and qualification of the institutions which are required to sign the certificate.

(9) It is important to establish personal contact between the two firms, and to note the names and addresses.

## 3.6.2 Checklist for the Importer When Applying

When applying for letter of credit, the importer must be sure of the following 13 points:

(1) Has a status report on the supplier been taken out to verify his ability to supply goods of the type and quality required?

(2) Has the contract been thoroughly vetted to ensure that the exact requirements as to the quantity, specification, delivery date, terms of sale, terms of payment, etc. are known?

(3) Has the question of finance to honor the credit been carefully considered and are funds available or budgeted for in a proper manner?

(4) Has the application form covered every instruction necessary for efficient conduct of the bank's undertakings? In particular:

• Is the credit to be irrevocable?

• Is it to be confirmed by a bank in the seller's country?

• How is the credit to be advised, by airmail or by SWIFT?

- What is the amount and currency of the credit, in words and figures?
- For how long is it to be valid and how and where is it to be paid?

(5) What documents are required?

- Invoice.
- Transport document.
- Proof of origin or value, or both.
- Proof of insurance.
- Proof of pre-shipment inspection, weighting, etc.
- Proof of packing.
- Proof of health, freedom from pest, etc.
- Consular invoices.
- A copy of the export license if applicable.

(6) What are the details of the goods required?

(7) If export licenses necessary, is the supplier aware that he is responsible for them?

(8) If import licenses necessary, are they in hand at the importer's end? The license number should be quoted in the L/C.

(9) What is the terms of trade, and whether Incoterms® 2020 is to be specified?

(10) Are partial shipments allowed? Is trans-shipment permitted?

(11) If the exporter is to insure, is it clearly stated about what level and value of cover is required?

(12) Are any other dates apart from the date of expiry of the credit important?

(13) Are there any restrictions on the flag of the ship chosen?

### 3.6.3　Checklist for the Issuing Bank When Opening the Credit

Before issuing a letter of credit, the issuing bank should make clear the following 7 points:

(1) Is the applicant known to us, and creditworthy to the extent of the amount required? Does he have an established line of credit? Does this request exceed it and, if so, what steps should we take?

(2) If the credit is irrevocable, we shall be bound by it, and consequently we must be sure of the applicant's reliability.

(3) Has the applicant signed our usual indemnity form? It is a certificate of pledge giving us rights over the document of title and the goods themselves.

(4) Any queries ambiguities, inconsistencies or omissions must be raised?

(5) Draw up a letter of credit for the correspondent bank in the exporter's country (the advising bank), ensuring absolute accuracy in all respects, particularly names, addresses, details of goods, prices and values, list of documents, details of amount, validity, time, place

and method of payment of credit; all dates and details part-shipments, transshipment, etc. should be checked.

(6) Is the consignment insured in a proper manner? Since the consignment represents part of our security for the credit, on which we, as issuing bank, may be liable, damage in transit may leave us with worthless goods in the event of the customer's default. It is therefore important, especially with FOB or CFR contracts, that our importer insures the goods in time after the exporter has notified the details of shipment as required by Incoterms. On CIF terms, the exporter must produce a valid insurance document when he presents the documents after shipment.

(7) Is the import license in order? If the goods are refused entry because no import license has been issued, the security for these operations is unable to enter the jurisdiction of our courts.

If all the points listed are in good order, the issuing bank should notify the credit by the method prescribed in the application, that is, to telex, airmail or facsimile copy of detailed instructions to the correspondent bank in the exporter's country, and ask them to advise the exporter that the credit is opened.

### 3.6.4 Checklist for the Advising Bank/Confirming Bank

Upon receipt of the credit, the exporter's bank should consider the following 6 issues and take proper actions:

(1) When the credit arrives, we must check it carefully to see that all necessary items have been raised.

(2) If confirmation is being requested, we are undertaking a commitment to the beneficiary which we will be obliged to honor.

(3) We must therefore check the status of the issuing bank and the stability of the country concerned.

(4) If we are unsure about this, we must require the transfer of funds from the issuing bank. These funds will be held in a suspense account until the credit is honored.

(5) We must advise the exporter of the existence of the credit, referring particularly to the following points:

- At whose request we are advising him.
- The exact terms of the credit as laid down by the applicant.
- Whether it is revocable or irrevocable; whether we are to confirm it or not. If not, we have no engagement personally to provide funds for the beneficiary.

(6) We must also deal with any changes notified by the issuing bank as a result of protests by the exporter, and advise the exporter of them so that he is reassured and can proceed with the order.

### 3.6.5 Checklist for the Beneficiary on Receipt of the Credit

Upon receipt of the letter of credit, the beneficiary must check the following points and take actions accordingly:

(1) Whether it conforms to the original agreement with the foreign customer as to the following points:

- Irrevocable or not.
- Confirmed or not.
- Names and addresses of the parties.
- Does the shipping date specified give sufficient time to manufacture or obtain the goods, pack and ship them?
- Is it sight or term credit? If the latter, what is the period or usance?
- Does the expiry date allow enough time to prepare and present the documents?
- Is the amount sufficient to cover the original quotation and any variable items specified in it?
- Is the currency correct?
- Is the place of validity correct?
- Is the description of the goods correct?
- Is partial shipments permitted if necessary?
- Is the port of final discharge as agreed?
- A list of document and a note of which language is to be used.
- If "on deck" shipment is needed, does the letter of credit authorize it?
- If a vessel is being chartered, does the letter of credit specify that a charter party bill of lading is acceptable?
- Are the terms of the sales contract in accordance with the original Incoterms specified in the contract?
- Are the transportation documents correct for the mode of transport envisaged?
- Does the letter of credit call for an insurance policy or an insurance certificate? Does it call for notification to the foreign insurer who will arrange cover?
- Are all the license and documentation requirements of a country met?

(2) Raise any queries directly with customer and urge him to send immediately authorized amendments via his issuing bank, for onward transmission to the exporter.

(3) Preparing goods and processing documentation:

- Obtain, assemble and pack the goods.
- Process documents in accordance with the letter of credit.
- Ship goods according to the letter of credit.

● Obtain a bill of lading or other document proving dispatch of goods.

(4) Presenting documents for payment:

● Present documents to the advising bank in accordance with the letter of credit, including sight draft for payment or term draft for acceptance or negotiation.

● If credit is not a confirmed one it may be necessary to wait until payment is remitted or "accepted" term bill arrives from abroad before funds can be obtained.

● Acknowledge conclusion of contract to importer and solicit further business.

### 3.6.6 Checklist of Letter of Credit Amendments

After careful examination on letter of credit, the beneficiary may find that some terms and conditions of L/C do not comply with the sales contract, or they may find some clauses with which they are unable to comply. Under these circumstances, the exporter should communicate with his buyer, the applicant of L/C, to arrange appropriate L/C amendments. When amending L/C, the following points should be kept in mind by parties concerned[①].

(1) Once the beneficiary applies for L/C amendment, it is the applicant who is entitled to decide whether to amend an L/C or not.

(2) In order to avoid additional charges and expenses, the beneficiary should put forward all items being amended at one time.

(3) Once the applicant decides to amend an L/C, the amendment should be issued by the original issuing bank and advised by the original advising bank to the beneficiary.

(4) Usually, a credit can not be amended without the agreement of the issuing bank, the confirming bank, if any, and the beneficiary.

(5) An issuing bank is irrevocably bound by an amendment as of the time it issues the amendment.

(6) A confirming bank may extend its confirmation to an amendment and will be irrevocably bound as of the time it advises the amendment. A confirming bank may, however, choose to advise an amendment without extending its confirmation and, if so, it must inform the issuing bank without delay and inform the beneficiary.

(7) The terms and conditions of the original credit (or a credit incorporating previously accepted amendments) will remain in force for the beneficiary until the beneficiary communicates its acceptance of the amendment to the bank that advised such amendment. The beneficiary should give notification of acceptance or rejection of an amendment. If the beneficiary fails to give such notification, a presentation that complies with the credit and to any not yet accepted amendment will be deemed to be notification of acceptance by the beneficiary of such amend-

---

① UCP600 Article 10.

ment. As of that moment the credit will be amended.

(8) A bank that advises an amendment should inform the bank from which it received the amendment of any notification of acceptance or rejection.

(9) Partial acceptance of an amendment is not allowed and will be deemed to be notification of rejection of the amendment.

(10) A provision that the amendment shall enter into force unless rejected by the beneficiary within a certain time shall be disregarded.

### 3.6.7 Checklists of Possible Problems and Discrepancies

Letter of credit is usually available by the issuing bank, or confirming bank (if any), against complying presentation. Where complying presentation means a presentation that is in accordance with the terms and conditions of the credit, the applicable provisions of these rules and international standard banking practice. That is to say, the inconsistency with the credit, the violation of the applicable provisions, and the deviation from the international standard banking practice may all constitute discrepancies and result in dishonor. The following checklists are frequently occurred problems and discrepancies in international trade practice[1].

(1) Letter of Credit. As for L/C, the frequently occurred problems are:

• Late Presentation. Documents not presented within 21 days after the date of the transport document or within the stipulated time period.

It is quite often the case that documents are dishonored for reasons that could have been corrected or for which an indemnity may be given, but by the time the exporter has attended to this, the time period has elapsed and thus the corrected documents are refused when presented due to "late presentation".

Care should be taken not to exceed this period when correcting documents and representing.

• Credit Expired & Late Shipment. Documents are regularly refused for reasons that the credit has expired or that the shipment is late. A large number of rejections could be avoided by timely planning.

(2) Transport Documents. As for the transport documents, the frequently occurred discrepancies are:

• Presentation of incomplete Bills of Lading.

• The "on board" date of the transport document not being within the time limit allowed.

• "Received for shipment Bill of Lading" converted into an "on board" Bill by notation without the notation being dated or a "received for shipment" Bill being presented when an "on

---

① http://www. esatclear. ie/~irish. trade/tgindex. htm.

board" Bill is required.

- Transport document not marked "Freight paid" or "Freight payable at destination", as required.
- Bill of Lading evidencing shipment "on deck" when not authorized by L/C.
- Incorrect notify party or notify party address.
- B/L indicating "intended" ports of shipment and discharge instead of named ports.
- Marks and numbers, numbers of cases or packages, weight etc. shown on transport documents being inconsistent with other documents.
- The name of the carrier does not appear on the face of the transport document.
- It does not cover transshipment when it is being effected.
- Incorrectly signed transport documents in accordance with articles 19-27 of the UCP 600.
- Signature may be absent, or inadequate signatures of the country concerned, such as facsimile signatures may have been given when original signatures are required.

(3) Invoices. As for invoices, such problems should be consider:

- Made to the buyer in an incorrect name and/or address.
- Goods, prices and terms of delivery described incorrectly and in the case of the latter, not always being stated.
- Invoice amount exceeding the credit amount.
- Goods or charges being invoiced in addition to those permitted by the credit.
- Invoices not being legalized or certified when this is required.
- Invoices not being signed when this is required.

(4) Insurance. As for insurance, the frequently occurred problems are:

- Often issued for an incorrect amount (CIF, CIP + 10% is usually called for) or different currency.
- Does not cover all the risks required.
- The insurance policy or certificate is dated later than the date of the transport document without stating that the cover is effective from the date of shipment or dispatch.
- It is not endorsed as required.
- It does not state where claims are payable when it is required by the L/C.

(5) Others.

- Other documents called for by the credit not being issued by the party stipulated in the credit and not containing the correct wording or data content.
- Copy letter, telexes etc. to the issuing bank, the buyer or other specified party not properly addressed, or dated, or containing incorrect information.
- There may be errors on the bill of exchange, such as the wrong party drawn on, the wrong amount, inadequate dating, and incorrect endorsement.

## Questions and Problems

### I . Choose the best answer to fill in the blank.

1. According to the UCP 600, Letter of Credit means any arrangement, however named or described, that is irrevocable and thereby constitutes a definite undertaking of the _____ to honor a complying presentation.

    A. issuing bank      B. nominated bank    C. advising bank      D. negotiating bank

2. According to the UCP 600, _____ means the purchase by the nominated bank of drafts and/or documents under a complying presentation, by advancing or agreeing to advance funds to the beneficiary on or before the banking day on which reimbursement is due to be paid to the nominated bank.

    A. confirmation      B. negotiation        C. honor           D. payment

3. All parties concerned in a letter of credit deal with _____ .

    A. goods or services               B. goods and documents

    C. services and documents        D. documents

4. Under L/C payment term, the obligation of the advising bank is _____ .

    A. to authenticate the L/C and notify the seller of the arrival of the L/C

    B. to issue the L/C upon the application of the importer

    C. to purchase a documentary draft

    D. to honor a complying presentation

5. If a B/L contains the following date(s) simultaneously, _____ will be deemed to be the date of shipment.

    A. the date of receiving the goods

    B. the date of issuing the B/L

    C. the actual date of shipment in a specific notation

    D. the sailing date of the carrying vessel

6. In documents other than _____ , the description of the goods, services or perfor-mance, if stated, may be in general terms not conflicting with their description in the credit.

    A. the commercial invoice           B. the bill of lading

    C. the packing list                 D. the inspection certificate

7. The description of goods in the L/C (subject to the UCP 600) is "about 10, 000 metric tons of rice, total amount: about USD 10, 000. 00". The permitted maximum quantity of ship-ment is _____ metric tons.

    A. 11, 000          B. 10, 500          C. 10, 000          D. 95, 000

8. If the beneficiary finds out discrepancies between terms/conditions of L/C and sales

contract, he should contact the＿＿＿＿at the first place for L/C amendment.

    A. issuing bank     B. negotiating bank   C. advising bank   D. applicant

9. If the negotiating bank finds out discrepancies between documents and terms/conditions of L/C, he should contact the＿＿＿＿at the first place for documents correction.

    A. issuing bank     B. beneficiary     C. confirming bank   D. applicant

10. If the issuing bank finds out MINOR discrepancies between documents and terms/conditions of L/C, he usually contacts the＿＿＿＿at the first place for documents acceptance.

    A. negotiating bank   B. beneficiary     C. confirming bank   D. applicant

## II. True (T) or false (F).

1. According to the UCP 600, branches of a bank in different countries are not considered to be separate banks.

2. According to the UCP 600, the undertaking of a bank to honor, to negotiate or to fulfill any other obligation under the credit is subject to claims or defenses by the applicant resulting from its relationships with the issuing bank or the beneficiary.

3. A credit available with a nominated bank is also available with the issuing bank.

4. If credit does not state an expiry date for presentation, the expiry date stated for honor or negotiation will be deemed to be an expiry date for presentation.

5. A bank utilizing the services of an advising bank or second advising bank to advise a credit must use the same bank to advise any amendment thereto.

6. A document may be dated prior to the issuance date of the credit, but must not be dated later than its date of presentation.

7. Partial acceptance of an amendment is allowed and will not be deemed to be notification of rejection of the amendment.

8. If a credit requires presentation of copies of documents, presentation of either originals or copies is permitted.

9. The date of issuance of the bill of lading will be deemed to be the date of shipment unless the bill of lading contains an on board notation indicating the date of shipment, in which case the date stated in the on board notation will be deemed to be the date of shipment.

10. A clean transport document is one bearing no clause or notation expressly declaring a defective condition of the goods or their packaging.

11. If a drawing or shipment by installments within given periods is stipulated in the credit and any installment is not drawn or shipped within the period allowed for that installment, the credit ceases to be available for that and any subsequent installment.

12. A bank has no obligation to accept a presentation outside its banking hours.

13. A bank will, upon resumption its business, honor or negotiate under a credit that

expired during such interruption of its business.

14. Bank assumes liability or responsibility for errors in translation or interpretation of technical terms and may transmit credit terms without translating them.

15. A bank assumes no liability or responsibility for the consequences arising out of the interruption of its business by Acts of God, riots, civil commotions, insurrections, wars, acts of terrorism, or by any strikes or lockouts or any other causes beyond its control.

**III. Fill in the blank form L/C application according to the following contract.**

---

### CONTRACT No. AC4789

**Sellers:** Jiahe Trading Company, 60 Niujie Road, Beijing, China

**Buyers:** Global Trading Company , 30 Fifth Avenue, New York, U. S. A.

The undersigned Sellers and Buyers have agreed to close the following transaction according to the terms and conditions stipulated below:

**Commodity:** "YONGJIU" Brand Bicycle

**Specifications:** Model YE110

**Quantity:** 1,000 Bicycles

**Unit Price:** At USD100 each CIF New York

**Total Value:** USD100, 000 ( Say United States Dollars One Hundred Thousand Only)

**Packing:** In wooden cases

**Shipping Mark:** At Sellers' option

**Insurance:** To be covered by the Sellers for 110% of the invoice value against All Risks and War Risk as per CIC dated 1st January, 1981.

**Time of Shipment:** To be effected not later than 31st March, 2024, allowing partial shipments and prohibiting transshipment.

**Port of Shipment:** China Port

**Port of Destination:** New York

**Terms of Payment:** By irrevocable L/C at sight to reach the Sellers a month prior to the time of shipment and remain valid for negotiation in China until the 15th day after the final date of shipment.

Done and signed in Beijing on this 11th day of October, 2023.

The sellers                                        The buyers

_____                        _____

---

# IRREVOCABLE DOCUMENTARY CREDIT APPLICATION

TO: BANK OF New York                                                    Date:

| Beneficiary (full name and address) | L/C No.<br>Ex-Card No.<br>Contract No. |
|---|---|
| | Date and place of expiry of the credit |

| Partial shipments<br>☐allowed<br>☐not allowed | Transshipment<br>☐allowed<br>☐not allowed | ☐Issue by airmail<br>☐With brief advice by teletransmission<br>☐Issue by express delivery<br>☐Issue by SWIFT |
|---|---|---|

| Loading on board/dispatch/taking in charge at/<br>from<br>Not later than<br>for transportation to | Amount (both in figures and words) |
|---|---|

| Description of goods: | Credit available with<br>☐ by sight payment　☐ by acceptance<br>☐ by negotiation　　☐ by deferred payment at<br>against the documents detailed herein<br>☐ and beneficiary's draft for　% of the invoice value<br>At<br>on |
|---|---|
| Packing: | |
| | ☐FOB　☐CFR　☐CIF　☐or other terms |

Documents required: (marked with ✗)

    1. (　) Signed Commercial Invoice in copies indicating invoice no. , contract no.

    2. (　) Full set of clean on board ocean Bills of Lading made out to order and blank endorsed, marked "freight (　) to collect / (　) prepaid (　) showing freight amount" notifying

    3. (　) Air Waybills showing "freight (　) to collect / (　) prepaid (　) indicating freight amount" and consigned to__

    4. (　) Memorandum issued by_____ consigned to_____

    5. (　) Insurance Policy / Certificate in copies for__% of the invoice value showing claims payable in China in currency of the draft, blank endorsed, covering (　) Ocean Marine Transportation / (　) Air Transportation / (　) Over Land Transportation(　) All Risks, War Risks.

    6. (　) Packing List / Weight Memo in__copies indicating quantity / gross and net weights of each package and packing conditions as called for by the L/C.

    7. (　) Certificate of Quantity / Weight in__copies issued an independent surveyor at the loading port, indicating the actual surveyed quantity / weight of shipped goods as well as the packing condition.

    8. (　) Certificate of Quality in__copies issued by (　) manufacturer / (　) public recognized surveyor / (　)?

9. （   ） Beneficiary's certified copy of FAX dispatched to the accountee with__days after shipment advising （   ） name of vessel / （   ） date, quantity, weight and value of shipment.

10. （   ） Beneficiary's Certificate certifying that extra copies of the documents have been dispatched according to the contract terms.

11. （   ） Shipping Company's Certificate attesting that the carrying vessel is chartered or booked by accountee or their shipping agents:

12. （   ） Other documents, if any:

（   ） a) Certificate of Origin in__copies issued by authorized institution.

（   ） b) Certificate of Health in__copies issued by authorized institution.

Additional instructions:

1. （   ） All banking charges outside the opening bank are for beneficiary's account.

2. （   ） Documents must be presented with__days after the date of issuance of the transport documents but within the validity of this credit.

3. （   ） Third party as shipper is not acceptable. Short Form / Blank Back B/L is not acceptable.

4. （   ） Both quantity and amount__% more or less are allowed.

5. （   ） prepaid freight drawn in excess of L/C amount is acceptable against presentation of original charges voucher issued by Shipping Co. / Air line / or it's agent.

6. （   ） All documents to be forwarded in one cover, unless otherwise stated above.

7. （   ） Other terms, if any:

---

Advising bank: Bank of China, Beijing Branch

---

Account No. : with （name of bank）

Transacted by: Applicant（name, signature of authorized person）

Telephone No. : （with seal）

## Ⅳ. Issue a documentary credit by SWIFT according to the application in problem Ⅲ above.

### Issue of a Documentary Credit

| | | |
|---|---|---|
| Issuing Bank | | |
| Destination Bank | | |
| Type of Documentary Credit | 40A | |
| Letter of Credit Number | 20 | |
| Date of Issue | 31G | |
| Date and Place of Expiry | 31D | |
| Applicant Bank | 51D | |
| Applicant | 50 | |
| Beneficiary | 59 | |

| | | |
|---|---|---|
| Currency Code, Amount | 32B | |
| Available with. . . by. . . | 41D | |
| Drafts at | 42C | |
| Drawee | 42D | |
| Partial Shipments | 43P | |
| Transshipment | 43T | |
| Shipping on Board/Dispatch/Packing in Charge at/ from | 44A | |
| Transportation to | 44B | |
| Latest Date of Shipment | 44C | |

Description of Goods or Services: 45A

Documents Required: 46A

1. SIGNED COMMERCIAL INVOICE IN 5 COPIES.

2. FULL SET OF CLEAN ON BOARD OCEAN BILLS OF LADING MADE OUT TO ORDER AND BLANK ENDORSED, MARKED "FREIGHT PREPAID" NOTIFYING ACCOUNTEE.

3. PACKING LIST/WEIGHT MEMO IN 4 COPIES INDICATING QUANTITY/GROSS AND NET WEIGHTS OF EACH PACKAGE AND PACKING CONDITIONS AS CALLED FOR BY THE L/C.

4. CERTIFICATE OF QUALITY IN 3 COPIES ISSUED BY PUBLIC RECOGNIZED SURVEYOR.

5. BENEFICIARY'S CERTIFIED COPY OF FAX DISPATCHED TO THE ACCOUNTEE WITH 3 DAYS AFTER SHIPMENT ADVISING NAME OF VESSEL, DATE, QUANTITY, WEIGHT, VALUE OF SHIPMENT, L/C NUMBER AND CONTRACT NUMBER.

6. CERTIFICATE OF ORIGIN IN 3 COPIES ISSUED BY AUTHORIZED INSTITUTION.

7. CERTIFICATE OF HEALTH IN 3 COPIES ISSUED BY AUTHORIZED INSTITUTION.

ADDITIONAL INSTRUCTIONS: 47A

| | | |
|---|---|---|
| Charges | 71B | ALL BANKING CHARGES OUTSIDE THE OPENNING BANK ARE FOR BENEFICIARY'S ACCOUNT. |
| Period for Presentation | 48 | DOCUMENTS MUST BE PRESENTED WITHIN 15 DAYS AFTER THE DATE OF ISSUANCE OF THE TRANSPORT DOCUMENTS BUT WITHIN THE VALIDITY OF THE CREDIT. |
| Confirmation Instructions | 49 | WITHOUT |

续表

| Instructions to the Paying/Accepting/Negotiating Bank: 78 | | |
|---|---|---|
| 1. ALL DOCUMENTS TO BE FORWARDED IN ONE COVER, UNLESS OTHERWISE STATED ABOVE. 2. DISCREPANT DOCUMENT FEE OF USD 50.00 OR EQUAL CURRENCY WILL BE DEDUCTED FROM DRAWING IF DOCUMENTS WITH DISCREPANCIES ARE ACCEPTED. | | |
| "Advising Through" Bank | 57A | BANK OF CHINA, BEIJING BRANCH 135 RENMING RD NANTONG, CHINA TEL:0513-5341234 |
| ******** other wordings between banks are omitted ******** | | |

## V. Examine the following L/C with the following contract to see whether the stipulations in the L/C are exactly the same as those in the contract. If not, please make necessary amendments.

### The First National City Bank
### New York, U. S. A.

No. 9524/86

Date: 5 June 2024

Documentary Letter of Credit

Confirmed, Irrevocable

To: Shanxi Ceroilfood Imp. & Exp. Corp. Xi'an, P. R. China

Advising Bank: Bank of China, Xi'an Branch, Xi'an, China

Dear Sirs,

You are authorized to draw on Messrs. Macdnoald & Evans Co., for a sum not exceeding USD60,700 (SAY US DOLLARS SIXTY THOUSAND SEVEN HUNDRED ONLY) available by draft drawn in duplicate on them at 30 days after sight, accompanied by the following documents:

1. Full set of Clean on Board Bills of Lading made out to order and blank endorsed, marked "FREIGHT PREPAID".
2. Signed Commercial Invoice in triplicate, including S/C No 95/4527 dated May 3, 2024.
3. Weight Memo/Packing list in duplicate, indicating gross and net weight of each package.
4. One original insurance Policy/Certificate.

Packing: Packed in seaworthy wooden cases.

Shipment from Shanghai to Boston. Partial Shipments and Transshipment are allowed, through B/L required. Shipment to be made on or before 10 July, 2024

This credit is valid in China on or before 10 July, 2024, for negotiation and all drafts drawn hereunder must be marked "DRAWN UNDER THE FIRST NATIONAL CITY BANK, Credit No, 9524/86." ①

---

① Source: http://metc.gdut.edu.cn/trade/drill/drill3.asp.

# Sales Contract

No. 95/3527

Date: May 3, 2024

Sellers: Shanxi Ceroilfood Imp. & Exp. Co.

Buyers: Messrs. Macdonald & Evans Co.

Commodity: Canned Fruit

Specification: A Grade, Art. No. 123

Quantity: 2,000 cartons 24 can each

Unit Price: US $28 per carton CIF New York.

Total Value: US $56,000 (Say US Dollars Fifty Six Thousand Only)

Packing: in seaworthy reinforced cardboard box.

Insurance: to be effected by the sellers for 110% of the invoice value against All Risks as per China Insurance Clauses of Jan. 1,1981.

Shipment: to be effected in July, 2024 from Shanghai to New York, with partial shipments allowed and transshipment prohibited.

Shipping Marks: at the buyer's option.

Terms of Payment: by confirmed and irrevocable sight L/C.

 This contract is signed in Xi'an on this third day of May, 2024.

The sellers          The buyers

_____     _____

# Appendix

## SWIFT Telex Field Definitions[1]

| NUMBER | SWIFT FIELD 700/701 DEFINITIONS | SWIFT Field Explanation |
|---|---|---|
| :700 | ISSUE OF DOC CREDIT | type of transmission |
| :20 | DOC CREDIT NUMBER | credit number assigned by the issuing bank |
| :21 | RECEIVER'S REFERENCE | |
| :23 | REFERENCE TOP PRE-ADVISE | |
| :26E | NUMBER OF AMENDMENTS | number of amendments |
| :27 | SEQUENCE OF TOTAL | page number of total pages |
| :30 | DATE CONTACT AGREED / AMENDED | date amended |
| :31C | ISSUE DATE | the date the letter of credit is issued |
| :31D | DATE AND PLACE OF EXPIRY | the date the letter of credit expires |
| :31E | MATURITY DATE | |
| :32B | CURRENCY / AMOUNT | the currency and value of the credit |
| :39A | PERCENTAGE CREDIT AMOUNT TOLE-RANCE | |
| :39B | MAXIMUM CREDIT AMOUNT | |
| :39C | ADDITIONAL AMOUNTS COVERED | additional amounts covered |
| :40A | FORM OF DOC CREDIT | irrevocable and/or transferable |
| :41A | AVAILABLE WITH ... BY | |
| :41D | AVAILABLE WITH / BY | bank the credit is available to be paid by |
| :42C | DRAFTS AT | sight or days after sight for payment |
| :42A | DRAWEE | bank the draft is drawn on |
| :42M | MIXED PAYMENT DETAILS | |
| :42P | DEFERRED PAYMENT DETAILS | deferred payment details |
| :43P | PARTIAL SHIPMENTS | partial shipments allowed or not allowed |
| :43T | TRANSSHIPMENT | transshipments allowed or not allowed |
| :44A | LOADING ON BOARD / DISPATCH / TAKING IN CHARGE AT / FROM | commercial port loading from |
| :44B | FOR TRANSPORT TO | destination commercial port |
| :44C | LATEST SHIPMENT DATE | last date shipment letter of credit is valid for |

[1] http://www.internetlc.com/ILCpresenations/ILCeTradeFintrain116A346A_files/frame.htm.

续表

| NUMBER | SWIFT FIELD 700/701 DEFINITIONS | SWIFT Field Explanation |
|---|---|---|
| :44D | SHIPMENT PERIOD | |
| :45 | GOODS | goods to be delivered |
| :45A | DESCRIPTION OF GOODS AND/OR SERVICES | goods description |
| :46 | DOCUMENTS REQUIRED | |
| :46A | DOCUMENTS REQUIRED | documents required for payment |
| :47 | ADDITIONAL CONDITIONS | |
| :47A | ADDITIONAL CONDITIONS | additional requirements of the letter of credit |
| :47B | ADDITIONAL CONDITIONS | additional conditions to be complied with |
| :48 | PERIOD FOR PRESENTATION OF DOCUMENTS | number of days after shipment allowed for document presentation |
| :49 | CONFIRMATION INSTRUCTIONS | confirmation by the paying bank is allowed or not allowed |
| :50 | APPLICANT | the applicant (usually the buyer) of the letter of credit |
| :50 | ORDERING CUSTOMER | ordering customer |
| :51A | APPLICANT BANK | |
| :51D | SENDING INSTITUTION | sending institution |
| :53A | REIMBURSEMENT BANK | paying bank to negotiating bank |
| :53D | REIMBURSEMENT | reimbursement instructions between the paying and issuing bank |
| :57A | "ADVISE THROUGH" BANK | |
| :57D | ACCOUNT WITH BANK | issuing banks account relationship bank |
| :59 | BENEFICIARY | the beneficiary (usually the seller) of the Letter of Credit |
| :71B | CHARGES | applicant and beneficiary responsibility for bank charges |
| :72 | SENDER TO RECEIVER INFORMATION | send and receive information |
| :78 | INSTRUCTIONS TO PAY / ACCEPT / NEGOTIATING BANK | instructions to paying, accepting, or negotiating bank |
| :79 | NARRATIVE | |
| I/O | INSTEAD OF | |

# Chapter 4  Delivery Documents

## 【本章提要】

按照合同和信用证规定交货是卖方最基本的义务。交货单据就是证明卖方所交货物情况的单据,主要包括商业发票、装箱单和重量单。

在对外贸易中,商业发票通常被简称为发票,是出口方开给进口方的载有货物名称、规格、数量、单价、总金额等内容的清单,是出口方所交货物的总说明,也是进口方办理进口报关、收受货物和支付货款不可缺少的文件。在全套出口单据中,商业发票是核心单据,其余单据的制作均需参照商业发票。

商业发票的格式并无统一规定,一般会因出具商业发票的单位不同而不同。商业发票的项目内容则大同小异,一般包括首文、文本和结文三部分内容。首文部分主要包括发票名称、发票号码、合同号码、发票的出票时间和地点、船名、装运港、卸货港、发货人、收货人等项目。文本部分主要包括运输标志、商品名称,货物数量,规格,单价,总价毛重/净重等内容。结文部分一般包括信用证中加注的特别条款或文句,以及发票出票人必要时的签字。

出于不同需要,发票可分为海关发票、领事发票、税收发票、厂商发票、形式发票、商业发票等。本章着重说明商业发票的制作。

装箱单是由发货人缮制的表明装箱货物的名称、规格、数量、运输标志、箱号、件数、重量以及包装情况的单据,是商业发票的补充单据,是进口方收受货物、进口国海关核验货物的重要依据。如果信用证明确要求提交装箱单,出口方就必须严格按信用证规定制作独立的装箱单;如果信用证未明确要求提交装箱单,出口方则可以将有关内容加列在商业发票上。

重量单是出口方向进口方提供的证明所装货物的重量与合同规定相符的文件。除装箱单上的内容之外,重量单上的内容需要尽可能清楚地列明商品单位包装的毛重、净重和总重量。和装箱单一样,重量单也是商业发票的补充单据,是进口方收受货物和进口国海关验收货物的主要依据,是信用证交易中常用的结汇单据。

Delivery documents are those documents evidencing the detailed information of the goods delivered. They are closely related to the seller's obligation of goods delivery, and usually include commercial invoice, packing list, and weight list.

This chapter covers the essentials of delivery documents in international transactions, containing definition, governing rules and usual practices, functions, types, contents and the specimen, checklists for their practical application, and some relevant sample L/C clauses.

## 4.1 Commercial Invoice

### 4.1.1 Definition

A commercial invoice, also called a bill of sale, or invoice[1] for short, is a non-negotiable commercial instrument issued by a seller to a buyer.

Generally, commercial invoice is a commercial document identifying the seller and buyer of goods or services, identifying numbers such as invoice number, date, shipping date, mode of transport, delivery and payment terms, and a complete list and description of the goods or services being sold including prices, discounts and quantities[2].

Commercial invoice has different meanings to different parties involved.

From the seller's point of view, an invoice is a sales invoice, specifying and evidencing type of goods, quantity and price of each type and terms of goods sold. It is also the core document, on the basis of which the seller is to prepare and process all other documents required by documentary credit or documentary collection.

From the buyer's point of view, an invoice is a purchase invoice, specifying and evidencing type of goods, quantity and price of each type and terms of goods purchased. It is also the basic document, on the basis of which the buyer is to check the compliance of documents to terms and conditions of relevant L/C and the consistence among other documents.

From the point of governments, an invoice is a document required by customs to determine true transaction value of goods for the assessment of customs duties/taxes, to prepare customs declaration and consular documentation, to record trade statistics, and to exercise import control. Governments using the commercial invoice to control imports often specify its form, content, language to be used, number of copies, and other characteristics[3].

In certain cases, especially when signed by the seller or seller's agent, an invoice serves as a demand for payment and becomes a document of title when paid in full[4].

### 4.1.2 Functions

As the starting or initiating document that underpins the rest of the international transaction,

---

[1]  The term invoice indicates money is owed or owing. In English, the context of the term invoice is usually used to clarify its meaning, such as "We sent them an invoice" (they owe us money) or "We received an invoice from them" (we owe them money).

[2]  Edward G. Hinkelman. Longman Dictionary of International Trade. Longman and China Renmin University Press, 2000.

[3]  Edward G. Hinkelman. Longman Dictionary of International Trade. Longman and China Renmin University Press, 2000.

[4]  http://www.businessdictionary.com/definition/invoice.html.

the commercial invoice is considered a very important document in trade practice. As the core document in which detailed description of the goods can be found, the commercial invoice can be used in many aspects, and play many leading roles accordingly.

- To evidence the fulfillment of seller's contractual obligation of delivering goods.
- To obtain the necessary export documents and to enable the consignment to be exported.
- To prove ownership and claim payment from the buyer for the value of the goods being supplied.
- To keep business record for both the seller and the buyer.
- To facilitate the import of the goods into the country in question.
- To act as the basis for assessing duties, for customs clearance, and for consular documentation.
- To act as the basis for recording trade statistics.
- To act as the basis for insurance claims and settlements.
- To act as the instrument of import control.
- To replace the drafts in case no drafts are required.
- Etc.

### 4.1.3 Governing Rules and Usual Practices

(1) UCP (Uniform Customs and Practices for Documentary Credit). Most trade documents are used under letters of credit, and most letters of credit are subject to UCP, the universally recognized set of rules governing the use of the documentary credits in international trade.

UCP was originally formulated in 1933 by the International Chamber of Commerce (ICC), and the current revision (the UCP 600) came into effect on 1st July 2007. Most general documentary requirements referred to in this chapter (and in this book) are in accordance with the UCP 600[1].

(2) ISBP (International Standard Banking Practice for the Examination of Documents). ISBP was first published in 2003 as ICC publication No. 645, and has been updated three times (in 2007, 2013, and 2023) as ICC publication No. 681, 745, and 821 respectively.

ISBP is a list of procedures for document checkers to examine the documents presented under letters of credit and serves as a practical companion to UCP 600. It reflects international standard banking practice for all parties to a documentary credit under the revised rules. Not as a substitute for the UCP, ISBP demonstrates how the UCP is to be integrated into day-to-day practice.

It is estimated that the global percentage of documents refused on first presentation under

---

[1] http://www.sitpro.org.uk/trade/lettcredintro.html.

documentary credits ranges between 65% ~ 80%. ISBP, by encouraging a uniformity of practice worldwide, should reduce that number dramatically and thereby facilitate the flow of world trade[1].

(3) Relevant laws and usual practices of specific countries. Different countries may have different statutory stipulations on contents and requirements of commercial invoice, and have varied usual customs and practices.

Some countries require that the invoice take effect only after being signed by the beneficiary. For instance, when goods are exported to Mexico, commercial invoice must be manually signed, and certified by the consular. If there is no Mexican consular, it may be signed by the embassy, marking "There is no Mexican consular here". When goods are exported to Bahrein Islands, commercial invoice need to be manually signed and indicate country of origin. When goods are exported to Panama, commercial invoice must be signed by the CCPIT (China Council for the Promotion of International Trade), marking "There is no panama consular here".

Some countries levy preferential tariff on goods imported from developing countries, and commercial invoice must indicate "country of origin" or be certified by some competent authorities. For instance, when goods are exported to Australia, the commercial invoice must show developing country declaration that the final process of manufacture of the goods for which special rates are claimed has been performed in China and that not less than one half of the factory or works cost of the goods is represented by the value of the labor or materials of China and Australia. When goods are exported to Lebanon, commercial invoice must bear the wording of "We hereby certify that this invoice is authentic, that it is the only one issued by us for the goods herein, that the value and price of the goods are correct without any deduction of payment in advance and its origin is exclusively China". When goods are exported to Arabian Area, commercial invoice must show country of origin, or be accompanied by a certificate of origin issued by the CCPIT.

Some countries may have special requirements on commercial invoice. For instance, when goods are exported to Chile, commercial invoice must indicate freight, insurance premium and FOB value. When goods are exported to Kuwait, commercial invoice must indicate the name of manufacture and vessel, gross weight and net weight in kilograms.

As for the detailed and latest requirements, the businessmen are recommended to visit the relevant official websites of your potential importing countries.

### 4.1.4  Contents

Although there is no standard format, a commercial invoice mainly consists of three parts:

---

[1]  http://www.iccwbo.org/policy/banking/iccbfdfc/index.html.

the heading, the body, and the complementary clause. Specifically, a typical invoice may contain the following items:

(1) The term "invoice" or "commercial invoice". It is required to differentiate commercial invoice from other trade documents. To avoid unnecessary discrepancies, it must be in compliance with the specific term of L/C.

When a credit requires presentation of an "invoice" without further description, this will be satisfied by the presentation of any type of invoice (commercial invoice, customs invoice, tax invoice, final invoice, consular invoice, etc.) However, an invoice is not to be identified as "provisional", "pro-forma" or the like.

When a credit requires presentation of a "commercial invoice", this will also be satisfied by the presentation of a document titled "invoice", even when such document contains a statement that it has been issued for tax purposes (ISBP 821 C1).

Terms as "combined invoice" or "sworn invoice" are not recommended.

(2) A unique reference number. In case of correspondence about the invoice, a unique reference number is usually given by exporting company itself.

(3) Date of the invoice. Unless required by the credit, an invoice need not be dated (ISBP 821 C11, UCP 600 Article 18).

(4) A commercial invoice must appear to have been issued by the beneficiary of the relevant L/C. However, if the credit has been transferred, a commercial invoice may be issued by the second beneficiary (ISBP 821 C2).

(5) Name and address of the buyer/consignee/recipient/applicant. It refers to the buyer's full company name and address, including street address, city, country, post code, telephone number, and e-mail address. In the case of L/C transaction, it refers to the applicant, and its name and address should be strictly in accordance with the stipulation of L/C.

According to the UCP 600 article 18, a commercial invoice must be made out in the name of the applicant.

Depending on the L/C specific requirements, an invoice may be made out as "for account of ×××", "to the order of ×××", etc.

However, according ISBP 821 A17(b), there is no requirement for the applicant name, address and contact details (if any) to appear in a specific box, field or space on an invoice. These details need not be identified by the heading or prefix "Applicant".

(6) Contract number. An invoice is a document evidencing the seller's fulfillment of the relevant contract, and relevant contract number is required to be mentioned on the invoice.

Alternatively, it may be named as "purchase order No. ", "sales contract No. ", "sales confirmation No. ", or similar tracking numbers.

(7) Customs Commodity Code (if known). Customs Commodity Code (CCC), also known

as Harmonized Tariff Schedule (HTS), is optional information. If the Customs Commodity Code for the items within the shipment is known, they may be indicated to a six-digit level.

(8) Country of manufacture. Country of manufacture indicates the country where the goods were grown, produced, or manufactured into a finished product.

In particular, when the importing country adopt import control (via import quota) or impose discriminatory tariffs on goods from different exporting countries, country of manufacture is necessarily required.

(9) Marks and numbers. It refers to the shipping marks on the outer packing of packed goods.

If the goods do not need to be packed, the word "naked" or "in bulk" may be noted.

If specific shipping marks are required by L/C, it must be filled accordingly. Internationally accepted standard shipping mark consists of four parts: the abbreviated name of consignee, reference number (contract No., order No., or invoice No.), named port/place of destination, and number of packing units. A typical example is given below:

ABC

ASAKA

AZF08128

No. 1-100

If no shipping marks are required by L/C, "N/M" may be filled in a proper box of invoice.

However, the marks and numbers in an invoice must be strictly consistent with that on the packing of goods actually provided.

(10) The port/place of shipment, the port/place of destination, and the mode of transportation. The named port/place of shipment and destination must comply with the L/C requirement, and they must be specific name of port/place, name of country/continent is not acceptable. It is usually expressed in a brief way, for instance, "From Shanghai to Osaka by Air".

If transshipment is allowed, the port of transshipment must be marked. For example, "From Qingdao to Helsinki W/T (with transshipment) Hong Kong by Vessel".

(11) Description of the goods. The description of the goods, services or performance in a commercial invoice must correspond with that appearing in the credit. However, there is no requirement for a mirror image. For example, details of the goods may be stated in a number of areas within the invoice which, when collated together, represents a description of the goods corresponding to that in the credit.

The description of goods, services or performance in an invoice must also reflect what has actually been shipped or provided. An invoice showing the description of the entire goods as stated in the credit, then stating what has actually been shipped is also acceptable ( UCP 600 Article 18, ISBP 821 C3, C4, C5).

In addition, if a trade term is part of the goods description in the credit, or stated in connection with the amount, the invoice must state the trade term specified, and if the description provides the source of the trade term, the same source must be identified ( e. g. a credit term "CIF Singapore Incoterms® 2020" would not be satisfied by "CIF Singapore Incoterms") ( ISBP 821 C9).

(12) Unit price. The unit price of international trade consists of currency, measurement unit, value, and trade terms. These four parts should keep in accordance with L/C strictly. For instance, "USD 5,000. 00 Per Set CIF New York" is a typical unit price expression for exporting to New York on CIF trade term.

According to the UCP 600 Article 18, a commercial invoice must be made out in the same currency as the credit.

However, when a credit is issued in USD, and the invoice currency is shown as a " $ " sign, without further qualification, the invoice will fulfil the requirement of UCP 600 subarticle 18 ( a ) ( iii ) of being made out in the same currency as the credit, unless data in the invoice itself, such as the domicile of the beneficiary is in a country whose currency is denominated in dollars and/or is commonly referred to with a " $ " sign, or another presented document implies that the " $ " sign may refer to a currency other than USD[1].

The invoice may show any discounts or deductions required in the credit. The invoice may also show a deduction covering advance payment, discount, etc. which is not stated in the credit ( ISBP 821 C6(d) ).

(13) The quantity of merchandise, weights and measurements. The quantity of merchandise, weights and measurements shown on the invoice must not conflict with the same quantities appearing on other documents ( ISBP 821 C12).

If merchandise is valued on weight basis, the gross weight and net weight must be noted on the invoice respectively.

The quantity of the goods required in the credit may vary within a tolerance of +/− 5%. This does not apply if a credit states that the quantity must not be exceeded or reduced, or if a credit states the quantity in terms of a stipulated number of packing units or individual items. A variance of up to +5% in the goods quantity does not allow the amount of the drawing to exceed the amount of the credit ( ISBP 821 C14).

Even when partial shipments are prohibited, a tolerance of 5% less in the credit amount is

[1]  ISBP 821, C7.

acceptable, provided that the quantity is shipped in full and that any unit price, if stated in the credit, has not been reduced. If no quantity is stated in the credit, the invoice will be considered to cover the full quantity (ISBP 821 C15).

If a credit calls for installment shipments, each shipment must be in accordance with the installment schedule (ISBP 821 C16).

(14) Total amount charged. Total amount is the product of unit price and total quantity. It is the base value for customs to calculate tariffs, and for trading parties to calculate insurance premium, discount, or commission when necessary. It thus deserves utmost careful calculation and repeating examinations.

Usually total amount is expressed both in figure and in words, and cannot exceed the highest amount stipulated in L/C.

However, a nominated bank acting on its nomination, a confirming bank, if any, or the issuing bank may accept a commercial invoice issued for an amount in excess of the amount permitted by the credit, and its decision will be binding upon all parties, provided the bank in question has not honored or negotiated for an amount in excess of that permitted by the credit (UCP 600 Article 18).

For instance, when the words "about" or "approximately" are used in connection with the amount of the credit, they are to be construed as allowing a tolerance not exceeding 10% more or 10% less than the amount to which they refer (UCP 600 Article 30a).

Charges and costs must be included within the value shown against the stated trade term in the credit and invoice. Any charges and costs shown beyond this value are not allowed (ISBP 821 C6).

(15) Payment terms. Payment terms include method of payment, date of payment, and details about charges of late payment, etc. They must be in strict accordance with L/C requirements.

(16) Declaration of truth. Indication of validity of the invoice information, i. e. "I/we hereby certify that the information on this invoice is true and correct and that the contents of this shipment are as stated above."

(17) Signature of beneficiary. Unless required by the credit, an invoice doesn't need to be signed (ISBP 821 C11, UCP 600 Article 18).

If the credit requires an invoice to be signed, it must be signed by the beneficiary. However, if the issuing bank requires that the transport or other documents may show a shipper other than the beneficiary, then an invoice may be issued by a party other than the beneficiary.

The beneficiary's signature needs not be handwritten. Facsimile signatures, perforated signatures, stamps, symbols (such as chops) or any electronic or mechanical means of authentication are sufficient. A requirement for a commercial invoice to be "signed and stamped", or a similar requirement, is also fulfilled by a signature and the name of the party typed, or stamped, or handwritten, etc. A signature on a company letterhead paper will be taken to be the signature of that company, unless otherwise stated. The company name need not be repeated next to the signature. (UCP 600 Article 18, ISBP 821 C2(b))

For the detailed contents, please refer to commercial invoice specimens in the appendix of this chapter.

Specimens 1, 2 and 3 are all commonly used commercial invoices in international trade. While specimen 4 is a typical commercial invoice used in China, and is of bilingual, both in Chinese and in English.

### 4.1.5 Variants

There are many variants of commercial invoice, including customs invoice, consular invoice, tax invoice, pro-forma invoice, electronic invoice, and etc.

(1) Customs invoice. Customs invoice is a special invoice required by customs of some importing countries to determine the values in order to assess customs duties and taxes, especially to ensure whether there is a dumping, and to determine origin of the imported goods in order to implement import control.

It is an extended form of commercial invoice, in which the exporter states the description, quantity and selling price, freight, insurance, packing costs, terms of delivery and payment, weight and/or volume of the goods, and origin of the merchandise exported, for the purpose of determining customs import value at the port of destination. However, the form and contents of a customs invoice are determined by the customs of relevant country and vary from country to country.

Different countries use customs invoice for different purposes. For instance, U. S. A. requires Form 5519 Invoice details for cotton fabrics and linens, Form 5523 Invoice details for footwear, and Form 5520 Special Summary Steel Invoices; Canada requires Canada Customs Invoice (1985/1/1) when the value of exporting to Canada exceeds CAD1, 200; New Zealand requires Certificate of Origin for Exports to New Zealand Form 59A; Ghana uses Combined Certificate of Invoice in respect of Goods for Importation into Ghana Form C61; Jamaica uses Invoice and Declaration of Value Required for Shipments to Jamaica C23; and Caribbean Common Market countries require CARICOM, etc.

A Canada Customs Invoice Specimen is attached in the appendix of this chapter.

(2) Consular invoice. Consular invoice is a special invoice required by some foreign countries, describing a shipment of goods and showing information such as the consignor, consignee, and value of shipment. Certified by a consular official of the foreign country, consular invoice is used by the country's customs officials to verify the value, quantity, and nature of the

shipment, in order to ensure that there is no dumping of the goods exported. The form of a consular invoice is usually made by the consulate of the importing country, and the exporter should first fill up the form and then have it signed by the consular.

It is also an extended form of commercial invoice. It serves to exercise control over imports, and help prevent over-invoicing and under-invoicing.

Both customs invoices and consular invoices are considered obstacles to the development of international trade, and thus diminishing, though still found.

(3) Tax invoice. Tax invoice is a document issued by a supplier which stipulates the amount charged for goods or services as well as the amount of Goods and Services Tax payable.

(4) Manufacturer's invoice. Manufacturer's invoice is an invoice issued in domestic currency by the manufacturer to the exporter. Evidencing the domestic market condition, it is usually used in customs valuation, tariff verification, and anti-dumping duty levying. The description of goods must be the same as those in the commercial invoice. The unit price may be lower than that in the commercial invoice. If the exporter themselves are the manufacturer, they may indicate in the commercial invoice "we, ourselves, are the manufacturer", and no manufacturer's invoice shall be presented.

(5) Pro-forma invoice. Pro-forma invoice is commonly used as a preliminary invoice with a price quotation, either for import license application or for customs purposes in importation. It is usually issued by the exporter to importer before concluding an export contract.

The contents of such a pro-forma invoice include the name of the goods, unit price, measurement, etc. It is not a true invoice, because the seller does not record a pro-forma invoice as an accounts receivable and the buyer does not record a pro-forma invoice as an accounts payable[1].

A sample pro-forma invoice is attached in the appendix of this chapter.

According to the ISBP 821 C1, if a credit requires an "invoice" but without further definition, it will be satisfied by any type of invoice presented (commercial invoice, customs invoice, consular invoice, tax invoice, etc.). However, invoices identified as "provisional", "pro-forma" or the like are not acceptable. When a credit requires presentation of a commercial invoice, a document titled "invoice" will be acceptable.

(6) Electronic invoice. Some invoices are no longer paper-based, but rather transmitted electronically over the internet.

Standards for electronic invoicing vary widely from country to country. Electronic Data Interchange (EDI) standards such as the United Nation's EDIFACT standard include message encoding guidelines for electronic invoices. The EDIFACT, abbreviated for the United Nations

---

① http://www. businessdictionary. com/definition/pro-forma-invoice. html.

standard for electronic invoices (INVOIC), includes standard codes for transmitting header information (common to the entire invoice) and codes for transmitting details for each of the line items (products or services).

The most common electronic invoice is PDF formatted invoice over e-mail from providers such as NetSuite, Saasu. com, NetAccounts, SimpleBill, Freshboks, Invoice. com and Microsoft Dynamics[1].

However, it is still common to have electronic remittance or invoicing printed to maintain paper records.

### 4. 1. 6　Checklists

To sum up, in the case of a documentary credit, the parties involved in a commercial invoice must check the following aspects:

● The document must be headed as per requirements, e. g. Invoice, Commercial Invoice, etc.

● Unless otherwise specified, the invoice must be made out by the beneficiary and addressed to the applicant.

● The description of the goods must correspond exactly to the description in the Credit.

● The currency and the amount stated in the invoice, as well as the individual items, must correspond to the terms of the credit.

● Credit numbers must be specified if required. A request to insert the credit number on a document is usually at the instigation of the issuing bank in order to facilitate the collation of documents should one or more documents become detached from the presentation. Provided all the stipulated documents are received by the issuing bank, the absence of a credit number or the mistyping of that number on a document does not constitute a reason for refusal. The exception to this position is where it is a requirement of the importing country that the credit number be stated on one or more documents. In such circumstances, the credit must clearly indicate that this is the reason for the number to be shown on that or those documents. [2]

● The invoice needs to be signed only if the Credit specifically requires the signature of the exporter.

● The invoice must be authenticated, validated, legalized, certified, etc.

● The contents of the commercial invoice must be consistent with all other stipulated documents.

### 4. 1. 7　Sample L/C Clauses of Commercial Invoice

As for L/C clauses concerning commercial invoice, some sample clauses are listed below.

● Signed commercial invoice in duplicate, showing FOB value and freight charges.

---

① http://en. wikipedia. org/wiki/Special:Search? search = Invoice&fulltext = Search.

② ISBP 821 Preliminary consideration viii.

• Signed commercial invoice in triplicate, showing deduction of USD 500. 00 being commission.

• Signed commercial invoice in quadruplicate, showing merchandise to be of Chinese origin and certified by competent authority.

• Manually signed commercial invoice in quintuplicate indicating issuing bank name, L/C No. and contract No.

• Commercial invoice in sextuplicate indicating the following: ( 1 ) each item has been marked "made in China"; ( 2 ) one set of non-negotiable shipping documents has been airmailed in advance to buyer.

• Commercial invoice in septuplicate less 5% discount.

• Signed commercial invoice in octuplicate for value not exceeding the purchase order amount, certifying that the goods are as per purchase order No. JP1588 dated 18, August 2008 of the applicant.

• Signed commercial invoice in nonuplicate showing the credit number.

• Signed commercial invoice in decuplicate, original of which must be certified by the chamber of commerce and legalized by the CCPIT.

## 4.2  Packing List

When exporter prepares goods for shipment, he may be required to prepare a detailed packing list.

### 4.2.1  Definition

Packing list, sometimes known as a packing slip, a packaging slip or customer receipt, is a shipping document that always accompanies delivery packages of the shipment. It is a detailed document provided by the exporter that spells out how many containers there are in the shipment and which merchandise is packaged in each container. It is usually inside an attached shipping pouch or inside the package itself. It commonly includes an itemized detail of the package contents and may or may not include customer pricing[1]. It serves to inform all parties, including transport agencies, government authorities, and customers about the contents of the package. It helps them deal with the package accordingly.

A packing list is to be issued by the entity stated in the credit[2].

When a credit does not indicate the mane of an issuer, any entity may issue a packing list. [3]

---

[1]  http://en. wikipedia. org/wiki/ Packing_slip.

[2]  ISBP 821, M2.

[3]  ISBP 821, M3.

### 4.2.2 Functions

Packing lists may be used by different parties in different aspects.

• Used by the shipper to evidence the detailed weight, volume, size, packing and packaging of the cargo delivered.

• Used by the forwarding agent to determine the total shipment weight and volume and whether the correct cargo is being shipped.

• Used by the carrier to calculate freight or carriage.

• Used by both local and foreign customs officials to check the cargo, to impose duty and trade control.

• Used by the consignee to check the cargo and determine appropriate objects of being claimed when necessary.

Packing lists can be obtained from the freight forwarder, and filled out by the seller. They are usually attached to the outside of a package in a waterproof envelope or plastic sheath marked "Packing list enclosed".

### 4.2.3 Contents

Different trading company may use different formats of packing list. However, a typical packing list usually contains the following items:

• Name and contact details of the issuer/seller/shipper/sender/beneficiary.

• Name, address and contact details of the buyer/consignee/recipient/applicant.

• The gross, tare and net weights of the cargo.

If you are exporting to a market using imperial measures (such as the U. S. or the U. K.), provide weights and dimensions in both metric (kg and mm), as well as imperial (lbs and inches).

• The description of the goods, services or performance in a weight list should correspond with that appearing in the commercial invoice. However, if stated, it may be in general terms not conflicting with their description in the credit (UCP 600 Article 14e).

• The quantity of the cargo.

• The mode of packing and type of package (such as pallet, box, crate, drum, carton, etc.).

For instance: Packed in polythene bags of 3 kgs each, and then in inner box, 20 boxes to a carton.

• The measurements/dimensions of each package.

• The number of pallets/boxes/crates/drums, etc.

• The contents of each pallet or box (or other container).

• The package markings, if any, as well as shipper's and buyer's reference numbers.

Similar to a commercial invoice, a packing list contains basic information about the seller, the buyer, and the goods.

Dissimilar to a commercial invoice, a packing list contains more detailed information (such as the types, measurement, contents, and marking, etc.) about packing and packaging, and it does not require pricing information. To some extent, a packing list is complementary to a commercial invoice.

It is essential that the packing list must agree exactly with all the terms and conditions of the commercial invoice and other trade documents. Any mistake on the packing list may cause subsequent troubles and difficulties, for instance a delay in customs clearance at the port of destination. Should the packing list be incomplete or incorrect, customs authorities in the importing country have the right to delay the clearance of the shipment until the importer provides a packing list reflecting the real contents of the container.

When a credit indicates specific requirements, without stipulating the document to indicate compliance with these requirement, any data regarding the packing of the goods mentioned on a packing list, if presented, are not to conflict with those requirements. ①

A packing list may indicate a different invoice number, invoice date and shipment routing to that indicated on one or more other stipulated documents, provided the issuer of the packing list is not the beneficiary. ②

Banks only examine total values, including, but not limited to, total quantities, total weights, total measurements, or total packages, to ensure that the applicable total does not conflict with a total shown in the credit and on any other stipulated document. ③

Three packing list specimen, in fairly standard forms, are given in the appendix part of this chapter. They are all frequently used in China.

## 4.2.4  Electronic Packing List

According to "the World in 2008" of the Economist, a growing number of entrepreneurs will buy in volume from China on sites like Alibaba and sell to consumers on Western sites such as eBay④. And electronic packing list is getting more popular in the practice of e-trade.

Unlike paper formed packing list, electronic packing list is transmitted electronically over the internet (EDI), and it is beneficial to parties concerned in many aspects.

● By electronic packing list, ports and wharfs can collect detailed information of packing list in advance, and confirm the cargo soon after its arrival at the transit gate. This will un-

---

① ISBP 821, M4.
② ISBP 821, M5.
③ ISBP 821, M6.
④ http://www. economist. com/theworldin/china/displayStory. cfm? story_id = 10125658&d = 2008.

doubtedly increase the operation efficiency of loading port.

- By electronic packing list, the shipper can realize trade documents automation, reduce time of documents preparation, correction and presentation, and avoid any delay in the drawback of export tax.

- By electronic packing list, the forwarding agent can provide related information to shipping company beforehand, smooth and expedite the interlinkage of cargo and ship.

Many important ports, such as Shanghai, Qingdao, Lianyungang, and the like, have published the detailed instructions on the use of electronic packing list, useful websites are: http://www. sdeport. com/; http://www. spict. com/port/help. doc; and http://www. lygedi. com/, etc.

The professional system of electronic packing list can be freely downloaded from local EDI centre.

## 4.2.5  Checklists

To sum up, in the case of a documentary credit, the parties involved in a packing list must check the following aspects:

- When a credit requires the presentation of a packing list, this will be satisfied by the presentation of a document titled as called for in the credit, or bearing a similar title or untitled, that fulfils its function by containing any information as to the packing of the goods. [1]

- The packing list doesn't need to be signed unless the Credit specifically requires the signature of the exporter. If a credit requires neutral packing, the name of exporter must not appear on the packing list.

- If all the information required for the packing list is already stated in the commercial invoice, the packing list may be unnecessary.

- If all the information required for the packing list is not stated in the commercial invoice, the packing list is necessary. And the contents of the packing list must be consistent with all other stipulated documents and related L/C.

- Keep the content of the document appears to just fulfill the function of the required "Packing List". To avoid getting enmeshed in a web of one's own spinning, never provide too much information.

- If neural packing is required, information related to the exporter should not be appeared.

- Etc.

---

[1]  ISBP 821, M1.

### 4.2.6 Sample L/C Clauses of Packing List

As for L/C clauses concerning packing list, some sample clauses are listed below.

• Separate packing list in full details required.

• Combined packing list is not acceptable.

• Packing list showing gross and net weights expressed in kilos of each type of goods required.

• Packing list in 3 copies manual signed by the beneficiaries.

• Packing list detailing the complete inner packing specification and contents of each package.

• Packing list in duplicate issued by beneficiary indicating quantity, gross weight, net weight and measurement of each package.

• Packing list in four copies showing the total weight, total net weight, number of packages.

## 4.3　Weight List

### 4.3.1 Definition

A weight list, sometimes known as a weight note, weight memo, or weight certificate, is also a shipping document that accompanies delivery packages, usually inside an attached shipping pouch or inside the package itself, describing the weight of each piece of goods.

A weight list is to be issued by the entity stated in the credit. Where a credit does not indicate the name of an issuer, any entity may issue a weight list (ISBP821 N2, N3).

### 4.3.2 Issuer

A weight list is to be issued by the entity stated in the credit. [1]

When a credit does not indicate the name of an issuer, any entity may issue a weight list. [2]

### 4.3.3 Functions

When a credit requires a packing list and a weight list, such requirement will be satisfied by presentation of two separate documents, or by presentation of two original copies of a combined packing and weight list, provided such document states both packing and weight details. That is, documents listed in a credit should be presented as separate documents. [3]

A weight list may be used in several cases:

• Used by the shipper to evidence the gross weight and net weight of each unit of package, and the total weight of the cargo delivered.

---

① ISBP821 N3.
② ISBP821 N3.
③ ISBN821, N1.

- Used by the forwarding agency to determine the total shipment weight.
- Used by the carrier to calculate freight or carriage.
- Used by both local and foreign customs officials to check the cargo, to impose duty.
- Used by the consignee to check the cargo and determine appropriate objects of being claimed when necessary.

### 4.3.4 Contents

- The term "weight list", "weight note", or "weight memo".
- The reference number, which must be consistent with that on the commercial invoice. A weight list may indicate a different invoice number, invoice date and shipment, routing to that indicated on one or more other stipulated documents, provided the issuer of the weight list is not the beneficiary. [1]
- The underlying sales contract/confirmation number.
- The Shipping Mark must comply with that in the commercial invoice. It may be noted as the actual shipping mark, or just indicate"as per invoice No. ×××".
- Actual number of packages. "Case No. 1-UP" is required by some credit, here the word "UP" refers to total number of cases.
- Description of the goods. The description of the goods, services or performance in a weight list should correspond with that in the commercial invoice. However, if stated, it may be in general terms not conflicting with their description in the credit( UCP 600 article 14e).
- Gross Weight. Gross Weight ( G. W. or GW) , sometimes called laden weight, is a term that is generally used in commerce or trade, and refers to the total weight of a product and its packaging. It is important to note G. W. in a weight list, particularly in the case of calculating freight/carriage on weight basis. For detailed weight list, subtotal gross weight of each article number or specification, the gross weight of each package, and the total gross weight of the whole lot of cargo, must be noted.
- Net Weight. Net Weight ( N. W. or NW) is the weight of the product alone. It is important to note N. W. in a weight list, particularly in the case of computing the cost of the goods carried for purposes of taxation ( sometimes called a tariff) or for tolls related to barge, rail, road, or other transportation.

Net Weight is obtained by subtracting Tare Weight from the Gross Weight. Tare weight, sometimes called unladen weight, is the weight of an empty vehicle or container. When goods are transported via railway, tare weight is often published upon the sides of railway cars to

---

[1] ISBN821, N5.

facilitate the computation of the load carried[1]. When goods are shipped via container, tare weight is standardized for different specifications of container. For example, the tare weight of 20′ Dry Container and Refrigerated Container (with height of 8′ 6″ ) is 1,630 kg/3,594 lbs, and 2,820 kg/6,217 lbs respectively, while the tare weight of 40′ Refrigerated Container with height of 8′6″ is 4,100 kg/9,036 lbs[2].

When a credit indicates specific weight requirement, without stipulating the document to indicate compliance with these requirements, any data regarding the weight of the goods mentioned on a weight list. , if presented are not to conflict with those requirements. [3]

To be noted, banks only examine total values,including , but not limited to, total quantities, total weights, total measurements or total packages, to ensure that the applicable total does not conflict with a total shown in the credit and on any other stipulated document. [4]

See specimens of weight list, and packing/weight list in the appendix of this chapter.

## 4.3.5　Checklists

In the case of a documentary credit, the following issues should be considered by relevant parties:

● When required by L/C, the "Weight List" should be headed as per L/C requirements. However, a credit requirement for a "Weight List" may also be satisfied by a document containing weight details whether titled "Weight Memo", "Packing and Weight List", etc. or an untitled document, on condition that the contents of the document appear to fulfill the function of the required "Weight List".

● When a credit requires total measurement appear on the Weight List, such requirement should be satisfied, and the measurement should be consistent with that on bill of lading.

● If neural packing is required, information related to the exporter should not appear.

● If "Plain Paper" is required to make out packing/weight list, names of beneficiary and opening bank should not appear on the Weight List, and no signature is required.

In addition to packing list and weight list, a measurement list may be required when necessary.

To sum up, packing/weight/measurement lists are complementary to commercial invoice with more detailed information of goods and packing, and have several common characteristics[5]:

---

① http://en. wikipedia. org/wiki/Tare_weight.

② http://www. easipass. com/ytsce/ys/ytsce_jzx_04. htm.

③ ISBN821, N4.

④ ISBN821, N6.

⑤ http://wiki. mbalib. com/wiki/%E8%A3%85%E7%AE%B1%E5%8D%95.

- They share the same reference number and date with commercial invoice.
- Price related information may not be noted.
- The description of the goods on them may be in general terms not conflicting with their description in the credit.
- They are all issued on the basis of S/C, L/C, and commercial invoice.
- They have similar formats and basic contents.

However, they have emphasis on different aspects. For example, packing list stresses the detailed information of packing and packaging, weight list stresses gross weight and net weight, while measurement list stresses the volume or cubic of the goods and packaging.

### 4.3.6 Sample L/C Clauses of Weight List

- Manually signed weight certificate in five folds.
- Signed original weight memo in 3 copies issued by beneficiary showing quantity, gross weight and net weight for each carton.

## Questions and Problems

I. True (T) or false (F).

1. According to the UCP 600, unless required by the credit, an invoice need not be dated.

2. According to the UCP 600, a commercial invoice must appear to have been issued by the beneficiary, and must be made out in the name of the applicant.

3. According to the UCP 600, a commercial invoice must be made out in the same currency as the credit.

4. According to the UCP 600, a commercial invoice must be signed.

5. If the credit requires an invoice to be signed, it must be signed by the beneficiary.

6. According to the UCP 600, the description of the goods, services or performance in a commercial invoice must correspond with that appearing in the credit.

7. If an invoice is to be dated, the date of invoice should be earlier than the date of shipment and draft.

8. When listed in a credit, the "Packing List" should be presented as a separate document.

9. Unless required by the credit, a packing list need not be dated.

10. Unless required by the credit, a weight list need not be dated.

11. The description of the goods, services or performance in a weight list may be in general terms not conflicting with their description in the credit.

12. In the case of calculating freight/carriage on weight basis, it is particularly important to note net weight (N. W.) in a weight list.

13. It is important to note Gross Weight ( G. W. ) in a weight list, particularly in the case of computing the cost of the goods carried for purposes of tariff.

14. Packing/weight lists are all complementary to commercial invoice with more detailed information of goods and packing.

15. Price related information must be noted in a packing list or weight list.

## II. Translate the following into Chinese.

| In Duplicate | 2-Fold | |
|---|---|---|
| In Triplicate | 3-Fold | |
| In Quadruplicate | 4-Fold | |
| In Quintuplicate | 5-Fold | |
| In Sextuplicate | 6-Fold | |
| In Septuplicate | 7-Fold | |
| In Octuplicate | 8-Fold | |
| In Nonuplicate | 9-Fold | |
| In Decuplicate | 10-Fold | |

## III. Examine the following items of commercial invoices presented by the beneficiary, and determine whether they are acceptable ( √ ), or not acceptable ( × )?

| Letter of Credit | Documents | | acceptable |
|---|---|---|---|
| | Type | Items | /not acceptable |
| Commercial Invoice | I | Without signature of beneficiary | |
| 5,000 bags bombazine | N | 4,950 bags bombazine | |
| 5,000 Metric Ton peanut oil | V O | 4,692 Metric Ton peanut oil | |
| Amount: USD 100,000.00 | I C | USD 110,000.00 (B/E value:USD 110,000.00) | |
| Amount: USD 100,000.00 | E | USD 110,000.00 (B/E value:USD 100,000.00) | |
| CIFC5 Hong Kong USD 145,935.00 | | USD 137,638.25 (Total Amount) | |
| CIF Hong Kong 147,550.00 Freight fee:HKD 10,560.00 Insurance fee:HKD 140.00 | | CIF Hong Kong HKD 147.550.00 Less F HKD 10,560.00 Less I HKD 140.00 FOB HKD 136,850.00 | |

## IV. Make a commercial invoice based on the particulars given below.

- L/C NO. 281-12-6222571 DATED APRIL 2ND, 2024

- DATE AND PLACE OF EXPIRY : OCT. 15, 2024 IN COUNTRY OF BENEFICIARY

- APPLICANT: WOODLAND LIMITED

    450 CASTLE PEAK ROAD, KOWLOON, HONG KONG, CHINA

- BENEFICIARY: ZHEJIANG ANIMAL BY-PRODUCTS IMP. & EXP. CORPORATION

    76 WULIN RD, HANGZHOU, CHINA

- L/C AMOUNT: USD 17,540.00

- LOADING IN CHARGE: SHANGHAI PORT, CHINA

- FOR TRANSPORTATION TO: HONGKONG

- LATEST DATE OF SHIP: 240930

- DESCRIPTION OF GOODS: 42,500 PIECES OF STUFFED TOY AS PER SALES CONTRACT 24ZA16IA0019 DATED 24.03.13

| STYLE NO. | QUANTITY | UNIT PRICE |
|---|---|---|
| ZEAPEL01 | 7,000PCS | USD0. 345/PC |
| ZEAPEL02 | 500PCS | USD0. 65/PC |
| ZEAPEL04 | 5,000PCS | USD1. 10/PC |
| ZEAPEL05 | 30,000PCS | USD0. 31/PC |

CIFC5 HONGKONG AS PER INCOTERMS 2020

- DOCUMENTS REQUIRED:
    + COMMERCIAL INVOICE IN 1 ORIGINAL AND 3 COPIES LESS 5% COMMISSION AND HANDSIGNED BY BENEFICIARY.

- ADDITIONAL COND. : +PACKING IN CARTONS OF 50 PCS EACH.
    +CARTONS TO BE MARKED WITH:
    Z. J. A. B
    HONGKONG
    24ZA16IA0019
    C/NO. 1-

- Issuing bank: HSBC, HONGKONG.

续表

| ZHEJIANG ANIMAL BY-PRODUCTS IMP. & EXP. CORPORATION |
| :---: |
| 76 WULIN RD,HANGZHOU,CHINA |

## COMMERCIAL INVOICE

| To: | | | Invoice No. : | |
| | | | Invoice Date: | |
| | | | S/C No. : | |
| | | | S/C Date | |
| From: | | To: | | |
| L/C No. : | | | | |
| Date of Issue: | | Issued By: | | |
| | | | | |

| Marks and Numbers | Number and kind of package description of goods | Quantity | Unit Price | Amount |
| :---: | :---: | :---: | :---: | :---: |
| | | | | |
| | TOTAL: | | | |
| SAY TOTAL: | | | | |
| | ZHEJIANG ANIMAL BY-PRODUCTS IMP. & EXP. CORPORATION | | | |

## V. Make a packing list based on the particulars given below.

L/C NO.：3/0146/35

DATE OF ISSUE：2024-02-10

EXPIRY DATE：2024-03-21 PLACE：AT CHINA

APPLICANT：F-I-T FRANCE INTERNATIONAL TRADE 24 AVENUE HENRI FREVILLE 352006

BENEFICIARY：COFCO NINGBO CEREALS AND OILS CO.，LTD.

AMOUNT：USD 25,000.00

AVAILABLE WITH：BY DRAFTS AT SIGHT AT ISSUING BANK

PARTIAL SHIPMENT：ALLOWED

TRANSSHIPMENT：ALLOWED

PORT IN CHARGE：SHANGHAI,CHINA

TRANSPORT TO：ROTTERDAM NETHERALANDS

LATEST DATE OF SHIPPMENT：2024-02-28

DESCRIPTION OF GOODS

160PCS LADIES'JACKETS STYLE NO.70019 PO NO.D42067 AT USD 31.00 EACH

25 CARTONS, NET WEIGHT：150KGS, GROSS WEIGHT：230KGS, MEASUREMENT：1.500CBM

320PCS LADIES'JACKETS STYLE NO.70016 PO NO.D42067 AT USD 30.00 EACH

50 CARTONS, NET WEIGHT：300KGS, GROSS WEIGHT：420KGS, MEASUREMENT：3.000CBM

320PCS LADIES'JACKETS STYLE NO.70094 PO NO.D42067 AT USD 32.50 EACH

50 CARTONS, NET WEIGHT：300KGS, GROSS WEIGHT：420KGS,MEASUREMENT：3.000CBM

OPEN POLICY NO.：009284/53/EAL/JUNU

INVOICE NO. AND DATE：2024-02-01；20240201

DOCUMENTS REQUIRED：

+THREE COPIES OF ORIGINAL PACKING LIST

+THREE COPIES OF ORIGINAL COMMERCIAL INVOICE

+COPY FORMA CERTIFICATE OF CHINESE ORIGIN

+STATEMENT：

（A）ONE ORIGINAL INVOICE, ONE PACKING LIST, ONE FORMA CERTIFICATE OF CHINESE ORIGIN AND 1/3

BILL OF LADING MUST BE SEND TO APPLICANT BY COURIER WITHIN 7 DAYS OF SHIPMENT DATE

（B）SHIPMENT ADVICE MUST BE FAX TO APPLICANT WITHIN 24 HOURS OF SHIPMENT DATE

+ TWO COPYS OF BENEFICIARY's CERTIFICATE AND DECLARATION OF SHIPMENT

+ THREE COPYS OF EXPORT ADDMISSION

续表

| COFCO NINGBO CEREALS AND OILS CO. , LTD. | | | | | | |
|---|---|---|---|---|---|---|
| **PACKING LIST** | | | | | | |

| To: | | Invoice No. : | | |
|---|---|---|---|---|
| | | Invoice Date: | | |
| | | S/C No. : | | |
| | | S/C Date: | | |
| From: | | To: | | |
| Letter of Credit No. : | | Date of Shipment: | | |
| Date of Issue: | | | | |

| Marks and Numbers | Number and kind of package Description of goods | Quantity | Package | G. W | N. W | Meas. |
|---|---|---|---|---|---|---|
| | | | | | | |
| | TOTAL: | | | | | |
| SAY TOTAL: | | | | | | |

113

# Appendix

**Commercial Invoice Specimen 1**[1]

| COMMERCIAL INVOICE | | | | | | |
|---|---|---|---|---|---|---|
| SENDER: <br> ABC Company <br> 3 N. Main St. <br> Anytown, State, U. S. A. <br> Phone:999-999-9999 <br> Fax: 999-999-9999 <br> Tax ID/VAT/EIN# nnnnnnnnnn | | | RECIPIENT: <br> XYZ Company <br> 3 Able End <br> There, Shropshire, U. K. <br> Phone:99-99-9999 | | | |
| Invoice Date: 12 December 2024 | | | Invoice Number: 0256982 | | | |
| Carrier tracking number: 526555598 | | | Sender's Reference: 5555555 | | | |
| Carrier: GHI Transport Company | | | Recipient's Reference: 5555555 | | | |
| Quantity | Country of Origin | Description of Contents | Harmonized Code | Unit Weight | Unit Value | Subtotal (USD) |
| 1,000 | United States of America | Widgets | 999999 | 2 | 10. 00 | 10,000 |
| Total Net Weight(lbs): | 2,000 | Total Declared Value (USD): | 10,000 | | | |
| Total Gross Weight (lbs): | 2,050 | Freight and Insurance Charges (USD): | 300. 00 | | | |
| Total Shipment Pieces: | 1,000 | Other Charges (USD): | 30. 00 | | | |
| Currency Code: | USD | Total Invoice Amount (USD): | 10,000 | | | |
| Type of Export: Permanent | | | Terms of Trade: Delivery Duty Unpaid | | | |
| Reason for Export: stated reason | | | | | | |
| General Notes: notes and comments | | | | | | |
| The exporter of the products covered by this document—customs authorization number—declares that, except where otherwise clearly indicated, these products are of United States of America preferential origin. <br><br> I/We hereby certify that the information on this invoice is true and correct and that the contents of this shipment are as stated above. <br><br> Name, Position in exporting company, company stamp, signature | | | | | | |

---

[1]  http://en. wikipedia. org/wiki/Commercial_invoice.

**Commercial Invoice Specimen 2①**

| COMMERCIAL INVOICE | | |
|---|---|---|
| Exporter reference no. | Importer order/reference no. | Invoice expiration date |

| | |
|---|---|
| Exporter/Shipper (Name and physical address)<br><br>Tel:　　　　Fax:<br>E-mail: | Importer/Consignee (Name and physical address)<br><br>Tel:　　　　Fax:<br>E-mail: |
| Intermediate consignee (Name and physical address)<br><br>Tel:　　　　Fax:<br>E-mail: | Buyer (name and physical address)<br><br>Tel:　　　　Fax:<br>E-mail: |
| Notify party (Name and physical address)<br><br><br>Tel:　　　　Fax:<br>E-mail: | Terms and conditions of delivery and payment (including Inco-terms):<br>■ Freight (please mark): Prepaid ____ Collect ____<br>■ Title transfer occurs at:<br>■ Payment terms: |

| Marks and numbers | Total number of packages | Total gross weight (kg) | Dimensions H×W×L (m$^3$) |
|---|---|---|---|
| Port of loading | Port of discharge | Total net weight (kg) | Currency of sale |
| Final destination | BOL/AWB No. | Transportation method:<br>Vessel/flight No. | Date of shipment:<br>L/C No. |

| Complete and accurate description of the goods, including item no., product description, HS/tariff classification code and country of origin | Quantity (Unit of measure) | Unit price | Total price |
|---|---|---|---|
| ■　Packing costs<br>■　Freight costs<br>■　Other transportation-related costs<br>■　Handling<br>■　Insurance costs<br>■　Assists<br>■　Additional fees<br>■　Duties and taxes | | | |
| | | Grand Total | |

| Signature, initials, name, title and position | Date | Place |
|---|---|---|

---

① http://ww. exporthelp. co. za/.

**Commercial Invoice Specimen 3**

# SHANGHAI FOREIGN TRADE CORP.

# SHANGHAI, CHINA

COMMERCIAL INVOICE

| To: | | Invoice |
| --- | --- | --- |
| | | No. : _____ |
| | | Invoice |
| | | Date: _____ |
| | | S/C No. : _____ |
| | | S/C Date: |

| From: | To: |
| --- | --- |
| Letter of Credit No. : | Issued By: |

| Marks and No. | No. and kind of package Description of goods | Quantity | Unit Price | Amount |
| --- | --- | --- | --- | --- |
| | | | | |
| | TOTAL: | | | |
| SAY TOTAL: | | | | |

**Commercial Invoice Specimen 4**

COMMERCIAL INVOICE 商业发票

RECEIVER DETAILS（收件人详细资料，请务必准确填写收件人信息、联系电话和人名，将有助于加快货物通关速度）

| Company Name（收件人公司名称） | Consignment / Invoice No.（货物发票号码） | TNT Consignment Number（运单号） |
|---|---|---|
| Street（街道，门牌号码） | Total No. of Packages（货物总件 / 箱数） | |
| City/States（城市 / 州名） | Total Weight（货物总重量） | Dimensions（货物总体积） |
| Country（国家） | Fax / Telex（联系人传真/电传） | |
| Post / Zip Code（邮政编码） | Telephone（联系人电话） | |
| Contact Name（联系人姓名） Mr. / Ms. | Trade Terms (e. g. CIF / FOB)（贸易条件 例如：CIF / FOB） | |

CONSIGNMENT DETAILS（货物详细信息）

| Package Number（箱号） | Full Description of Goods（详细的货物名称） | Weight(重量) Net（净重） | Weight(重量) Gross（毛重） | No. of Items（数量） | Dimensions L×W×D( $m^3$ )（体积 长×宽×高 立方米） | Unit Value（单价） | Total Value and Currency（报关总价和货币） |
|---|---|---|---|---|---|---|---|
| | | | | | | | |

EXPORT INFORMATION（出口信息）

| Name and Address of Manufacturer / Importer (if know)（生产商或货物进口商的地址，如果知道请提供） | |
|---|---|
| Reason for Export（出口原因） | Origin of Goods（货物原产国/地） |

SHIPPER DECLARATION(发件人声明)

I (name) _____ NRIC No. _____ certify that the particulars and quantity of goods specified in this documents and the goods which are submitted for clearance for export out of (country).
声明：兹证实本发票已列明所有出口货件的详情、数量及价值，各项交运货件并没有签发其他发票。

| Signature（发件公司签章） | Name & Designation of Authorized Signatory（发件人签章） |
|---|---|
| Name and Stamp of Company (Shipper) / Firm（发件公司名称） | Address of Company (Shipper) / Firm（发件公司地址） |

117

## Canada Customs Invoice

Revenue Canada       Revenu Canada

Customs and Excise     Douanes et Accise FACTURE DES DOU ANES CANADIENNE

| 1 Vendor ( Name and Address ) / Vendeur ( Name et adresse ). | 2 Date of Direct Shipment to Canada / Date d' expedition directe vers le Canada |
| | 3 Other References ( Include Purchaser's Order No. ) Autres references ( Inclure le n de commande de l' acheteur) |

| 4 Consignee ( Name and Address )/ Destinataire ( Nom et adresse ) | 5 Purchaser's Name and Address ( if other than Consignee ) Nom et adresse de l' acheteur ( S' il differe du destinataire ) |
| | 6 Country of Transshipment / Pays de transbordement |
| | 7 Country of Origin of Goods    IF SHIPMENT INCLUDES GOODS Pays d' origine des marchandises  OF DIFFERENT ORIGINS ENTER GOODS OF DIFFERENT     ORIGINS AGAINST ITEMS IN 12. |

| 8 Transportation Give Mode and Place of Direct Shipment to Canada Transport/Preciser mode et point d' expedition directe Vers le Canada | 9 Conditions of Sale and Terms of Payment ( i. e. Sale, Consignment Shipment. Leased Goods, etc. ) Conditions de vente et modalites de paiement ( p. ex. vente, expedition en consignation, location de marchandises. etc. ) |
| | 10 Currency of Settlement / Devises du paiement |

| 11 No of Pkgs/ ND' e De colis | 12 Specification of Commodities ( Kind of Packages, Marks and Numbers, General Description and Characteristics, i. e. Grade, Quality) | 13 Quantity (State Unit) ( Preciser I' unite) | Selling Price / Prix de vente | |
| | | | 14 Unit Price /Prix unitaire | 15 Total |

| 18 If any of fields 1 to 17 are included on an attached commercial invoice. Check this box ☐ Commercial Invoice No. _____ | 16 Total Weight / Poids Total | | 17 Invoice Total |
| | Net | Gross / Bru | |

| 19 Exporter's Name and Address ( If other than Vendor) Nom et adresse de l' exportatur ( S' il deffere du vendeur) | 20 Originator ( Name and Address ) / Expediteur d' origine ( Nom et adresse) |

| 21 Departmental Ruling ( If applicable) / Decision du Ministere( S' il y a lieu) | 22 If fields 23 to 25 are not applicable, check this box ☐ /Si les zones 23 a 25 sont sans object, cocher cette boite |

| 23 If included in field 17 indicate amount/ /Si compris dans le total a la zone 17. Preciser<br>( i ) Transportation charges, expenses and insurance from the place of direct shipment to Canada<br>$ _____<br>( ii ) Costs for construction, erection and assembly incurred after importation into Canada<br>$ _____<br>( iii ) Export packing<br>$ _____ | 24 If not included in field 17 indicate amount/Si non copris dans le total a la zone 17 preciser<br>( i ) Transportation charges. Expenses and insurance to the place of direct shipment to Canada<br>$ _____<br>( ii ) Amounts for commissions other than buying commissions<br>$ _____<br>( iii ) Export packing<br>$ _____ | 25 Check ( If applicable) : /Cocher ( S' il y a lieu) :<br>( i ) Royalty payments or subsequent proceeds are paid or payable by the purchaser<br>☐<br>( ii ) The purchaser has supplied goods or services for use in the production of these goods<br>☐ |

DEPARTMENT OF NATIONAL REVENUE CUSTOMS AND EXCISE       MINISTERE DU REVENU NATIONAL DOUANES ET ACCISE

Pro-forma Invoice Specimen 1

# 世格国际贸易有限公司

# DESUN TRADING CO. ,LTD.

**Room 2901, HuaRong Mansion, Guanjiaqiao 85#, Nanjing 210005, P. R. CHINA**

**TEL: 025-4715004, 025-4715619 FAX: 4691619**

## PROFORMA INVOICE

TO:

INVOICE NO. :_____

INVOICE
DATE: _____

S/C NO. : _____

S/C DATE: _____

TERM OF PAYMENT: _____
PORT TO LOADING: _____
PORT OF DESTINATION: _____
TIME OF DELIVERY: _____
INSURANCE: _____
VALIDITY: _____

| Marks and Numbers | Number and kind of package Description of goods | Quantity | Unit Price | Amount |
|---|---|---|---|---|
| | | | | |
| | | | | |

Total Amount:

SAY TOTAL:

BENEFICIARY:

ADVISING BANK:

NEGOTIATING BANK:

119

**Pro-forma Invoice Specimen 2①**

# JIAHE IMPORT & EXPORT CO. ,LTD.

## 嘉 禾 进 出 口 有 限 公 司

**ADD：60，NONGJU RD QUTANG NANTONG JIANGSU CHINA**

**TEL：86-513-8603269 FAX：86-513-8603144**

## 形 式 发 票
### PROFORMA INVOICE

号码 NO：PRO-01-22

　　TO：LEBRUN

日期 DATE：November 16，2024

　　FRANCE.

NOTE：THIS PROFORMA INVOICE IS VALID UP TO SEP. 20，2000.

| 唛头 Marks | 货品名称及规格<br>Commodities & Specifications | 数量<br>Quantity | 单价<br>Unit Price | 总价<br>Amount |
|---|---|---|---|---|
| LEBRUN SE-RIE 5 CASSEROLES 'OSLO' 6 SE-RIES | S/S COOKWARE（WITH BLUE RING BAKELITE HANDLES）SAUCEPAN 5 PCS SETS CASSE-ROLES DIAM 20CM × 10CM CASSEROLES DIAM 24CM × 12CM | 1,800 SETS / 300CTNS<br>600 SETS / 100CTNS<br>1,200 SETS / 200CTNS<br>1,200 SETS / 300CTNS | CNF<br>USD 9.75<br>USD 4.20<br>USD 5.60<br>USD 7.65<br>TOTAL: | ANTWERP<br>USD 17,550.00<br>USD 2,520.00<br>USD 6,720.00<br>USD 9,180.00<br>USD 35,970.00 |

1. 付款方式

PAYMENT：L/C AT SIGHT

---

① http：//service. xjftec. gov. cn：7001.

2. 包装条款

PACKING：EACH PACKED IN COLOR BOX，THEN IN CARTONS.

3. 装运港

PORT OF LOADING ：GUANGZHOU，CHINA

4. 卸货港／目的港

PORT OF DISPATCHING/DESTINATION：ANTWERP

5. 交货期

DELIVERY：ON/BEFORE DECEMBER 15，2024

6. 其他

OTHERS：(如输入银行信息)

有 错 当 查

E. &. O. E

Packing List Specimen 1

长城贸易有限公司

## GREAT WALL TRADING CO. , LTD.

Room 201 HUASHENG BUILDING NINGBO P. R. CHINA

TEL：0574-24704015 FAX：24691619

# PACKING LIST

To：L. BALOUSHI TRADING EST JEDDAH.

Invoice No. :      AC05AR031

Invoice Date：    APR. 25 ,2024

S/C No. :      05AR225031

S/C Date：

From： NINGBO        To：    JEDDAH BY APL

Letter of Credit No. :       Date of Shipment： APR. 29 ,2024

| Marks and Numbers | Number and kind of package Description of goods | Quantity | Package | G. W | N. W | Meas. |
|---|---|---|---|---|---|---|
| ROYAL 05AR225031 JEDDAH C/N：1-460 | P. P INJECTION CASES  14″/22″/27″/31″ ART NO. ：ZL0322+BC05 | 230SET | 230CTNS | 18.5/4,255 KGS | 16.5/3,795 KGS | 34m³ |
| | 14″/19″/27″/31″ ART NO. ：ZL0319+BC01 | 230SET | 230CTNS | 18.5/4,255 KGS | 16.5/3,795 KGS | 34m³ |
| | 460 CARTONS OF ONE SET EACH | | | | | |
| TOTAL： | | 460SET | 460CTNS | 8,510KGS | 7,590KGS | 68m³ |

SAY TOTAL：FOUR HUNDRED AND SIXTY CARTONS ONLY

**Packing List Specimen 2**

上海纺织品进出口有限公司
**SHANGHAI TEXTILES I/E CORP.**
**PACKING LIST**
ADD：27, CHUNGSHAN ROAS E1.
TEL：8621-65342517 FAX：8621-65724743

MESSR：
CRYSTAL KOBE LTD. ,
1410 BROADWAY, ROOM 3000
NEW YORK N. Y. 10018 U. S. A.

INVOICE NO：STP015088
S/C NO：21SSG-017
DATE：NOV. 8th, 2024

| DESCRIPTION OF GOODS | SHINPPING MARKS： |
|---|---|
| 55% ACRYLIC 45% COTTON LADIES' KNITTED BLOUSE STYLE NO. H32331SE： <br><br> PAYMENT BY L/C NO. L-02-I-03437 <br> SHIPPING S/C NO. | CRYSTAL KOBE LTD. , <br> NEW YORK <br> ORDER NO. 21SSG-017 <br> STYLE NO. H32331SE L-02-I-03437 <br> CARTON/NO. 1-120 <br> MADE IN CHINA |

COLOUR BREAKDOWN：　　　SIZE

| COLOR | PACK | S | M | L | XL | XXL | XXXL | TOTAL（PCS） |
|---|---|---|---|---|---|---|---|---|
| IVORY | | 120 | 360 | 240 | | | | 720 |
| BLACK | | 320 | 360 | 440 | | | | 1,120 |
| NAVYBLUE | | 180 | 180 | 100 | | | | 460 |
| RED | | 432 | 580 | 440 | | | | 1,452 |
| WHITE | | 78 | 234 | 156 | | | | 468 |
| BROWN | | 160 | 280 | 220 | | | | 660 |
| TAWNY | | 32 | 360 | 440 | | | | 1,120 |
| TOTAL(PCS)： | | | | | | | | 6 000 |

SIZE ASSORTMENT　　　　　　　　　QUANTITY

| CTN NO. | COLOR | CTNS | S | M | L | XL | XXL | XXXL | （PCS） |
|---|---|---|---|---|---|---|---|---|---|
| 1-20 | IVORY | 20 | 6 | 18 | 12 | | | | 720 |
| 21-40 | BLACK | 20 | 16 | 18 | 22 | | | | 1,120 |
| 41-50 | NAVYBLUE | 10 | 18 | 18 | 10 | | | | 460 |
| 51-66 | RED | 16 | 16 | 28 | 22 | | | | 1,056 |
| 67-79 | WHITE | 13 | 6 | 18 | 12 | | | | 468 |
| 80-89 | BROWN | 10 | 16 | 28 | 22 | | | | 660 |
| 90-109 | TAWNY | 20 | 16 | 18 | 22 | | | | 1,120 |
| 110-120 | RED | 11 | 16 | 12 | 8 | | | | 396 |

TOTAL：　6,000　PCS　IN　120　CARTONS　ONLY.

GROSS WT：　　2,584KGS　　NET WT：　　2,326KGS
MEASUREMENT：　60×40×40CBCM　　11.58CBM

For and on behalf of
上海纺织品进出口有限公司
SHANGHAI TEXTILES I/E CORP.

Authorized Signature（s）

Packing List Specimen 3

# SHANGHAI FOREIGN TRADE CORP.
# SHANGHAI, CHINA

## PACKING LIST

| To: | | Invoice No. : | |
| --- | --- | --- | --- |
| | | Invoice Date: | |
| | | S/C No. : | |
| | | S/C Date: | |

| From: | | To: | |
| --- | --- | --- | --- |
| Letter of Credit No. : | | Date of Shipment: | |

| Marks and Numbers | Number and kind of package Description of goods | Quantity | Package | G. W | N. W | Meas. |
| --- | --- | --- | --- | --- | --- | --- |
| | | | | | | |
| | TOTAL: | | | | | |

| SAY TOTAL: | |
| --- | --- |

**Weight List Specimen**①

# WEIGHT LIST

No. 重量单号码           Date: 日期

WEIGHT LIST of      出货品名      MARKS & NOS.

For account and risk of Messrs.     买方     唛头

Shipped by      卖方

Per S. S.      运输方式

Sailing on or about     运输日期

From    起运地    to    目的地

| Packing No. | Description | Quantity | Net Weight | Gross Weight |
|---|---|---|---|---|
| 箱号 | 品名 | 数量 | 净重 | 毛重 |

---

①   http://club.china.alibaba.com/forum/iask_thread/view/51_20764947_.html.

Packing/Weight List Specimen[①]

# Packing/Weight List

No. 包装号码                             Date: 日期

Packing/Weight List of      出货品名               Marks & No.

For account and risk of Messrs.      买方              唛头

Shipped by                    卖方

Per S. S.                    运输方式

Sailing on or about             运输日期

From      起运地       to       目的地

| Packing No. | Description | Quantity | Net Weight | Gross Weight | Measurement |
|---|---|---|---|---|---|
| 箱号 | 品名 | 数量 | 净重 | 毛重 | 尺码 |

---

① http://post-service.speedy.com.tw/files/packing_sample.doc.

# Chapter 5　Transport Documents

## 【本章提要】

对外贸易中的运输单据是承运人签发给托运人（通常是卖方）的证明所收到货物情况，以及承运人和托运人之间权利义务的文件，是交接货物、处理索赔与理赔，以及货款结算的重要单据。

根据运输方式的不同，运输单据可以分为海运提单/海运单、铁路运单、航空运单、邮包收据、多式联合运输单据。其中，海运提单是本章的学习重点。

和其他运输单据一样，海运提单可用作货物收据和运输契约的证明，此外，海运提单还是货物所有权的凭证，可以进行流通和转让。

基于不同视角，海运提单可分为记名提单/凭指示提单/来人提单，清洁提单/不清洁提单、已装船提单/备运提单、直运提单/转运提单、联运提单/多式联合运输提单、全式提单/略式提单、班轮提单/租船提单/集装箱提单、预借提单/迟期提单/倒签提单/顺签提单、正本提单/副本提单、船东提单/货代提单、舱面提单等。

海运提单的格式并无统一规定，一般会因出具海运提单的运输公司不同而不同。海运提单的项目内容则大同小异，一般包括基本当事人、运输事宜、货物信息和其他规定四大部分，具体包括托运人、收货人、提单号码、通知人、船名及航次、装运港、卸货港、唛头和包装件数、货物描述、毛重和尺码、运费和费用、正本提单份数、提单日期和签发地点、签署，以及其他杂项规定。

海运提单的填写应遵循单证一致、单单一致的原则。此外，还要参照适用国际惯例的相关规定。比如，根据 INCOTERMS 的规定，买卖双方选择使用的贸易术语不同，负责办理运输事宜的当事人不同，运费的支付时间也不同。因此，以 CIF/CFR 为贸易术语的交易项下的海运提单，运费支付情况一栏应填写"运费预付"（FREIGHT PREPAID）；而以 FOB 为贸易术语的交易项下的海运提单，其运费支付情况一栏则应填写"运费到付"（FREIGHT TO COLLECT）。再比如，根据 UCP 规定，海运提单表面应注明承运人名称，并由承运人或其代理人、船长或其代理人签署。签署人签署时须表明身份。若为代理人签署，还须表明被代理一方的名称和身份。

International sales often involve large-distance transportation of the goods sold. This means that either the seller or the buyer needs to make arrangements relating to the transportation, and some transport documents are required to evidence the fulfillment of their obligations.

This chapter covers the essentials of transport documents in international transactions, containing definition, governing rules and usual practices, functions, types, contents and the specimen, and others.

## 5.1 Introduction

### 5.1.1 Definition

Generally, transport documents are all types of documents evidencing acceptance, receipt and shipment of goods. Typical examples are ocean bill of lading, sea waybill, air waybill, rail waybill, etc. [1]

Both the UCP 600 and the ISBP 821 define transport documents as original documents evidencing contracts of carriage between the carrier and the consignor. Some documents commonly used in relation to the transportation of goods, e. g. Delivery Order, Forwarder's Certificate of Receipt, Forwarder's Certificate of Shipment, Forwarder's Certificate of Transport, Forwarder's Cargo Receipt and Mate's Receipt do not reflect a contract of carriage thus are not transport documents.

### 5.1.2 Functions

Different types of transport documents may play different functions in international trade. The general functions of transport documents are:

(1) Receipt for the goods. It operates as a receipt providing evidence that goods conforming to the contract have been shipped as agreed and in the physical possession of the carrier for delivery to the consignee at destination. This evidentiary aspect of the document is important, both as between the seller and the buyer, in relation to obligations under the sale contract, and as between a potential cargo-claimant and the carrier, should goods be lost or damaged during transit.

(2) Evidence of a carriage contract. It contains or evidences the relevant terms of contract with the carrier. Where goods are lost or damaged in transit or short-delivered, these terms are the basis on which cargo interests may be able to pursue a claim against the carrier.

(3) Document of title. It operates as a transferable document of title. A document of title in this context is a document, which provides its holder with the exclusive right to demand delivery from the carrier. As the goods will only be released at the port of discharge against surrender of the bill of lading, possession of the document amounts to constructive possession of the goods.

If the document is "negotiable", the right embodied in the document can be transferred along a chain of sale contracts by delivery, with any necessary endorsement, of the document alone. While goods are in the physical possession of a carrier during transit, a seller is able to

---

[1]  Edward G Hinkelman. Longman Dictionary of International Trade. Longman and China Renmin University Press, 2000.

pass possession and property in the goods to a subsequent buyer simply by passing on the negotiable document of title. By the same token, the document can be pledged to a bank and thus may be used as a security to raise finance.

It is this aspect that sets the negotiable transport document apart from non-negotiable transport documents as sea waybills, air waybills, road waybills, rail waybills, etc.

## 5.1.3 Types

Transport documents may be categorized into different types from different perspectives.

(1) Negotiable/Non-negotiable transport documents. According to the negotiability/transferability of documents, transport documents may be grouped into negotiable documents and non-negotiable ones.

A negotiable transport document, a transport document issued by a carrier upon shipment of goods, is usually made out "to order", or "to the order of a named party", or "to the bearer", and the right embodied in the document can be transferred accordingly.

Primary reason for negotiable documents is security under documentary credits and re-sale of goods in transit. Because when goods are sold in transit, documentary security is a vital concern to the parties involved in an export transaction. The negotiable document needs to be physically transferred to the final consignee, possibly along a chain of buyers and banks.

However, a number of problems may be associated with the use of negotiable transport document. These include higher administrative costs related to the issuing, processing and transfer of paper documentation, and additional costs due to delayed arrival of the document at the port of discharge, in particular where travel time is short, e. g. in short-sea shipping.

Instead, commercial parties have, over recent years, been increasingly encouraged to use non-negotiable transport documents (including straight bill of lading, non-negotiable sea waybill, air waybill, etc.) in all cases where sale of goods in transit is not envisaged.

Non-negotiable transport documents operate as a receipt for the goods and an evidence of a carriage contract, but not a document of title. They are advantageous where the distinct characteristics of a document of title are not required, as the need for physical transmission of the document and thus the potential for delayed arrival of the document do not arise.

When the master (captain) signs a non-negotiable sea waybill, the signature may be accompanied by a stamp that incorporates the name of the vessel. Even if the stamp also mentions the name of the owner, the non-negotiable sea waybill will be considered to have been signed by the master (captain). This stamp is often referred to as the "ship's stamp". [1]

(2) Ocean bill of lading / Sea waybill / Air waybill/ Rail waybill. According to the modes

---

[1]  ISBP821, D5(e).

of transportation, transport documents may be classified into ocean bill of lading, sea waybill, air transport document, road waybill, rail or inland waterway transport documents, certificate of posting, etc.

Ocean bill of lading is a document issued by a carrier to a shipper, signed by the captain, agent, or owner of a vessel, furnishing written evidence regarding receipt of the goods, the conditions on which transportation is made (contract of carriage), and the engagement to deliver goods at the prescribed port of destination to the lawful holder of the bill of lading. A bill of lading is, therefore, a receipt for merchandise, an evidence of contract of carriage, and a contract to deliver it as freight[1]. It is one commonly used negotiable transport document, in particular when goods are sold in transit. It can be transferred by delivery, with any necessary endorsement, or the document alone.

Sea waybill is a non-negotiable document that also functions as a receipt for shipment and as evidence of the contract of carriage. Sea waybill is typically used in cases where sale of goods in transit is not intended, where no letter of credit is in place, or where the parties' relationship is close (business partners are known to each other or are part of the same organization) and documentary security is not required.

When the master (captain) signs a non-negotiable sea waybill, the signature may be accompanied by a stamp that incorporates the name of the vessel. Even if the stamp also mentions the name of the owner, the non-negotiable sea waybill will be considered to have been signed by the master (captain). This stamp is often referred to as the "ship's stamp".[2]

Air waybill is a shipping document used by the airlines for air freight. It is a contract for carriage that includes carrier conditions of carriage, including such items as limits of liability and claims procedures. The air waybill also contains shipping instructions to airlines, a description of the commodity and applicable transportation charges.

Rail waybill is a freight document that indicates goods have been received for shipment by rail. A duplicate is given to the shipper as a receipt for acceptance of the goods.[3]

Road waybill is a transport document that indicates goods have been received for shipment by road haulage carrier.[4]

Inland waterway transport document is a transport document that indicates goods have been

---

[1]  Edward G Hinkelman. Longman Dictionary of International Trade. Longman and China Renmin University Press, 2000.

[2]  ISBP821, F4(e).

[3]  Edward G Hinkelman. Longman Dictionary of International Trade. Longman and China Renmin University Press, 2000.

[4]  Edward G Hinkelman. Longman Dictionary of International Trade. Longman and China Renmin University Press, 2000.

received for shipment by inland waterway.

Certificate of posting is a transport document that indicates goods have been received for shipment by post.

(3) Multimodal or combined transport document. Multimodal or combined transport document is a transport document covering at least two different modes of transport. Standard form documents are often designed to be used both for carriage of goods by sea (port of loading to port of discharge) and for transport from point-to-point (receipt to delivery).

Documents for multimodal transport may be made out in negotiable form (e. g. "to order"), so as to operate as a negotiable document of title; or may be made out in non-negotiable form, so as to operate as a non-negotiable transport document.

When the master (captain) signs a multimodal transport document, the signature may be accompanied by a stamp that incorporates the name of the vessel. Even if the stamp also mentions the name of the owner, the multimodal transport document will be considered to have been signed by the master(captain). This stamp is often referred to as the "ship's stamp". [1]

(4) E-alternatives to traditional transport documents. For their increased speed and reduced cost, electronic means of communication, including electronic data interchange (EDI), internet based tracking and tracing systems, customs clearing programs and e-mail, etc. are generally used by commercial parties. Furthermore, it is of importance that the use of electronic alternatives may help avoid liability arising from delayed arrival of documents at destination. This suggests that problems, currently associated with the use of negotiable transport documents, in particular in the context of short sea voyages, are of considerable concern to commercial parties.

However, electronic alternatives to traditional transport documents do not currently appear to play a significant role in commercial practice. Comparatively, the transition to an electronic environment is easier for non-negotiable transport documents than for negotiable transport documents. It is broadly recognized that the document of title aspect of negotiable transport documents continues to present a major challenge in the effort to encourage the use of electronic alternatives. [2]

## 5. 1. 4  Contents

Most of the discrepancies discovered in L/C operations are associated with the transport document. It is of great necessity to learn about the detailed items of transport documents.

---

[1]  ISBP821, D5(e).

[2]  Several generally accepted obstacles to the use of electronic transport documents are: infrastructure/market/trading partners not yet ready; legal framework is not clear enough or is not adequate; electronic equivalents are not sufficiently secure; technology and/or switch to electronic environment is too costly; confidentiality concerns; and others.

Generally, the details on the transport document should include the following information:

- An indication that it has been issued by a "named carrier or his agent".
- A description of the goods in general terms not conflicting with description in the L/C.
- Identifying marks and numbers.
- The name of the carrying vessel in the case of a Marne Bill of Lading, or the name of the intended carrying vessel in the case of a multimodal transport document including sea transport.
- An indication of dispatch or taking in charge of the goods or loading on board, as the case may be.
- An indication of the place of such dispatch or taking in charge or loading on board and the place of final destination.
- The name of shipper, consignee (if not made out "to order") and the name and address of any "notify" party.
- Whether freight has been paid or still to be paid.
- The number of originals issued to the consignor if issued in more than one original.
- Date of issuance of the transport document.

Traders are also to scrutinize and ensure that if a transport document bears a superimposed clause or notation which expressly declares a defective condition of the goods and/or the packaging. A claused transport document will not be acceptable unless acceptance of such clause is authorized in the L/C.

A transport document specifically stating that the goods are or will be loaded on deck is also not acceptable unless expressly authorized in the L/C. [1]

### 5.1.5 Governing Usual Customs and Practices

There are many laws, uniform rules and usual practices relevant to transport documents. However, only those laws and usual practices closely related to transport documents under letter of credit transaction are discussed here.

(1) UCP 600. It's the latest revision of Uniform Customs and Practices for documentary credits which took effect on 1 July 2007, provides guidance for documents under different modes of transportation, covering combined/multiple transport documents, bill of lading, non-negotiable sea waybill, charter party bill of lading, air transport document, road, rail or inland waterway transport documents, courier receipt, post receipt or certificate of posting, clean transport document; etc. (UC P600 Articles 19-27).

The relevant stipulations mainly concern such items as the signature, shipped on board notation, transshipment definition, and place of taking in charge, dispatch, loading on board and

---

[1] http://resources. alibaba. com/topic/294489/Transport_Document. htm.

destination, etc.

(2) ISBP 821. ISBP provides detailed governance for documents under different modes of transportation, covering combined/multiple transport documents; bill of lading; non-negotiable sea waybill; charter party bill of lading; air transport document; road, rail or inland waterway transport documents; courier receipt, post receipt or certificate of posting; clean transport document; and etc.

The relevant stipulations of ISBP(E3-28) concerning the application of the UCP 600 article 19, 20, 22, 23, and 24, provide detailed standards for transport documents, including the interpretation of the following terms:

- Full set of originals.
- Signature.
- On board notations.
- Place of loading and ports of discharge.
- Consignee, order party, shipper and endorsement, notify party.
- Partial shipment and transshipment.
- Clean transport documents.
- Goods description.
- Corrections and alterations.
- Freight and additional costs.

However, when the master (captain) signs a non-negotiable sea waybill, the signature may be accompanied by a stamp that incorporates the name of the vessel. Even if the stamp also mentions the name of the owner, the non-negotiable sea waybill will be considered to have been signed by the master (captain). This stamp is often referred to as the "ship's stamp". [1]

## 5.2 Bill of Lading

Statistical data indicates that more than 2/3 of the total volume of global trade is transported via sea way, and the percentage for China is even as high as 90%. Accordingly, bill of lading is the most popularly used document of transport in international trade.

### 5.2.1 Definition

The term bill of lading, sometimes referred to as BOL, Ocean Bill of Lading, Marine Bill of Lading, Port to Port Bill of Lading, derives from the noun "bill", which means a schedule of costs for services supplied or to be supplied, and from the verb "to lade" which means to load a cargo onto a ship or other forms of transport.

---

[1] ISBP 821, F4(e).

A bill of lading may be defined into different versions. Some typical definitions are given below:

- It is a document issued by a carrier to a shipper, signed by the captain, agent, or owner of vessel, furnishing written evidence regarding receipt of the goods (cargo), the condition on which transportation is made (contract of carriage), and the engagement to deliver goods at the prescribed port of destination to the lawful holder of the bill of lading. [1]

- It is a document issued by a carrier, e. g. a ship's master or by a company's shipping department, acknowledging that specified goods have been received on board as cargo for conveyance to a named place for delivery to the consignee who is usually identified. [2]

- It is a document issued by a carrier, or its agent, to the shipper as a contract of carriage of goods. It is also a receipt for cargo accepted for transportation, and must be presented for taking delivery at the destination. It serves as a proof of ownership (title) of the cargo, and may be issued either in a negotiable or non-negotiable form. In negotiable form, it is commonly used in letter of credit transactions, and may be bought, sold, or traded; or used as security for borrowing money. A B/L is required in all claims for compensation for any damage, delay, or loss; and for the resolution of disputes regarding ownership of the cargo. [3]

- Bill of lading, a written account of goods shipped by any person, signed by the agent of the owner of the vessel, or by its master, acknowledging the receipt of the goods, and promising to deliver them safe at the place directed, dangers of the sea excepted. It is usual for the master to sign two, three, or four copies of the bill; one of which he keeps in possession, one is kept by the shipper, and one is sent to the consignee of the goods. [4]

- A bill of lading, however named, must appear to indicate the name of the carrier and be signed by qualified parties; appear to indicate that the goods have been shipped on board a named vessel at the port of loading stated in the credit by pre-printed wording, or an on board notation indicating the date on which the goods have been shipped on board; appear to indicate shipment from the port of loading to the port of discharge stated in the credit; be the sole original bill of lading or, if issued in more than one original, be the full set as indicated on the bill of lading; contain terms and conditions of carriage or make reference to another source containing the terms and conditions of carriage in the case of short form or blank back bill of lading; and contain no indication that it is subject to a charter party. [5]

- A bill of lading is a receipt from a shipping company for goods shipped for transport

---

[1]  Edward G. Hinkelman. Longman Dictionary of International Trade. Longman and China Renmin University Press, 2000.

[2]  http://en. wikipedia. org/wiki/Bill_of_lading.

[3]  http://www. businessdictionary. com/definition/bill-of-lading-B-L. html.

[4]  http://dictionary. die. net/bil of lading.

[5]  Article 20 of UCP 600.

from one destination to another. It is signed by or on behalf of the master of the carrying vessel, or by the carrier or a named agent, for or on behalf of the master or carrier, and sets out the terms and conditions under which the goods are to be carried.

## 5.2.2  Functions

A bill of lading may, therefore, be used as a receipt for merchandise, a contract to deliver it as freight, and as a traded object. It serves a number of purposes:

• It is evidence that a valid contract of carriage, or a chartering contract, exists, and it may incorporate the full terms of the contract between the consignor and the carrier by reference.

• It is a receipt signed by the carrier confirming whether goods matching the contract description have been received in good condition.

• It is also a document of transfer, being freely transferable but not a negotiable instrument in the legal sense. It governs all the legal aspects of physical carriage, and, like a cheque or other negotiable instrument, it may be endorsed affecting ownership of the goods actually being carried. It binds the carrier to its terms, irrespectively of the actual holder of the B/L, and owner of the goods, may be at a specific moment. [1]

In addition, a B/L may also play important roles in business correspondence, payment and freight settlement, and trade/transportation/insurance claims settlement.

## 5.2.3  Types

There are a number of different types of bills of lading, depending on the standards of categorization.

(1) Straight/Order/Bearer B/L. According to the way of stipulating consignee, a bill of lading may be a straight bill of lading, an order bill of lading, or a bearer bill of lading.

A straight B/L is made out directly to the consignee, i. e. the buyer under a sales contract. It is only the consignee named in the bill of lading that has the right to pick up the goods from the carrier. In this case, the B/L itself does not give title to the goods. The consignee needs only to identify himself to claim the goods. It is thus known as a non-negotiable bill of lading, and cannot be transferred. It is often used when payment for the goods has been made in advance.

An order B/L is made out to the order of a named party, in terms of "to order", "to order of the shipper", "to order of the issuing bank", or, "to order of the buyer". An order bill of lading is a title document to the goods, thus it is negotiable, and can be bought, sold, or traded while goods are in transit. It is the most commonly used bill of lading in international trade

---

[1]  http://en. wikipedia. org/wiki/Bill_of_lading.

practice, in particular under documentary L/C transactions. In this case, the shipper should endorse blankly before submitting them to the negotiating bank. The buyer usually needs the original or a copy as proof of ownership to take possession of the goods.

A bearer B/L, sometimes known as blank bill of lading, or open bill of lading, indicates that delivery shall be made to whosoever holds the bill. Such a bill of lading may be created explicitly or it is an order bill that fails to nominate the consignee whether in its original form or through an endorsement in blank. A bearer bill of lading could be negotiated simply by physical delivery. If the bearer bill of lading was lost or stolen, anyone could be the bearer claiming for the goods. It is, therefore, relatively risky and seldom used in the practice of international trade.

B/L can, therefore, be grouped into negotiable bill of lading and non-negotiable bill of lading. The former contains order B/L and bearer B/L, while the latter only refers to straight B/L.

(2) Clean/Claused B/L. According to the existence of notations or clauses specifying deficient condition(s) of the goods and/or packaging, a bill of lading may be a clean bill of lading, or a claused bill of lading.

A clean B/L is a bill of lading where the carrier has noted that the merchandise/packaging has been received in apparent good condition (no apparent damage, loss, etc.).

A claused B/L, sometimes known as an unclean bill of lading, is a bill of lading containing notations which specify deficient condition (s) of the goods and/or packaging, for instance, "rusty of the goods", "breakage of the package", "insufficiently packed for ocean voyage", "three cases short ship", "a few drums leaking", "the cloth bags have been stained", "about 3% of goods have been crushed", etc. Under a letter of credit, banks will not accept bill of lading bearing such clauses or notations, unless otherwise stipulated in the credit.

(3) Shipped on board / Received for shipment B/L. According to whether the goods has been shipped on board the named vessel, a bill of lading may be a shipped on board bill of lading, or a received for shipment bill of lading.

A shipped on board B/L, sometimes known as "laden on board B/L", or "clean on board B/L", means that the goods have been shipped on board the vessel in apparent good order and condition. It usually indicates so by a clause such as "shipped on board the vessel named above...". If no such a clause is printed on the bill of lading, there should be a notation "On Board" accompanied by the date of boarding, which will be deemed as the date of shipment. To assure the seller's actual delivery of goods, a shipped on board bill of lading is usually required by a sales contract and the relevant letter of credit.

A received for shipment B/L is a bill of lading bearing no notation of "On Board". It means that the goods have been received by the carrier and ready for shipment, and is commonly used for transportation by containers. Under a letter of credit, banks usually do not accept received for shipment bill of lading. However, a received for shipment bill of lading can be transferred into a shipped on board bill of lading by the carrier's adding the notation of "On Board" on the face of the bill of lading, and in this case, the date of shipment is later than the date of issuance of the B/L.

(4) Direct/Transshipment B/L. According to whether transshipment is involved or not, a bill of lading may be a direct bill of lading, or a transshipment bill of lading. Where transshipment means unloading and reloading from one vessel to another during the course of ocean carriage from the port of loading to the port of discharge stipulated in the credit. [1]

A direct B/L is a bill of lading indicating that the goods will be transported from the port of loading directly to the port of discharge. If the letter of credit does not allow transshipment, banks will only accept direct bills of lading.

A transshipment B/L is a bill of lading indicating that the goods will be transported from the port of loading, transshipped at the port of transshipment, and indirectly to the port of discharge. Unless transshipment is prohibited by the terms of the credit, banks will accept a bill of lading indicating that the goods will be transshipped, provided that the entire ocean carriage is covered by one and the same bill of lading. A bill of lading indicating that transshipment will or may take place is acceptable, even if the credit prohibits transshipment, if the goods have been shipped in a container, trailer or LASH barge as evidenced by the bill of lading. [2]

As for the owner of the goods, direct bills of lading are preferred to transshipment bills of lading, because transshipment will increase costs and probably result in damage to or loss of the goods, and the arrival time of the goods will probably be delayed due to unexpected reasons. Thus, only when there is no direct shipment between the port of loading and the port of discharge can transshipment be used.

(5) Through/Combined B/L. According to the multimodes of shipment, a bill of lading may be a through bill of lading, or a combined transport bill of lading.

A through B/L involves the use of at least two different modes of transport from road, rail, air, and sea, and the first of which should be ocean transport, such as ocean-land, ocean-river, ocean-air, or ocean-ocean, etc. A through bill of lading is issued by the first leg ocean carrier.

A combined transport B/L is issued by combined transport operator that covers the multimodal transport on a door to door basis in one contract of carriage. It is ideal for container movements. It differs from "through B/L" in that combined transport is operated by only one

---

① UCP600 Article 20 b.
② UCP600 Article 20 c.

carrier.

(6) Long Form/Short Form B/L. According to the existence of the items on the rights and liabilities of the carrier and the shipper, a bill of lading may be a long form bill of lading, or a short form one.

A long form B/L contains detailed items on the rights and liabilities of the carrier and the shipper, which are usually printed on the back of B/L in very small sized words, and thus called "SMALL PRINT" or "MINUTE PRINT". This form of bills of lading is widely used in practice of international trade, particularly in the case of liner transportation.

A short form B/L only contains the essential items on the face of B/L, the detailed clauses on the rights and liabilities of the carrier and the shipper on the back are omitted. It is frequently used in the case of affreightment, and the detailed items on the rights and liabilities of the carrier and the shipper are subject to a charter party concluded between them.

Unless otherwise stipulated in the credit, banks only accept long form bills of lading.

(7) Liner/Charter Party/Container B/L. According to the vehicles of shipment, a bill of lading may be a liner bill of lading, a charter party bill of lading, or a container bill of lading.

A liner B/L is usually a long form bill of lading, and contains detailed items on the rights and liabilities of the carrier and the shipper.

A charter party B/L is a short form bill of lading, and usually contains some basic provisions but not detailed items on the rights and liabilities of the carrier and the shipper, which are usually subject to a charter party.

Unless otherwise stipulated in the credit, banks will not accept a charter party bill of lading.

A container B/L is a bill of lading indicating that the goods will be transported in containers. It usually bears the notation of "containerized". A container bill of lading is a kind of received for shipment bill of lading. It is, therefore, important to see the notation of "On Board" on such bills of lading.

(8) Advanced/ Stale / Ante-dated / Post-dated B/L. According to the issuing/presenting date of bill of lading, a B/L may be an advanced B/L, a stale B/L, an ante-dated B/L, or a post-dated B/L.

An advanced B/L is a bill of lading issued by the carrier to the shipper when the expiry date of the L/C is due but the exporter has not yet got the goods ready for shipment. The purpose of issuing such a bill of lading is to negotiate payment with the bank in time within the validity of the L/C. It is regarded as unlawful and risky and should be avoided.

A stale B/L is a bill of lading presented to its consignee after the arrival date of goods at the named port of destination, or presented to a bank after the last date for presentation specified in the relevant letter of credit. The latter case is not acceptable as a valid document. Sometimes especially in the case of short sea voyages, it is a usual practice for a B/L to be presented later than the date of arrival of the shipment, it is, therefore, necessary to add a clause of "Stale B/L is acceptable" in the relevant L/C.

Neither the UCP 600 nor the ISBP 821 gives stipulations about stale bill of lading. However, according to the uniform commercial code (UCC), a B/L may be rejected if presented more than 21 days after the date of arrival of the shipment.

An ante-dated B/L, sometimes known as back-dated B/L, is a bill of lading issued by the carrier to the shipper when the actual shipment date is later than that stipulated in the L/C. It is dated before the date of the goods actually shipped on board the named vessel. The purpose of issuing such a bill of lading is to guarantee the date of signature of the B/L to suit the L/C requirement, to make it retroactively effective, and to avoid non-acceptance by the bank. Despite of its necessities in certain practical cases, it is regarded as illegal and risky and should be avoided.

A post-dated B/L is a bill of lading issued by the carrier to the shipper when the actual shipment date is earlier than that stipulated in the L/C. It is dated after the date of the goods actually shipped on board the named vessel. Similar to an ante-dated B/L, the purpose of issuing a post-dated bill of lading is also to guarantee the date of signature of the B/L to suit the L/C requirement, to make it retroactively effective, and to avoid non-acceptance by the bank.

In practice of international trade, the shipper may request the carrier to issue an ante-dated B/L or a post-dated B/L against "an indemnity" or "a guarantee".

(9) Original/Copy B/L. According to the existence of the carrier's signature, a B/L may be an original bill of lading or a copy one.

Bills of lading are usually made out in sets, consisting of a number of originals (usually three) and a number of copies and marked "original" and "copy" respectively. Only the originals signed by the carrier enable the consignee to take delivery of the goods. The copies are just for reference.

(10) Others. Furthermore, there are some other types of B/L, such as on deck B/L, groupage B/L, house B/L, etc.

An on-deck B/L is issued only when the cargo is loading on ship's deck. It applies to goods like livestock, plants, dangerous cargo, or awkwardly-shaped goods that can not fit into the ship's holds. In this case, the goods are exposed to greater risks and therefore specific insurance must be covered against additional risks. Unless otherwise stipulated in the credit, banks will not accept on deck bills of lading, for there is no assurance of the safety of the goods during the course of transportation.

A groupage B/L is a bill of lading issued by the ship-owner to the "groupage operator", covering a number of consignments from different shippers with a common destination. The "groupage operator" refers to person/company who consolidates cargo from several exporters into a full container load ( FCL ), and then presents the packed container as an FCL to the container operator. The ship-owner issues a groupage bill of lading to the "groupage operator", and the "groupage operator" issues "house bills" to the individual shippers.

A house B/L is a bill of lading issued by a groupage operator/freight forwarder to each individual shipper. Usually, house B/L is issued by the freight forwarder before he gets on groupage B/L from the ship-owner.

An FIATA B/L is a document designed as a multimodal or combined transport document with negotiable status which has been developed by the International Federation of Forwarding Agents' Associations ( FIATA ).

To be noted, all the above-mentioned bills of lading are not independent of each other. Several types may be combined into one like "Clean on board, to order, blank endorsed B/L". A received for shipment B/L may also be a straight and clean bill.

### 5.2.4  Contents and Specimens

The contents of a bill of lading cover all the items on both the front and the back of the document. On the back of a bill of lading are the conditions of the transport contract between the shipper and the carrier, usually including the liabilities and disclaimers of the carrier, which are governed generally either by the older Hague rules, by the more recent Hague-Visby rules, or by the latest Hamburg rules, and will be briefly discussed in 5.2.5.

The main contents on the front of B/L include four general parts: basic parties, items on marine transportation, items on goods, and miscellaneous. 15 detailed fields are listed as follows:

( 1 ) Shipper or consignor. The shipper/consignor is the party who consigns the goods to the carrier. It is usually the seller under the sales contract, i. e. the beneficiary under the letter of credit.

However, the shipper or consignor of the goods is not necessarily the beneficiary of the credit. Sometimes the credit requires the buyer as shipper. The reason may be that the buyer is not the final buyer but a middleman. In this event, the phrase "third party bill of lading is acceptable" should be stated in the credit.

( 2 ) Consignee. The consignee is the party who has the right to pick up the goods from the carrier against bills of lading at the port of destination, usually the buyer under the sales contract, i. e. the applicant under the letter of credit.

If a credit requires a bill of lading to show that the goods are consigned to a named party, this B/L is the so-called "straight bill of lading", and it must not contain words such as "to order" or "to order of" that precede the name of that named party, whether typed or pre-printed.

Likewise, if a credit requires the goods to be consigned "to order" or "to order of" a named party, the bill of lading is the so-called "order bill of lading", and it must not show that the goods are consigned straight to the named party.

If a bill of lading is issued to order or to order of the shipper, it must be endorsed by the shipper. An endorsement indicating that it is made for or on behalf of the shipper is acceptable.

In practice of international trade, goods may be consigned to a named party, or to order of a named party (usually the consignee, or the shipper). However, the consignee may be the shipper (seller), the negotiating bank, or the issuing bank. When the bills of lading are made out "to the order of shipper", the shipper (seller) must endorse them blankly before submitting them to the negotiating bank. An endorsement indicating that it is made for or on behalf of the shipper is acceptable.

Three commonly used methods of stipulating the consignee of B/L in L/C are:
- "Full set of B/L consigned to A. B. C. Co".
- "Full set of B/L made out to order".
- "B/L issued to order of ×××".

Accordingly, you should make out B/L respectively:
- "Consigned to A. B. C. Co. ".
- "To order".
- "To order of ×××".

To be noted, the aforementioned methods frequently used to stipulate the consignee of B/L are not always acceptable to all countries. For instance, Bs/L consigned "to the order" will not be accepted by Brazil, the complete information (full address, telephone, fax, city and contact person) for both the consignee and notify party will be required. While in U. S. A. , especially since 2 February, 2003, the date on which THE NEW U. S. CUSTOMS REGULATIONS REQUIRING FILING OF CARGO DECLARATIONS 24 HOURS PRIOR TO LOADING came into full force, where the bill of lading is drawn "to order", and no consignee is named, the actual consignee must appear in the cargo declaration by name and address, otherwise the carrier may be penalized.

(3) B/L No. Each B/L has its unique number, which is usually located on the right head of B/L.

B/L No. is a reference number given by the shipping company or its agent to the consignor for later correspondence and easy checking, and is usually incorporated in other documents as insurance policy, and shipping advice.

(4) Notify party. The notify party, sometimes known as notify party addressed to, is the party whom the carrier will notify of the arrival of the goods. It may be the applicant of the

credit, the party nominated in the credit, and its address and contact details must be as stated in the credit. If a credit does not state a notify party, the respective field on the bill of lading may be left blank or completed in any manner.

To sum up, if the B/L is straight bill of lading, the notify party's address is written in details; if it states otherwise, fill in the blank as the requirement in the L/C. Moreover, the notify party under documentary collection is usually the payer, that is the buyer under a sales contract.

In practice of international trade, to switch off the direct connections between the real supplier and the end buyer, the middlemen usually request that the detailed name and address of the notify party should NOT appear in the letter of credit (e. g. transferable L/C, back-to-back L/C).

(5) Ocean vessel and voyage No. A bill of lading must appear to indicate the name of the ocean vessel used by the carrier to carry the goods from the port of loading to the port of destination. If the transshipment is not allowed, only one ship's name is filled in the B/L; if the transshipment is allowed, the second ship's name should be filled in. In the case of liner shipment, a bill of lading must appear to indicate the Voyage Number.

(6) Place of receipt or port of loading. A bill of lading must appear to indicate shipment from the port of loading to the port of discharge stated in the credit.

When the named port of loading is required by the credit, it should appear in the port of loading field within the bill of lading. However, it may instead be stated in the field headed "place of receipt" or the like, if it is clear that the goods were transported from that place of receipt by vessel, and provided there is an on board notation evidencing that the goods were loaded on the named vessel at the port stated under "place of receipt" or like term.

If a credit does not require the named port of loading, but just gives a geographical area or range of ports of loading ( e. g. "any China ports" ) , the bill of lading must indicate the actual port of loading, which must be within the geographical area or range stated in the credit.

(7) Port of discharge or final destination. When the named port of discharge is required by the credit, it should appear in the field of port of discharge within the bill of lading. However, it may be stated in the field headed "place of final destination" or the like if it is clear that the goods were to be transported to that place of final destination by vessel, and provided there is a notation evidencing that the port of discharge is the one stated under "place of final destination" or like term. In practice, if transshipment is allowed, the port of discharge should be the port where the cargo is unloaded after the first voyage.

If a credit does not require the named port of discharge, but just presents a geographical area or range of ports of discharge ( e. g. "any European port" ) , the bill of lading must indicate the actual port of discharge, which must be within the geographical area or range stated in the credit.

(8) Shipping marks and numbers of packages. A bill of lading must appear to indicate shipping marks and numbers of packages, in accordance with the requirements of L/C. If there is no shipping marks, fill in "N/M", and the number of packages should be filled both in figures and in English words.

(9) Description of goods. Description of Goods in B/L should be consistent with that in L/C, commercial invoice and other documents, and the name of commodity is usually filled in the relevant field of B/L. However, a goods description in the bill of lading may be shown in General Terms not in conflict with that stated in the credit.

However, generic descriptions of the cargo, such as General Goods or Merchandise, "FAK" or "Freight of All Kinds", "General Cargo", "STC" or "Said to Contain", Generic or Miscellaneous Names, are not acceptable to some countries' customs (U. S. A. , Brazil, etc. ).

(10) Gross weight and measurement. The gross weight should be shown in kilogram as calculating weight unit. If there is no package or in bulk, "gross for net" is recommended to be written down.

When filling in the measurement, that is the cargo's volume, three decimal digits are usually kept.

(11) Freight and additional costs. If a credit requires that a bill of lading show that freight has been paid (e. g. under trade terms of CIF, CFR) or is payable at destination (e. g. under trade term of FOB), the bill of lading must be marked accordingly. In this case, the applicants and issuing bank should specify the requirements of documents to show whether freight is to be prepaid or collected.

If a credit states that costs additional to freight are not acceptable, a bill of lading must not indicate that costs additional to the freight have been or will be incurred. Such indication may be by express reference to additional costs or by the use of shipment terms which refer to costs associated with the loading or unloading of goods, such as Free In (FI), Free Out (FO), Free In and Out (FIO) and Free In and Out Stowed (FIOS).

However, a reference in the transport document to costs which may be levied as a result of a delay in unloading the goods or after the goods have been unloaded, e. g. costs covering the late return of containers, is not considered to be an indication of additional costs in this context.

(12) No. of original B(s)/L. The number of original B(s)/L to be issued and presented must be at least the number required by the credit, the UCP 600, or, the number stated on the document.

If the relevant L/C expressly stipulates the number of original B(s)/L, e. g. "full set 3/3 original clean on board ocean Bill of Lading···", the B/L is to be issued in three original, and all the three original B(s)/L should be presented to the bank.

If the relevant L/C stipulates as "full set of clean on board bill of lading issued…", then a B/L may be issued in sole original, or in more than one original①. And B/L issued in more than one original may be marked "Original", "Duplicate", "Triplicate", "First Original", "Second Original", etc. None of these markings will disqualify a B/L as an original, and all original B(s)/L should be presented to the bank. ②

In practice, it is usually written as "three", or "full set", and indicating "original".

(13) Place and date of issue. The place of issue should be the port of loading, while the date of issue refers to the date of shipment, which should be earlier than the validity of L/C.

If a pre-printed "shipped on board" bill of lading is presented, its issuance date will be deemed to be the date of shipment. If a bill of lading bears a separate dated on board notation, the date of the on board notation will be deemed to be the date of shipment, whether or not the on board date is before or after the issuance date of the bill of lading. ③

However, Ante-dated B/L, Post-dated B/L, and Advanced B/L are all unlawful and risky, and should be avoided.

(14) Signature. Original bills of lading must be signed by the carrier or a named agent for or on behalf of the carrier, the master or a named agent for or on behalf of the master.

Any signature by the carrier, master or agent must be identified as that of the carrier, master or agent. Any signature by an agent must indicate whether the agent has signed for or on behalf of the carrier or for or on behalf of the master. ④

For instance, if an agent signs a bill of lading on behalf of the carrier, the agent must be identified as agent and must identify on whose behalf it is signing, unless the carrier has been identified elsewhere on the bill of lading; if the master (captain) signs the bill of lading, the signature of the master (captain) must be identified as "master" ("captain"), and in this event, the name of the master (captain) need not be stated; if an agent signs the bill of lading on behalf of the master (captain), the agent must be identified as agent, and in this event, the name of the master (captain) need not be stated. ⑤

Three typical examples are given as follows:

     a. Signed by Carrier.

---

①   UCP 600 Article 20 a (4).
②   ISBP 821 E11.
③   ISBP 821 E6.
④   UCP 600 Article 20 a (1).
⑤   ISBP 821 E5.

```
┌─────────────────────────────────────────────────────────────┐
│                                                             │
│        Carrier's Name, e.g.  A.B.C SHIPPING CO. , LTD       │
│                                                             │
│                                                             │
│                      (Signature)                            │
│                 As Carrier or the Carrier                   │
│                                                             │
└─────────────────────────────────────────────────────────────┘
```

b. Signed by Agent.

```
┌─────────────────────────────────────────────────────────────┐
│                                                             │
│        Agent's Name, e.g.  A.B.C SERVICE CO. , LTD          │
│                                                             │
│                                                             │
│                      (Signature)                            │
│              As agent for and /or on behalf of the          │
│                      Carrier/COSCO/                         │
│                  Johnson, Master, etc.                      │
│                                                             │
└─────────────────────────────────────────────────────────────┘
```

c. Signed by Master.

```
┌─────────────────────────────────────────────────────────────┐
│                                                             │
│           Carrier's Name, e.g.  COSCO                       │
│                                                             │
│                                                             │
│                      (Signature)                            │
│                 As Master or the Master                     │
│                                                             │
└─────────────────────────────────────────────────────────────┘
```

However, if a credit states "freight forwarder's bill of lading is acceptable" or uses a similar phrase, then the bill of lading may be signed by a freight forwarder in the capacity of a freight forwarder, without the need to identify itself as carrier or agent for the named carrier. In this event, it is not necessary to show the name of the carrier. [1]

Moreover, a signature need not be handwritten. Facsimile signatures, perforated signatures, stamps, symbols (such as chops) or any electronic or mechanical means of authentication are sufficient. However, a photocopy of a signed document does not qualify as a signed original document, nor does a signed document transmitted through a fax machine, absent an original signature. A requirement for a document to be "signed and stamped", or a similar requirement, is also fulfilled by a signature and the name of the party typed, or stamped, or handwritten, etc. [2]

---

[1]   ISBP 821 E5.
[2]   ISBP 821 A35.

A signature on a company letterhead paper will be taken to be the signature of that company, unless otherwise stated. The company name need not be repeated next to the signature. [1]

(15) Others.

• On board notations. A credit usually requires a shipped on board B/L to be presented.

"Shipped in apparent good order", "laden on board", "clean on board" or other phrases incorporating words such as "shipped" or "on board" have the same effect as "shipped on board". [2]

• Clean bills of lading. Credit usually requires clean bill of lading. Claused bills of lading are not acceptable.

However, not all bill of lading bearing clauses are claused B/L. Clauses or notations which expressly declare a defective condition of the goods or packaging constitute discrepancies, while clauses or notations which do not expressly declare a defective condition of the goods or packaging do not constitute a discrepancy. For example, a statement "packaging may not be sufficient for the sea journey" is acceptable; a statement "packaging is not sufficient for the sea journey" would not be acceptable. [3]

If the word "clean" appears on a bill of lading and has been deleted, the bill of lading will not be deemed to be claused or unclean unless it specifically bears a clause or notation declaring that the goods or packaging are defective. [4]

• Corrections and alterations. A bill of lading may be corrected or altered.

Corrections and alterations on an original bill of lading must be authenticated. Such authentication must appear to have been made by the carrier, master (captain) or any of their agents (who may be different from the agent that may have issued or signed it), provided they are identified as an agent of the carrier or the master (captain). [5]

Non-negotiable copies of a bill of lading need not include authentication of any corrections that may have been made on the original. [6]

In shipping practice, different shipping companies may issue varied-formatted bill of lading, with detailed contents that depend on the modes of marine transportation, based on the shipper's letter of instructions. A sea freight shipper's letter of instruction specimen and two B/L specimens are given in the Appendix part of this Chapter. Among the latter, one is in filled form, another one is in blank form.

---

[1]  ISBP821 A36.
[2]  ISBP821 E6.
[3]  ISBP821 E20.
[4]  ISBP821 E21.
[5]  ISBP821 E24.
[6]  ISBP821, E25.

## 5.2.5 Usual Customs and Practices

Laws and usual customs and practices governing bill of lading may be discussed from two aspects. One aspect is related to the rights, responsibilities, and liabilities of the carrier and the shipper under a B/L, which is not the focus of this chapter. The other aspect is related to the standards of preparing and examining a B/L under an L/C, which is the focus of this chapter to be discussed in great details.

(1) Usual customs related to the rights, Responsibilities, and Liabilities of the Carrier and the Shipper under a B/L. The rights, responsibilities, and liabilities of the carrier and the shipper under a B/L are governed generally either by the older Hague Rules, by the more recent Hague–Visby Rules, or by the latest Hamburg Rules.

① The Hague Rules. the Hague Rules, the official title is "International Convention for the Unification of Certain Rules of Law relating to Bills of Lading", was drafted in Brussels in 1924, and took in effect on June 2, 1931. It represented the first attempt by the international community to find a workable and uniform means of dealing with the problem of ship-owners regularly excluding themselves from all liability for loss or damage of cargo. The objective of the Hague Rules was to establish a minimum mandatory liability of carriers which could be derogated from.

Under the Hague Rules, the shipper bears the cost of lost/damaged goods if they cannot prove that the vessel was unseaworthy, improperly manned or unable to safely transport and preserve the cargo, i. e. the carrier can avoid liability for risks resulting from human errors provided they exercise due diligence and their vessel is properly manned and seaworthy. These provisions have frequently been the subject of discussion between ship-owners and cargo interests on whether they provide an appropriate balance in liability.

The Hague Rules form the basis of national legislation in almost all of the world's major trading nations, possessing more than 100 member countries and entities, and probably cover more than 90 per cent of world trade. The Hague Rules have been updated by two protocols, but neither addressed the basic liability provisions, which remain unchanged. ①

② The Hague–Visby Rules. The Hague–Visby Rules are a set of international rules for the carriage of goods by sea. It was drafted in Brussels in 1924, and was amended by the Visby Amendments (officially the "Protocol to Amend the International Convention for the Unification of Certain Rules of Law Relating to Bills of Lading") in 1968, the rules became known as the Hague–Visby Rules. A final amendment was made in the SDR Protocol in 1979②. It is comparatively reasonable than the original Hague Rules, however, it plays a less important role in international trade transportation by sea.

---

① http://www. oecd. org/document/41/0,2340,en_2649_34367_2086825_1_1_1_1,00. html.

② http://en. wikipedia. org/wiki/Hague-Visby_Rules.

③ The Hamburg Rules. The Hamburg Rules are a set of rules governing the international shipment of goods, resulting from the United Nations International Convention on the Carriage of Goods by Sea adopted in Hamburg in 1978. [1]

The Convention establishes a uniform legal regime governing the rights and obligations of shippers, carriers and consignees under a contract of carriage of goods by sea. It was prepared at the request of developing countries, and its adoption by States has been endorsed by such intergovernmental organizations as the United Nations Conference on Trade and Development (UNCTAD), the Organization of American States (OAS) and the Asian – African Legal Consultative Committee (AALCO). A draft of the Convention was prepared by the UNCITRAL[2] and finalized and adopted by a diplomatic conference on March 31,1978.

On June 24, 2008, Kazakhstan became the 34th State party to the Convention. And the Convention entered into force for Kazakhstan on 1 July 2009. However, it plays an insignificant role in today's international transportation by sea.

China, the largest developing country in terms of value of international trade, is not the member country of the above mentioned three governing rules. However, the Hague Rules played a dominant role in China's practice of international trade transportation.

(2) Usual customs related to the standards of preparing and examining a B/L under an L/C. The standards for preparing and examining a B/L under an L/C are mainly governed by UCP 600 and ISBP 821.

① UCP 600. Article 20 of the UCP 600 gives detailed governance and explanations on:

a. The contents and related items of a bill of lading:

• The name of the carrier.

• The signature of qualified parties (the carrier or a named agent for or on behalf of the carrier, or the master or a named agent for or on behalf of the master).

• Shipped on board notation.

• Port of loading and port of discharging.

• Be the sole original bill of lading or, if issued in more than one original, be the full set as indicated on the bill of lading.

---

[1]  http://en. wikipedia. org/wiki/Hamburg_Rules.

[2]  The United Nations Commission on International Trade Law (UNCITRAL) is the core legal body of the United Nations system in the field of international trade law. Its mandate is to remove legal obstacles to international trade by progressively modernizing and harmonizing trade law. It prepares legal texts in a number of key areas such as international commercial dispute settlement, electronic commerce, insolvency, international payments, sale of goods, transport law, procurement and infrastructure development. UNCITRAL also provides technical assistance to law reform activities, including assisting Member States to review and assess their law reform needs and to draft the legislation required to implement UNCITRAL texts. The UNCITRAL Secretariat is located in Vienna, Austria. UNCITRAL maintains a website at www. uncitral. org.

- Contain terms and conditions of carriage or make reference to another source containing the terms and conditions of carriage in the case of short form or blank back bill of lading.
- Contain no indication that it is subject to a charter party.

b. Definition and interpretation of transshipment and related items:

- Transshipment means unloading from one vessel and reloading to another vessel during the carriage from the port of loading to the port of discharge stated in the credit.
- A bill of lading may indicate that the goods will or may be transshipped provided that the entire carriage is covered by one and the same bill of lading.
- A bill of lading indicating that transshipment will or may take place is acceptable, even if the credit prohibits transshipment, if the goods have been shipped in a container, trailer or LASH barge as evidenced by the bill of lading.
- Clauses in a bill of lading stating that the carrier reserves the right to transship will be disregarded.

② ISBP 821. Compare with UCP 600, ISBP 821 (E1~E28) provide even more detailed and workable guidance on presenting and examining bill of lading under letter of credit. The following 12 aspects are covered by ISBP, and they are just listed briefly. (It is strongly recommended to refer to ISBP 821 for detailed explanations. )

- Application of UCP 600 article 20 (ISBP 821, E1~E2).
- Full set of originals (ISBP 821, E11).
- Signing of bills of lading (ISBP 821, E3~E5).
- On board notations (ISBP 821, E6).
- Ports of loading and ports of discharge (ISBP 821, E6, E8).
- Consignee, order party, shipper and endorsement, notify party (ISBP 821, E12~E16).
- Transshipment and partial shipment (ISBP 821, E17~E19).
- Clean bills of lading (ISBP 821, E20~E21).
- Goods description (ISBP 821, E22).
- Corrections and alterations (ISBP 821, E24~E25).
- Freight and additional costs (ISBP 821, E26~E27).
- Goods covered by more than one bill of lading (ISBP 821, E28).

In addition to the usual customs and practices discussed above, an efficient and effective exporter and importer should always keep an eye on the introduction and development of new regulations related to import/export and customs clearance, both from the home country and the host country.

## 5.2.6 Frequently Found Discrepancies with a Bill of Lading

In practice of international trade, particularly in the case of L/C based exporting transaction, frequently found discrepancies with a B/L are listed below:

- The name of the consignee/notify party is not as per L/C.
- Port of loading/transship/discharge is not consistent with the stipulation of L/C.
- Claused/Unclean B/L submitted.
- No "on board" notation.
- Description of goods does not comply with the stipulation of L/C.
- Number of packages, gross weight, net weight conflict with those on other documents.
- The shipping marks and numbers are not consistent with the marks and numbers on the other documents.
- The number of original B(s)/L is less than full set.
- No evidence that freight has been paid, and the amount of freight paid is not listed when required by L/C.
- The date of shipment or the "on board" notation is later than the latest shipment date on L/C.
- Stale B/L presented.
- B/L marked "on deck".
- Chartered party B/L submitted.
- No endorsement, when required.
- Payment of freight notations "freight prepaid" or "freight collect" not in conformity with the terms of delivery (Incoterms® 2020).
- The issuer is not the qualified party (the carrier or its agent, the master or its agent).

To keep the smooth going of international trade and payment, it is of necessity and importance for the exporter to prepare and present B/L and other like documents in due time and in sound condition.

## 5.2.7 Sample Clauses Concerning Bill of Lading under L/C

- Full set of clean shipped on board ocean bills of lading made out to order of shipper and endorsed to the order of Nanyang Commercial Bank Ltd. Hongkong marked with the documentary credit no. "freight prepaid" and notify buyers.
- Full set clean on board ocean bill of lading consigned to ××× marked "freight prepaid" and notify A. B. C. Co. In case transshipment is effected name and sailing date of second ocean vessel calling Rotterdam must be shown on B/L.
- 3/3 original +3 copies clean on board marking bills of lading issued to order and endorsed in blank marked "freight paid" notify applicant.
- Original shipped on board bill of lading in triplicate, made out to order and endorsed in our favour, marked freight prepaid and notify applicant, B/L must bear a written signature, if

signed by a facsimiles stamp they can not be acceptable.

- Bill of lading must specifically state that the merchandise has been shipped on board on a named vessel and/or bill of lading must evidence that merchandise has been shipped or loaded on board on a named vessel in the on-board notation.

## 5.3 Charter Party Bill of Lading

### 5.3.1 Definition

Charter party bill of lading is a bill of lading containing an indication that it is subject to a charter party. [1]

A charter party bill of lading is not accepted by banks under letter of credit unless the credit requires presentation of a charter party bill of lading or allows presentation of a charter party bill of lading.

### 5.3.2 Contents and Specimen

A charter party bill of lading, however named, must appear to contain the following items.

(1) Originals. A charter party bill of lading must be the sole original charter party bill of lading or, if issued in more than one original, be the full set as indicated on the charter party bill of lading.

Unlike other types of transport documents, charter party bills of lading need not be marked "original", and this is acceptable under a credit.

(2) The issuer's signature. Original charter party bills of lading must be signed by the master or a named agent for or on behalf of the master, the owner or a named agent for or on behalf of the owner, or the charterer or a named agent for or on behalf of the charterer.

If the master (captain), charterer or owner signs the charter party bill of lading, the signature of the master (captain), charterer or owner must be identified as "master" ("captain"), charterer or "owner".

If an agent signs the charter party bill of lading on behalf of the master (captain), charterer or owner, the agent must be identified as agent of the master (captain), charterer or owner. In this event, the name of the master (captain) need not be stated, but the name of the charterer or owner must appear.

(3) On board notations and the dates of issuance/shipment. A charter bill of lading must indicate that the goods have been shipped on board a named vessel at the port of loading stated in the credit, by pre-printed wording, or by an on board notation indicating the date on which the goods have been shipped on board.

---

[1] UCP 600 Article 22.

If a charter party bill of lading bears a pre-printed wording "shipped on board", its issuance date will be deemed to be the date of shipment. If a charter party bill of lading bears an on board notation, the date of the on board notation will be deemed to be the date of shipment.

"Shipped in apparent good order" "laden on board" "clean on board" or other phrases incorporating words such as "shipped" or "on board" have the same effect as "shipped on board".

(4) Ports of loading and ports of discharge. A charter party bill of lading must indicate shipment from the port of loading to the port of discharge stated in the credit.

If a credit gives a geographical area or range of ports of loading or discharge (e. g. "any European port"), the charter party bill of lading must indicate the actual port or ports of loading, which must be within the geographical area or range stated in the credit but may show the geographical area or range of ports as the port of discharge.

(5) Consignee, order party, shipper and endorsement, notify party. If a credit requires a charter party bill of lading to show that the goods are consigned to a named party, e. g. "consigned to bank ×" (a "straight" bill of lading), rather than "to order" or "to order of Bank ×", the charter party bill of lading must not contain words such as "to order" or "to order of" preceding the name of that named party, whether typed or pre-printed.

Likewise, if a credit requires the goods to be consigned "to order" or "to order of" a named party, the charter party bill of lading must not show that the goods are consigned straight to the named party.

If a charter party bill of lading is issued to order or to order of the shipper, it must be endorsed by the shipper. An endorsement indicating that it is made for or on behalf of the shipper is acceptable.

If a credit does not state a notify party, the respective field on the charter party bill of lading may be left blank or completed in any manner.

(6) Clean charter party bills of lading. Clauses or notations on charter party bills of lading which expressly declare a defective condition of the goods or packaging are not acceptable.

Clauses or notations that do not expressly declare a defective condition of the goods or packaging (e. g. "packaging may not be sufficient for the sea journey") do not constitute a discrepancy. A statement "the packaging is not sufficient for the sea journey" would not be acceptable.

If the word "clean" appears on a charter party bill of lading and has been deleted, the charter party bill of lading will not be deemed to be claused or unclean unless it specifically bears a clause or notation declaring that the goods or packaging are defective.

(7) Goods description. A goods description in charter party bills of lading may be shown in general terms not in conflict with that stated in the credit.

(8) Partial shipment. If a credit prohibits partial shipments, and more than one set of original charter party bills of lading are presented covering shipment from one or more ports of

loading (as specifically allowed, or within the geographical area or range stated in the credit), such documents are acceptable, provided that they cover the shipment of goods on the same vessel and same journey and are destined for the same port of discharge, range of ports or geographical area. In the event that more than one set of charter party bills of lading are presented and incorporate different dates of shipment, the latest of these dates of shipment will be taken for the calculation of any presentation period and must fall on or before the latest shipment date specified in the credit. Shipment on more than one vessel is a partial shipment, even if the vessels leave on the same day for the same destination.

(9) Corrections and alterations. Corrections and alterations on charter party bills of lading must be authenticated. Such authentication must appear to have been made by the owner, charterer, master (captain) or any of their agents (who may be different from the agent that may have issued or signed it), provided they are identified as an agent of the owner, charterer or the master (captain).

Non-negotiable copies of charter party bills of lading do not need to include any signature on, or authentication of, any alterations or corrections that may have been made on the original.

(10) Freight and additional costs. If a credit requires that a charter party bill of lading show that freight has been paid or is payable at destination, the charter party bill of lading must be marked accordingly.

Applicants and issuing banks should be specific in stating the requirements of documents to show whether freight is to be prepaid or collected.

If a credit states that costs additional to freight are not acceptable, a charter party bill of lading must not indicate that costs additional to the freight have been or will be incurred. Such indication may be by express reference to additional costs or by the use of shipment terms which refer to costs associated with the loading or unloading of goods, such as Free In (FI), Free Out (FO), Free In and Out (FIO) and Free In and Out Stowed (FIOS). A reference in the transport document to costs which may be levied as a result of a delay in unloading the goods, or after the goods have been unloaded, is not considered to be an indication of additional costs in this context.

(11) The wording "subject to charter party ×××". A charter party bill of lading is usually subject to a specific charter party contract. Where a charter party contract is a contract, according to which the precisely designed freight room of a ship or the whole ship is leased by the owner to a charterer for a specific period, specific voyage or voyages.

However, a bank will not examine charter party contracts, even if they are required to be presented by the terms of the credit.

## 5.4　Sea Waybill

Difficulties as well as costs associated with the use of bills of lading have led to calls by the international community (the UNCTAD, etc.) for the increased use of non-negotiable sea waybills, in particular whenever there is no intention to transfer ownership of the goods while in transit. To minimize the problems associated with delayed arrival of bills of lading, more commercial parties, over recent years, have been increasingly using non-negotiable sea way-bill in international trade, in particular in the case of short sea transportation and e-commerce.

## 5.4.1 Definition

A Sea Waybill is a non-negotiable document which evidences a contract for the carriage of goods by sea and the taking over or loading of the goods by the carrier, and by which the carrier undertakes to deliver the goods to the consignee named in the document. In certain countries, e.g. Canada, sea waybill is deemed as synonymous with "straight" or "non-negotiable bill of lading". ①

The sea waybill indicates the "on board" loading of the goods and can be used in cases where no ocean bill of lading, i.e. no document of title is required. For receipt of goods, presentation of the sea waybill by the consignee named therein is required, which can speed up processing at the port of destination. ②

## 5.4.2 Functions

It is the title document aspect that differentiates a non-negotiable sea waybill from a negotiable bill of lading. However, a sea waybill also functions as a receipt for shipment and as evidence of the contract of carriage.

Moreover, the increasing use of sea waybill may have the following significant roles in the promotion and facilitation of international trade:

(1) Make the shipping of cargo simple, speedy and cost-efficient. A specific advantage of using non-negotiable seaway bill is that goods are released without production of the document. That is to say, the document need not be presented in order to obtain delivery of the goods from the carrier. Accordingly, procedures associated with the discharge and delivery of the cargo is simple, speedy and cost-efficient. In particular, the issue of delayed arrival of documents, which may be a particular problem in the context of short sea transit times, does not arise.

(2) Expedite establishing e-alternatives to traditional paper documents. Under existing rules and regulations, electronic alternatives to traditional transport documents are not yet recognized as documents of title. In the context of e-commerce, it is thus the document of title aspect of the negotiable bill of lading, which constituted a major obstacle in establishing electronic al-

---

① UN/EDIFACT D.03A, Data Element 1001.

② Edward G Hinkelman. Longman Dictionary of International Trade. Longman and China Renmin University Press, 2000:553.

ternative to traditional paper documents. Comparatively, the transition to an electronic environment is easier for non-negotiable sea waybill than for negotiable bill of lading.

However, sea waybills do not provide constructive possession of the goods covered, and thus they cannot be used to transfer possession and property. In other words, the use of non-negotiable sea waybills may be considered advisable if sale of goods in transit is not envisaged, or if independent documentary security is not required by the parties, because they are known to each other or they are part of the same organization.

Some commercial parties use non-negotiable bill of lading in cases where transit time is short and the transport documents may arrive later than the carrying vessel, e. g. coastal traffic and short sea voyages. As far as specific routes and trades are concerned, non-negotiable bill of lading are primarily used for trade to and from North America and the Far East, as well as for intra-European routes and to some extent for trade between Europe and Middle East and North Africa.

### 5.4.3 Contents and UNeDocs Specimen

(1) Contents. The contents of non-negotiable sea waybill are quite similar to that of negotiable ocean bill of lading, including:

- Name and address of relevant parties (consignor, shipper, forwarder, consignee, carrier, notify party, additional notify party, and carrier, etc. ).
- Information about shipment (place of receipt, port of lading, vessel/voyage No. , port of discharge, final place of delivery by on-carrier, container No. , seal No. , etc. ).
- Information about goods (marks and numbers, transport unit, number and kind of packages, shipping description of goods, gross weight, measurement, etc. ).
- Information about freight (freight details and charge, freight rate, basis of freight calculation, the freight amount that is prepaid or collect, name of the location where freight is payable, etc. ).
- Information about sea waybill itself (bill of lading No. , number of original bill of lading, place and date of issue, and authenticating signature, etc. ).
- Disclaimer sentence: received for carriage as above in apparent good order and condition, unless otherwise stated hereon, the goods described in the above particulars.

(2) UNeDocs specimen. UNeDocs (United Nation electronic documents sets), was developed by the UNCTAD, one of the influential international organizations who encourage commercial parties to use non-negotiable sea waybill, on the basis of the SITPRO TOP-FORM Common Short Form Bill of Lading (Version 2.0). UNeDocs provides standard form layout for non-negotiable sea waybill, which are given below and in the Appendix part of this chapter.

## UNeDocs 2.02    Non-negotiable Sea Waybill Specimen

| | | |
|---|---|---|
| Consignor ( name, address, tax reference )<br><br>01 | Shipper's reference<br><br>02a | Bill of Lading No.<br><br>02b |
| | Forwarder's reference<br><br>02c | |
| | Unique consignment reference<br><br>02d | |
| Consignee ( name, address, tax reference )<br>03 | Carrier ( name, address, tax reference )<br>04 | |
| Notify party ( name, address, tax scheme )<br>05 | Additional notify party ( name, address, tax reference )<br>06 | |

| | | |
|---|---|---|
| Pre-carriage by<br>07a | Place of receipt<br>UN/LOCODE<br>07b | |
| Vessel / voyage No.<br>07c | Port of loading<br>UN/LOCODE<br>07d | 08 |
| Port of discharge<br>UN/LOCODE<br>07e | Final place of delivery by<br>on-carrier UN/LOCODE<br>07f | |

| Marks and numbers; transport unit  ID<br>09a | Number and kind of packages; shipping description of goods<br>09b | | | Gross weight<br>10a | Measurement<br>10b |
|---|---|---|---|---|---|
| Container No.<br>11a | Seal No.<br>11b | Freight details, charge etc.<br>12 | Rate<br>13 | Per<br>14 | Prepaid<br>15 | Collect<br>16 |

| | | |
|---|---|---|
| 17 | Freight payable at<br>UN/LOCODE<br>18 | Carrier's name<br><br>19 |
| | Number of original<br>Bill of Lading<br>20 | Place ( + ISO code ) and date<br>of issue ( yyyy-mm-dd )<br>21 |
| Received for carriage as above in apparent good order and condition, unless otherwise stated hereon, the goods described in the above particulars | Authenticating signature<br><br>22 | |

Source: http://www. unece. org/etrades/unedocs/V04/UNSWB/UNPLK/UNSWB_FORM_N. pdf.

UNeDocs also provides very detailed completion guidelines for non-negotiable sea waybill box. The main completion directions are summed up as following:

Box 01: Consignor (name, address, tax reference)

Enter the name and address of the party consigning the goods as stipulated in the contract by the party ordering the transport; this may be the exporter or seller (Mandatory).

Enter the tax identifier, which is a number assigned to a party by a tax authority. If the company is registered for VAT, enter the relevant VAT number for EC supplies only, and the number should be prefixed with the country code for the state. E. g. GB is the code for United Kingdom (Mandatory if registered for VAT).

Box 02a: Consignor's reference

Enter the consignor's number used to reference this consignment. (Recommended)

Box 02b: Bill of Lading number

Enter the Bill of Lading number which is usually assigned by the carrier. (Optional)

Box 02c: Forwarder's reference

Enter the forwarder's number used to reference this consignment. (Optional)

Box 02d: Unique consignment reference

Enter unique reference of a consignment used for identification purposes. This unique reference assigned to a consignment also known as UCR. (Recommended)

Box 03: Consignee (name, address, tax reference)

Enter the name and address of party to which goods are consigned. If the company is registered for VAT, enter the relevant VAT number for EC supplies only. The number should be prefixed with the country code for the state. E. g. GB is the code for United Kingdom. (Mandatory)

Box 04: Carrier (name, address, tax reference)

Enter the name and address of party providing the transport of goods between named points. The carrier is the party in whose name the transport contract is issued and signed[1]. (Recommended)

If the company is registered for VAT enter the relevant VAT number for EC supplies only. The number should be prefixed with the country code for the state. E. g. GB is the code for United Kingdom. (Optional)

Box 05: Notify party (name, address, tax reference)

Enter name and address of a party to be notified. To be completed if another party other than the consignee is to be notified on the arrival of the consignment. (Optional)

---

[1] In practice, the party providing the transport services will send a Non-negotiable Sea Waybill, usually after receipt of the shipping instruction.

If the company is registered for VAT enter the relevant VAT number for EC supplies only. The number should be prefixed with the country code for the state. E. g. GB is the code for United Kingdom. (Optional)

Box 06: Additional notify party (name, address, tax reference)

Enter the name of a party, who can be a notify party, buyer's or seller's agent or any other interested party. It is recommended that this party is either mutually agreed between the trading partners or UNTDED, and is also transmitted to confirm the role of the party. (Optional)

Party function code refers to a code giving specific meaning to the function of a party. Use this only if the role of the party has not been mutually agreed. (Optional)

If the company is registered for VAT enter the relevant VAT number for EC supplies only. The number should be prefixed with the country code for the state. E. g. GB is the code for United Kingdom. (Optional)

Box 07a: Pre-carriage by

Enter pre-carriage transport mode, normally this is the first mode of transport for through transport consignments (e. g. road). (Optional)

Box 07b: Place of receipt

Enter pre-carrier receipt location, that is, the name of the place at which goods are to be, or have been, taken over for carriage prior to the main transport. Normally it is the first place of loading for through transport consignments. (Recommended)

Use UN/ECE Recommendation No. 16: United Nations Codes for Ports and other Locations (UN/LOCODE)[①] if Pre-carrier Receipt Location Text is used. (Mandatory)

Box 07c: Vessel/ voyage number

Enter name of a specific means of transport such as the vessel name, specified by the carrier, or the number used to identify the means of transport. (Recommended)

Box 07d: Port of loading

Enter name of the seaport, airport, freight terminal, rail station or other place at which the goods (cargo) are loaded onto the means of transport being used for their carriage. (Recommended)

Use the UN/ECE Recommendation No. 16: United Nations Codes for Ports and other Locations (UN/LOCODE). (Mandatory if Consignment Loading Location Text is used)

Box 07e: Port of discharge

Consignment Discharge Location: Name of the seaport, airport, freight terminal, rail station or other place at which the goods (cargo) are unloaded onto the means of transport being used for their carriage (Recommended).

---

① http://www.unece.org/cefact/cf_plenary/plenary99/docs/99trd227.pdf.

Use UN/ECE Recommendation No. 16: United Nations Codes for Ports and other Locations (UN/LOCODE). (Mandatory if Port of Discharge Location Text is used)

Box 07f: Final place of delivery by on-carrier

Delivery Location:The name of the place at which the cargo leaves the custody of the carrier under the terms and conditions of the transport contract. This is the place where the cargo is finally delivered. (Optional)

Use UN/ECE Recommendation No. 16: The United Nations Codes for Ports and other Locations (UN/LOCODE). (Mandatory if Delivery Location Text is used)

Box 08: Enter code specifying information details, which is used to identify the information text. (Optional)

Box 09a: Marks and numbers; Transport unit ID

Enter goods item sequence identifier, a sequence number differentiating a specific goods item within a consignment. Often this is a simple sequence such as 1, 2, 3, 4 etc. (Recommended, and recommended to use UN Trade Recommendation 15: Simpler Shipping Marks)

Enter transport equipment identification identifier: marks (letters and/or numbers) which identify equipment. Use the unique container number if applicable. (Recommended)

Box 09b: Number and kind of packages; shipping description of goods

Enter number of packages per goods item packaged in such a way that they cannot be divided without first undoing the package. No blanks or other separators allowed. (Recommended)

Enter Packaging details such as unpacked, boxes, cases, pallets etc. Use UN/ECE Recommendation No. 21: Codes for Packages. [1](Recommended)

Goods Item Description: use plain language description of the nature of a goods item sufficient to identify it for customs, statistical or transport purposes. Description of the good in common trade terms, if possible using terminology of the applicable customs or freight tariffs (Mandatory). In practice, goods items may reflect either the contractual or operational description of the goods.

Box 10a: Gross weight

Enter weight (mass) of goods including packaging but excluding the carrier's equipment. (Recommended)

Enter measurement unit code: indication of the unit of measurement in which weight (mass), capacity, length, area, volume or other quantity is expressed. Use UN/ECE Recom-

---

[1] http://www.unece.org/cefact/recommendations/rec21/rec21rev1_ecetrd195e.pdf. UN/ECE Recommendation No. 21 has 6 revisions during 1994 and 2008.

mendation No. 20①: Codes for Units of Measurement (Mandatory if Item Gross Weight Measure is other than 'kg').

Box 10b: Measurement

Item gross volume/measure: measurement normally arrived at by multiplying the maximum lengths, widths and heights of the pieces or packages.

The use of cubic meters as unit of measurement is mandatory. And no blanks or separators other than decimal point (comma) allowed. (Optional)

Box 11a: Container number

When a goods item is transported in one or more containers, it is necessary to enter marks (letters and/or numbers) which identify equipment. (Optional)

Box 11b: Seal number

Enter the exact number as shown on the seal fixed to the equipment. (Optional)

Box 12: Freight details, charge etc

Enter code specifying a charge such as freight and other charges. Use UN/ECE Recommendation No. 23②: Freight Cost Code. (Optional)

Free form description of a charge according to tariffs, such as "Sea Freight", "Local Freight", "Heavy Lift", "5% Bunker surcharge", etc. (Optional)

The Non Negotiable Sea Waybill might contain information concerning charges, however, it should not be seen as a replacement for the invoice.

Box 13: Rate

To specify the rate per unit specified in the unit price basis. (Optional)

Box 14: Per

Enter unit of quantity for the calculation of freight charges and other charges, the basis of calculation in plain language. (Mandatory if charges are specified)

Box 15: Prepaid

Enter the freight charge amount that is prepaid. (Mandatory if charges are specified)

Enter payment arrangement code: code specifying the arrangements for a payment. Code P specifies that the charges are prepaid. (Recommended)

Box 16: Collect

Enter the freight charge amount that is collect. (Mandatory if charges are specified)

Enter payment arrangement code: code specifying the arrangements for a payment. Code C

---

① http://www.unece.org/cefact/recommendations/rec20/rec20_00cf20a1-3e.pdf. UN/ECE Recommendation No. 20 has 5 revisions during the period of the 2000 and 2008.

② http://www.unece.org/cefact/recommendations/rec23/rec23_ecetrd170.pdf. UN/ECE Recommendation No. 23 has 6 revisions during the period of the 1990 and 2008.

specifies that the charges are collect. (Recommended)

Box 18: Freight payable at ... UN/LOCODE

Enter the name of the location where the freight has been or should be paid. (Optional)

Use UN/ECE Recommendation No. 16: United Nations Codes for Ports and other Locations (UN/LOCODE). (Mandatory if Payment Location Text is used)

Box 19: Carriers name

Use the first line of the name and address to specify the carrier's name. (Optional)

Box 21: Place (+ ISO code) and date of issue (yyyy-mm-dd)

Enter name of place where document is signed or otherwise authenticated. (Optional)

Use the United Nations Code for Trade and Transport Locations (UNLOCODE, UN Trade Recommendation 16). (Mandatory if Document Issue Location Text is used)

Enter date when a document is issued and—when appropriate—signed or otherwise authenticated. Recommend to use calendar date according to UN Trade Recommendation 7[①]: numerical representation of year, month and day in descending order, separated by hyphen. Example: 19 December in 2008 is written as 2008-12-19. (Mandatory)

Box 22: Authenticating signature

Provide the authentication code of the person signing the document. (Optional)

Provide the name of the person signing the document. (Recommended)

### 5.4.4 Usual Customs and Practices

(1) Usual customs related to the rights, responsibilities, and liabilities of relevant parties under a non-negotiable sea waybill.

① The Hague Rule and the Hague–Visby Rule. Unlike negotiable bill of lading, non-negotiable sea waybills are not expressly covered by the Hague Rule and the Hague–Visby Rule, since they are restricted to "bill of lading or similar documents of title".

However, non-negotiable sea waybills are also standard form documents, issued by a carrier and operating as a receipt and as evidence of a contract of carriage. The parties involved in non-negotiable sea waybill may effectively incorporate the Rules in the document, and therefore the application of the rules is triggered.

Under English law, the rules are applicable to sea waybills. However, the evidentiary value of statements in the document relating to the goods shipped may be less strong. For instance, in a cargo claim, the description of the goods in a bill of lading is final evidence, and thus a third-party endorsee of a bill of lading may rely conclusively on it, but the description of the goods in a sea waybill is only prima facie evidence.

---

① http://www.unece.org/cefact/recommendations/rec07/rec07_1988_infl08.pdf.

② The Hamburg Rules 1978. Non-negotiable sea waybills are expressly covered by the Hamburg Rules 1978, as they apply to all contracts for the carriage of goods by sea, including contracts covered by negotiable as well as non-negotiable transport documents, but excluding charter parties contract of carriage.

③ The CMI Uniform Rules for Sea Waybills. The CMI (Committee Maritime International) Uniform Rules for Sea Waybills, which are designed for incorporation into commercial contracts, also set out a mechanism for the transfer of the right of control from shipper to consignee.

According to rule 6(ii), the shipper shall have the option, to be exercised not later than the receipt of the goods by the carrier, to transfer the rights of control to the consignee. And the exercise of this option must be noted on the sea waybill or similar document, if any. Where the option has been exercised the consignee shall have such rights to give instructions to the carrier in relation to the contract of carriage and the shipper shall cease to have such rights.

(2) Usual customs related to the standards of preparing and examining a non-negotiable sea waybill under an L/C. The UCP 600 Article 21 and ISBP 821 (F1 ~ F25) provides detailed governance on non-negotiable sea waybill, which are quite similar to that on negotiable bill of lading.

① Basic requirements for a non-negotiable sea waybill.

• A non-negotiable sea waybill must appear to indicate the name of the carrier and be signed by qualified party.

• A non-negotiable sea waybill must indicate that the goods have been shipped on board a named vessel at the port of loading stated in the credit by pre-printed wording, or by an on board notation indicating the date on which the goods have been shipped on board.

• The date of issuance of the non-negotiable sea waybill will be deemed to be the date of shipment unless the non-negotiable sea waybill contains an on board notation indicating the date of shipment, in which case the date stated in the on board notation will be deemed to be the date of shipment.

If the non-negotiable sea waybill contains the indication "intended vessel" or similar qualification in relation to the name of the vessel, an on board notation indicating the date of shipment and the name of the actual vessel is required.

• Shipment must be effected from the port of loading to the port of discharge stated in the credit.

If the non-negotiable sea waybill does not indicate the port of loading stated in the credit, or if it contains the indication "intended" or similar qualification in relation to the port of loading, an on board notation indicating the port of loading as stated in the credit, the date of shipment and the name of the vessel is required. This provision applies even when loading on board or shipment on a named vessel is indicated by pre-printed wording on the non-negotiable sea waybill.

- The number of original non-negotiable sea waybill must be the sole original non-negotiable sea waybill or, if issued in more than one original, be the full set as indicated on the non-negotiable sea waybill.

- For short form or blank back non-negotiable sea waybill, terms and conditions of carriage may be applied to another source containing the terms and conditions of carriage. In this case, contents of terms and conditions of carriage will not be examined.

- Charter party non-negotiable sea waybill is not acceptable.

② Definition and Interpretation of Transshipment. Transshipment means unloading from one vessel and reloading to another vessel during the carriage from the port of loading to the port of discharge stated in the credit.

A non-negotiable sea waybill may indicate that the goods will or may be transshipped provided that the entire carriage is covered by one and the same non-negotiable sea waybill.

A non-negotiable sea waybill indicating that transshipment will or may take place is acceptable, even if the credit prohibits transshipment, if the goods have been shipped in a container, trailer or LASH barge as evidenced by the non-negotiable sea waybill.

Clauses in a non-negotiable sea waybill stating that the carrier reserves the rights to transship will be disregarded.

In practice of international trade, non-negotiable sea waybill is not as popularly used as some international institutes expected. In particular, banking requirements and security considerations may make the use of non-negotiable inappropriate. Moreover, legal and regulatory requirements may prevent more widespread use of non-negotiable transport documents in circumstances where a document of title is not required by commercial parties.

## 5.5 Air Waybill

### 5.5.1 Definition

Air Waybill (also referred to as AWB, air consignment note, or airway bill of lading) refers to a documentary receipt issued by a carrier (i. e. airline) in favour of a shipper for goods received and is evidence of the contract of carriage to carry the goods to a specified airport under specified conditions.

The air waybill is a document proving the transport contract between the consignor and the carrier's company. It is issued by the carrier's agent and falls under the provisions of the Warsaw Convention.

A single air waybill may be used for multiple shipments of goods; it contains three originals and several extra copies. One original is kept by each of the parties involved in the transport (the consignor, the consignee and the carrier). The copies may be required at the airport of departure/destination, for the delivery and in some cases, for further freight carriers. The air waybill is a freight bill which evidences a contract of carriage and proves receipt of goods.

The IATA Standard Air Waybill is used by all carriers belonging to the International Air Transport Association (IATA) and it embodies standard conditions associated to those set out in the Warsaw Convention. ①

The AWB must indicate that the goods have been accepted for carriage, and it must be signed or authenticated by the carrier or the named agent for or on behalf of the carrier. The signature or authentication of the carrier must be identified as carrier, and in the case of agent signing or authenticating, the name and the capacity of the carrier on whose behalf the agent signs or authenticates must be indicated. ②

Unlike a bill of lading, an AWB is not a document of title to the goods, hence, it is non-negotiable. In addition, an AWB does not specify on which flight the shipment will be sent, or when it will reach its destination. ③

### 5.5.2 Types

In addition to direct AWB, which has actual consignor and consignee, there are two types of air waybills used for the international transportation of air cargo: the Master Air Waybill and House Air Waybill.

In air freight, the shipper (exporter, consignor) often engages a freight forwarder to handle the forwarding of goods. The freight forwarder may consolidate the consignments of several independent shippers that are intended for the same airport of destination and dispatch them together under one air waybill (AWB) issued by the carrier, known as Master Air Waybill (MAWB), with a cargo manifest detailing such consignments attached to the MAWB. The freight forwarder in turn issues to each shipper its own AWB, known as a House Air Waybill (HAWB) or freight forwarder's waybill.

MAWB may differ from HAWB in the following aspects:

(1) Issuer. The issuer of MAWB is the actual carrier, while the issuer of HAWB is the forwarder (contractual carrier) who gains profit by consolidation, putting together cargoes from different shippers under one MAWB to earn a more favourable bulk quantity freight rate and charges the shippers a higher freight rate, whilst does not provide the aircraft for carriage.

(2) Consignor and consignee. The consignor and consignee on MAWB are the freight forwarder's handling agent, while the consignor and consignee on HAWB are the actual shipper

---

① http://www.prochile.cl/nexos/madrid_manzanas_anexo9.pdf.
② UCP600 Article 23.
③ http://www.iata.org/whatwedo/cargo/standards_procedures/montreal-protocol-4.htm.

and consignee.

(3) Logo of carrier and No. of air waybill. The actual carrier's logo is usually pre-printed in the space at the top right-hand corner of MAWB, bearing the air waybill number assigned by the airline as MAWB 1234/5678. As for the HAWB, the space at the top right-hand corner is left blank and stamped with the forwarder's name, indicating the air waybill number as "HAWB 1234/5678".

(4) Governing usual customs and rules. An MAWB is subject to IATA rules, the international air conventions (Warsaw Convention, Hague Amendment, Guadalajara Convention, etc.) and related protocols (Montreal Protocol, and Guatemala Protocol). These are the "Basel II" equivalents in the air carriage industry to regulate the performance of air carriers, and clear stipulations are provided to protect the interests of the consignor/shipper and the consignee. As a result, the applicant of an L/C can be well protected under an MAWB.

However, an HAWB need not be subject to IATA Rules (unless the forwarder is also an IATA member), and certainly not subject to those "Basel II" conventions and protocols named above. So the shipper and the consignee have no protection in case the goods are damaged or lost in transit. They are not a party in the MAWB and hence cannot sue the actual air carrier. They can only sue the forwarder in the HAWB.

(5) Risk Management. From a risk management point of view, an MAWB is like a credit issued by world noted bank, and an HAWB is like a credit issued by a non-bank. In case the goods are damaged or lost in transit, a forwarder, can be an SME(Small Medium sized Enterprise), may not have readily disposable cash to meet big claims or it may be reluctant to sue the actual carrier on the consignee's behalf for obvious reasons. Moreover, cargoes may be withheld by the actual carrier on arrival due to freight being unpaid by the forwarder that has exceeded its credit limit extended by the actual carrier.

To be practical and reasonable, if the credit does not expressly require an MAWB, an HAWB from an FIATA member (such as Schenkers, Penalpina and Crown Pacific) should be acceptable, as FIATA has strict supervision over the operations of its members, and an FIATA member has good financial strength, at least adequate to meet the claims.

To avoid unpleasant surprises, it is prudent to add in the credit wording such as "One original and × copies of Master air waybill issued and signed by an actual carrier. Signature or issuance by an agent or forwarder is not acceptable. This provision overrides UCP 600 sub-article 23(a)(i)". [1]

Furthermore, the air waybill can be either an air waybill referred to as an "airline air way-

---

[1] Master air waybill vs. house air waybill, ICC "Documentary Credits Insight" Magazine, Volume 13 No. 4, Oct - Dec 2007 Issue; http://www.free-logistics.com/.

bill", with preprinted issuing carrier identification, or an air waybill referred to as a "neutral air waybill" without preprinted identification of the issuing carrier in any form and used by other than an air carrier.

### 5.5.3 Functions

Air waybills can be used for both domestic flights and international ones, and they usually serve as:

- Proof of receipt of the goods for shipment.
- Evidence of the contract of carriage.
- An invoice for the freight, reflecting the shipper, the consignee and the goods being shipped, as well as the full freight amount.
  - A certificate of insurance (if carriers insurance is requested by the shipper).
  - A guide to airline staff for the handling, dispatch and delivery of the consignment.
  - A means of clearing the goods through customs.

Usually, the AWB has a tracking number (consists of a three digits airline identifier issued by IATA and an 8-digit number) which can be used to check the status of delivery, and current position of the shipment. However, it is still risky for the consignor to consign the goods directly to the party (the consignee) named in the letter of credit, as the importer can obtain the goods from the carrier at destination without paying the issuing bank or the consignor. Therefore, consigning goods directly to the importer is safe only when a cash payment has been received by the exporter, or the buyer's integrity is unquestionable. [1]

### 5.5.4 Usual Customs and Practices

As for the laws and usual customs governing the rights and liabilities of the shipper and the air carrier, they contain the following rules, conventions and protocols: [2]

- The Warsaw Convention (1929) and the Hague Protocol (1955).
- The Montreal Inter-carrier Agreement (1966).
- The Guadalajara Convention (1961).
- The Guatemala City Protocol (1971).
- The 1975 Montreal Protocols.
- The IATA and ATA Inter-carrier Agreements (1997).
- The Montreal Protocol No. 4 and Cargo Operations.
- The 1999 International Conference on Air Law.
- The 1999 Montreal Convention on Air Carrier Liability.

---

[1] http://www. exporthelp. co. za/modules/17_documentation/transportation/air_waybill. html, http://en. wikipedia. org/wiki/Air_waybill.

[2] http://www. cargolaw. com/presentations_montreal_cli. html.

Moreover, the IATA Cargo Services Conference (CSC) is responsible for the development and maintenance of Air Waybill specifications and standards. For instance, Resolution 600a provides the governing rules on the use of air waybill, technical specifications, completion instructions, distribution of copies and applicable conditions when transmitting air waybill information electronically, while Resolutions 600b and 600b(II) provide the guidelines for the Conditions of Contract and notices included in the air waybill.

In particular, the IATA air waybill Conditions of Contract (Cargo Services Conference Resolution 600b) was approved and declared effective March 17,2008. CSC Resolution 600b is the abbreviated and modernized "Conditions of Contract" that invokes both Warsaw Convention and Montreal Convention. ①

In addition, the UCP 600 (Article 23) provides the explanations and interpretations on air transport documents, covering essential contents and functions, and transshipment in the case of air freight. Furthermore, the ISBP 821(H3 ~ H27) provides a very detailed guidance for preparing and examining air transport documents.

## 5.5.5 Contents and Specimen

In the practice of international trade, it is usually the shipper—the exporter (or their agent) that completes the AWB, and it is of great necessity for the exporter to be familiar with the detailed items of a typical air transport document.

The main contents on the front of AWB usually include four general parts—basic parties, items on airway transportation, items on goods, and miscellaneous. Detailed items are listed below. ②

(1) The term "air waybill" or similar title. To differentiate from other types of transport documents, air transport documents usually bear the title of "air waybill", "air consignment note" or similar.

According to the UCP 600 article 23, if an air transport document appears to cover an airport-to-airport shipment, it need not be titled "air waybill", "air consignment note" or similar.

(2) Original. The air transport document must appear to be the original for consignor or shipper. A requirement for a full set of originals is satisfied by the presentation of a document indicating that it is the original for consignor or shipper.

Traditionally, air transport documents are usually issued in ten: the Blue Original 1 for consignor or Shipper; the Green Original 1 for Issuing Carrier; the Pink Original 2 for Consignee; the Goldenrod one for Delivery Receipt; three White ones for Invoice, Remittance Copy, and Destination Agent's Copy respectively; and other three White ones as Extra

---

① http://www. iata. org/NR/rdonlyres/9B4A04A3-2383-4D62-84B5-B632DD42D2BB/0/Resolution_600b. pdf.
② UCP 600 article 23 and ISBP 821 H3 ~ H27.

Copies.

However, IATA encourages the air cargo industry to make plans to migrate to the non-colored coded air waybills (air waybill printed on plain paper), to move to automated production of a plain paper version. With the new Conditions of Contract on the reverse side, the air cargo industry participants will be well-positioned to meet the ad hoc printing requirements in an e-freight environment. [1]

(3) Terms and conditions of carriage. An air transport document must contain terms and conditions of carriage or make reference to another source containing the terms and conditions of carriage. Contents of terms and conditions of carriage will not be examined.

(4) The carrier and signature. An air transport document, however named, must appear to indicate the name of the carrier.

An original air transport document must be signed by the carrier, or a named agent for or on behalf of the carrier.

Any signature by the carrier or agent must be identified as that of the carrier or agent. Any signature by an agent must indicate that the agent has signed for or on behalf of the carrier.

If a credit states "House air waybill is acceptable" or "Freight Forwarder's air waybill is acceptable" or uses a similar phrase, then the air transport document may be signed by a freight forwarder in the capacity of a freight forwarder without the need to identify itself as a carrier or agent for a named carrier. In this event, it is not necessary to show the name of the carrier.

(5) Goods accepted for carriage. An air transport document, however named, must appear to indicate that the goods have been accepted for carriage.

(6) Date of issuance / shipment and requirement for an actual date of dispatch. An air transport document, however named, must appear to indicate the date of issuance. This date will be deemed to be the date of shipment unless the air transport document contains a specific notation of the actual date of shipment, in which case the date stated in the notation will be deemed to be the date of shipment.

Any other information appearing on the air transport document relative to the flight number and date will not be considered in determining the date of shipment.

(7) Airports of departure and destination. An air transport document must indicate the airport of departure and airport of destination as stated in the credit. The identification of airports by the use of IATA codes instead of writing out the name in full (e. g. LHR instead of London Heathrow) is not a discrepancy.

---

[1]  http://www. iata. org/whatwedo/cargo/resolution600b. htm.

If a credit gives a geographical area or range of airports of departure or destination ( e. g. "Any European Airport" ) , the air transport document must indicate the actual airport of departure or destination, which must be within the geographical area or range stated in the credit.

(8) Consignee, order party and notify party. An air transport document should not be issued "to order" or "to order of" a named party, because it is not a document of title. Even if a credit calls for an air transport document made out "to order" or "to order of" a named party, a document presented showing goods consigned to that party, without mention of "to order" or "to order of", is acceptable.

If a credit does not state a notify party, the respective field on the air transport document may be left blank or completed in any manner.

(9) Clean air transport documents. Clauses or notations on an air transport document which expressly declare a defective condition of the goods or packaging are not acceptable. Clauses or notations on the air transport document which do not expressly declare a defective condition of the goods or packaging ( e. g. "packaging may not be sufficient for the air journey") do not constitute a discrepancy. A statement that the packaging "is not sufficient for the air journey" would not be acceptable.

If the word "clean" appears on an air transport document and has been deleted, the air transport document will not be deemed to be claused or unclean unless it specifically bears a clause or notation declaring that the goods or packaging are defective.

(10) Goods description. A goods description in an air transport document may be shown in general terms not in conflict with that stated in the credit.

(11) Freight and additional costs. If a credit requires that an air transport document show that freight has been paid or is payable at destination, the air transport document must be marked accordingly.

Applicants and issuing banks should be specific in stating the requirements of documents to show whether freight is to be prepaid or collected.

If a credit states that costs additional to freight are not acceptable, an air transport document must not indicate that costs additional to the freight have been or will be incurred. Such indication may be by express reference to additional costs or by the use of shipment terms that refer to costs associated with the loading or unloading of goods.

A reference in the transport document to costs which may be levied as a result of a delay in unloading the goods or after the goods have been unloaded is not considered an indication of additional costs in this context.

Air transport documents often have separate boxes which, by their pre-printed headings, indicate that they are for freight charges "prepaid" and for freight charges "to collect", respectively. A requirement in a credit for an air transport document to show that freight has been pre-paid will be fulfilled by a statement of the freight charges under the heading "Freight Prepaid" or a similar expression or indication, and a requirement that an air transport document shows that freight has to be collected will be fulfilled by a statement of the freight charges under the heading "Freight to Collect" or a similar expression or indication.

(12) Corrections and alterations. Corrections and alterations on air transport documents must be authenticated. Such authentication must appear to have been made by the carrier or any of its agents (who may be different from the agent that may have issued or signed it), provided it is identified as an agent of the carrier.

Copies of air transport documents do not need to include any signature of the carrier or agent (or shipper, even if required by the credit to appear on the original air transport document), nor any authentication of any alterations or corrections that may have been made on the original.

(13) Transshipment and partial shipment. Transshipment is the unloading from one air-craft and reloading to another aircraft during the carriage from the airport of departure to the air-port of destination stated in the credit. If it does not occur between these two airports, unloa-ding and reloading is not considered to be transshipment.

If a credit prohibits partial shipments and more than one air transport document is presen-ted covering dispatch from one or more airports of departure (as specifically allowed, or within the geographical area or range stated in the credit), such documents are acceptable, provided that they cover the dispatch of goods on the same aircraft and same flight and are destined for the same airport of destination. In the event that more than one air transport document is pres-ented incorporating different dates of shipment, the latest of these dates of shipment will be taken for the calculation of any presentation period and must fall on or before the latest shipment date specified in the credit.

Shipment on more than one aircraft is a partial shipment, even if the aircraft leave on the same day for the same destination.

The specimen of an air freight shipper's instruction and an air waybill is attached in the appendix of this chapter.

## 5.5.6 Specific Programs for Preparing Air Waybill

Moreover, some specific programs are developed and used in air transportation. The cus-tomer can simply enter basic information required to print an Air Waybill[1]. The essential items are:

---

[1]  http://www. bmsi. com/bmsi/doc/awld/awawed1. html.

(1) AWB (Air Waybill) number. The Air Waybill (AWB) number consists of a 3-digit airline number and an 8-digit serial number, usually assigned by the airline. Most airlines will assign a block of numbers to agents. Pressing F4 in this field will display the template inquiry.

(2) M/H/D (Type of AWB). Air Waybills may be Master, House or Direct. Enter the appropriate letter in this field, M for Master, H for House, and D for Direct.

(3) DEP airport of departure. Enter airport codes, a valid 3-letter airport code in this field. The departure and destination airports may be modified on the WYSIWYG screen.

(4) MAWB (Master AWB). If this is a house air waybill, you must enter the MAWB in this field. You may enter a 3-digit airline code and the system will assign the next AWB number from inventory. This does not create the MAWB, but does reserve the number. You must later manually enter the number and provide the necessary data. If this is a Master AWB, the system will automatically copy the AWB number when you select the M code in the M/H/D field. Leave this field blank if this is a Direct AWB.

(5) Date AWB date. Dates are entered as MMDDYY. If you enter DD, the current month and year will be assumed. If you enter MMDD, the current year will be assumed. Leading zeros must be entered for days and years but are not necessary for months.

(6) Customer codes. Enter a valid customer number in this field.

(7) FILE company's reference number. You may enter a file number in the File field. If you do not, the system will automatically assign one.

(8) DEPT accounting department number. Enter your department number in this field. This is assigned by your accounting department and, normally will default to the proper value. The department number will have an effect on the automatic file number and the AWB inventory routines.

(9) Consignee. Enter the consignee name and address information in these fields. If more space is required, you may expand on the WYSIWYG screen, which is reached by pressing F14 (shift F4). You should always complete the information of this screen because it is only transmitted on electronic versions of the Waybill. You may press F4 to access the Consignee database. You may store an unlimited number of consignees for each shipper in this database.

(10) Contact number. Enter the consignee's contact number: FAX (FX), Telephone (TE), or Telex (TL). All these 3 numbers may be transmitted with an electronic Waybill if you use the Consignee database.

(11) Country. Enter the 2-letter country code. You may access the country database by pressing F4.

(12) Shipper. For international shipments, the shipper must have a valid IRS (Interna-

tional Revenue Service) number in the customer database. The Shipper on a Master AWB must be the consol shipper designated in the system default file. The Shipper name and address may be modified on the WYSIWYG screen.

(13) Billing. The system will automatically create an invoice for the appropriate party. Use the Bill to field only in the case of a separate Bill to address. The system will properly handle the billing on collect direct and house AWB's. No billing should be done on Master AWB's. An invoice record is created for Master AWB's, but only for the purpose of setting up sales report data.

(14) Rating airline. If you are using the automatic rating system, you may enter a 2-letter airline code in this field. That airline will then be used to rate the waybill.

(15) To—By Table. Use this table to enter the freight movement routing. Enter the 3-letter code for the destination airport of each leg in the "TO" field. Enter the 2-letter airline code in the "BY" field. In both fields, you may access the appropriate database by pressing F4. Enter the flight number in the "FLIGHT" field. This may be alpha or numeric or a combination. Finally, you must enter the flight date. If any one of the fields on a line has data, all fields on the line must be completed.

(16) Currency. Enter the 3-letter currency code used on this waybill.

(17) Carriage value. Enter the value for carriage in this field. This value will be used to calculate valuation charges. Normally, NCV (No Commercial Value) is entered in this field.

(18) Customs Value. Enter the customs value in this field. This value will be shown on the waybill and carried over to the export declaration. You may enter NVD (No Value Declared) in this field.

(19) Insurance value. Use this field to enter the value to be insured with the airline. This value will be multiplied by the rate shown in the INS % field to calculate the insurance charge due to the airline. You may enter NIL in this field.

(20) Accounting information. Text entered in this field will be printed in the accounting information block of the waybill. It will also be used in the Reference number field for tracking. If you enter multiple reference numbers separated by ";", each will be shown separately as a reference number for this waybill.

## 5.6  Road, Rail or Inland Waterway Transport Documents

### 5.6.1  Definition

Road, rail or inland waterway transport documents refer to transport documents covering cargo movement by road, rail or inland waterway.

Rail waybill is a freight document that indicates goods have been received for shipment by rail. A duplicate is given to the shipper as a receipt for acceptance of goods (also called duplicate way-bill)[1].

Road waybill is a transport document that indicates goods have been received for shipment by road haulage carrier[2].

Inland waterway bill is a transport document that indicates goods have been received for shipment by inland waterway carrier.

### 5.6.2 Functions

Road, rail or inland waterway transport documents can be used for both domestic freight and international ones, and they usually serve:

- Proof of receipt of the goods for shipment.
- Evidence of the contract of carriage.
- An invoice for the freight, reflecting the shipper, the consignee and the goods being shipped, as well as the full freight amount.

However, they can not be used as documents of title, and thus are not transferable from one party to another.

### 5.6.3 Contents

The UCP 600 Article 24 and the ISBP 821 J2 ~ J20 provide specific guidance and requirements for preparing such kinds of transport documents. They usually contain the following detailed items.

(1) The carrier and its signature. A road, rail or inland waterway transport document, however named, must appear to indicate the name of the carrier, and be signed by the carrier or a named agent for or on behalf of the carrier, or indicate receipt of the goods by signature, stamp or notation by the carrier or a named agent for or on behalf of the carrier.

Any signature, stamp or notation of receipt of the goods by the carrier or agent must be identified as that of the carrier or agent. Any signature, stamp or notation of receipt of the goods by the agent must indicate that the agent has signed or acted for or on behalf of the carrier.

If a rail transport document does not identify the carrier, any signature or stamp of the railway company will be accepted as evidence of the document being signed by the carrier.

(2) Date of shipment/received for shipment/dispatch. A road, rail or inland waterway transport document, however named, must appear to indicate the date of shipment or the date

---

[1] Edward G. Hinkelman, Longman Dictionary of International Trade, Longman and China Renmin University Press, 2000.

[2] Edward G. Hinkelman, Longman Dictionary of International Trade, Longman and China Renmin University Press, 2000.

the goods have been received for shipment, dispatch or carriage at the place stated in the credit. Unless the transport document contains a dated reception stamp, an indication of the date of receipt or a date of shipment, the date of issuance of the transport document will be deemed to be the date of shipment.

(3) Place of shipment and destination. A road, rail or inland waterway transport document must indicate the place of shipment and the place of destination stated in the credit.

(4) Original and duplicate. A road, rail or inland waterway transport document must appear to be the original for consignor or shipper or bear no marking indicating for whom the document has been prepared.

If a credit requires a rail or inland waterway transport document, the transport document presented will be accepted as an original whether or not it is marked as an original.

With respect to rail waybills, the practice of many railway companies is to provide the shipper or consignor with only a duplicate (often a carbon copy) duly authenticated by the railway company's stamp. Such a duplicate will be accepted as an original. A rail transport document marked "duplicate" will, therefore, be accepted as an original.

In the absence of an indication on the transport document as to the number of originals issued, the number presented will be deemed to constitute a full set.

(5) Order party and notify party. A road, rail or inland waterway transport document is not documents of title, and thus should not be issued "to order" or "to order of" a named party.

Even if a credit calls for a road, rail or inland waterway transport document to be made out "to order" or "to order of" a named party, such a document, showing goods consigned to that party, without mention of "to order" or "to order of", is acceptable.

If a credit does not stipulate a notify party, the respective field on the transport document may be left blank or completed in any manner.

(6) Goods description. A goods description in a road, rail or inland waterway transport document may be shown in general terms not in conflict with that stated in the credit.

(7) Corrections and alterations. Corrections and alterations on a road, rail or inland waterway transport document must be authenticated. Such authentication must appear to have been made by the carrier or any one of their named agents, who may be different from the agent that may have issued or signed it, provided they are identified as an agent of the carrier.

However, copies of road, rail or inland waterway transport documents do not need to include any signature on, or authentication of, any alterations or corrections that may have been made on the original.

(8) Transshipment. A road, rail or inland waterway transport document may indicate that

the goods will or may be transshipped provided that the entire carriage is covered by one and the same transport document.

A road, rail or inland waterway transport document indicating that transshipment will or may take place is acceptable, even if the credit prohibits transshipment.

Here, transshipment means unloading from one means of conveyance and reloading to another means of conveyance, within the same mode of transport, during the carriage from the place of shipment, dispatch or carriage to the place of destination stated in the credit.

(9) Partial shipment. Shipment on more than one truck (lorry), train, vessel, etc. is a partial shipment, even if such means of conveyance leave on the same day for the same destination.

(10) Freight and additional costs. If a credit requires a road, rail or inland waterway transport document show that freight has been paid or is payable at destination, the transport document must be marked accordingly.

Applicants and issuing banks should be specific in stating the requirements of documents to show whether freight is to be prepaid or collected.

### 5.6.4  International Conventions

There are two important conventions governing international carriage by rail and by road.

(1) The convention concerning international carriage by rail 1980 (COTIF-CIM). The rail waybill (CIM) is a document required for the transportation of goods by rail. It is regulated by the convention concerning international carriage by rail 1980 (COTIF-CIM). The CIM is issued by the carrier in five copies, the original accompanies the goods, and the duplicate of the original is kept by the consignor, and the three remaining copies are intended for internal purposes of the carrier. It is considered the rail transport contract.

(2) The convention for the contract of the international carriage of goods by road 1956 (the CMR Convention). Road waybill (CMR): The road waybill is a document containing the details of the international transportation of goods by road, set out by the convention for the contract of the international carriage of goods by road 1956 (the CMR Convention). It enables the consignor to have the goods at his disposal during the transportation. It must be issued in quadruplicate and signed by the consignor and the carrier. The first copy is intended for the consignor; the second remains in the possession of the carrier; and the third accompanies the goods and is delivered to the consignee. Usually, a CMR is issued for each vehicle. The CMR note is not a document of title and is non-negotiable.

## Questions and Problems

### I. Choose the best answer to fill in the blank.

1. According to the UCP 600, a tolerance not to exceed＿＿＿＿more or＿＿＿＿less than the quantity of the goods is allowed, provided the credit does not state the quantity in terms of a stipulated number of packing units or individual items and the total amount of the drawings does not exceed the amount of the credit.

    A. 10%, 10%        B. 5%, 5%        C. 10%, 5%        D. 5%, 10%.

2. An L/C (subject to the UCP 600) stipulates that "time of shipment: on or about January 16, 2023", this means that the shipment is to occur during the period of＿＿＿＿.

    A. January 10, 2023–January 20, 2023

    B. January 11, 2023–January 21, 2023

    C. January 13, 2023–January 19, 2023

    D. January 06, 2023–January 26, 2023

3. The L/C (subject to the UCP 600) stipulates that: Shipment is to be effected in two equally monthly lots during March and April. The actual shipment dates are April 1st for the 1st lot and April 23rd for the 2nd lot. Which statement is correct＿＿＿＿.

    A. the credit ceases to be available for the 1st shipment, but is available for the 2nd shipment

    B. the credit is available for the 1st shipment, but ceases to be available for the 2nd shipment

    C. the credit is available for both of the 1st shipment and the 2nd shipment

    D. the credit ceases to be available for both the 1st shipment and 2nd shipment

4. A(n)＿＿＿＿B/L refers to the one that is made out to a designated consignee.

    A. straight        B. order        C. bearer        D. blank endorsed

5. The B/L presented to the consignee or buyer or his bank after the stipulated expiry date of presentation or after the goods are due at the port of destination is a＿＿＿＿.

    A. stale B/L        confirmed B/L        C. ante-dated B/L    D. straight B/L

6. According to the UCP 600, if a B/L contains the following date(s) simultaneously,＿＿＿＿will be deemed to be the date of shipment.

    A. the date of receiving the goods

    B. the date of issuing the B/L

    C. the actual date of shipment in a specific notation

    D. the sailing date of the carrying vessel

7. According to the UCP 600, a presentation consisting of 2 sets of transport documents will be regarded as covering a partial shipment when 2 sets of bill of lading are presented show-

ing port to port shipment_____.

    A. from Shanghai to Rotterdam on vessel B and from Tianjin to Bremerhaven on vessel C

    B. from Shanghai to Rotterdam on vessel B and from Shanghai to Rotterdam on vessel C

    C. from Shanghai to Rotterdam on vessel B and from Shanghai to Bremerhaven on vessel B

    D. from Shanghai to Rotterdam on vessel B and from Tianjin to Rotterdam on vessel B

    8. The description of goods in the L/C (subject to the UCP 600) is "about 100, 000 metric tons of wheat, Total amount: USD 100, 000. 00". The permitted maximum quantity of shipment is_____metric tons.

    A. 110, 000        B. 100, 500        C. 100, 000        950, 000

    9. In the case of a credit requiring Bill of Lading to be made out "to order of issuing bank", _____ of following Bills of Lading is acceptable?

    A. Bill of Lading to be made out "consigned to the issuing bank"

    B. Bill of Lading to be made out "to order of the issuing Bank"

    C. Bill of Lading to be made out "to order", and endorsed by the shipper in blank

    D. Bill of Lading to be made out "to order of negotiating bank", and endorsed by the negotiating bank in blank

    10. If an Air transport document contains the following date(s) simultaneously, _____ will be deemed to be the date of shipment?

    A. the date of issuance

    B. the actual date of shipment in a specific notation

    C. an information appearing on the air transport document relative to the flight number and date

    D. the date of receiving the goods

**II. True (T) or false (F).**

    1. If the transport document indicates, by stamp or notation, a date of dispatch, taking in charge or shipped on board, this date will be deemed to be the date of shipment.

    2. The shipper or consignor of the goods indicated on any document must be the beneficiary of the credit.

    3. According to the UCP 600, transshipment means unloading from one means of conveyance and reloading to another means of conveyance (whether or not in different modes of transport) during the carriage from the place of dispatch, taking in charge or shipment to the place of final destination stated in the credit.

    4. The date of issuance of the bill of lading will be deemed to be the date of shipment unless the bill of lading contains an on board notation indicating the date of shipment, in which case the date stated in the on board notation will be deemed to be the date of shipment.

5. According to the UCP 600, a bank will only accept a clean transport document.

6. A clean transport document is one bearing no clause or notation expressly declaring a defective condition of the goods or their packaging.

7. The word "clean" must appear on a transport document, if a credit has a requirement for that transport document to be "clean on board".

8. According to the UCP 600, a presentation consisting of more than one set of transport documents evidencing shipment commencing on the same means of conveyance and for the same journey, provided they indicate the same destination, will not be regarded as covering a partial shipment, even if they indicate different dates of shipment or different ports of loading, places of taking in charge or dispatch.

9. According to the UCP 600, if the presentation consists of more than one set of transport documents, the latest date of shipment as evidenced on any of the sets of transport documents will be regarded as the date of shipment.

10. If a drawing or shipment by instalments within given periods is stipulated in the credit and any instalment is not drawn or shipped within the period allowed for that instalment, the credit ceases to be available for that and any subsequent instalment.

**III. Practical application.**

1. Fill in the blank form bill of lading according to the particulars below:

---

√APPLICANT: ABC TRADING CO., KARACHI

√BENEFICIARY: ZHEJIANG LIGHT INDUSTRIAL PRODUCTS IMPORT AND EXPORT CORPORATION

√EXPIRY DATE : SEP 15, 2024

√PARTIAL SHIPMENT:ALLOWED    TRANSSHIPMENT:ALLOWED

√SHIPMENT: FROM NINGBO TO KARACHI

√DESCRIPTION OF GOODS:"GOLD ELEPHANT" BRAND WATCH

√FULL SET OF"SHIPPED ON BOARD"OCEAN BILL OF LADING MADE OUT TO ORDER OF SHIPPER AND BLANK ENDORSED,SHOWING FREIGHT PREPAID AND NOTIFY APPLICANT

√QUANTITY OF GOODS: 1,000PCS;    PACKING IN 40 CTNS

√THE NAME OF STEAMER: CHANGJIANG    VOV. NO.: V.123

√B/L NO.: CJ2651_____    B/L DATE: SEP 5, 2024

√GROSS WEIGHT: @ 16KGS/CTN    NET WEIGHT: @ 15KGS/CTN

√MEASUREMENT: 0.012M$^3$

---

续表

| Shipper | B/L NO. _____ |
|---|---|

**PIL**

**PACIFIC INTERNATION LINES (PTE) LTD**

( Incorporated in Singapore )

**COMBINED TRANSPORT BILL OF LADING**

Received in apparent good order and condition except as otherwise noted the total number of container or other packages or units enumerated below for transportation from the place of receipt to the place of delivery subject to the terms hereof. One of the signed Bills of Lading must be surrendered duly endorsed in exchange for the Goods or delivery order. On presentation of this document ( duly ) Endorsed to the Carrier by or on behalf of the Holder, the rights and liabilities arising in accordance with the terms hereof shall ( without prejudice to any rule of common law or statute rendering them binding on the Merchant ) become binding in all respects between the Carrier and the Holder as though the contract evidenced hereby had been made between them.

**SEE TERMS ON ORIGINAL B/L**

**Consignee**

**Notify Party**

| Vessel and Voyage Number | Port of Loading | Port of Discharge |
|---|---|---|
| Place of Receipt | Place of Delivery | Number of Original Bs/L |

**PARTICULARS AS DECLARED BY SHIPPER – CARRIER NOT RESPONSIBLE**

| Container Nos/Seal Nos. Marks and/Numbers | No. of Container / Packages / Description of Goods | Gross Weight ( Kilos ) | Measurement ( cu-meters ) |
|---|---|---|---|
| | | | |

**FREIGHT & CHARGES**

Number of Containers/Packages ( in words )

Shipped on Board Date:

Place and Date of Issue:

In Witness Whereof this number of Original Bills of Lading stated Above all of the tenor and date one of which being accomplished the others to stand void.

for PACIFIC INTERNATIONAL LINES ( PTE ) LTD as Carrier

2. Fill in the blank form bill of lading according to the particulars below:

---

√LETTER OF CREDIT NO. : LC-515

√EXPIRY DATE:240315   PLACE IN CHINA

√APPLICANT:BLUE SKY HOLDINGS LTD. HONGKONG

√BENEFICIARY: ZHEJIANG LIGHT INDUSTRIAL PRODUCTS IMPORT AND EXPORT CORPORATION

√AMOUNT: CURRENCY USD AMOUNT 25,000.00

√PARTIAL SHIPMENTS: ALLOWED

√TRANSSHIPMENT: ALLOWED

√LOADING IN CHARGE: SHANGHAI, CHINA

√FOR TRANSPORT TO: HAMBURG

√LATEST DATE OF SHIPMENT:240228

√DESCRIPTION OF GOODS: TOYS DETAILS AS PER ORDER NO. P01009 FOB SHANGHAI

√FULL SET (3/3) OF ORIGINAL CLEAN ON BOARD MARINE BILLS OF LADING MADE OUT TO ORDER OF APPLICANT MARKED "FREIGHT COLLECT" AND NOTIFY APPLICANT.

√B/L MUST SHOW THIS LETTER OF CREDIT NO.

√PACKING: TOTAL PACKED IN 200 CARTONS

√QUANTITY: 1,000PCS

√BILL OF LADING NO. : YB5008_____     B/L DATE:240220

√VESSEL VOV. NO. : SUNFENG V. 188   CONTAINER NO. :GVDU2041118/SEAL 21281

√NET WEIGHT: 20KGS/CARTON     GROSS WEIGHT:21KGS/CARTON

√MEASUREMENT: 0.086CBM/CARTON

√PORT OF TRANSSHIPMENT:HONG KONG

---

| Shipper | B/L No. _____ |
|---|---|
| | **≡≡PIL** |
| | **PACIFIC INTERNATION LINES (PTE) LTD** |
| | (Incorporated in Singapore) |
| **Consignee** | **COMBINED TRANSPORT BILL OF LADING** |
| | Received in apparent good order and condition except as otherwise noted the total number of container or other packages or units enumerated below for transportation from the place of receipt to the place of delivery subject to the terms hereof. One of the signed Bills of Lading must be surrendered duly endorsed in exchange for the Goods or delivery |
| **Notify Party** | order. On presentation of this document (duly) Endorsed to the Carrier by or on behalf of the Holder, the rights and liabilities arising in accordance with the terms hereof shall (without prejudice to any rule of common law or statute rendering them binding on the Merchant) become binding in all respects between the Carrier and the Holder as though the contract evidenced hereby had been made between them. |
| | **SEE TERMS ON ORIGINAL B/L** |

续表

| Vessel and Voyage Number | Port of Loading | Port of Discharge |
|---|---|---|
| Place of Receipt | Place of Delivery | Number of Original Bs/L |

PARTICULARS AS DECLARED BY SHIPPER – CARRIER NOT RESPONSIBLE

| Container Nos/Seal Nos. Marks and/Numbers | No. of Container / Packages / Description of Goods | Gross Weight ( Kilos ) | Measurement ( cu-metres ) |
|---|---|---|---|
| | | | |

**FREIGHT & CHARGES**

Number of Containers/Packages ( in words )

Shipped on Board Date:

Place and Date of Issue:

In Witness Whereof this number of Original Bills of Lading stated
Above all of the tenor and date one of which being accomplished
the others to stand void.

for PACIFIC INTERNATIONAL LINES ( PTE ) LTD as Carrier

# Appendix

## Sea Freight Shipper's Letter of Instruction / Interim Wharf Receipt Specimen[1]

| SHIPPER | | YOUR LOCAL OFFICE | PHONE / FAX NUMBERS |
|---|---|---|---|
| | **ICE** INTERNATIONAL CARGO EXPRESS | ☐ ICE BRISBANE<br>☐ ICE FREMANTLE<br>☐ ICE MELBOURNE<br>☐ ICE SYDNEY | 07 3868 1777 / 3868 1776<br>08 9430 7822 / 9430 7821<br>03 9338 4755 / 9338 4010<br>02 9669 7800 / 9669 7802 |

| CONSIGNEE | SHIPPING REFERENCES / SPECIAL INSTRUCTIONS TO ICE | | |
|---|---|---|---|
| | | | |

| NOTIFY PARTY | E. C. N. TO BE ARRANGED BY | | |
|---|---|---|---|
| | ☐ SHIPPER ( INDICATE # ) _____<br>☐ ICE ( PLEASE DECLARE FOB VALUE ) AUD _____<br>☐ ICE TO ARRANGE DRAWBACK | | |

| VESSEL | VOYAGE | PORT OF LOADING | ETD | CONTAINER # |
|---|---|---|---|---|
| | | | | |

| PORT OF DISCHARGE | FINAL DESTINATION | INSURANCE TO BE COVERED BY ICE<br>☐ NO<br>☐ YES ( PLEASE APPLY ) | | SEAL # |
|---|---|---|---|---|
| | | | | |

| MARKS AND NUMBERS | NUMBER AND KIND OF PACKAGES | DESCRIPTION OF GOODS | GROSS WEIGHT ( KILOGRAMS ) | DIMENSIONS ( LENGTH × WIDTH × HEIGHT IN METRES ) |
|---|---|---|---|---|
| TOTALS | | | | |

---

[1] http://www.icecargo.com.au/online/downloads.html.

| CHARGES PAYABLE BY | SHIPPER | CONSIGNEE | PICK UP BY ICE |
|---|---|---|---|
| LOCAL CARTAGE | ☐ | ☐ | ☐ NO ( PLEASE ATTACH IWR TO CARGO ) |
| EXPORT CLEARANCE | ☐ | ☐ | ☐ YES ( PLEASE INDICATE ADDRESS ) |
| OCEAN FREIGHT | ☐ | ☐ | _____ |
| PORT CHARGES | ☐ | ☐ | _____ |
| INSURANCE | ☐ | ☐ | _____ |
| OTHER ( PLEASE SPECIFY ) | ☐ | ☐ | _____ |
| | | ☐ | |

**INCOTERM** ☐ ☐ ☐

PLACE

_____

WE CERTIFY THAT NO PROHIBITED PACKING
MATERIALS HAVE BEEN USED IN THE PACKING
NOR THAT RESTRICTED CARGO FORMS PART
OF THE ABOVE GOODS.

CO. / DATE / SIGNATURE

---

**SHIPPING DOCUMENTS TO BE DESPATCHED
TO**
☐   SHIPPER
☐   CONSIGNEE
☐   OTHER ( INDICATE ADDRESS ) _____

_____

_____

**RELEASE OF CARGO AT DESTINATION**
☐   AGAINST ORIGINAL BILL OF LADING
☐   EXPRESS RELEASE

**ALL BUSINESS HANDLED IS IN ACCORDANCE
WITH OUR STANDARD TRADING CONDI-
TIONS PRINTED ON THE BACK HEREOF AND
ALSO AVAILABLE SEPARATELY.**

**RECEIVED**
NUMBER AND KIND OF PACKAGES

_____

CO. / DATE / TIME / SIGNATURE

GOODS RECEIVED IN APPARANT GOOD ORDER FOR FOR-
WARDING IN ACCORDANCE WITH THE TERMS, CONDI-
TIONS AND EXCEPTIONS CONTAINED IN THE STAMPED
BILL OF LADING.

# Bill of Lading Specimen 1

| Shipper<br>CHINA WEIFANG RC OIL AND FAT CO., LTD.<br>2, BEIHAI, KUIWEN, WEIFANG, SHANDONG, 261041 CHINA | B/L NO.: COS271234<br><br>中国远洋运输总公司<br>**CHINA OCEAN SHIPPING CO.** |
|---|---|
| Consignee<br>TO OPENING BANK's ORDER | **DIRECT TRANSPORT** |
| Notify Party<br>GISBERT BRINKSCHULTE<br>GMBH & CO., KG<br>UNIVERSITAETSALLEE11-13,<br>D-2800<br>BREMEN 33. F. R. GERMANY | **BILL OF LADING**<br><br>**ORIGINAL** |

| Pre-carriage by | Place of Receipt |
|---|---|
| Ocean Vessel<br>Voy. No.<br>YUN FENG 9455 | Port of Loading<br>QINGDAO |

| Port of Discharge<br>ROTTEDAM | Final Destination | Freight Payable at<br>QINGDAO | Numbers of Original B/L<br>THREE (3) |
|---|---|---|---|

| Marks & No.<br>Container. No./Seal No.<br>GB BREMEN<br>NO. 1-UP DIN-NO.<br>Container No./Seal No.<br>1×20′ FULL<br>FBZU<br>0032453-0032462 | No. of Containers or<br>Packages<br>180 PALLETS<br>3,600 BAGS | Kind of Packages:<br>Destination of Goods<br>FIRST GRADE 12-HSA<br>IN 50KG BAG | Gross Weight<br>180,000KGS | Measurement<br>180CBM |
|---|---|---|---|---|

Total Packages (in words): ONE HUNDRED AND EIGHTY PALLETS ONLY

| Freight & Charges<br><br>CLEAN ON BOARD<br><br>FREIGHT PREPAID | Place and Date of Issue:<br>QINGDAO OCT 23, 2024 |
|---|---|
| | Signed for the Carrier:<br>中国外轮代理公司青岛分公司<br>CHINA OCEAN SHIPPING AGENCY QINGDAO BRANCH<br>王　伟　(盖章)<br><br><br>FOR THE CARRIER NAMED ABOVE |

Source: http://www.sdwfvc.com/jpkc/swyyhd/html/documents/BL.htm.

## Bill of Lading Specimen 2

| 1. Shipper Insert Name, Address and Phone | B/L No. |
|---|---|

| 2. Consignee Insert Name, Address and Phone |  中远集装箱运输有限公司<br>COSCO CONTAINER LINES<br><br>TLX: 33057 COSCO CN<br>FAX: +86(021) 6545 8984<br>ORIGINAL<br>Port-to-Port or Combined Transport<br>**BILL OF LADING** |

3. Notify Party Insert Name, Address and Phone

(It is agreed that no responsibility shall attach to the Carrier or his agents for failure to notify)

RECEIVED in external apparent good order and condition except as otherwise noted. The total number of packages or unites stuffed in the container, the description of the goods and the weights shown in this Bill of Lading are furnished by the Merchants, and which the carrier has no reasonable means of checking and is not a part of this Bill of Lading contract. The carrier has issued the number of Bills of Lading stated below, all of this tenor and date, one of the original Bills of Lading must be surrendered and endorsed or signed against the delivery of the shipment and whereupon any other original bills of Lading shall be void. The Merchants agree to be bound by the terms and conditions of this Bill of Lading as if each had personally signed this Bill of Lading.

SEE clause 4 on the back of this Bill of Lading (Terms continued on the back hereof, please read carefully).

* Applicable Only When Document Used as a Combined Transport Bill of Lading.

| 4. Combined Transport * Pre-carriage | 5. Combined Transport * by Place of Receipt |
|---|---|
| 6. Ocean Vessel Voy. No. | 7. Port of Loading |
| 8. Port of Discharge | 9. Combined Transport * Place of Delivery |

| Marks & No. Container/ Seal No. | No. of Containers or Packages | Description of Goods (If Dangerous Goods, See Clause 20) | Gross Weight (Kgs) | Measurement |
|---|---|---|---|---|
| | | Description of Contents for Shipper's Use Only (Not part of This B/L Contract) | | |

10. Total number of containers and/or packages (in words)

| Subject to Clause 7 Limitation | |
|---|---|

续表

| 11. Freight & Charges | Revenue Tons | Rate | | Per | Prepaid | | Collect |
|---|---|---|---|---|---|---|---|
| Declared Value Charge | | | | | | | |

| Ex. Rate: | Prepaid at | | Payable at | | Place and date of issue | |
|---|---|---|---|---|---|---|
| | Total Prepaid | | No. of Original B(s)/L | | Signed for the Carrier, COSCO CONTAI-NER LINES | |

LADEN ON BOARD THE VESSEL

| DATE | | BY | |
|---|---|---|---|

## UNeDocs 2. 02 Non-negotiable Sea Waybill Specimen

| Consignor ( name, address, tax reference) | Shipper's reference | Bill of Lading No. |
|---|---|---|
| | Forwarder's reference | |
| | Unique consignment reference | |
| Consignee ( name, address, tax reference) | Carrier ( name, address, tax reference) | |
| Notify party ( name, address, tax scheme) | Additional notify party ( name, address, tax reference) | |

| Pre-carriage by | Place of receipt   UN/LOCODE | |
|---|---|---|
| Vessel / voyage No. | Port of loading      UN/LOCODE | |
| Port of discharge UN/ LOCODE | Final place of delivery by on-carrier   UN/LOCODE | |

| Marks and numbers; transport unit ID | Number and kind of packages; shipping description of goods | | Gross weight | Measurement |
|---|---|---|---|---|
| Container No.                    Seal No. | Freight details, charge | Rate | Per | Prepaid | Collect |

| | Freight payable at UN/LOCODE | Carrier's name |
|---|---|---|
| | Number of original Bill of Lading | Place ( + ISO code ) and date of issue ( yyyy-mm-dd ) |
| Received for carriage as above in apparent good order and condition, unless otherwise stated hereon, the goods described in the above particulars | Authenticating signature | |

# Air Freight Shipper's Letter of Instruction Specimen

<table>
<tr>
<td colspan="2">SHIPPER</td>
<td colspan="3">
ice<br>
INTERNATIONAL<br>
CARGO EXPRESS
</td>
</tr>
<tr>
<td colspan="2" rowspan="2">CONSIGNEE</td>
<td>YOUR LOCAL OFFICE</td>
<td>PHONE / FAX NUMBERS</td>
</tr>
<tr>
<td>
☐ ICE BRISBANE<br>
☐ ICE FREMANTLE<br>
☐ ICE MELBOURNE<br>
☐ ICE SYDNEY
</td>
<td>
07 3868 1777 / 3868 1776<br>
08 9430 7822 / 9430 7821<br>
03 9338 4755 / 9338 8789<br>
02 9669 7800 / 9669 7802
</td>
</tr>
<tr>
<td colspan="2">ALSO NOTIFY</td>
<td colspan="2">THE SHIPPER HEREBY DECLARES THAT THESE PARTICULARS ARE CORRECT AND THAT THEY ARE AWARE OF AND ACCEPT THE CONDITIONS OF TRADING REFERRED TO ON THE REVERSE SIDE OF THE FORM</td>
</tr>
<tr>
<td colspan="2">AIRPORT OF DEPARTURE<br>AIRPORT OF DESTINATION</td>
<td colspan="2">IF PAYMENT METHOD NOT INDICATED BELOW ALL CHARGES WILL BE AUTOMATICALLY PREPAID TO YOUR ACCOUNT</td>
</tr>
<tr>
<td colspan="2">SPECIAL INSTRUCTIONS</td>
<td colspan="2">SIGNED ON BEHALF OF SHIPPER<br>BY: _____<br>DATE: _____</td>
</tr>
</table>

<table>
<tr>
<th>NO. OF<br>PACKAGES</th>
<th>GROSS<br>WEIGHT</th>
<th>MEASUREMENTS</th>
<th>MARKS AND<br>NUMBERS</th>
<th></th>
<th>NATURE AND QUANTITY<br>OF GOODS</th>
</tr>
</table>

| | PREPAID | | VALUE FOR CUSTOMS |
|---|---|---|---|
| **TICK APPLICABLE BOX:** | | | ECN NO. : |
| COLLECT | ☐ | ☐ | INSURANCE BY ICE YES / NO |
| AIR/FREIGHT | ☐ | ☐ | AMOUNT $ _____ |
| AWB FEE | ☐ | ☐ | COD        YES / NO |
| AGENCY | ☐ | ☐ | AMOUNT $ _____ |
| ECN | ☐ | ☐ | |
| CARTAGE | ☐ | ☐ | |
| AIRLINE HANDLING ( ADF) | ☐ | ☐ | DELIVERY DUTY UNPAID    YES / NO |
| INSURANCE | ☐ | ☐ | |
| DOCUMENT RETURN BY COURIER | ☐ | ☐ | DELIVERY DUTY PAID    YES / NO |

HAZARDOUS CARGO – YES /NO

THE GOODS HEREIN DESCRIBED ARE ACCEPTED IN APPARENT GOOD ORDER AND CONDITION EXCEPT AS NOTED HEREIN

SIGNATURE _____
_____
FOR **INTERNATIONAL CARGO EXPRESS**

Source: http://www. icecargo. com. au/online/downloads. html.

# Air Waybill Specimen

| Shipper's name and address<br>MATSUDA TELEVISION SYSTEMS CO.<br>LOT5, PRESIAN TENKU APUAN<br>SITE 400 SHA ALAM<br>SELANG DE MALAYSIA | NOT NEGOTIABLE<br>**Air Waybill**<br>Issued by<br><br>Beijing Kinte World Express Co. , Ltd. |
|---|---|

| Consignee's name and address<br>MATSUDA QINGDAO CO. , LTD.<br>NO. 128 WUHAN ROAD<br>QINGDAO<br>CHINA | It is agreed that the goods described herein are accepted in apparent good order and condition (except as noted) for carriage SUBJECT TO THE CONDITIONS OF CONTRACT ON THE REVERSE HEREOF, ALL GOODS MAY BE CARRIED BY ANY OTHER MEANS. INCLUDING ROAD OR ANY OTHER CARRIER UNLESS SPECIFIC CONTRARY INSTRUCTIONS ARE GIVEN HEREON BY THE SHIPPER. THE SHIPPER'S ATTENTION IS DRAWN TO THE NOTICE CONCERNING CARIER'S LIMITATION OF LIABILITY.<br>Shipper may increase such limitation of liability by declaring a higher value of carriage and paying a supplemental charge if required. |
|---|---|
| Issuing Carrier's Agent Name and City<br><br>Beijing Kinte World Express Co. , Ltd. | |

Agents IATA Code   Account No.

| Airport of Departure (Add. of First Carrier) and Requested Routing K. LUMPUR, MALAYSIA | Accounting Information<br><br>FREIGHT COLLECT |
|---|---|

| to QAO | By first carrier KE | to | by | to | by | Currency USD | Declared Value for Carriage NVD | Declared Value for Customs NVD |
|---|---|---|---|---|---|---|---|---|

| Airport of Destination QINGDAO, CHINA | Flight/Date KE855/17JUN | Amount of Insurance | INSURANCE–If carrier offers insurance and such insurance is requested in accordance with the conditions thereof indicate amount to be insured in figures in box marked "Amount of Insurance" |
|---|---|---|---|

Handling Information

"NOTIFY PARTY–SAME AS CONSIGNEE"

| No. of Pieces | Gross Weight | Rate Class | Chargeable Weight | Rate/ Charge | Total | Nature and Quantity of Goods |
|---|---|---|---|---|---|---|
| 52 | 510. 00 | | 211 | AS ARRANGED | | TV-PARTS<br><br>12. 638m$^3$ |

| | | Other Charges |
|---|---|---|
| Prepaid Weight charge Collect<br>AS ARRANGED | | |
| Valuation Charge | | |
| Tax | | |
| Total Other Charges Due Agent | | Shipper certifies that the particulars on the face hereof are correct and that insofar as any part of the consignment contains dangerous goods, such part is properly described by name and is in proper condition for carriage by air according to the applicable Dangerous Goods Regulations. |
| Total Other Charges Due Carrier | | |
| | | Signature of Shipper or his agent |
| Total Prepaid | Total Collect<br>AS ARRANGED | JUN. 10,2024 QINGDAO KEWQAO<br>Executed on＿＿at＿＿Signature of issuing Carrier or as Agent |
| Currency<br>Conversion Rates | CC Charges in<br>des. Currency | |
| For Carrier's Use<br>Only at Destination | Charges at Destination | Total Collect Charges | AIR WAYBILL NUMBER<br>KEW-51000788 |

Source：http://bguide.ec.com.cn/article/mycydj/200606/210478_1.html.

# Chapter 6    Insurance Documents

## 【本章提要】

对外贸易货物通常要经过跨国长途运输,容易遭遇海上风险和意外事故引致的损失和费用。按损失程度,保险损失可分为全部损失或部分损失。按损失性质,全部损失可分为实际全损和推定全损,部分损失可分为共同海损和单独海损。按补偿对象,保险费用可分为施救费用和救助费用。

对外贸易中的货物运输保险单据,是指保险人(承保人)签发给被保险人(投保人)的,在按一定费率收取保险费的基础上对保险货物承保一定范围的保险险别的重要单据。保险单据是证明保险合同成立的法律文件,是保险人对被保险人的承保证明,是保险人和被保险人之间权利义务关系的证明。在被保险货物遭受承保责任范围内的损失时,保险单据是被保险人索赔和保险人理赔的法律依据。

按保险单据的形式,保险单据可分为保险单、保险凭证、暂保单等。

保险单:俗称"大保单",是保险人与被保险人之间订立的正式保险合同的书面证明,一般由被保险人逐笔投保,由保险人逐笔签发。保险单的格式通常因保险人而异,但内容基本一致,分为正面和背面。保险单正面主要包括:①发票号码和保单号码;②投保人即被保险人名称;③货物描述、唛头和件数;④保险金额和货币单位;⑤船名、起讫地、预计起运日期;⑥承保险别;⑦理赔地点;⑧出单日期;⑨保险公司签章等具体内容。保险单背面主要载明保险条款,主要包括适用的保险条款(如英国协会货物条款,中国保险条款),不同险别的责任范围、除外责任、责任起讫、被保险人的义务、索赔期限等。

保险凭证:俗称小保单,是一种只有正面内容、背面没有载明保险条款的简化的保险单。小保单有与大保单同等的法律效力,在预约保险单或流动保险单的情况下会用到,但在整个对外贸易实践中使用较少。

暂保单:又称"临时保险单",是保险人签发正式保单前所出立的临时证明。在规定的有效期内(一般为30天),暂保单的效力与正式保险单相同。在按 FOB、CFR 条件进口时,进口商可以预先办理投保获取暂保单,一旦收到出口方发来的装运通知,再将装运细节通知保险人,换取正式保险单。

以 CIF、CIP 为贸易术语的交易,若信用证要求卖方提交保险凭证,卖方提交保险单将视为可接受,反之则不然。

保险单据必须注明签发日期。除非信用证另有规定,保险单据的签发日期不得迟于运输单据的签发日期。

中国对外贸易中常用的保险条款主要有中国保险条款和英国协会货物条款。UCP 600 和 ISBP 相关条款对保险单据的制作和提交有具体要求。

International trade usually involves long-distance travel of goods from one country to another, during which the goods are out of the physical control of both the buyer and the seller, and may face all kinds of damages or losses. Therefore, the cargo transported must be insured against loss or damage at each stage of the journey.

Cargo insurance is a contract whereby the insurer (insurance company), on the base of a premium paid, undertakes to indemnify the insured against loss from certain risks or perils to which the cargo insured may be exposed. It is an indispensable adjunct of international trade.

Transport insurance provides cover for goods transported by sea, air, land and inland waterway. In addition to providing indemnity against transit-related risks, transport insurance also embraces conveyance-related transfers and warehousing. The goods are insured against loss and damage.

This chapter mainly refers to marine cargo insurance, and covers four parts: the essentials of marine cargo insurance, the various insurance documents used in international trade transactions, the legal and commercial functions of each of those documents, and the basic contents and items of insurance documents.

## 6.1 Marine Cargo Insurance: Essentials

### 6.1.1 Types of Risks Covered

There are two types of risks to be covered by marine cargo insurance.

One type is the perils of the sea, including both natural calamities and unexpected accidents. Where natural calamities include heavy weather, lightning, Tsunami, earthquake, volcanic eruption and so on; and accidents refer to fire, explosion, vessel being stranded, grounded, sunk or capsized, collision or contact of vessel with any external object other than water, etc.

The other type of risks is external (extraneous) risks including general external risks and special external risks. Where general external risks include theft and pilferage, contamination, leakage, breakage, sweating and/or heating, taint of odor, rusting, hook damage, fresh and/or rain water damage, short-delivery and non-delivery, shortage in weight, clashing and so on; and special risks include war, strike, failure to delivery due to some special laws or regulations.

### 6.1.2 Types of Losses Covered

There are two types of losses covered by marine cargo insurance, one is total loss and the other is partial loss.

Total loss is divided into Actual Total Loss (ATL) and Constructive Total Loss (CTL), where actual total loss means the complete loss of the insured cargo in value, and a constructive total loss occurs when the cost of salvaging the shipment would be more than the salvaged value of the merchandise. Most insurance policies provide for the payment of a total loss up to the insured amount.

Partial loss means the total loss of part of the insured cargo. It can be divided into general average and particular average.

General average is based upon the relationship between the ship owner and the shippers who have cargo aboard the same vessel on a particular voyage. All these parties are bound together in the "adventure". Sometimes, when the whole ship was threatened by a peril of the sea or some other hazard, in order to save the ship and some of the cargo, part of the cargo has to be sacrificed; in this case an act of general average would be declared. According to marine law, those interests whose property was saved must contribute proportionally to cover the loss of the one whose property was voluntarily sacrificed.

Particular average means a partial loss suffered by part of the cargo. It occurs when a storm or fire damages part of the shipper's and no one else's cargo has to be sacrificed to save the voyage. The cargo owner whose goods were damaged or lost should refer to his insurance company, provided his policy covers the specific type of loss suffered.

### 6.1.3 Types of Expenses Covered

Ocean cargo insurance also covers the expense incurred to avoid or reduce the damage or loss of the subject matte insured. There are two main types of expenses. One is sue and labor expense paid by the assured or his agent; the other is salvage charge paid by the party other than the insurer and/or the insured.

### 6.1.4 Types of Insurance Coverage

According to China Insurance Clause (CIC, dated Jan. 1, 1981), there are mainly two types of insurance coverage, basic coverage and additional coverage. Where basic coverage mainly includes FPA, WPA and All Risks, and additional coverage includes General Additional Coverage and Special Additional Coverage.

FPA (Free from Particular Average) is a limited form of cargo insurance coverage under which no partial loss or damage is recoverable. It only provides coverage for total losses and general average emerging from the actual "marine perils" like vessel being stranded, grounded or sunk.

WPA (With Particular Average) covers wider coverage than FPA. It provides extensive coverage against all loss or damage due to marine perils throughout the duration of the policy, including partial loss or damage which may be attributed to natural calamities like heavy weather.

All Risks is the most comprehensive type of basic insurance coverage, under which the insurer is responsible for all total or partial loss of or damage to the goods insured either arising from sea perils or general external causes. However, it does not cover loss, damage or expense caused by delay, inherent vice or nature of the goods insured, or special external risks of war, strike, etc.

General Additional Risks include TPND (Theft, Pilferage and Non-delivery), FWRD (Fresh Water Rain Damage), Risk of Shortage, Risk of Intermixture and Contamination, Risk of Leakage, Risk of Clash and Breakage, Risk of Odor, Damage caused by Heating and Sweating, Hook Damage, Risk of Rust, etc. These additional risks can not be covered independently and should go with FPA or WPA and are included in All Risks coverage.

Special Additional Risks include War Risk, Strike Risks, Failure to Delivery Risk, Import Duty Risk, Rejection Risk, etc. among which War Risk and Strike Risk are more common. These special additional coverage are usually taken out with FPA, WPA and All Risks.

To choose an insurance coverage that is both economical and effective, the exporter or the importer should be aware of the possible losses to be expected of a particular consignment. Different items have different natures and may apply to different insurance types. For instance, cargo like iron ore faces little risk of partial loss, so FPA will be sufficient. Most manufactured goods are covered against All Risks as they are prone to damage caused by sea perils or external risks. [1]

## 6.2　Insurance Documents

### 6.2.1　Definition

Insurance documents are documents evidencing a contract of insurance, describing the term, coverage, premiums and deductibles.

Where term means a period of time, such as for a policy, bond, or contract; coverage means the amount and extent of risk covered by an insurer; premium means a regular periodic payment for an insurance policy, here also called insurance premium; deductible means the amount of a loss that an insurance policy holder has to pay out-of-pocket before reimbursement begins in accordance with the coinsurance rate. [2]

Insurance documents often accompany transport documents in documentary sale transactions, particularly CIF contracts, which form the bases of the analysis in this chapter.

### 6.2.2　Types

Insurance documents usually contain three types: insurance policy, insurance certificate, and declaration under an open cover.

(1) Insurance policy. The insurance policy is a formal insurance document usually required

---

[1]　http://business-heaven. blogspot. com/2007/07/international-cargo-transportation. html.

[2]　http://www. investorwords. com/2517/insurance_policy. html.

to accompany transport and other documents for tender under documentary sale transactions. Execution and issuance of a marine insurance policy is a statutory requirement, non-compliance with which renders the contract inadmissible in evidence in an action for the recovery of loss.

A policy is usually required to specify the name of the assured or his agent, the subject-matter insured and the risk insured against, the voyage or period of time or both, the sum or sums insured, and the name or names of the insurer(s); and it must be signed by or on behalf of the insurer.

(2) Insurance certificate. The insurance certificate is a provisional insurance document furnishing information and certifying that a consignment has been insured. It is now common to tender instead of the policy with transport documents. One of the most important reasons is that preparation of the policy takes time, particularly when a number of underwriters or several insurance companies are involved, and documents may be required promptly. While waiting for the policy to be issued, brokers or leading insurers issue certificates of insurance to certify that an insurance cover of the required description has been effected.

(3) Declaration under an open cover. The declaration under an open cover is sometimes used instead of the insurance policy, particularly under open cover. Open policies are a method of insuring recurring shipments of goods, and cover future transactions, the details of which are unknown at the time. An open policy usually covers a specified value and period. When goods are ordered, the exporter effects the insurance of the shipment by sending to the insurers a declaration of details of the consignment. Each shipment covered by the policy must be shipped within the specified period and the value of each declaration is deducted from the value of the policy. The broker or assured usually receives one policy document for the open cover. The broker or assured or sometimes the insurer issues in respect of each consignment a certificate of insurance within the terms of the cover, certifying that he or she is holding the policy of insurance. [1]

## 6.2.3 Functions

Generally, insurance documents are used to evidence the insurance contract, and as one important document for international trade payment. Specifically, different types of insurance play different roles.

(1) Functions of the insurance policy. The functions of the insurance policy may be summarized as follows:

First, the insurance policy satisfies statutory requirements for the enforcement of marine insurance contracts.

Second, the insurance policy evidences protection against marine perils and offers an im-

---

[1] Laryea Emmanuel T. Demateralisation of Insurance Documents in International Trade Transactions: A Need for Legislative Reform [J]. The University of New South Wales Law Journal, 2000-23 (1): 78-104.

portant assurance required by CIF buyers who pay against shipping documents and finances of documentary credit transactions who often take security over the documents.

Third, the insurance policy is assignable to the buyer or other parties, to transfer the beneficial interest in the insurance contract to them. Assignment of the insurance policy does not operate to confer "holder in due course" status, as the assignee takes the document subject to any equities, claims, counter-claims and defenses that the insurer may have against the assignor.

(2) Functions of the insurance certificate. Generally, the CIF seller must tender the insurance policy himself, but the parties may stipulate that a certificate of insurance be tendered instead of the policy.

Owing to the wide use of certificates of insurance in modern trade, however, it appears that a practice has evolved whereby a certificate of insurance that entitles the assured (or transferee) to demand the issue of a policy is regarded as equivalent to a formal policy. Such certificates should incorporate all the terms of the contract of insurance.

However, authorities at least in England and Australia, suggest that a certificate of insurance be not in law equivalent to an insurance policy. In some typical cases[1], the insurance certificate was rejected as not equating to the policy. One reason is that the buyer can not ascertain from the certificate whether the terms of the insurance contract are usual and customary in the trade as required under a CIF contract. Another reason is that the certificate cannot be assigned under the relevant marine insurance laws.

The decisive criterion in determining whether the certificate of insurance operates similarly to the policy and should be accepted under a CIF contract is whether it entitles the holder at any time to demand the issue of a formal policy.

According to the UCP 600 article 28, an insurance policy is acceptable in lieu of an insurance certificate, but an insurance certificate is not acceptable in lieu of an insurance policy.

(3) Functions of the insurance declaration under an open cover. Under CIF trade terms, the declaration under an open cover is usually sent by the seller to the insurer, to declare details of the consignment, and to effect the open cover. Under FOB and similar trade terms, the declaration under an open cover is usually sent by the buyer, basing on the contents of shipping advice from the seller, to the insurer, to declare details of the goods ordered and to make the open cover operative.

### 6.2.4 Contents and Specimen

A typical insurance document usually contains the following items:

(1) The words "Insurance Policy", or "Insurance Certificate".

---

① Diamond Alkali Export Corp v Fl Bourgeois.

(2) The unique reference number.

(3) Issuers and their signatures. The issuers of insurance documents may be insurance company, underwriter, and their agents.

According to the UCP 600 Article 28 and the ISBP 821 K2, insurance documents must appear to have been issued and signed by insurance companies or underwriters or their agents or proxies. If required by the insurance document or in accordance with the credit terms, all originals must appear to have been countersigned.

An insurance document is acceptable if issued on an insurance broker's stationery, provided the insurance document has been signed by an insurance company or its agent or proxy, or by an underwriter or its agent or proxy. A broker may sign as agent for the named insurance company or named underwriter. [1]

When an insurance document appears to have been signed by an agent or proxy, for or on behalf of the insurance company or underowriter, the name of the agent or proxy need not be stated. [2]

Insurance documents must be signed in accordance with the provisions of the UCP 600.

(4) Insured party and endorsement. The insured depends on the trade terms and L/C stipulations, for instance, under CIF trade term, the insured is usually the exporter, under FOB trade term, the insured is usually the importer.

Where necessary, the insurance document should be endorsed by the party to whose order claims are payable. A document issued to bearer is acceptable where the credit requires an insurance document endorsed in blank and vice versa. [3]

If a credit is silent as to the insured party, an insurance document evidencing that claims are payable to the order of the shipper or beneficiary would not be acceptable unless endorsed. An insurance document should be issued or endorsed so that the right to receive payment under it passes upon, or prior to, the release of the documents. [4]

(5) Date of issuance. Insurance documents must be dated even if a credit does not expressly so require, and the date of issuance must not be later than the date of shipment, except that such stipulation as "This cover is effective latest from the date of loading on board" or similar words included in the insurance document. [5]

(6) Goods description. This item refers to the relevant information of subject matter,

---

[1]  ISBP 821 K3.

[2]  ISBP 821 K2(b)

[3]  ISBP 821 K20.

[4]  ISBP 821 K21(a).

[5]  UCP 600 Article 28.

usually including name of commodity, quantity, numbers, shipping marks, etc.

Some insurance documents only note that subject matter is subject to Invoice No. or B/L No.

(7) Percentage and amount. An insurance document must be issued in the currency of and, as a minimum, for the amount required by the credit.

If there is no indication in the credit of the insurance coverage required, the amount of insurance coverage must be at least 110% of the CIF or CIP value of the goods.

An insurance document may indicate that the cover is subject to a franchise or excess (deductible).

If a credit requires the insurance cover to be irrespective of percentage, the insurance document must not contain a clause stating that the insurance cover is subject to a franchise or an excess deductible. ①

If it is apparent from the credit or from the documents that the final invoice amount only represents a certain part of the gross value of the goods (e. g. due to discounts, pre-payments or the like, or because part of the value of the goods is to be paid at a later date), the calculation of insurance cover must be based on the full gross value of the goods. ②

In addition, the rule of "round" is not applicable to the number after the decimal points of the invoice value, otherwise, inadequate amount insured.

(8) Premium and rate, transport vehicle . The premium and rate is simply written as arranged, while the transport vehicle is usually filled in brief, such as: by VICTORIA, by VICTORIA and EASTWIND, by VICTORIA and or steamer, by airplane or by air, by parcel post, by train Wagon No. 36, etc. depending on the mode of transportation.

(9) Sailing date and route. The sailing date and route is usually written as per B/L or as per AWB.

(10) Risks to be covered. An insurance document must cover the risks defined in the credit. Even though a credit may be explicit with regard to risks to be covered, there may be reference to exclusion clauses in the document.

If a credit requires "all risks" coverage, this is satisfied by the presentation of an insurance document evidencing any "all risks" clause or notation, even if it is stated that certain risks are excluded. An insurance document indicating that it covers Institute Cargo Clauses (A) satisfies a condition in a credit calling for an "all risks" clause or notation. ③

(11) Expiry date. An insurance document that incorporates an expiry date must clearly indicate that such expiry date relates to the latest date that loading on board or dispatch or taking

---

① ISBP 821 K14.
② ISBP 821 K15.
③ ISBP 821 K18.

in charge of the goods (as applicable) is to occur, as opposed to an expiry date for the presentation of any claims there-under. ①

(12) Copies of original. The insurance document may be issued in one original or in more than one original.

When the insurance document indicates that it has been issued in more than one original, all originals must be presented. ②

(13) Place of insurance claim payment . For convenience, place of insurance claim payment should be the port of destination.

(14) Amendment. The insurer is the only party who is entitled to make any amendments to insurance documents when necessary.

Furthermore, the insurance document must indicate that risks are covered at least between the place of taking in charge or shipment and the place of discharge or final destination as stated in the credit.

Two specimens of insurance documents are attached in the appendix part of this chapter.

## 6.3 Usual Customs and Practices

Usual customs and practices relevant to cargo insurance can be categorized into two types: usual customs and practices governing insurance coverage and conditions, and usual customs and practices governing insurance documents preparation and examination.

### 6.3.1 Insurance Documents Preparation and Examination

As for the preparation of and examination on the L/C based insurance documents, the UCP 600 Article 28 and the ISBP 821(K1~K23) provide very detailed interpretation and instruction, on the basis of which we have discussed the contents and items requirements in Section 6.2.4.

### 6.3.2 Insurance Coverage and Conditions

As for the coverage and conditions of marine cargo insurance, there are two influential clauses, I. C. C. (Institute Cargo Clauses) and C. I. C. (Marine Cargo Insurance Clause of PICC).

(1) I. C. C. (Institute Cargo Clauses). I. C. C. is a set of terms for cargo insurance policies voluntarily adopted as standard terms by many international marine insurance organizations, including the Institute of London Underwriters and the American Institute of Marine Under-writers. Widest insurance cover is provided under "Institute Cargo Clause A", a more restrictive cover under "Institute Cargo Clause B", and the most restrictive cover under "In-

---

① ISBP 821 K9.
② UCP 600 Article 28.

stitute Cargo Clause C". These clauses have replaced the older "All Risks", "With Average", and "Free from Particular Average" clauses. It is also called American Institute cargo clauses. ① The prevailing version of I. C. C. was revised in the year 2008 and took into effect in 2009.

Following is a summary of the risks covered under the three main sets of clauses. Each is subject to listed exclusions. ②

①Institute Cargo Clauses "C" cover loss of or damage to the subject matter insured, "reasonably attributable to":

- Fire or explosion.
- Vessel of craft being stranded, grounded, sunk or capsized.
- Overturning or derailment of land conveyance.
- Collision or contact of vessel, craft or conveyance with any external object other than water.
- Discharge of cargo at a port of distress.
- Loss of or damage to the subject matter insured caused by general average sacrifice.

To sum up, the "C" clauses provide major casualty coverage during the land, air or sea transit.

②Institute Cargo Clauses "B" provide all the cover available under the "C" clauses, and additional cover for loss of or damage to the subject matter insured "reasonably attributable to":

- Earthquake, volcanic eruption or lightening.

The insurance also covers loss of or damage to the subject matter caused by:

- Washing overboard.
- Entry of sea, lake or river water into the vessel, craft, hold, conveyance, container, lift-van or place of storage.
- Total loss of any package lost overboard or dripped while loading on to or unloading from vessel or craft.

The "B" clauses provide significant additional coverage; wet damage from sea, lake or river water and accidents in loading and discharging, but there is no coverage for theft, shortage and non-delivery.

③Institute Cargo Clauses "A" provide coverage for all risks of loss or damage to the subject matter insured. The words "all risks" should be understood in the context of the "A" clause to cover "fortuitous loss", but not "loss that occurs inevitably. "

General Exclusions including:

---

① http://www. businessdictionary. com/definition/institute-cargo-clauses. html.

② http://www. dtgruelle. com/articles/nuinsabc. html.

- Willful misconduct of the assured.
- Ordinary leakage, ordinary losses in weight or volume or ordinary wear and tear.
- Insufficient or unsuitability of packing or preparation of the subject matter insured.
- Inherent vice or nature of the subject matter insured.
- Delay.
- Insolvency or financial default of carrier.
- Deliberate damage to or deliberate destruction of the subject matter insured.
- Loss arising from nuclear weapons.

(2) C. I. C. (Marine Cargo Insurance Clause of the PICC). Under CIF based sales transaction, most Chinese exporters prefer to effect marine cargo insurance subject to C. I. C (dated Jan. 1, 1981). It thus deserves a detailed introduction as bellow. The C. I. C. contains 5 parts in total. [1]

①Part I. Scope of cover.

This insurance is classified into the following three Conditions: Free from Particular Average (F. P. A.), With Particular Average (W. P. A.) and All Risks. Where the goods insured hereunder sustain loss or damage, the company shall undertake to indemnify therefore according to the Insured condition specified in the Policy and the provisions of these clauses.

Following is a summary of the risks covered under the three main sets of clauses.

a. Free from Particular Average (F. P. A) covers:

- Total or constructive total loss caused by natural calamities.
- Total or partial loss caused by accidents.
- Partial loss of the insured goods attributable to heavy weather, lightning and/or tsunami, where the conveyance has been grounded, stranded, sunk or burnt, irrespective of whether the event or events took place before or after such accidents.
- Partial or total loss consequent on falling of entire package or packages into sea during loading, transshipment or discharge.
- Reasonable salvage cost incurred by the Insured, provided that such cost shall not exceed the sum insured of the consignment so saved.
- Losses attributable to discharge of the insured goods at a port of distress following a sea peril as well as special charges arising from loading, warehousing and forwarding of the goods at an intermediate port of call or refuge.
- Sacrifice in and contribution to General Average and Salvage Charges.
- Such proportion of losses sustained by the ship-owners as to be reimbursed by the Cargo Owner under the Contract of Affreightment "Both to Blame Collision" clause.

---

① http://www. julie8. cn/article. asp? id=914.

b. With Particular Average ( W. P. A. ). Aside from the risks covered under F. P. A. condition as above, this insurance also covers partial losses of the insured goods caused by heavy weather, lightning, tsunami, earthquake and/or flood.

c. All Risks. Aside from the risks covered under the F. P. A. and W. P. A. conditions as above, this insurance also covers all risks of loss of or damage to the insured goods whether partial or total, arising from external causes in the course of transit.

②Part II. Exclusions.

This insurance does not cover:

a. Loss or damage caused by the intentional act or fault of the insured.

b. Loss or damage falling under the liability of the consignor.

c. Loss or damage arising from the inferior quality or shortage of the insured goods prior to the attachment of this insurance.

d. Loss or damage arising from normal loss, inherent vice or nature of the insured goods, loss of market and/or delay in transit and any expenses arising there-from.

e. Risks and liabilities covered and excluded by the Ocean Marine Cargo War Risks Clauses and Strike, Riot and Civil Commotion Clauses of this Company.

③Part III. Commencement and termination of cover.

a. Warehouse to warehouse clause. This insurance attaches from the time the goods hereby insured leave the warehouse or place of storage named in the Policy for the commencement of the transit and continues in force in the ordinary course of transit including sea, land and inland waterway transits and transit in lighter until the insured goods are delivered to the consignee's final warehouse or place of storage at the destination named in the Policy or to any other place used by the Insured for allocation or distribution of the goods or for storage other than in the ordinary course of transit. This insurance shall, however, be limited to sixty (60) days after completion of discharge of the insured goods from the seagoing vessel at the final port of discharge before they reach the above mentioned warehouse or place of storage. If prior to the expiry of the above mentioned sixty (60) days, the insured goods are to be forwarded to a destination other than that named in the Policy, this insurance shall terminate at the commencement of such transit.

b. Special cases. If, owing to delay, deviation, forced discharge, reshipment or transshipment beyond the control of the Insured or any change or termination of the voyage arising from the exercise of a liberty granted to the ship-owners under the contract of affreightment, the insured goods arrive at a port or place other than that named in the Policy, subject to immediate notice being given to the Company by the Insured and an additional premium being paid, if required, this insurance shall remain in force and shall terminate as hereunder:

● If the insured goods are sold at port or place not named in the Policy, this insurance shall terminate on delivery of the goods sold, but in no event shall this insurance extend beyond sixty (60) days after completion of discharge of the insured goods from the carrying vessel at such port or place.

• If the insured goods are to be forwarded to the final destination named in the Policy or any other destination, this insurance shall terminate in accordance with Section 1 above.

④Part IV. Duty of the insured

It is the duty of the insured to attend to all matters as specified hereunder, failing which the company reserves the right to reject his claim for any loss if and when such failure prejudice the rights of the company:

a. The insured shall take delivery of the insured goods in good time upon their arrival at the port of destination named in the policy. In the event of any damage to the goods, the Insured shall immediately apply for survey to the survey and/or settling agent stipulated in the Policy. If the insured goods are found short in entire package(s) or to show apparent traces of damage, the Insured shall obtain from the carrier, bailee or other relevant authorities (customs and port authorities etc.) certificate of loss or damage and/or short-landed memo. Should the carrier, bailee or the other relevant authorities be responsible for such shortage or damage, the Insured shall lodge a claim with them in writing and, if necessary, obtain their confirmation of an extension of the time limit of validity of such claim.

b. The Insured shall, and the company may also, take reasonable measures immediately in salvaging the goods or prevention or minimizing a loss or damage thereto. The measures so taken by the insured or the company shall not be considered respectively, as a waiver of abandonment hereunder, or as an acceptance thereof.

c. In case of a change of voyage or any omission or error in the description of the interest, the name of the vessel or voyage, this insurance shall remain in force only upon prompt notice to this company when the Insured becomes aware of the same and payment of an additional premium if required.

d. The following documents should accompany any claim hereunder made against this company: Original Policy, Bill of Lading, Invoice, Packing List, Tally Sheet, Weight Memo, Certificate of Loss or Damage and/or Short-land Memo, Survey Report, Statement of Claim.

If any third party is involved, documents relative to pursuing of recovery from such party should also be included.

e. Immediate notice should be given to the company when the cargo owner's actual responsibility under the contract of affreightment "Both to Blame Collision" clause becomes known.

⑤Part V. The time of validity of a claim

The time of validity of a claim under this insurance shall not exceed a period of two years counting from the time of completion of discharge of the insured goods from the seagoing vessel at the final port of discharge.

## Questions and Problems

### I. True (T) or false (F).

1. An insurance policy is acceptable in lieu of an insurance certificate or a declaration under an open cover.

2. An insurance certificate is acceptable in lieu of an insurance policy.

3. The date of the insurance document must be no later than the date of shipment, unless it appears from the insurance document that the cover is effective from a date not later than the date of shipment.

4. The insurance document must indicate the amount of insurance coverage and be in the same currency as the credit.

5. The insurance document must indicate that risks are covered at least between the place of taking in charge or shipment and the place of discharge or final destination as stated in the credit.

6. An insurance document must not indicate that the cover is subject to a franchise or excess (deductible).

### II. Choose the best answer to fill in the blank.

1. A Chinese company concluded an export transaction with a foreign company under CIF term. To insure the cargoes from being stolen, the Chinese exporter shall cover_____.

A. W. P. A.          B. F. P. A.          C. A. R.          D. A. R. + TPND

2. A Chinese company concluded an export transaction with a foreign company under CIF term. If there are no specific stipulations concerning the insurance, the Chinese exporter shall effect_____.

A. W. P. A.          B. F. P. A          C. A. R.          D. A. R. and W. R.

3. The loss of the general average shall be borne by_____.

A. the carrier                          B. the party who suffers the loss

C. All parties proportionally          D. all parties equally

4. The invoice showing value counted as follows:

FOB Value: USD 9, 800. 00

Freight: USD 100. 00

Insurance: USD 100. 00

CIF Xiamen USD 10, 000. 00

Less discount USD 500. 00

Total amount payable: USD 9, 500. 00

The minimum amount of insurance coverage is_____.

A. USD 10,780. 00                          B. USD 10,450. 00

C. USD 11,000.00                    D. USD 12,000.00

5. An insurance document, such as an insurance policy, an insurance certificate or a declaration under an open cover, must appear to be issued and signed by_____.

A. an insurance company                    B. an underwriter

C. their agents                    D. their proxies

6. If there is no indication in the credit of the insurance coverage required, the amount of insurance coverage must be at least 110% of the_____value of the goods.

A. CIF                    B. CIP                    C. FCA                    D. CPT

### III. Calculation questions.

1. A Chinese Seller Co. in Shanghai exported a specific product to a U.S. Buyer Co. at USD 9,000 per metric ton CIF New York (subject to the Incoterms® 2020), and insurance was effected by the seller for 110% of CIF based invoice value, against all risks at 1% of insurance premium rate, as per C.I.C. dated 1/1/1981.

(1) Please calculate the insurance premium.

(2) Suppose the goods suffered damage in transit from Shanghai to New York, which accounts for 10% of the total lot, and the insurance company agreed to compensate the insured with I.O.P. (irrespective of percentage), please calculate the value of remedy covered by the insurance company.

(3) Suppose that the goods suffered damage in transit from Shanghai to New York, which accounts for 10% of the total lot, and the insurance company agreed to compensate the insured with deductible franchise of 5%, please calculate the value of remedy covered by the insurance company.

2. Supposing that there is a sales contract concluded on the basis of CIF trade term. Major terms and conditions are as follows:

• Quantity: 50,000 dozen

• Unit Price: USD 2.0/dozen CIF London

• Freight to named port of destination: USD 5,000

• Insurance: to be covered by the seller for 110% of invoice value, against WPA and War Risk at 0.4% and 0.6% respectively, as per C.I.C.

• Prevailing exchange rate: USD 100 = CNY 611.93/614.39

Please calculate:

(1) Total CIF based invoice value in USD.

(2) Payable Insurance Premium in USD.

(3) FOB based invoice value in USD.

(4) Net export income in (CNY).

## IV. Practical application.

1. Answer questions based on the insurance policy below：

(1) Invoice No.

(2) The Seller：

(3) Commodity：

(4) Quantity：

(5) Unit Price：

(6) Total Invoice Value：

(7) Packing：

(8) Shipping Mark：

(9) Insurance：

(10) Time of Shipment：

(11) Port of Shipment：

(12) Port of Destination：

(13) No. and Date of the insurance policy

(14) Place of claims payable：

| | | | |
|---|---|---|---|
| 中保财产保险有限公司<br>**The People's Insurance（Property）Company of China, Ltd** | | | |
| 发票号码<br>Invoice No. | INV52148 | 保险单号次<br>Policy No. | PICC241019 |
| 海洋货物运输保险单<br>**MARINE CARGO TRANSPORTATIONINSURANCE POLICY** | | | |
| 被保险人：<br>Insured： | NANJING FOREIGN TRADE IMP. AND EXP. CORP.<br>318 TIANSHI ROAD NANJING, CHINA | | |

中保财产保险有限公司(以下简称本公司)根据被保险人的要求,及其所缴付约定的保险费,按照本保险单承担险别和背面所载条款与下列特别条款承保下列货物运输保险,特签发本保险单。

This policy of Insurance witnesses that the People's Insurance（Property）Company of China, Ltd.（hereinafter called "The Company"）, at the request of the Insured and in consideration of the agreed premium paid by the Insured, undertakes to insure the under mentioned goods in transportation subject to conditions of the Policy as per the Clauses printed overleaf and other special clauses attached hereon.

续表

| 保险货物项目<br>Descriptions of Goods | 包装单位数量<br>Packing Unit Quantity | 保险金额<br>Amount Insured |
|---|---|---|
| LADIES LYCRA LONG PANT | 200 CTNS(2,400 PCS) | USD 5,280.00 |

| 承保险别<br>Conditions | 货物标记<br>Marks of Goods |
|---|---|
| ICC(A)and WAR RISKS | CBD/LONDON/NOS1-200 |

| 总保险金额:<br>Total Amount Insured: | UNITED STATES DOLLARS FIVE THOUSAND TWO HUNDRED AND EIGHTY ONLY | | | |
|---|---|---|---|---|
| 保费<br>Premium | AS ARRANGED | 载运输工具<br>Per conveyance S.S | DAFENG | 开航日期<br>Slg. on or abt | 2024-10-20 |
| 起运港<br>Form | NANJING | 目的港<br>To | | LONDON |

所保货物,如发生本保险单项下可能引起索赔的损失或损坏,应立即通知本公司下述代理人查勘。如有索赔,应向本公司提交保险单正本(本保险单共有 2 份正本)及有关文件。如一份正本已用于索赔,其余正本则自动失效。

In the event of loss or damage which may result in acclaim under this Policy, immediate notice must be given to the Company's Agent as mentioned here under. Claims, if any, one of the Original Policy which has been issued in two original(s) together with the relevant documents shall be surrendered to the Company. If one of the Original Policy has been accomplished, the others to be void.

| 赔款偿付地点<br>Claim payable at | LONDON | | |
|---|---|---|---|
| 日期<br>Date | 2024-10-19 | 在<br>at | NANJING (IN USD) |
| 地址:<br>Address: | ××××××××,NANJING,CHINA | | |

2. Fill in the blank form insurance policy according to the particulars below:

A. Relevant L/C terms and conditions

√APPLICANT: ZELLERS IMP & EXP CORP.

401 BAY STREET, 10/FL.

TORONTO ON MJH. 2Y4, CANADA

√BENEFICIARY: G. M. G. HARDWEAR & TOOLS IMP & EXP CO. LTD.

726 DONGFENG EAST STREET, GUANGZHOU, CHINA

√LOADING IN CHARGE: GUANGZHOU, CHINA

√FOR TRANSPORT TO···: VANCOUVER, CANADA

√DESCRIPT. OF GOODS: HANDLE TOOLS

| ITEM NO. | QUANTITY | UNIT PRICE CIF VANCOUVER |
|---|---|---|
| A0214 | 2,000 DOZ | USD 10.50 |
| A0012 | 1,000 DOZ | USD 11.50 |
| M0102 | 500 DOZ | USD 28.00 |

√AS PER SALES CONFIRMATION NO. 09GP520471 DD 03 JAN. 2024

√DOCUMENTS REQUIRED: +MARINE INSURANCE POLICY OR CERTIFICATE IN DUPLICATE, ENDORSED IN BLANK, FOR FULL INVOICE VALUE PLUS 10 PERCENT, STATING CLAIM PAYABLE IN CANADA COVERING ICC(A) AND WAR RISKS.

B. Other relevant information.

√Invoice No.: KW-240419; Invoice Date: 2024-04-10; Invoice Value: USD 46,500.00

√B/L Date: 2024-04-19

√S. S.: CHAOHE/ZIM CANADA V. 44E(TRANSSHIPPED AT HONGKONG)

√Shipping Marks: ZELLERS CANADA/VANCOUVER

√Insurance Policy No: KC03-85362

√Packing and No. of Packages: 10 DOZ/PACKAGE   350 PACKAGES

# 中保财产保险有限公司

### The People's Insurance (Property) Company of China, Ltd

| 发票号码<br>Invoice No. | | 保险单号次<br>Policy No. | |
|---|---|---|---|

# 海洋货物运输保险单

### MARINE CARGO TRANSPORTATIONINSURANCE POLICY

被保险人:
Insured:

中保财产保险有限公司(以下简称本公司)根据被保险人的要求,及其所缴付约定的保险费,按照本保险单承担险别和背面所载条款与下列特别条款承保下列货物运输保险,特签发本保险单。

This policy of Insurance witnesses that the People's Insurance (Property) Company of China, Ltd. (hereinafter called "The Company"), at the request of the Insured and in consideration of the agreed premium paid by the Insured, undertakes to insure the under mentioned goods in transportation subject to conditions of the Policy as per the Clauses printed overleaf and other special clauses attached hereon.

| 保险货物项目<br>Descriptions of Goods | 包装单位数量<br>Packing Unit Quantity | 保险金额<br>Amount Insured |
|---|---|---|
| | | |

| 承保险别<br>Conditions | 货物标记<br>Marks of Goods |
|---|---|
| | |

总保险金额:
Total Amount Insured:

| 保费<br>Premium | AS ARRANGED | 载运输工具<br>Per conveyance S. S | 开航日期<br>Slg. on or abt | |
|---|---|---|---|---|

| 起运港<br>Form | | 目的港<br>To | |
|---|---|---|---|

所保货物,如发生本保险单项下可能引起索赔的损失或损坏,应立即通知本公司下述代理人查勘。如有索赔,应向本公司提交保险单正本(本保险单共有　份正本)及有关文件。如一份正本已用于索赔,其余正本则自动失效。

 In the event of loss or damage which may result in acclaim under this Policy, immediate notice must be given to the Company's Agent as mentioned here under. Claims, if any, one of the Original Policy which has been issued in＿＿＿＿ original (s) together with the relevant documents shall be surrendered to the Company. If one of the Original Policy has been accomplished, the others to be void.

| 赔款偿付地点<br>Claim payable at | | |
|---|---|---|
| 日期<br>Date | 在<br>at | |
| 地址:<br>Address: | | |

# Appendix

## Marine Cargo Transportation Insurance Policy Specimen[1]

---

### MARINE CARGO TRANSPORTATION INSURANCE POLICY

**Invoice No.**

**Policy No.**

This policy of Insurance witnesses that the Insurance company ( hereinafter called "the Company" ) , at the Request of _____ ( hereinafter called the "Insured" ) and in consideration of the agreed premium being paid to the company by the Insured, undertakes to insure the under-mentioned goods in transportation subject to the conditions of this policy as per the Clauses printed overleaf and other special Clauses attached hereon.


Marks & Nos.

Quantity

Description of Goods

Amount Insured

Total Amount Insured _____

Premium as arranged

Rate as arranged

Per conveyance S. S. _____

Slg. on or abt. _____ from _____ to _____

Conditions _____

Claims, if any, payable on surrender of this Policy together with other relevant documents. In the event of accident whereby loss or damage may result in a claim under this Policy immediate notice applying for survey must be given to the Company's Agent as mentioned hereunder.

_____ Insurance Company

Claim payable at _____

Address of Issuing Office _____

BUSINESS DEPARTMENT

Our Contract Template Database is complied in accordance with laws of P. R. China. This English document is translated.

---

① http://www. julie8. cn/article. asp? id＝914.

## Cargo Transportation Insurance Policy Specimen

中国人民保险公司

**PICC**

The People's Insurance Company of China

总公司设于北京　一九四九年创立

Head Office Beijing　Established in 1949

# 货物运输保险单
## CARGO TRANSPORTATION INSURANCE POLICY

发票号(INVOICE NO.)
合同号(CONTRACT NO.)
信用证号(L/C NO.)
被保险人
INSURED：

保单号次
POLICY NO.

中国人民保险公司(以下简称本公司)根据被保险人的要求,由被保险人向本公司缴付约定的保险费,按照本保险单承保险别和背面所载条款与下列特款承保下述货物运输保险,特立本保险单。

THIS POLICY OF INSURANCE WITNESSES THAT THE PEOPLE's INSURANCE COMPANY OF CHINA (HEREINAFTER CALLED "THE COMPANY") AT THE REQUEST OF THE INSURED AND IN CONSIDERATION OF THE AGREED PREMIUM PAID TO THE COMPANY BY THE INSURED, UNDERTAKES TO INSURE THE UNDERMENTIONED GOODS IN TRANSPORTATION SUBJECT TO THE CONDITIONS OF THIS POLICY AS PER THE CLAUSES PRINTED OVERLEAF AND OTHER SPECIAL CLAUSES ATTACHED HEREON.

| 标　记<br>MARKS&NOS | 包装及数量<br>QUANTITY | 保险货物项目<br>DESCRIPTION OF GOODS | 保险金额<br>AMOUNT INSURED |
|---|---|---|---|
|  |  |  |  |

总保险金额：
TOTAL AMOUNT INSURED＿＿＿＿＿＿＿＿＿

保费：　　AS
PERMIUM <u>ARRANGED</u>
自
FROM：＿＿＿＿＿

起运日期
DATE OF
COMMENCEMENT＿＿＿＿＿
经
VIA＿＿＿＿＿

装载运输工具：
PER CONVEYANCE：＿＿＿＿＿
至
TO＿＿＿＿＿＿

承保险别：
CONDITIONS

所保货物,如发生保险单项下可能引起索赔的损失或损坏,应立即通知本公司下述代理人查勘。如有索赔,应向本公司提交保单正本(本保险单共有＿＿＿＿份正本)及有关文件。如一份正本已用于索赔,其余正本自动失效。

IN THE EVENT OF LOSS OR DAMAGE WHICH MAY RESULT IN A CLAIM UNDER THIS POLICY, IMMEDIATE NOTICE MUST BE GIVEN TO THE COMPANY's AGENT AS MENTIONED HEREUNDER. CLAIMS, IF ANY, ONE OF THE ORIGINAL POLICY WHICH HAS BEEN ISSUED IN＿＿＿＿ORIGINAL(S) TOGETHER WITH THE RELEVANT DOCUMENTS SHALL BE SURRENDERED TO THE COMPANY. IF ONE OF THE ORIGINAL POLICY HAS BEEN ACCOMPLISHED,THE OTHERS TO BE VOID.

中国人民保险公司
The People's Insurance Company of China

赔款偿付地点
CLAIM PAYABLE AT＿＿＿＿＿＿
出单日期
ISSUING DATE＿＿＿＿＿

Authorized Signature

212

# Chapter 7　Payment Documents

【本章提要】

对外贸易货款结算多采用非现金结算,即多以汇票、本票、支票等金融票据为结算工具进行。金融票据具备无因性、要式性、文义性和流通性等特点。

汇票是一个人开给另一个人的,由发出命令者签名,要求受票人在见票时或将来某一固定时间或在将来某一可确定时间,将一定的货币金额付给特定人或特定人指定的人或来人的无条件的书面支付命令。

汇票有三个基本当事人:出票人、受票人/付款人、受/收款人。必要时汇票还会有背书人、保证人、承兑人和被背书人。所有在汇票上做过亲笔签名的人,都对持票人负有付款责任。

根据出票人,汇票可分为商业汇票和银行汇票。跟单信用证和跟单托收项下的汇票出票人都是出口方,均为商业汇票;票汇(D/D)项下汇票的出票人为进口方银行,为银行汇票。

根据付款期限,汇票可分为即期汇票和远期汇票。使用即期汇票需要一次提示,即向受票人/付款人提示汇票要求付款。使用远期汇票需要两次提示,向受票人提示汇票要求承兑和向承兑人提示汇票要求付款。根据承兑人不同,远期汇票可分为商业承兑汇票和银行承兑汇票。

根据是否随附商业单据,汇票可分为跟单汇票和光票。跟单信用证和跟单托收项下使用的汇票通常为跟单汇票,票汇项下的汇票为光票。

根据中国票据法,一份有效汇票应包括:①"汇票"字样;②无条件支付命令;③确定的货币金额;④受票人/付款人;⑤受/收款人;⑥出票日期;⑦出票人签字。未记载以上事项之一的,汇票无效。

汇票的使用通常包括:①出票;②提示;③承兑和/或付款;④背书和贴现;⑤拒付和追索等票据行为。

本票是由一个人开给另一个人的,由出票人签名,保证凭票或在规定日期,或在将来某一可确定的日期,将一定的货币金额付给特定的人或特定人指定的人或来人的无条件的书面的支付承诺。

本票有两个基本当事人:出票人和受/收款人。

根据出票人,本票可分为商业本票和银行本票;根据付款期限,本票可分为即期本票和远期本票;根据对持票人的付款责任,有多个出票人的本票可分为共同本票、共同和个别本票。

根据中国票据法,一份有效本票应包括:①"本票"字样;②无条件支付承诺;③确定的货币金额;④受/收款人;⑤出票日期;⑥出票人签字。未记载以上事项之一的,本票无效。

支票是以银行为付款人的即期汇票,可以看作汇票的特例。

根据中国票据法和《支付结算办法》,一份支票必须包括:①"支票"字样;②无条件支付委托;③确定的金额;④付款人名称;⑤出票日期;⑥出票人签章。未记载以上事项之一的,支票无效。不过,支票的金额和收款人名称两项可以通过出票人以授权补记的方式记载,未补记前不得使用。

Payment, one most important process in international trade, has been settled more commonly by documents/instruments than by cash. Consequently, payment documents are playing dominant roles in the practice of international trade payment and settlement.

This chapter will discuss payment documents, including general introduction, bill of exchange, promissory note and cheque (check)[1], etc.

# 7.1　General Introduction

## 7.1.1　Definition

Payment documents, most commonly known as negotiable instruments, are contracts for the payment of money. Just as the name implies, they are instruments used in international trade payment and settlement, and they are negotiable. That is, the rights on them can be transferred from one person to another. [2]

In a broad sense, negotiable instruments refer to any commercial title ownership. In a narrow sense, negotiable instruments are written documents that contain an unconditional promise (promissory note) by the drawer to pay the payee or an unconditional order (bill of exchange or cheque) by the drawer to the drawee to pay the payee a fixed amount of money at a definite time.

This chapter is about to discuss negotiable instruments in a narrow sense.

## 7.1.2　Players

According to the roles played, parties to payment documents can be divided into basic players and derivative players.

(1) Basic players. Basic players are those parties who exist in every typical negotiable instrument, including Drawer/Maker, Drawee/Payer, and Payee.

①Drawer. The drawer is the party that gives an unconditional order or promised to pay,

---

① Check(American English) and cheque(British and Canadian English) may be used interchangeably.

② http://en. wikipedia. org/wiki/Negotiable_instrument.

engages that the instrument will be accepted or paid on due presentation. If dishonor occurs, the drawer will compensate the holder or any endorser who is compelled to pay the instrument, on condition that the requisite proceeding on dishonor is duly taken.

In the case of promissory note and cheque, the drawer is also called the maker.

②Drawee. The drawee is the party that is directed by the drawer to pay, also known as the payer. The drawee of a bill of exchange is the person to whom the payment order is given, the drawee of a promissory note is the drawer himself, and the drawee of a cheque is the drawee bank.

③Payee. The payee is the party who has the right to ask the drawee to pay. When a negotiable instrument is payable to order, the payee may transfer the instrument by endorsement and delivery; when a negotiable instrument is payable to bearer, the payee may transfer the instrument by mere delivery. When non-payment or non-acceptance occurred, the payee has the right of recourse to the drawer.

Sometimes one party may play two roles. For instance, when a bill of exchange is drawn payable to the drawer, then the drawer and the payee are identical to each other.

(2) Derivative players. Several derivative players may appear depending on different circumstances.

①Transferor /Transferee. The payee or holder may transfer a negotiable instrument to another person. In this case, the payee or holder is called the transferor, while the person to whom the negotiable instrument is transferred is called the transferee.

②Endorser/Endorsee. When a negotiable instrument is payable to a named person or order, the payee or holder of the negotiable instrument may sign his name on the back of the instrument and transfer it to another party. The payee or holder who has signed his name on the back of the instrument and has transferred it is called an endorser, and the person to whom the instrument is transferred is called an endorsee.

③Prior party /Subsequent party. To the endorsee, all the endorsers on the instrument before him are called its prior parties, and to the endorser, all the endorsees after him are called its subsequent parties.

④Acceptor. The acceptor is the drawee that has accepted a time draft. By signing his name on the face of a time draft, the drawee accepts the time draft and engages that he will pay it as stated in the instrument or as accepted by.

⑤Guarantor. A guarantor is the person who guarantees the payment or acceptance of a negotiable instrument. Typically, he is not a party already liable to the instrument.

⑥Holder. The holder of a negotiable instrument is the person who possesses the instrument. He may be the payee, endorsee or bearer.

⑦Holder for value. The holder for value is a person who possesses an instrument for which value has been given by himself or by some other person prior to him. The value can be given in the forms of money, goods, or services. If a person has a lien on the instrument, the person is also deemed to be a holder for value.

⑧Holder in due course. The holder in due course, may also known as bona fide holder, refers to an individual who acquires a negotiable instrument in good faith. Good faith means the observance of honorable intent in business relations and the avoidance of any attempts to deceive in assuming and performing contractual obligations.

Typically, a holder in due course is the holder who meets the following four requirements:

● The instrument should be complete and regular on its face.

● The instrument is before maturity and the holder did not notice its previous dishonor, if any.

● The holder took it in good faith and for value.

● The holder did not notice any infirmity in the instrument or defect in the title of the person negotiating it.

To be noted, a holder for value may or may not be a holder in due course, but a holder in due course must be a holder for value.

### 7.1.3 Characteristics

Compare with documents of delivery, transport and insurance, payment documents have the following characteristics.

(1) Non-causative nature. The so-called "non-causative" implies that the existence of a negotiable instrument is independent of the underlying commercial or financial relationship between the drawer and the drawee.

When the payee transfers the draft to a transferee, the latter will not mind how the instrument was generated and his only concern is that the instrument must be in a qualified form and contain the essential item required by the relative negotiable instrument law.

(2) Literally determined. The "non-causative" nature of negotiable instruments demands that all rights and liabilities of negotiable instruments must be literally determined. Specifically, in addition to the fact that the act related to negotiable instruments must be taken in accordance with the lawful procedures and forms, the contents and items of negotiable instruments must be in strict conformity with the relevant statutory requirements, otherwise the instruments will be void.

(3) Requisite in form. The fact that all rights and liabilities of negotiable instruments are determined literally indicates that negotiable instruments must meet some mandatory legal requirements on their forms. For instance, according to the Uniform Law for Bills of Exchange and Promissory Notes of Geneva (1930), a negotiable instrument must be in the form of a

document containing certain required items as follows:

- The word "bill of exchange"/"promissory note"/"cheque".
- Be in writing.
- Be signed by the maker or drawer.
- Be an unconditional promise or order to pay.
- Certain amount in figures and in words.
- Date and place of issue.
- Be payable on demand or at a definite time.
- Name of payee.
- Name and address of drawee.

(4) Negotiability. The three above mentioned characteristics determine the negotiability of negotiable instruments. That is, the title to a negotiable instrument can be transferred by delivery or by endorsement plus delivery. Here the title refers to the rights embodied in a negotiable instrument, including the holder's claim for a fixed sum of money payment on the obligor and the right of recourse on the prior party.

When a negotiable instrument is payable to bearer, it may be transferred by mere delivery and no endorsement is required. When a negotiable instrument is payable to a named person or order, it may be transferred by endorsement and delivery.

### 7.1.4  Guidance

There are several laws and usual customs and practices governing negotiable instruments, including:

- The Bills of Exchange Act of 1882 of U. K.
- The Uniform Commercial Code of 1962 (Article 3) of U. S.
- French and German law.
- The Uniform law for Bills of Exchange and Promissory Notes of Geneva of 1930 of UN.
- The Convention Providing a Uniform Law for International Bills of Exchange and International Promissory Notes and Convention Providing a Uniform Law for International Checks (1988) of UN.
- The Negotiable Instrument Law of People's Republic of China (2004 Revision).

## 7.2  Bill of Exchange

### 7.2.1  Definition

Bill of exchange, one of the key financial instruments in international trade, can be defined into different versions by different laws. In general, the two most influential definitions come from the two world-wide used negotiable instrument laws—the U. K. Bills of Exchange Act of 1882 and the Uniform Law for Bills of Exchange and Promissory Notes of Geneva of 1930.

(1) Definition from the U. K. Bills of Exchange Act of 1882 . A bill of exchange is "an unconditional order in writing addressed by one person to another, signed by the person giving it, requiring the person to whom it is addressed to pay on demand or at a fixed or determinable future time a sum certain in money to or to the order of a specified person or to bearer".

In fact, it is an almost perfect definition, as good as any group of Parliamentary draftsman has drafted[1], and has been generally used in almost all the textbooks on International Trade Payment and Settlement in China, and many other countries[2] that are all under the U. K. Bills of Exchange Act of 1882.

(2) Definition from the Uniform Law for Bills of Exchange and Promissory Notes of Geneva of 1930. A bill of exchange is an instrument that must:

• Be inserted with the words "Bill of Exchange" in the body of the instrument and expressed in the language employed in drawing up the instrument.

• Bear unconditional order to pay a determinable sum of money.

• Bear the name of the person who is to pay.

• Bear a statement of the time of payment.

• Bear a statement of the place where payment is to be made.

• Bear the name of the person to whom or to whose order payment is to be made.

• Bear a statement of the date and of the place where the bill is issued.

• Bear the signature of the person who issues the bill.

This definition is popularly used world widely, because more than 40 countries[3] all over the world are under the influence of the Geneva Uniform Law.

However, a bill of exchange can be briefly defined as a three-party instrument that is an unconditional written order by one party that orders the second party to pay money to a third party.

### 7.2.2  Specimens

To have a better understanding of bill of exchange, four specimens are given below: the first one is a demand draft, the second one is a time draft, and the last two are drafts under L/Cs.

---

① Geoffrey Whitehead (1983). Elements of International Trade and Payment. Great Britain: Wood head-Faulkner Ltd.

② Ireland, Cyprus, Hong Kong China, India, Israel, Malaysia, Pakistan, Philippines, Singapore, Sri Lanka, Australia, Fiji, New Zealand, and Tonga.

③ Germany, Denmark, Finland, France, Greece, Iceland, Italy, Luxembourg, Malta, the Netherlands, Norway, Portugal, Spain, Sweden, Switzerland, Turkey, Indonesia, Poland, etc. and some Asian countries such as Japan, Indonesia, Korea, etc.

## Specimen 1: A bill of exchange payable on demand

Exchange for US $1,000.00                                                      Shanghai, March 5, 2024

    At sight pay to the order of ABC Bank the sum of one thousand US dollars only value received.

To: The ... Bank

New York, U. S. A.

                                               For China...Import & Export Co.

                                                  (Authorized Signature)

## Specimen 2: A bill of exchange payable at future time

Exchange for US $1,000.00                                                   SHANGHAI, MARCH 5, 2024

    At 30 days after sight pay to the order of ABC Bank the sum of one thousand US dollars only value received.

To: The... Bank

New York, U. S. A.

                                             For China ... Import & Export Co.

                                                  (Authorized Signature)

## Specimen 3: A bill of exchange drawn under an L/C

Drawn under Credit Commercial de France, Hong Kong, irrevocable L/C No. LC654321 dated July 3,... payable with interest @... % No. 56789.

Exchange for USD 5,000.00                                                        Jiangsu,July,2024

at 30 days sight of this First of Exchange (Second of Exchange unpaid)

Pay to the order of Bank of Communications the sum of U. S. Dollars Five Thousand only.

To: Credit Commercial de France, Hong Kong

                                                    General Manager

                                                    (Signature)

## Specimen 4: Bill of exchange under an irrevocable L/C both in English and Chinese

### BILL OF EXCHANGE

凭
Drawn Under

不可撤销信用证
Irrevocable    L/C No.

日期
Date

支 取 Payable
With interest     @      % 按 息      付款

号码
No.

汇票金额
Exchange for

南京
Nanjing

见票
at

日后(本汇票之副本未付)付交
sight of this FIRST of Exchange (Second of Exchange Being unpaid)

Pay to the order of

金额
the sum of

此致
To

### 7.2.3 Players

Players involved in a bill of exchange can be classified into basic players and derivative players.

(1) Basic players. As a three party instrument, a draft has three basic players.

①Drawer. The drawer is the party that gives an unconditional order to pay. In the practice of international trade, the drawer is usually the exporter, the beneficiary of relevant L/C.

The drawer of a bill, by drawing it – (A) engages that on due presentment it shall be accepted and paid according to its tenor, and that if it be dishonored he will compensate the holder or any endorser who is compelled to pay it, provided that the requisite proceedings on dishonor be duly taken; (B) is precluded from denying to a holder in due course the existence of the payee and his then capacity to endorse. ①

②Drawee. The drawee of a bill of exchange is the person to whom the unconditional payment order is given, also known as the payer. The drawee of the bill under collection is usually the importer, while the drawee of the bill under credit is usually the L/C-issuing bank.

③Payee. The payee is the party who has the right to ask the drawee to pay. In the practice of international trade, the payee of the bill under collection is usually the exporter, and that under credit is usually the beneficiary of relevant L/C or its bank.

In practice, a bill may be drawn payable to, or to the order of, the drawer; or it may be drawn payable to, or to the order of, the drawee. Where in a bill drawer and drawee are the same person, or where the drawee is a fictitious person or a person not having capacity to contract, the holder may treat the instrument, at his option, either as a bill of exchange or as a promissory note. ②

(2) Derivative players.

①Acceptor. The acceptor is the person (usually the drawee) who takes the bill and either writes "Accepted" and his own name on it, or just signs it.

The acceptor of a bill, by accepting it – (A) engages that he will pay it according to the tenor of his acceptance; (B) is precluded from denying to a holder in due course: (a) the existence of the drawer, the genuineness of his signature, and his capacity and authority to draw the bill; (b) in the case of a bill payable to drawer's order, the then capacity of the drawer to endorse, but not the genuineness or validity of his endorsement; (c) in the case of a bill payable to the order of a third person, the existence of the payee and his then capacity to endorse, but not the genuineness or validity of his endorsement. ③

---

① U. K. Bill of Exchange Act 1882 Article 55(1).
② U. K. Bill of Exchange Act 1882 Article 5.
③ U. K. Bill of Exchange Act 1882 Article 54.

The acceptor for honour is liable to the holder and to all parties to the bill subsequent to the party for whose honour he has accepted. ①

②endorser. The endorser is the person who writes on the back of an order bill, either writes "pay to × or to order of ×" and his name on it, or just signs it.

The endorser of a bill, by endorsing it—( A ) engages that on due presentment it shall be accepted and paid according to its tenor, and that if it be dishonored he will compensate the holder or a subsequent endorser who is compelled to pay it, provided that the requisite proceedings on dishonour be duly taken; ( B ) is precluded from denying to a holder in due course the genuineness and regularity in all respects of the drawer's signature and all previous endorsements; ( C ) is precluded from denying to his immediate or a subsequent endorsee that the bill was at the time of his endorsement a valid and subsisting bill, and that he had then a good title thereto. ②

③Bearer/Holder. The bearer means the person in possession of a bill which is payable to bearer.

The holder means the payee or endorsee of a bill who is in possession of it, or the bearer thereof.

The rights and powers of the holder of a bill are as follows: ( A ) He may sue on the bill in his own name. ( B ) Where he is a holder in due course, he holds the bill free from any defect of title of prior parties, as well as from mere personal defenses available to prior parties among themselves, and may enforce payment against all parties liable on the bill. ( C ) Where his title is defective ( a ) if he negotiates the bill to a holder in due course, that holder obtains a good and complete title to the bill, and ( b ) if he obtains payment of the bill, the person who pays him in due course gets a valid discharge for the bill. ③

Where a bill has been lost before it is overdue, the person who was the holder of it may apply to the drawer to give him another bill of the same tenor, giving security to the drawer if required to indemnify him against all persons whatever in case the bill alleged to have been lost shall be found again. If the drawer on request as aforesaid refuses to give such duplicate bill, he may be compelled to do so. ④

④Referee in case of need. The drawer of a bill and any endorser may insert therein the name of a person to whom the holder may resort in case of need, that is to say, in case the bill is dishonored by non-acceptance or non-payment. Such person is called the referee in case of

---

① The Bills of Exchange Act 1882 Article 66.
② The Bills of Exchange Act 1882 Article 55( 2 ).
③ The Bills of Exchange Act 1882 Article 38.
④ The Bills of Exchange Act 1882 Article 69.

need. It is in the option of the holder to resort to the referee in case of need or not as he may think fit. ①

⑤Guarantor. A guarantor is the person who guarantees the payment or acceptance of a bill of exchange. Typically, he is not a party already liable to the instrument.

⑥Accommodation party. An accommodation party to a bill is a person who has signed a bill as drawer, acceptor, or endorser, without receiving value therefore, and for the purpose of lending his name to some other person. An accommodation party is liable on the bill to a holder for value; and it is immaterial whether, when such holder took the bill, he knew such party to be an accommodation party or not. ②

To be noted, no person is liable as drawer, endorser, or acceptor of a bill who has not signed it as such: provided that (A) where a person signs a bill in a trade or assumed name, he is liable thereon as if he had signed it in his own name; (B) the signature of the name of a firm is equivalent to the signature by the person so signing of the names of all persons liable as partners in that firm. ③

Where a person signs a bill as drawer, endorser, or acceptor, and adds words to his signature, indicating that he signs for or on behalf of a principal, or in a representative character, he is not personally liable thereon; but the mere addition to his signature of words describing him as an agent, or as filling a representative character, does not exempt him from personal liability. In determining whether a signature on a bill is that of the principal or that of the agent by whose hand it is written, the construction most favourable to the validity of the instrument shall be adopted. ④

(3) The relationship of the parties to a bill of exchange. The relationship of the parties to a bill of exchange is discussed under the following two circumstances.

①Sight draft. As shown in figure 7. 1, the party D, the holder of this sight/demand draft, is the only obligee. Parties including A, B, C, E, F are all obligors, among whom the drawer A is the principal obligor who is primarily liable for the payment of the draft, and B, C, E, F are the secondary obligors who are secondarily liable for the payment of the draft. The party E, the guarantor of party C in this case, can be any obligor's guarantor. ⑤

---

① The Bills of Exchange Act 1882 Article 15.
② The Bills of Exchange Act 1882 Article 28.
③ The Bills of Exchange Act 1882 Article 23.
④ The Bills of Exchange Act 1882 Article 26.
⑤ Zhao Wei. International Settlement: Payment Techniques in International Trade Finance. Nanjing: South-eastern University Press, 2005.

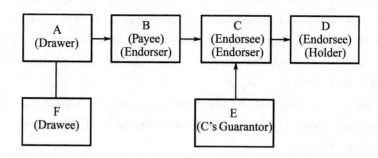

**Figure 7. 1   The relationship of the parties to a sight bill of exchange**[1]

②Time draft.   As shown in figure 7. 2, the party D, the holder of this usance/time draft, is the only obligee. Before acceptance, the party F, the drawee, is the secondary obligor, and the party A, the drawer, is the principal obligor. After acceptance, however, F, the acceptor, becomes the principal obligor, and A, B, C, and E secondary obligors. Although after acceptance F becomes the principal obligor, if he dishonors the accepted draft, the obligee has to enforce his right of recourse against C, E, B, and finally to A for payment.

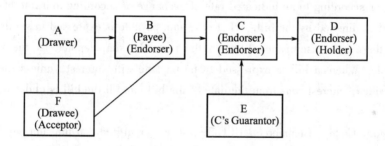

**Figure 7. 2   The relationship of the parties to a usance bill of exchange**[1]

## 7.2.4   Essential Items

The above four specimens of bill of exchange can help us to sum up the essential items contained in a typical draft.

( 1 ) The word "Exchange", "Bill of Exchange" or "Draft" . In order to distinguish a bill of exchange from a promissory note or a check, the word "Exchange" or similar word is usually clearly indicated on the face of a bill of exchange.

---

① Zhao Wei. International Settlement: Payment Techniques in International Trade Finance. Nanjing: South-eastern University Press,2005.

The Uniform Law for Bills of Exchange and Promissory Notes of Geneva of 1930 stipulated clearly that the term "Bill of Exchange" must be inserted in the body of a bill and expressed in the language employed in drawing up the bill. Negotiable Instrument Law of People's Republic of China also has identical stipulation. However, the U. K. Bills of Exchange Act of 1882 has no specific requirement for it.

Both the Bills of Exchange Act of 1882 of the U. K. and the Uniform Law for Bills of Exchange and Promissory Notes of Geneva of 1930 stipulate that a bill of exchange should contain an unconditional order to pay.

The correct way of expressing an unconditional order is "Pay ···" or "Please pay ... ". Sentences like "If the goods meet the requirements, please pay A Co. $1,000" or "I should be pleased if you would kindly pay ... "are not unconditional orders, but requests.

According to the Bills of Exchange Act of 1882, "Pay from my No. 2 A/C to Mary Malt by the sum of £ 10" is not valid, while "Pay Mary Malt by the sum of £ 10 and debit my No. 2 A/C" is valid.

(2) A sum certain in money. The Bills of Exchange Act of 1882 stipulated that the sum payable by a bill is a sum certain in money. However, it may be paid with interest; by stated installments; with a provision that upon default in payment of any installments the whole shall become due; or according to an indicated rate of exchange or according to a rate of exchange to be ascertained as directed by the bill. Where the sum payable is expressed in words and also in figures, and there is a discrepancy between the two, the sum denoted by the words is the amount payable. Where a bill is expressed to be payable with interest, unless the instrument otherwise provides, interest runs from the date of the bill, and if the bill is undated from the issue thereof.

The Uniform Code of Commerce [ UCC 3-104( a ) ] required that the sum payable by a bill must be a fixed amount in money. The amount must be on the face of the instrument, and it may include payment of interest, discount, and costs of collection. Moreover, the amount must be payable in money, i. e. in U. S. or foreign country's currency. If payment is to be made in goods, services, or non-monetary items, the instrument is nonnegotiable.

A draft is to be drawn for the amount demanded under the presentation[1]. The amount may be expressed both in figures and in words. If both are shown, the amount in words must accurately reflect the amount in figures. The currency must be indicated as stated in the credit. [2] When the amount in words and figures are in conflict, the amount in words is to be examined as

[1]  ISBP 821, B13.
[2]  ISBP 821, B14.

the amount demanded. ①

Some countries customarily use the smaller one as the amount, though. According to the Negotiable Instrument Law of the People'Republic of China, a discrepancy between the two amounts will render the instrument invalid. In addition, the amount may be paid with interest. In this, the interest rate must be indicated clearly on the bill.

(3) Name and address of the drawee. Under L/C transaction, A draft, when required, is to be drawn on the bank stated in the credit. ②, usually the issuing bank or its nominated bank. A credit may be issued requiring a draft drawn on the applicant as one of the required documents, but must not be issued available by drafts drawn on the applicant.

The name and address of the drawee must be reasonably clear and definite. If there are two drawees, A and B, it indicates that both A and B will be liable for the payment jointly and severally, and the drawee item in a draft should be written as "To A and B", not "To A or B".

(4) The signature of the drawer. Under L/C transaction, the draft must be drawn by the beneficiary③.

Even if not stated in the credit, drafts require a signature. A signature means "a handwritten signature, its facsimile or an equivalent authentication effected by any other means" ④. Without the signature of the drawer, a draft is invalid.

The drawer of a bill of exchange may be an individual or a legal entity. If it is an individual, the person himself signs the bill; if it is a legal entity, the authorized manager signs on behalf of the entity.

Unauthorized or forged signature of the drawer makes a draft invalid.

(5) Date and place of issue. Drafts must be dated even if a credit does not expressly so require⑤. The date of issue can be used to determine the expiry date of the draft. For instance, the Uniform Law for Bills of Exchange and Promissory Notes of Geneva of 1930 stipulated that the validity period for a sight bill should be "one year from the date of issue". The issuing date can also be used to calculate the paying date when a bill is payable at 30/60/90 days after date. Moreover, the date of issue can be used to determine the date of presentment and the date of acceptance; they should not be prior to this date.

Where a bill expressed to be payable at a fixed period after date is issued undated, or where the acceptance of a bill payable at a fixed period after sight is undated, any holder may

---

① ISBP 821, B14.
② ISBP 821, B1.
③ ISBP 821, B8.
④ the United Nations Commission on International Trade Law (UNCITRAL) Convention on International Bills of Exchange and International Promissory Notes of 1988.
⑤ ISBP 821, B5.

insert therein the true date of issue or acceptance, and the bill shall be payable accordingly. Provided that (A) where the holder in good faith and by mistake inserts a wrong date, and (B) in every case where a wrong date is inserted, if the bill subsequently comes into the hands of a holder in due course the bill shall not be avoided thereby, but shall operate and be payable as if the date so inserted had been the true date. [1]

Place of issue is usually not a mandatory of a draft. However, it may be used to determine the applicable law for an international draft. If there is no indication of such a place, the place where the drawer resides is considered the place of issue.

(6) Name of the payee. A draft may be payable to a named person only, a named person or order, or bearer; there are thus three different ways of writing the payee of a draft.

A bill of exchange, payable to a named person only or to a named person not transferable, is a restricted order, and thus is a non-negotiable instrument. It can not be transferred to another person. The ways of writing such an order are: "Pay A Co. only" "Pay A Co. not transferable" "Pay A Co." plus "Not Transferable" on the face of the bill.

A bill of exchange, payable to the order of a particular person or to a particular person without any words indicating the prohibition of further transfer, is a demonstrative order. The frequent ways of writing such an order are: "Pay to A Co. or order" "Pay to the order of A Co." "Pay A Co.". There are no words like "Not Transferable" on the face of the bill.

A draft may be payable to bearer without a specific person as the payee. For example: "Pay bearer" "Pay A Co. or bearer".

To sum up, the payee must be indicated with certainty. Where a bill is not payable to bearer, the payee must be named or otherwise indicated therein with reasonable certainty. A bill may be made payable to two or more payees jointly, or it may be made payable in the alternative to one of two, or one or some of several payees. A bill may also be made payable to the holder of an office for the time being. Where the payee is a fictitious or non-existing person the bill may be treated as payable to bearer[2].

(7) Tenor. Tenor means the due date of a bill on which the drawer or the acceptor should effect payment. A bill may be payable on demand or at a future time.

When a bill is payable on demand, it is expressed to be payable on demand, or at sight, or on presentation; or in which no time for payment is expressed. When a bill is payable at a future time, it may be expressed to be payable (A) at a fixed period after date or sight; or (B) on or at a fixed period after the occurrence of a specified event which is certain to happen, though the time of happening may be uncertain. An instrument expressed to be payable on a

---

[1] The Bills of Exchange Act of 1882, Article 12.
[2] The Bills of Exchange Act of 1882, Article 7.

contingency is not a bill, and the happening of the event does not cure the defect. [1]

Under L/C transaction, the tenor of a draft must be in accordance with the terms of the credit[2].

If a draft is drawn at a tenor other than sight, or other than a certain period after sight, it must be possible to establish the maturity date from the data in the draft itself.

As an example of where it is possible to establish a maturity date from the data in the draft, if a credit calls for drafts at a tenor 60 days after the bill of lading date, where the date of the bill of lading is July 12,2024, the tenor could be indicated on the draft in one of the following ways:

- "60 days after bill of lading date July 12, 2024", or
- "60 days after July 12, 2024", or
- "60 days after bill of lading date" and elsewhere on the face of the draft state "bill of lading date July 12, 2024", or
- "60 days date" on a draft dated the same day as the date of the bill of lading, or
- "September 10, 2024", i. e. 60 days after the bill of lading date.

If the tenor refers to ×××days after the bill of lading date, the on board date is deemed to be the bill of lading date even if the on board date is prior to or later than the date of issuance of the bill of lading.

The expression "on or about" or similar will be interpreted as a stipulation that an event is to occur during a period of five calendar days before until five calendar days after the specified date, both start and end dates included. The words "to", "until", "till", "from" and "between" when used to determine a period of shipment include the date or dates mentioned, and the words "before" and "after" exclude the date mentioned. The words "from" and "after" when used to determine a maturity date exclude the date mentioned. The terms "first half" and "second half" of a month shall be construed respectively as the 1st to the 15th and the 16th to the last day of the month, all dates inclusive. The terms "beginning", "middle" and "end" of a month shall be construed respectively as the 1st to the 10th, the 11th to the 20th and the 21st to the last day of the month, all dates inclusive. [3]

If a bill of lading showing more than one on board notation is presented under a credit which requires drafts to be drawn, for example, at 60 days after or from bill of lading date, and the goods according to both or all on board notations were shipped from ports within a permitted geographical area or region, the earliest of these on board dates will be used for calculation of

---

① The Bills of Exchange Act of 1882, Article 10, 11.

② ISBP 821 B2.

③ UCP 600 Article 3.

the maturity date. For example: the credit requires shipment from European port, and the bill of lading evidences on board vessel "A" from Dublin August 16 and on board vessel "B" from Rotterdam August 18. The draft should reflect 60 days from the earliest on board date in a European port, i. e. August 16.

If a credit requires drafts to be drawn, for example, at 60 days after or from bill of lading date, and more than one set of bills of lading is presented under the draft, the date of the last bill of lading will be used for the calculation of the maturity date[1].

(8) Place of payment. The place of payment means the place where the holder should present the bill for payment. A bill should be presented at the place specified in the bill, if there is no place of payment is specified, but the address of the drawee or acceptor is given in the bill, and the bill is there presented. Where no place of payment is specified and no address given, the bill is presented at the drawee's or acceptor's place of business if known. Where no place of payment is specified and no address given, and if the drawee's or acceptor's place of business not known, the bill is presented at the drawee's ordinary residence if known. In any other cases, a bill is presented to the drawee or acceptor wherever he can be found, or presented at his last known place of business or residence. [2]

(9) Writing. According to the U. K. Bills of Exchange Act of 1882, the order to pay must be in a form of writing, "written" includes printed, and "writing" includes print[3].

Apparently, ink is not the only medium used and, therefore, a bill drawn up in pencil is still valid. In practice, however, drawing a bill in pencil is usually not encouraged by banks, because of the easy opportunity for fraudulent alteration.

(10) Corrections and alterations. Corrections and alterations on a draft, if any, must appear to have been authenticated by the drawer. [4]

In some countries a draft showing corrections or alterations will not be acceptable even with the drawer's authentication. Issuing banks in such countries should make a statement in the credit to the effect that no correction or alteration must appear in the draft. [5]

## 7.2.5 Types

A bill of exchange may be grouped into different types according to different categorization criterion.

(1) Inland bill vs. foreign bill. Based on the places of issue and payment, a bill may be

---

[1]  ISBP 821, B2.
[2]  The Bills of Exchange Act 1882, Article 45.
[3]  The Bills of Exchange Act 1882, Article 2.
[4]  ISBP 821, B6.
[5]  ISBP 821, B17.

an inland bill or a foreign bill. If the places of issue and payment are the same, the bill is an inland bill; otherwise, it will be a foreign bill.

(2) Sight bill vs. usance bill. Based on the tenor, a bill may be classified into sight bill and usance bill. A sight bill is payable at sight, on demand, or on presentation while a usance bill is payable at a fixed or determinable future time.

A sight bill is sometimes called a sight draft or a demand draft. Sight bills are most commonly used in international trade. Under a sight payment documentary credit, for example, a sight bill is often required and the payment is on demand or on presentation of the negotiation documents to the paying bank.

A usance bill is also called a term draft or a time draft. Under an acceptance documentary credit, a usance bill is used and the payment is on the maturity date determinable in accordance with the stipulations of the credit.

(3) Clean bill vs. documentary bill. Based on whether shipping documents accompanied or not, a bill of exchange may be grouped into a clean bill and a documentary bill.

A clean bill, also known as a clean draft, is a bill of exchange with no shipping documents attached. It is most frequently used in the case of clean collection, under which the shipping documents are usually sent directly by the seller to the buyer.

A documentary bill is a bill to which shipping documents are attached, and most frequently used under documentary collection or documentary credit. Under a documentary collection, the buyer will be able to receive the shipping documents from the collecting bank only after it has accepted or paid the bill. Under a documentary credit, the buyer will be able to receive the shipping documents from the issuing/paying bank only after it has effected the payment.

(4) Banker's bill vs. trader's bill. According to whether the drawer is a bank or not, a bill of exchange may be categorized into a banker's bill or a trader's bill.

Banker's draft or bank draft is usually drawn by a bank on another bank. Both the drawer and drawer of bank draft are banks. A trader's bill or trade bill is usually issued by a trader on another trader or on a bank. The drawer of a trade bill is a trader, and the drawee may be a trader or a bank. Generally, a banker's draft is preferred to a trader's draft.

(5) Restrictive bill, order bill and bearer bill. According to the payee stipulated in a bill, it may be a restrictive bill, an order bill or a bearer bill.

A restrictive bill is made out directly to the payee. It is only the named payee in the bill that has the right to claim for payment from the payer. In this case, the bill is not negotiable, and usually bears stipulations as "Pay A Co. only", or "Pay A Co. not negotiable".

An order bill is made out to the order of a named party, the payee. An order bill can be transferred by endorsement plus delivery. In this case, the payee himself, or a third party (endorsee) are entitled to claim for payment from the payer. An order bill usually bears statements as "Pay A Co. or order", or "Pay to the order of A Co. "

A bearer bill, sometimes known as blank bill, indicates that payment shall be made to whosoever holds the bill, or bearer. Such a bill may be transferred only by delivery.

(6) Accommodation bill or party. An accommodation party to a bill is a person who has signed a bill as drawer, acceptor, or endorser, without receiving value therefore, and for the purpose of lending his name to some other person.

An accommodation party is liable on the bill to a holder for value; and it is immaterial whether, when such holder took the bill, he knew such party to be an accommodation party or not. [1]

### 7.2.6 Acts Relating to a Bill of Exchange

A typical bill of exchange usually involves the following acts.

(1) Issue. "Issue" means the first delivery of a bill, complete in form to a person who takes it as a holder. [2]

To issue a bill, the drawer should complete two acts: one is to draw and sign a bill; the other is to deliver it to the payee.

"Delivery" means transfer of possession, actual or constructive, from one person to another. [3]

Every contract on a bill, whether it be the drawer's, the acceptor's, or an endorser's, is incomplete and revocable, until delivery of the instrument in order to give effect thereto. [4]

For instance, if Mike draws a demand draft and leaves it in his desk from which they are stolen, Mike, the drawer, will not be liable on the grounds of non-delivery. But if the thief negotiates the bill to a holder in due course, the latter can enforce payment, and it will avail Mike nothing to plead non-delivery since a valid delivery will be conclusively presumed in favor of the holder in due course.

(2) Negotiation. A bill is negotiated when it is transferred from one person to another in such a manner as to constitute the transferee the holder of the bill. A bill payable to bearer is negotiated by delivery, while a bill payable to order is negotiated by the endorsement of the holder completed by delivery. Where the holder of a bill payable to his order transfers it for value without endorsing it, the transfer gives the transferee such title as the transferor had in the bill, and the transferee in addition acquires the right to have the endorsement of the transferor. Where any person is under obligation to endorse a bill in a representative capacity, he may en-

---

[1]   The Bills of Exchange Act 1882, Article 28.
[2]   The Bills of Exchange Act 1882, Article 2.
[3]   The Bills of Exchange Act 1882, Article 2.
[4]   The Bills of Exchange Act 1882, Article 21.

dorse the bill in such terms as to negative personal liability. [1]

(3) Endorsement. Endorsement contains two acts: the payee or holder signs on the back of a bill, and delivers it to the endorsee. Where a bill is payable to the order of a specified person, it can be negotiated by endorsement and delivery.

①Requisites of a valid endorsement. A valid endorsement must comply with the following conditions:

- It must be written on the bill itself and be signed by the endorser. The simple signature of the endorser on the bill, without additional words, is sufficient.

- It must be an endorsement of the entire bill. A partial endorsement, that is to say, an endorsement which purports to transfer to the endorsee a part only of the amount payable, or which purports to transfer the bill to two or more endorsees severally, does not operate as a negotiation of the bill.

- Where a bill is payable to the order of two or more payees or endorsees who are not partners all must endorse, unless the one endorsing has authority to endorse for the others.

- Where, in a bill payable to order, the payee or endorsee is wrongly designated, or his name is misspelt, he may endorse the bill as therein described, adding, if he thinks fit, his proper signature.

- Where there are two or more endorsements on a bill, each endorsement is deemed to have been made in the order in which it appears on the bill, until the contrary is proved.

- An endorsement may be made in blank or special. It may also contain terms making it restrictive. [2]

②Types of endorsement. An endorsement may fall into one of the following three types.

- Restrictive endorsement. An endorsement is restrictive which prohibits the further negotiation of the bill or which expresses that it is a mere authority to deal with the bill as thereby directed and not a transfer of the ownership thereof, as, for example, if a bill be endorsed "Pay D. only", or "Pay D. for the account of X.", or "Pay D. or order for collection".

A restrictive endorsement gives the endorsee the right to receive payment of the bill and to sue any party thereto that his endorser could have sued, but gives him no power to transfer his rights as endorsee unless it expressly authorize him to do so.

Where a restrictive endorsement authorizes further transfer, all subsequent endorsees take the bill with the same rights and subject to the same liabilities as the first endorsee under the restrictive endorsement. [3]

---

① The Bills of Exchange Act 1882, Article 31.
② The Bills of Exchange Act 1882, Article 32.
③ The Bills of Exchange Act 1882, Article 35.

• Special endorsement. Special endorsement, also called "endorsement in full", specifies the person to whom or to whose order the draft is to be payable in addition to the signature of the endorser. A bill with a special endorsement is capable of being transferred only by the endorsee. Special endorsement not only shows a chain of endorsers but also gives the holder full right of recourse against all the prior endorsers in the event of dishonor.

Conditional endorsement is a special endorsement with a condition for the endorsee to fulfill before the payment, i. e. the endorser is liable only if the condition is fulfilled. For example:

"Pay to B or order upon his delivery of goods. A (signed)"

"Pay to B without recourse to me. A (signed)"

However, not all the laws allow the use of conditional endorsement. For instance, the Uniform Law for Bills of Exchange and Promissory Notes of Geneva of 1930 stipulates, "an endorsement must be unconditional. Any condition to which it is made subject is deemed not to be written".

• Blank endorsement. Blank endorsement, also referred to as "general endorsement", is one that shows an endorser's signature only and specifies no endorsee. When a bill has been endorsed in blank, any holder may convert the blank endorsement into a special endorsement by writing above the endorser's signature a direction to pay the bill to or to the order of himself or some other person. [1]

According to the Uniform Law for Bills of Exchange and Promissory Notes of Geneva of 1930, there are three different ways for the holder to deal with a bill with a blank endorsement.

First, the holder may fill up the blank either with his own name or with the name of some other person, transferring the blank endorsement into a special endorsement.

Second, the holder may endorse the bill in blank and then transfers it to another person.

Third, the holder may transfer the bill to another person without filling up the blank and without endorsing it, i. e. by mere delivery. In this, the bill is deemed to be payable to bearer.

However, blank endorsement is not allowed in China, and only special endorsement can be used.

(4) Presentment. A bill must be duly presented for payment if it is a sight bill, or duly presented for acceptance first and then payment at maturity if it is a usance bill.

①When presentment for acceptance is necessary:

• Where a bill is payable after sight, presentment for acceptance is necessary in order to fix the maturity of the instrument.

• Where a bill expressly stipulates that it shall be presented for acceptance, or where a bill is drawn payable elsewhere than at the residence or place of business of the drawee, it must

---

[1]　The Bills of Exchange Act 1882, Article 34.

be presented for acceptance before it can be presented for payment. ①

②The time for presentment. A bill must be presented for payment or for acceptance at the specified time.

Different negotiable instrument laws may have different stipulations on the time for presentment for payment, see table 7. 1.

Similarly, different negotiable instrument laws may have different stipulations on the time for presentment for acceptance. According to U. K. Bill of Exchange Act 1882, a time bill should be presented for acceptance at a reasonable hour on a business day and before the bill is overdue. According to the Negotiable Instrument Law of the People's Republic of China, for a bill payable at a fixed future time or at a fixed time after date, the holder must present for accep-tance before the maturity. For a bill payable at a fixed time after sight, the holder should present it for acceptance within one month from the date of issue②.

Table 7. 1  Different stipulations on time for presentment for payment

| Types of Negotiable Instrument Law | Time for presentment for payment | |
|---|---|---|
| | Sight bill | An accepted bill |
| the Bills of Exchange Act (1882) | within a reasonable time and in business hours on a business day③ | on the due date |
| UN Uniform Law for Bills of Exchange and Promissory Notes of Geneva (1930) | one year | on the due date or within two days after the due date |
| the Negotiable Instrument Law of the People's Republic of China (2004 Revision) | within one month after its issue | within 10 days from the due date |

If the holder fails to present for payment within the specified time, the holder will lose its right of recourse to its prior parties.

③The place of presentment. The holder must present a bill for payment or acceptance at the place specified on the bill. If there is no such indication, the holder should present it at the drawer's business office, and if the drawer has no business office, his residential house will be the place of presentment.

---

① The Bills of Exchange Act 1882, Article 39.

② The Negotiable Instrument Law of the People's Republic of China (2004 Revision), Article 41.

③ In determining what is a reasonable time, regard shall be had to the nature of the bill, the usage of trade with respect to similar bills, and the facts of the particular case. (The Bills of Exchange Act 1882, Article 41)

(5) Acceptance. Acceptance of a bill of exchange is a process by which a drawee accepts the bill of exchange by signing under the words "accepted" on face of the bill. By this act, the drawee becomes the acceptor and converts the bill into a post-dated check an unconditional obligation to pay it on or before its maturity date. [1]

Like endorsement, acceptance includes two acts by the drawee: (A) to sign on the face of the bill; and (B) to deliver it to the person presenting for acceptance.

①Forms of acceptance. Usually the acceptance must be written on the bill and be signed by the drawee, and even the mere signature of the drawer without additional words is sufficient. When the drawer has signed his name on the bill, he is known as the acceptor and primarily liable for the payment of the bill.

It usually takes one of the following forms:

- Mere signature of the drawer.
- Signature of the drawer plus the word "accepted".
- Signature of the drawer plus date.
- Signature of the drawer plus the word "accepted" and the date.
- Any of the above four plus such words as "Payable at ××× Bank, London".

②Time for acceptance. A bill may be accepted, (A) before it has been signed by the drawer, or while otherwise incomplete; (B) when it is overdue, or after it has been dishonored by a previous refusal to accept, or by non-payment; (C) When a bill payable after sight is dishonored by non-acceptance, and the drawee subsequently accepts it, the holder, in the absence of any different agreement, is entitled to have the bill accepted as of the date of first presentment to the drawee for acceptance. [2]

③Types of acceptance. An acceptance is either general or qualified.

A general acceptance assents without qualification to the order of the drawer. An example of general acceptance is as follows:

---

Accepted

June 1, 2024

For ××× Bank

Signed

---

A qualified acceptance is one by which the acceptor agrees to pay a bill at maturity with qualification. In particular, an acceptance is qualified which is (A) conditional, that is to say,

---

[1] http://www.businessdictionary.com/definition/acceptance-of-a-bill-of-exchange.html.
[2] The Bills of Exchange Act 1882, Article 18.

which makes payment by the acceptor dependent on the fulfillment of a condition therein stated; (B) partial, that is to say, an acceptance to pay only part of the amount for which the bill is drawn; (C) local, that is to say, an acceptance to pay only at a particular specified place, an acceptance to pay at a particular place is a general acceptance, unless it expressly states that the bill is to be paid there only and not elsewhere; (D) qualified as to time; (E) the acceptance of some one or more of the drawees, but not of all. [1]

Several examples of qualified acceptance are as follows.

- Conditional acceptance.

---

Accepted

July 1, 2024

Payable providing goods fulfill the. . . Standard

For ×××Bank

Signed

---

- Partial Acceptance. Where the whole amount stated thereon is USD 100,000, a partial acceptance is written as:

---

Accepted

June 1, 2024

Payable for the amount of

USD 80,000 only

For ×××Bank

Signed

---

- Local Acceptance:

---

Accepted

June 1, 2024

Payable at ×××Bank,

London only

For. . . Bank

Signed

---

[1]　The Bills of Exchange Act 1882, Article 19.

• Time-qualified acceptance. When a bill drawn payable "60 days after date" is accepted as "payable at 90 days after date", it is a time-qualified acceptance. The qualification is the longer period than that stated on the bill.

In addition, when a bill is drawn on two or more drawers, the acceptance is made only by one or some of them, rather than by all of them, this acceptance is also a qualified acceptance. For instance, a bill is drawn on five persons jointly and only three of them consent to accept, then their acceptance, if taken by the holder, is known as a qualified one. The three acceptors must be liable for the whole amount of the bill.

④Duties as to qualified acceptances.

• The holder of a bill may refuse to take a qualified acceptance. If the holder does not obtain an unqualified acceptance, he may treat the bill as dishonored by non-acceptance.

• Where a qualified acceptance is taken, and the drawer or an endorser has not expressly or impliedly authorized the holder to take a qualified acceptance, or does not subsequently assent thereto, such drawer or endorser is discharged from his liability on the bill. However, this does not apply to a partial acceptance, whereof due notice has been given.

• When the drawer or endorser of a bill receives notice of a qualified acceptance, and does not within a reasonable time express his dissent to the holder he shall be deemed to have assented thereto. ①

(6) Payment.

①Payer. Payment of a bill is generally made by the drawee or acceptor.

②Payee. Payment of a bill is generally made to the holder of the instrument.

③Time and ways of payment. A bill can be paid in due course by any party to a bill providing that party pays the holder, at or after maturity, in good faith and without notice that his title is defective. And such payment is known as payment in due course.

④Effects of payment. A payment in due course can discharge the liability of the drawee or acceptor, that is, the obligation represented by the bill ceases to exist and all rights of action on the bill are extinguished, the whole transaction or series of transactions for which it has served as an instrument of payment are completed and settled, and the bill becomes history, a mere voucher evidencing what has happened and how it was concluded②.

In the event of dishonor, the holder may demand payment from any prior endorser or the drawer. However, payment in due course by an endorser or the drawer would not discharge the bill, because if an endorser is compelled to pay the bill, he may likewise recover from a prior

---

① The Bills of Exchange Act 1882, Article 44.

② To make certain that it remains only a voucher and not misused in any other way, the drawer or acceptor may cancel the signature of the drawer.

endorser or the drawer and in addition sue the acceptor for his dishonor. If the drawer is com-pelled to pay, he can still sue the acceptor for dishonor.

(7) Dishonor. Dishonor of a bill may be dishonor by non-acceptance or by non-payment.

①Dishonor by non-acceptance . When a bill is duly presented for acceptance and is not accepted within the reasonable or specified time, the person presenting it must treat it as dis-honored by non-acceptance. If he does not, the holder shall lose his right of recourse against the drawer and endorsers.

• Cases of dishonor by non-acceptance. A bill is dishonored by non-acceptance, (A) when it is duly presented for acceptance, and such an acceptance is refused or cannot be obtained; or (B) when presentment for acceptance is excused and the bill is not accepted. ①

• Consequences of dishonor by non-acceptance. When a bill is dishonored by non-accep-tance, an immediate right of recourse against the drawer and endorsers accrues to the holder, and no presentment for payment is necessary. ②

②Dishonor by non-payment. Dishonor by non-payment may cover non-payment of a sight bill or an accepted time bill.

• Cases of dishonor by non-payment. A bill is dishonored by non-payment: (A) when it is duly presented for payment and payment is refused or cannot be obtained, or (B) when pre-sentment is excused and the bill is overdue and unpaid.

• Consequences of dishonor by non-payment . When a bill is dishonored by non-payment, an immediate right of recourse against the drawer and endorsers accrues to the holder. ③

(8) Notice of dishonor and effects of non-notice. When a bill has been dishonored by non-acceptance or non-payment, notice of dishonour④ must be given to the drawer and each endor-ser.

If any drawer or endorser to whom such notice is not given, his liability is discharged. ⑤ That is to say, the holder who fails to give a notice of dishonor in due time may loose the right of recourse to the prior endorsers and the drawer.

To ensure that every prior party to a bill remains liable, the holder should advise every party when dishonor occurs. But it is equally effective if the holder gives notice to only his own transferor providing that notice is passed down through endorsers until the payee notifies the drawer.

---

①   The Bills of Exchange Act 1882, Article 43.
②   The Bills of Exchange Act 1882, Article 43.
③   The Bills of Exchange Act 1882, Article 47.
④   As for the rules to notice of dishonour, please refer to the Bills of Exchange Act 1882, Article 49.
⑤   The Bills of Exchange Act 1882, Article 48.

(9) Protest. When a bill has been dishonored by non-acceptance or non-payment, the holder may, within a reasonable time, have such dishonor certified by notary public. Such certificate is called a protest.

As to the making of a protest, different laws have different requirements, see table 7.2.

**Table 7.2　Different stipulations on the requirements for making a protest**

| Types of Negotiable Instrument Law | Requirements for making a protest | |
| --- | --- | --- |
| UN Uniform Law for Bills of Exchange and Promissory Notes of Geneva | √ | |
| the Negotiable Instrument Law of the People's Republic of China | √ | |
| the U.S. Uniform Commercial Code | √ | |
| the Negotiable Instrument Law of Japan | √ | |
| the Bills of Exchange Act | × Inland bill | √ Foreign bill |

In making a protest, the holder hands the bill to a notary public who again presents the bill for acceptance or payment as the case may be, so as to obtain legal proof of dishonor. If the acceptance or payment is still unobtainable, the notary public draws up a protest, evidencing the demand made to the drawer or acceptor and the answer received. On the reverse of the certificate is a copy of the bill.

This form of protest is recognized world-widely and international laws demand it as legal proof of dishonor. Failure to obtain a protest would imply that all parties excluding the acceptor would be released from their liability.

As to the time of protesting, there are some differences among the stipulations of various laws. The Uniform Law for Bills of Exchange and Promissory Notes of Geneva of 1930 states that protest for non-acceptance must be made within the limit of time fixed for presentment for acceptance. If in the case that the first presentment takes place on the last day of that time, the protest may nevertheless be drawn up on the next day. Protest for non-payment of a bill payable on a fixed day or at a fixed period after date or after sight must be made on one of the two business days following the day on which the bill is due. In the case of a bill payable at sight, the protest must be drawn up under the same conditions as protest for non-acceptance.

According to the Negotiable Instrument Law of the People's Republic of China, the time of making a protest should be within 10 days from the date of dishonor, and if the holder fails to do so within the specified time, it will lose its right of recourse to prior parties.

(10) Right of recourse. A holder in due course can, if necessary, sue every person who signed the instrument prior to him, including all the prior endorsers, the guarantor, and the drawer. This is known as a right of recourse and usually arises in the event of dishonor.

The holder claiming right of recourse must have (A) duly made presentation and been dishonored, (B) duly obtained the protest, and (C) duly noticed the prior party of the fact of dishonor. Otherwise, the holder may loose the right of recourse to all his prior parties and the drawer.

(11) Guarantee. The act of guarantee is usually performed by a third party called guarantor, who engages that the bill will be paid on presentment if it is a sight bill or accepted on presentment and paid at maturity if it is a time bill. The guarantor stands surely for a debtor such as drawer, endorser, or acceptor and assumes his indebtedness to the holder.

(12) Negotiation. A bill is negotiated when it is transferred from one person to another in such a manner as to constitute the transferee the holder of the bill.

A bill payable to bearer is negotiated by delivery. A bill payable to order is negotiated by the endorsement of the holder completed by delivery.

Where the holder of a bill payable to his order transfers it for value without endorsing it, the transfer gives the transferee such title as the transferor had in the bill, and the transferee in addition acquires the right to have the endorsement of the transferor.

Where any person is under obligation to endorse a bill in a representative capacity, he may endorse the bill in such terms as to negative personal liability. ①

In some cases, a bill may be waived, cancelled or altered.

(13) Express waiver. The holder of a bill may, at or after its maturity, absolutely and unconditionally renounce his rights against the acceptor. Once a bill is expressly waived, the bill is discharged.

Similarly, the liabilities of any party to a bill may be renounced by the holder before, at, or after its maturity.

The renunciation must be in writing, unless the bill is delivered up to the acceptor. ②

(14) Cancellation. The holder or his agent can intentionally cancel a bill. Once the bill is cancelled, and the cancellation is apparent thereon, the bill is discharged.

In like manner, any party liable on a bill may be discharged by the intentional cancellation of the holder or his agent.

A cancellation made unintentionally, or under a mistake, or without the authority of the

---

① The Bills of Exchange Act 1882, Article 12.
② The Bills of Exchange Act 1882, Article 62.

holder is inoperative. ①

(15) Alteration. Where a bill or acceptance is materially altered without the assent of all parties liable on the bill, the bill is avoided except as against a party who himself has made, authorized, or assented to the alteration, and subsequent endorsers.

Where a bill has been materially altered, but the alteration is not apparent, and the bill is in the hands of a holder in due course, such holder may avail himself of the bill as if it had not been altered, and may enforce payment of it according to its original tenor.

In particular, the following alterations are material, namely, any alteration of the date, the sum payable, the time of payment, the place of payment, and, where a bill has been accepted generally, the addition of a place of payment without the acceptor's assent. ②

## 7.2.7  Frequently Found Discrepancies with Drafts

Under credit-based transactions, the following discrepancies are usually found with bill of exchange.

- Draft is presented after the expiry date of the credit.
- The amount of the draft is greater than that of the credit.
- The tenor is not as shown in the credit.
- The drafts are not drawn on the bank specified in the credit.
- The drafts are not endorsed or endorsed incorrectly when L/C required.
- The drawer of the drafts is not the beneficiary of the credit required.
- There is no signature of the drawer.
- There is no drawn clause as specified in the credit.
- The number of the credit is omitted or incorrect.
- The credit requires no drafts, but the drafts are still included in the documents.

## 7.3  Promissory Notes

### 7.3.1  Definition

A promissory note is an unconditional promise in writing made by one person to another signed by the maker, engaging to pay, on demand or at a fixed or determinable future time, a sum certain in money, to, or to the order of, a specified person or to bearer. ③

A promissory note is an instrument written and issued by a drawer, promising to pay unconditionally a fixed amount of money to a payee or holder at the sight of the instrument. ④

---

① The Bills of Exchange Act 1882, Article 63.
② The Bills of Exchange Act 1882, Article 64.
③ The Bills of Exchange Act 1882, Article 83.
④ The Negotiable Instrument Law of the People's Republic of China, Article 73.

## 7.3.2　Players

Differing from a bill of exchange, a promissory note is a two-party negotiable instrument. The basic players are, namely, the drawer who makes an unconditional promise to pay, and the payee who has the right to demand payment from the drawer.

Depending on different circumstances, there may be some derivative players including the endorsers, the endorsees, the holder for value, the holder in due course, etc.

## 7.3.3　Essential Items and Specimens

According to the Uniform Law for Bills of Exchange and Promissory Notes of Geneva of 1930, a promissory note must contain:

● the term "Promissory Note" in the body of the note and expressed in the language employed in drawing up the note.

- An unconditional promise to pay a determinable sum of money.
- A statement of the time of payment.
- A statement of the place where payment is to be made.
- The name of the person to whom or to whose order payment is to be made.
- A statement of the date and of the place where the promissory note is issued.
- The signature of the maker.

Similarly, China's relevant law[1] stipulates that a promissory note shall record the following items:

● The characters indicating "Promissory Note".
- Unconditional promise to pay.
- Amount of money fixed.
- Name of the payee.
- Date of issue.
- Signature of the drawer.

A promissory note is invalid if any one of the above items is missing.

In addition, the place of payment, the place of issue and other items recorded on the promissory note shall be clear and definite. If the instrument does not bear the place of payment, the business site of the issuer shall be taken as the place of payment. If the instrument does not bear the place of issue, the business site of the issuer shall be taken as the place of issue. [2]

Two specimens of promissory note are given as follows:

---

①　The Negotiable Instrument Law of the People's Republic of China, Article 75.
②　The Negotiable Instrument Law of the People's Republic of China, Article 76.

**Specimen 1: A Time Promissory Note**

London, Sep. 15th, 2024

Promissory Note for GBP 1,000.00
    At 60 days after date we promise to pay Beijing Arts and Crafts Corp. or order the sum of one thousand pounds.

For Bank of Europe,

London.

<u>Signature</u>

**Specimen 2: A Banker's Promissory Note**

XYZ INTERNATIONAL BANK, LTD.

18 Park Street, Singapore

CASHIER's ORDER

Singapore, AUG. 8, 2024

Pay to the order of <u>ABC CO. LTD.</u>
The sum of HK DOLLARS EIGHTY THOUSAND AND EIGHT HUNDRED ONLY.

For XYZ International Bank, Ltd.

Manager

<u>Signature</u>

## 7.3.4 Types

Based on different standards of categorization and statutory stipulations of different countries, a promissory note may be grouped into different types.

(1) Demand note vs. time note. According to the tenor of payment, a promissory note may be a demand note or a time note. A demand note is payable on demand, while a time note is payable at a fixed future time.

Promissory notes mentioned in the Negotiable Instrument Law of the People's Republic of China only refer to demand note, and the maximum time limit of payment shall not exceed two months starting from the date of draft. [1]

(2) Trader's note vs. banker's note. According to the maker of a note, a promissory note may be a trader's note or a banker's note.

Where the maker of a promissory note is an individual or an enterprise, the note is a trader's note. When the maker is a small enterprise, this trader's note is not as acceptable and

[1]  The Negotiable Instrument Law of the People's Republic of China, Article 78.

negotiable as banker's note. Where the maker of a promissory note is a bank, the note is a banker's note.

A trader's note may be payable on demand or at a fixed future time. A banker's note can be made payable on demand or at a fixed future time, however, those payable at a fixed future time are rarely used. A banker's note payable on demand is customarily referred to as "Cashier's Order", and it can be converted into cash over the counter.

Promissory notes mentioned in the Negotiable Instrument Law of the People's Republic of China only refer to banker's notes. ①

(3) Joint note vs. joint and several note. A promissory note may be made by two or more makers, and they may be liable thereon jointly, or jointly and severally according to its tenor.

Where a note runs "I promise to pay" and is signed by two or more persons, it is deemed to be their joint and several note.

Where a note runs "We jointly and severally promise to pay", either maker is individually liable for the whole amount if the other does not pay his share; where a note runs "We promise to pay", each is liable for his share. ②

① Similarities. Each maker is individually liable for the full amount of the note. If called on to pay, any of the makers must pay the holder the whole amount involved individually. Afterwards, the maker who has made the payment can obtain from his fellow-makers whatever is their share of the liability.

In the event of the makers' refusal to pay, the holder can sue the makers and enforce payment.

② Differences. In a joint notes, the holder has only one right of action, i. e. he can sue in court but once. He can sue one maker alone, or sue some of the makers, or sue all the makers together. That is, there is only one debt and thus only one right of action in a joint note.

In a joint and several notes, the holder can sue each one of the makers in turn. That is, there are as many debts and thus as many rights of action as there are makers.

However, a holder is not allowed to recover more than the full amount of the note.

### 7.3.5 Related Acts

A typical note usually involves similar acts related to a bill.

(1) Issuance. By making a promissory note, the maker engages that he will pay it according to its tenor, and is precluded from denying to a holder in due course the existence of the payee and his then capacity to endorse. ③

---

① The Negotiable Instrument Law of the People's Republic of China, Article 73.
② The Bills of Exchange Act 1882, Article 85.
③ The Bills of Exchange Act 1882, Article 88.

A promissory note is inchoate and incomplete until delivery thereof to the payee or bearer. ①

In applying those provisions relating to bill of exchange, the maker of a note shall be deemed to correspond with the acceptor of a bill. ②

(2) Endorsement. A note may be transferred by endorsement and delivery.

In applying those provisions relating to bill of exchange, the first endorser of a note shall be deemed to correspond with the drawer of an accepted bill payable to drawer's order. ③

(3) Presentment. A note needs not to be presented for acceptance, because the maker is just the payer.

When the holder of a promissory note presents the instrument, the drawer shall be liable to pay. ④

①When presentment for payment is necessary. Depending on the tenor of a note, a presentment for payment may or may not be required by it.

In order to render the maker liable, presentment for payment must be made when a promissory note is written as it is payable at a particular place. In any other case, presentment for payment is not necessary to render the maker liable. ⑤

In order to render the endorser of a note liable, presentment for payment is necessary. Where a note is made payable at a particular place, presentment at that place is necessary in order to render an endorser liable.

If a holder has failed to present the instrument according to the prescribed time limit, the holder shall lose the right of recourse against the prior holders other than the drawer. ⑥

②Time for presenting note payable on demand. Similarly, the time for presenting a note payable on demand also depends on the tenor of it and relevant laws.

Where a note payable on demand has been endorsed, it must be presented for payment within a reasonable time of the endorsement. If it be not so presented , the endorser is discharged. In determining what is a reasonable time, regard shall be had to the nature of the instrument, the usage of trade, and the facts of the particular case. ⑦

(4) Negotiation. A promissory note may be negotiated when necessary. Where a note payable on demand is negotiated, it is not deemed to be overdue, for the purpose of affecting the

---

① The Bills of Exchange Act 1882, Article 84.
② The Bills of Exchange Act 1882, Article 89.
③ The Bills of Exchange Act 1882, Article 89.
④ The Negotiable Instrument Law of the People's Republic of China, Article 77.
⑤ The Bills of Exchange Act 1882, Article 87.
⑥ The Negotiable Instrument Law of the People's Republic of China, Article 79.
⑦ The Bills of Exchange Act 1882, Article 86.

holder with defects of title of which he had no notice, by reason that it appears that a reasonable time for presenting it for payment has elapsed since its issue. [1]

(5) Payment. The payment in due course made by the maker will discharge a note. The maximum time limit of payment shall not exceed two months starting from the date of note. [2]

However, some acts related to a bill are not involved in a note, including, presentment for acceptance, acceptance, acceptance supra protest, and protest in the case of dishonor of a foreign note, etc. [3]

### 7.3.6 Differences between a Bill and a Note

The detailed differences between a bill and a note are summed up in table 7.3.

**Table 7.3 Differences between a bill and a note**

| Items | Bill | Note |
|---|---|---|
| Nature | An unconditional order to pay | An unconditional promise to pay |
| Number of Basic Players | Two (maker and payee) | Three (drawer, drawee, payee) |
| Acceptance | Required when a bill payable after sight | Never required |
| Presentment for acceptance | Required when a bill payable after sight, to fix the maturity date of the bill, and to render the prior parties liable | Never accepted. However, a note must be presented for visa of the maker when it is made payable after sight, and to fix the maturity date of the note |
| A set | In a set (one or more) | Only one copy |
| Protest | Required in the case of a foreign bill dishonored, to retain the liability of prior parties | Never needed |
| Primary Debtor | Before acceptance, the drawer; after acceptance, the acceptor | Always the maker |
| When more than one obligors | Two or more acceptors of a bill are always jointly liable. | More than one maker, they can be liable jointly or jointly and severally according to the terms of the note |

## 7.4  Check

### 7.4.1  Definition

Different negotiable instrument law may define check into different versions.

---

[1]  The Bills of Exchange Act 1882, Article 86.

[2]  The Negotiable Instrument Law of the People's Republic of China, Article 78.

[3]  The Bills of Exchange Act 1882, Article 89.

A check is "a bill of exchange drawn on a banker payable on demand". ①

A check is an instrument issued by a drawer, at the sight of which the check deposit bank or other financial institutions unconditionally pay the fixed amount to the payee or holder. ②

Since a check is a kind of bill of exchange, the stipulations and provisions of negotiable instrument law applicable to a bill of exchange payable on demand apply to a cheque.

### 7.4.2 Players

Similar to a bill of exchange, a promissory note is also a three-party negotiable instrument. The basic players are, namely, the drawer who makes an unconditional order to pay and writes the check; the drawee, the bank to whom the order is to pay and on whom the check is drawn; and the payee who has the right to demand payment from the drawee.

### 7.4.3 Essential Items and Specimen

According to Negotiable Instrument Law of People's Republic of China, a check must record the following items:

- Characters denoting "Check".
- Commission to pay unconditionally.
- Amount fixed.
- Name of the payee.
- Date of draft.
- Signature of the drawer.

A check shall be invalid if any one of the above items is missing.

The amount of the check issued by the drawer shall not exceed the actual amount deposited by the payer at the time of payment. Otherwise, the check is a dishonorable check, which is strictly forbidden. ③

However, the amount on a check may be filled in afterwards by the holder with the authorization of the drawer; and if a check does not bear the name of the payee, it may be recorded afterwards with the authorization of the drawer, and a drawer can record himself as the payee on a check.

If a check does not bear the place of payment, the business site of the payer shall be taken as the place of payment; if a check does not bear the place of issue, the business site, residence of the drawer or the place where the drawer often lives shall be taken as the place of issue.

Two specimen of check are given as below.

---

① The BEA, 1957 supplementary version, Article 73.
② The Negotiable Instrument Law of the People's Republic of China, Article 81.
③ The Negotiable Instrument Law of the People's Republic of China, Article 87.

**Check Specimen 1**

---

Bank of Utopia

Pay Buyer Ltd or bearer
the sum of 10,000 dollars exactly

Signed ABC Limited

---

**Check Specimen 2**

---

London, Sep. 12th , 2024

Check for US $1,360. 00
    Pay to the order of <u>China National Textile Corp</u>.
The sum of US Dollars one thousand three hundred and sixty only.

To: National Westminster Bank Ltd.
    London

For London Export Co.
London
Signature

---

## 7.4.4 Types

Checks may be grouped into different types.

(1) Cashier's check vs. personal check. A check may be a cashier's check or a personal check.

A cashier's check (cashier's cheque, bank check, official check, demand draft, teller's check, bank draft or treasurer's check) is a check guaranteed by a bank. They are usually treated as cash since most banks clear them instantly. [1] Therefore, Cashier's checks are comparatively safer and faster, and most often used in infrequent transactions where the customer and merchant don't know each other, or when rapid settlement is necessary. This is because one can only get a cashier's check unless he actually has available funds in the account; and once his account is debited, the bank is responsible for paying the payee.

A personal check is issued by person who has available funds in his account to cover the check. Personal checks are relatively less safe and slower, and most often used in insignificant transactions, or when rapid settlement is not necessary. When one person writes a personal check, he is supposed to have available funds in his account to cover the check. His account

---

[1] http://en. wikipedia. org/wiki/Cashier%27s_check.

may not be debited for several business days after he writes the check, because the payee may not get the check to the bank for a few days, and that processing will take another few days. ①

(2) Order check vs. bearer check. According to the methods of stipulating the payee, checks may be payable to order or to bearer.

An order check is made out to the order of a named party, the payee. An order check can be transferred by endorsement plus delivery. In this case, the payee himself, or a third party (endorsee) are entitled to claim for payment from the payer. An order check usually bears statements as "Pay A Co. or order", or "Pay to the order of A Co. ".

A bearer check, sometimes known as blank check, indicates that payment shall be made to whosoever holds the check, or bearer. Such a check may be transferred only by delivery.

(3) General crossing check vs. special crossing check. Crossed check means a check bearing two parallel lines on the face. A crossing on a check is in fact an instruction by the drawer or holder to the paying bank to pay the fund to a bank only, so a crossed check will not be paid over the counter of the drawer bank, but must be presented for payment through a collecting bank. The drawer bank will also act as the collecting bank if both the drawer and the payee maintain current accounts with the drawer bank. Those bearing no crossing are called uncrossed checks, or open checks.

The crossing on a check can be a general crossing or a special one. A general crossing on a check specifies no name of the collecting bank and means that the check can be collected through any bank. A special crossing on a check usually contains the name of a bank and means that the fund can only be collected through the named bank. In practice, only one name of a bank is allowed, but the named bank can collect the fund through another bank by making another special crossing. But a check can bear no more than two special crossings.

(4) Certified check. A certified check is the check drawn by a customer of a bank which has been duly certified by the bank establishing enough balance in his account when the check is presented for payment. A certified check assures prompt payment, as the bank will embark the required amount to pay the certified check until its validity. ②

To be noted, not all relevant laws have stipulations on certified check. For instance, the US Uniform Commercial Code and the Negotiable Instrument Law of Japan have relevant stipulations on certified checks, while the U. K. Bills of Exchange Act of 1882, the Uniform Law for Checks of Geneva of 1930, and the Negotiable Instrument Law of the People's Republic of Chi-

---

① http://banking. about. com/od/checkingaccounts/a/cashierschecks. htm.
② http://www. legal-explanations. com/definitions/certified-check. htm.

na do not. ①

(5) Traveler's check. A traveler's check is a check issued by a financial institution which functions as cash but is protected against loss or theft. Traveler's checks are useful when traveling, especially in case of overseas travel when not all credit and debit cards carried by a person will be accepted. A charge or commission is usually incurred when a person exchanges cash for traveler's checks, though some issuers provide them free of charge. ②

Traveler's checks are available in several currencies such as U. S. dollars, Canadian dollars, pounds sterling, Japanese yen, and euro; denominations (usually being 20, 50, or 100×100 for Yen) of whatever currency, and are usually sold in pads of five or ten checks, e. g. 5×€20 for €100. Traveler's checks do not expire, so unused checks can be kept by the purchaser to spend at any time in the future. The purchaser of a supply of traveler's checks effectively gives an interest-free loan to the issuer, which is why it is common for banks to sell them "commission free" to their customers. The commission, where it is charged, is usually 1%~2% of the total face value sold. ③

(6) Euro-check. Euro-check was a type of cheque used in Europe. It was accepted across national borders and could be written in a variety of currencies. It originated in 1969 as an alternative to the traveler's cheque and for international payments for goods and services. The charges for clearing Euro-checks were substantially lower than those for cross-border use of domestic checks. Although still accepted as payment by a few bodies, the practice of issuing Euro-checks ceased on January 1,2002, which was, coincidentally, the same date that the euro currency was introduced. ④

(7) Substitute check. A substitute check (also called an Image Replacement Document or "IRD") is a United States negotiable instrument that represents the reproduction of the front and rear of an original paper check, and is to be electronically transmitted for payment collection through the Federal Reserve System.

Substitute checks are authorized as the legal equivalent of the original paper check under the Check Clearing for the 21st Century Act (Check 21 Act) as long as the substitute checks meet reproduction requirements of the original checks and the reconverting bank (the bank that creates the substitute check or the first bank that transfers or presents it during the clearing process) warranties the instruments.

---

① Zhao Wei. International Settlement: Payment Techniques in International Trade Finance. Nanjing: South-eastern University Press,2005.

② http://www. investorwords. com/5055/travelers_check. html.

③ http://en. wikipedia. org/wiki/Traveler's_cheque.

④ http://en. wikipedia. org/wiki/Eurocheque.

As a negotiable instrument, a substitute check maintains the status of a "legal check" in lieu of the original paper check as long as it meets specific requirements in the faithful reproduction of the original and meets requirements and standards for production of the instrument. A properly prepared substitute check can be accepted for payment in the same manner as the original paper check. All substitute checks are subject to existing federal and state check laws and new regulations specific to consumer rights related to substitute checks. [1]

### 7.4.5 Differences between a Bill and a Check

Since a check is a bill of exchange drawn on a bank and payable on demand, acts such as issue, endorsement, payment, right of recourse, etc. are all relevant to checks. However, there exist several differences between a bill and a check, and they are summarized as the following table 7.4.

**Table 7.4　Differences between a bill and a check**

| Items | Bill | check |
|---|---|---|
| Drawer | A trader or a bank | The customer of the drawer bank |
| Drawee/payer | A trader or a bank | Must be the bank, with which the drawer opens a checking account |
| Function | A payment instrument, and a credit instrument | A payment instrument only |
| Principal Obligor | For sight bill, or a usance bill before acceptance, the drawer is the principal obligor; for an accepted bill, the acceptor is the principal obligor | For certified check, the bank that has certified the check becomes the principal obligor and all other parties are discharged of liability |
| Certification or Acceptance | A bill can be accepted, guaranteed or accepted for honor | A check can be certified |
| Revocable or not | After acceptance, the payment is irrevocable | A check can be cancelled before payment |
| Payment time | A bill is payable on demand or at a determinable future time | A check is payable on demand |

## Questions and Problems

### I. True(T)or false(F).

1. Parties who have signed their names on a negotiable instrument are all debtors of the bona fide holder.

2. Before acceptance, the principal debtor of a time draft is the drawee.

3. Drawee of a time draft will become liable only when it endorses bill and becomes Acceptor.

---

[1]　http://en.wikipedia.org/wiki/Substitute_check.

4. According to the UCC, when no time is stated in a draft, it should be payable on demand.

5. Since the existence of a negotiable is independent of the underlying transaction, the payer can not defense against the drawer's non-performance of obligation under transaction contract.

6. The more the endorsers are, the higher the negotiable instrument's credit rate is.

7. When a drawer draws a draft on a drawee, there must be a commercial or funds relationship between them (excepting accommodation bills).

8. When the payee transfers a draft to the transferee, the latter will not mind how the instrument was generated and his only concern is that the instrument must be in a qualified form and contain the essential items required by the relative negotiable instrument law.

9. According to the UCC, if payment is conditional on the performance of another agreement, the instrument is non-negotiable.

10. The promise or order must be payable either on demand or at a specified time in the future.

11. A holder for value must be a holder in due course.

12. A bona-fide holder must be a holder for value.

13. The title to a B/E can only be transferred by endorsement plus delivery.

14. Parties who have signed their names on a draft are all obligee of the bona fide holder.

15. Drawee of a demand draft will only become primarily liable for payment when he accepts the bill and becomes Acceptor.

16. Once a bill is drawn, the debt/credit relationship of the bill is established.

17. The holder of a draft who fails to make presentation duly might lose the right of recourse to its prior parties.

18. The drawer cannot expect other people to honor the bill when he has received value for it and it is his customer who has dishonored the bill.

19. Time Draft gives drawee chance to have money ready.

20. Sometimes, drawee may require a reputable firm (Guarantor) to place its name on the bill if he is not sure of the reputation of drawer.

**II. Best choice.**

1. When payable to bearer, a negotiable instrument may be transferred by_____.

A. mere delivery                    B. endorsement

C. endorsement and delivery         D. pay the named payee

2. When payable to a named person or order, a negotiable instrument may be transferred by_____.

A. mere delivery                    B. endorsement

C. endorsement and delivery         D. pay the named payee

3. The drawer of a bill of exchange unconditionally orders the_____to pay a fixed

amount in money to the_____at a certain time.

    A. drawee, payee                      B. endorser, endorsee

    C. acceptor, drawer                  D. drawee, drawee

4. The party to whom the drawee is directed to make payment is_____.

    A. the payer                            B. the payee

    C. the drawer                          D. the endorser

5. _____is the only obligee on the instrument.

    A. The drawer                        B. The drawee

    C. The payee                         D. The payer

6. Negotiation of a draft without recourse means that the holder in due course has no recourse to the_____if such draft is dishonored.

    A. drawee                          B. payee

    C. payer                          D. drawer

7. The_____can transfer the title to a bill of exchange by endorsement plus delivery.

    A. drawer                         B. drawee

    C. holder                         D. bearer

8. In international trade payment, the drawer and the_____are usually the same person.

    A. payer                         B. payee

    D. drawee                      D. holder

9. Before acceptance, the_____of a time draft has primary liability to pay.

    A. drawee                        B. payer

    C. drawer                       D. payee

10. After acceptance of a time draft, the_____has primary liability to pay.

    A. drawer                        B. payee

    C. drawee                       D. acceptor

**Ⅲ. Practical application.**

1. Make out a draft based on the particulars below:

√L/C NO. 18/1234-B/128 DATED JUNE 2, 2024

√FROM: COMMERCIAL BANK OF KUWAIT

√ADVISING BANK: BANK OF CHINA, HANGZHOU

√APPLICANT: ABC TRADING & CONTRACTING EST. KUWAIT

√AMOUNT: USD 20,060.00

√BENEFICIARY: ZHEJIANG CHEMICALS IMPORT & EXPORT CORPORATION

√WE OPEN THIS IRREVOCABLE DOCUMENTARY CREDIT FAVOURING YOURSELVES FOR 97% OF THE INVOICE VALUE AVAILABLE AGAINST YOUR DRAFT AT SIGHT BY NEGOTIATION WITH ADVISING BANK ON U. S.

√QUANTITY OF GOODS: 1,000KGS NET

√UNIT PRICE: USD 20.00 PER KGS CIFC3 KUWAIT

√INVOICE NO.: 12469

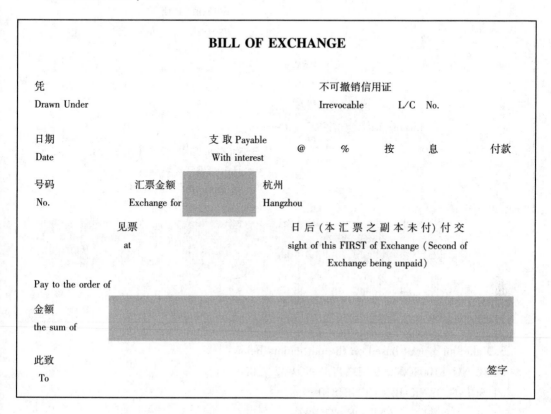

2. Make out a draft based on the particulars below:

√L/C NO. A-12B-34C DATED NOV.11, 2024

√ISSUING BANK: ISREAL DISCOUNT BANK OF NEW YORK, NEW YORK BRANCH

√APPICANT: THE BCD GROUP, INC.

√BENEFICIARY: ZHEJIANG TEXITILES IMPORT & EXPORT CORPORATION

√AMOUNT: USD 5,390.00

√COVERING: 1,000pcs of 100% COTTON CUSHIONS

√WE OPEN THIS IRREVOCABLE DOCUMENTARY CREDIT FAVOURING YOUR-SELVES AVAILABLE AGAINST YOUR DRAFT AT SIGHT BY NEGOTIATION

√OTHER TERMS AND CONDITIONS: INVOICE NOT TO SHOW ANY COMMISSION BUT TO SHOW TOTAL CFR NEW YORK USD 5,500.00

√COMMISSION OF 2% TO SHOW ONLY ON BILL OF EXCHANGE

√INVOICE NO.: 12346

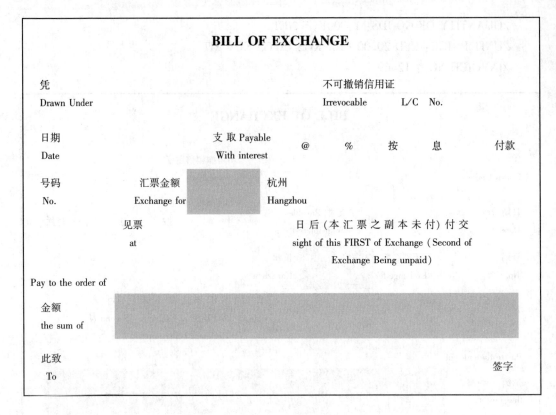

**BILL OF EXCHANGE**

| 凭<br>Drawn Under | | 不可撤销信用证<br>Irrevocable  L/C  No. |
| --- | --- | --- |

| 日期<br>Date | 支取 Payable<br>With interest | @    %    按    息    付款 |

| 号码<br>No. | 汇票金额<br>Exchange for | 杭州<br>Hangzhou |

见票
at

日后(本汇票之副本未付)付交
sight of this FIRST of Exchange (Second of
Exchange Being unpaid)

Pay to the order of

金额
the sum of

此致
To

签字

3. Make out a draft based on the particulars below:
√L/C NO. 810080000797 DATED NOV. 7, 2024
√ISSUING BANK: BKCHCNBJ810

BANK OF CHINA

QINGDAO

(SHANDONG BRANCH)

√APPICANT: QINGDAO TEXITILES IMPORT & EXPORT CORPORATION,

SHANDONG, CHINA

√BENEFICIARY: SUNKUONG LIMITED

(HSRO) C. P. O. BOX 1780

SEOUL, KOREA.

√AMOUNT: USD 738,000. 00
√COVERING: 630 CARTONS 1,000pcs of CANNED LITCHIS
√WE OPEN THIS IRREVOCABLE DOCUMENTARY CREDIT FAVOURING YOUR-
SELVES AVAILABLE AGAINST YOUR DRAFT AT 120 DAYS AFTER THE DATE OF SHIP-
MENT BY NEGOTIATION

√INVOICE No. :81609D3030

---

## BILL OF EXCHANGE

No. _____

For _____                    _____

      ( amount in figure )                              ( place and date of issue )

At _____  sight of this FIRST Bill of exchange ( SECOND being unpaid )

pay to _____              or order the sum of

_____

      ( amount in words )

Value received for _____ of _____

      ( quantity )                              ( name of commodity )

Drawn under _____

L/C No. _____ dated _____

For and on behalf of

To：

_____

( Signature )

# Chapter 8　Official Documents

【本章提要】

为了监控和管制对外贸易，国家有关部门必要时会要求进出口双方提交进出口许可证、原产地证明书、检验证书、进出口货物报关单等官方单据(又称公务单据)。

出口许可证是指国家对外经贸行政管理部门统一签发的、批准某项商品出口的、具有法律效力的证明文件，是海关查验放行出口货物的依据，也是银行办理结汇的依据。

出口许可证的内容主要包括：①出口商全称和代码；②发货人全称和代码；③许可证编号；④许可证有效截止日期；⑤贸易方式(一般贸易、易货贸易、补偿贸易、进料加工、来料加工、外商投资企业出口、边境贸易、出料加工、转口贸易、期货贸易、承包工程、归还贷款出口、国际展销、协定贸易、其他贸易)；⑥合同号；⑦报关口岸；⑧进口国(地区)；⑨支付方式(信用证、托收、汇付、本票、现金、记账和免费等)；⑩运输方式(海上运输、铁路运输、公路运输、航空运输、邮政运输、固定运输)；⑪货物标记、包装种类和件数；⑫商品名称和商品编码；⑬规格等级；⑭单位(计量单位)；⑮数量；⑯单价；⑰总值；⑱总值折美元；⑲总计；⑳备注；㉑发证机关签章及发证日期等。

原产地证明书，简称产地证，通常是进口方要求出口方提供的、证明货物原产地或制造地的书面文件，多在进口国/地区对进口产品实施差别性进口关税和进口配额时适用。

产地证可分为普通产地证和普惠制产地证①，前者可由中国进出口检验检疫局或中国贸促会签发，后者只能由中国进出口检验检疫局签发。

产地证的内容通常包括：①产地证编号；②出口商名称和地址；③收货人名称和地址；④运输工具及路线；⑤目的国或目的地；⑥证明文句；⑦货物标记；⑧货物包装种类、最大包装件数及货物名称；⑨H.S.编码；⑩商品数量；⑪发票号及日期；⑫出口商声明；⑬当局盖章；⑭原产地标准等项目。

检验证书是各种进出口商品检验证书、鉴定证书和其他证书的统称，是对外贸易有关当事人履行契约义务的证明文件，是处理争议索赔的法律依据，也是海关验放货物、征收关税的必要证明。

检验证书的种类繁多，比较常用的有：①品质检验证书；②重量检验证书；③数量检验证书；④价值证明书；⑤原产地证书；⑥卫生/健康证书；⑦消毒检验证书；⑧温度检验证书；⑨兽医检验证书；⑩货损检验证书等。

检验证书的内容因所要证明的内容不同而不同，通常包括：①检验证书的名称、发证

---

① 截至 2021 年 11 月 30 日，中国只需要对出口挪威、新西兰和澳大利亚三国的相关出口产品，签发普惠制产地证。

机关和地点;②发货人名称和地址;③收货人名称和地址;④商品的名称、数量/重量、包装种类及件数、运输标志;⑤起运地(港)、目的地(港)、运输工具等;⑥检验结果;⑦签证日期;⑧签字盖章。

进出口货物报关单是进出口货物的收发货人或其代理人,按照海关规定的格式对进出口货物的实际情况做出书面申明,是海关办理通关手续的法律文书。

按海关监管方式划分,进出口货物报关单可分为进料加工进出口货物报关单、来料加工及补偿贸易进出口货物报关单、一般贸易和其他贸易进出口货物报关单。按表现形式,可划分为纸质报关单和电子报关单。

报关单的内容比较复杂,主要包括:①预录入编号;②海关编号;③进口口岸/出口口岸;④备案号;⑤进口日期/出口日期;⑥申报日期;⑦经营单位;⑧运输方式;⑨运输工具名称;⑩提运单号;⑪收货单位/发货单位;⑫贸易方式(监管方式);⑬征免性质;⑭征税比例/结汇方式;⑮许可证号;⑯起运国(地区)/运抵国(地区);⑰装货港/指运港;⑱境内目的地/境内货源地;⑲批准文号;⑳成交方式;㉑运费;㉒保费;㉓杂费;㉔合同协议号;㉕件数;㉖包装种类;㉗毛重(千克);㉘净重(千克);㉙集装箱号;㉚随附单据;㉛用途/生产厂家;㉜标记唛码及备注;㉝项号;㉞商品编号;㉟商品名称和规格型号;㊱数量及单位;㊲原产国(地区)/最终目的国(地区);㊳单价;㊴总价;㊵币制;㊶征免;㊷税费征收情况;㊸录入员;㊹录入单位;㊺申报单位;㊻填制日期;㊼海关审批注栏等项目。

International trade involves complex flows of goods and services across national boarders. In order to monitor and control these flows, countries may require businessmen to provide a set of documents, known as government control documents, or official documents. These usually include Export License, Certificate of Origin, Inspection Certificate, Import License and Foreign Exchange Authorization, Consular Invoice, and Customs Invoice, etc. [1]

## 8.1　Export License

Ever since the emergence of international trade, many governments have been assisting and encouraging the export of goods, and there are usually very few barriers to exports erected by the exporting government. However, due to the nature of the product exported, the market to which the goods are exported or some other reasons, there are some occasions when a particular restriction on export might be encountered. Export license is one type of export restriction documents.

### 8.1.1　Definition

An export license is an export control document issued by the appropriate licensing agency. It grants permission to conduct a certain type of export transaction.

---

[1]　For detailed requirements on official documents by different countries, please refer to DHL Trade Automation Service: Trade document library (http://www.dhl-usa.com/tasclient/HandlerServlet? CLIENT=TD_DISPLAY_HANDLER).

Export license is most often used to monitor the export of sensitive technologies (such as advanced computer chips, encryption-decryption software), prohibited materials (drugs, genetically-modified plants), dangerous materials (explosives, radioactive substances), strategic materials (uranium, advanced alloys), or goods in short supply in the home market (foodstuffs, raw materials). [1]

### 8.1.2  Functions

Export licenses may be used to serve the following purposes:

• To adjust the exporting of specific goods according to the changes of trade policies and market conditions of importing countries.

• To control and supervise the exporting quantity and price so that out-of-order competition between similar exporters from one exporting countries can be avoided in international markets.

• To support the customs clearing and banking settlement.

### 8.1.3  Application

In practice, it is up to the exporter to determine whether the product requires a license and to research the end use of the product. To be a successful exporter, the first step is to acquire knowledge about the export licensing requirements that are most relevant to the company. The following procedures may be involved when applying for an export license.

(1) Exporters should learn which department or agency has jurisdiction over the item they are planning to export to find out if a license is required.

In China, as for the latest stipulations on import and export licenses, exporters are recommended to refer to the website of the Quota & License Administrative Bureau Ministry of Commerce of The People's Republic of China[2], which is responsible for export licenses application reviewing and granting. Other national agencies have licensing responsibilities for specialized articles or embargoes on certain countries.

(2) Since the licensed items of export (import) may be adjusted from time to time, exporters must keep up with the changes, and consider the following when they make the determination.

• What are you exporting?

• Where are you exporting?

• Who will receive your items?

• What will your items be used for?

For instance, as for China's dual use licensed items[3] which took effect on January 1,

---

① http://www.businessdictionary.com/definition/export-license.html.

② http://www.licence.org.cn/Web/xgxz/sqb/default.asp? Id=60.

③ Dual Use Licenses are required in certain situations involving national security, foreign policy, short-supply, nuclear non-proliferation, missile technology, chemical and biological weapons, regional stability, crime control, or terrorist concerns.

2009 and the restricted items of processing trade which took effect on February 1, 2009, exporters can refer to the following websites:

http://www. mofcom. gov. cn/accessory/200812/1230708815193. xls

http://www. mofcom. gov. cn/accessory/200812/1230724121365. xls

(3) Once exporters have acknowledged that export licenses are required for their exporting goods, they can fill in the export license application form accordingly. Two specimens of application form for export license of People's Republic of China is given in the appendix part of this chapter (Specimen 1 and Specimen 2).

(4) The detailed procedures of applying for an export license is portrayed in the internet flowchart indicated in the appendix of this chapter (Internet flowchart 1).

To be noted, in order to obtain an export license, the exporter should firstly obtain an electronic key (GFACA certificate) to ascertain their identities. As for a typical application form for a GFACA certificate, please refer to the appendix of this chapter (Specimen 3).

(5) Once exporters have obtained the export license[①], they can export their goods or products. However, exporters should first be familiar with the detailed items of an export license.

## 8. 1. 4　Contents

A typical export license may cover the following items in terms of varied boxes:

(1) Exporter. In this box, the exporter's name, and its identification code obtained from the relevant agency issuing export license should be filled in.

(2) Consignor. In this box, the exporters are required to fill in the export company's name and identification number.

(3) License No. This box covers the license number usually arranged by the export license issuing agency.

(4) Validity. The box of validity refers to the expiry date of export license. Depending on the types of goods, the validity of export license may differ from one month, three months to six months, starting from the date of license issuance.

(5) Terms of trade. In this box, the alternative terms of trade may be filled in one of the following items, general trade, barter trade, compensation trade, trade of processing with imported materials, trade of processing with customer's materials, exporting of foreign-funded enterprises, frontier trade, outward processing, entrepot trade, forward trade, contract project, export for reimbursement loan, international sales exhibition, agreement trade, and etc. The term of trade filled in here should be consistent with that of the customs declaration.

(6) Contract number. This box is for the contract number used in applying for export li-

---

① From January 1,2009, Chinese exporters can obtain export licenses, without paying licensing issuing fees, from the relevant agencies.

cense, customs clearing and banking settlement.

(7) Port of shipment. In practice, three ports of shipment may be filled in this box. However, customs can only be declared in one of them.

(8) Country of destination. This refers to the contracted country of destination. Usually the name of a continent (e. g. Europe) is not allowed.

(9) Terms of payment. This refers to the contracted terms of payment. Alternatives may include L/C, D/P, D/A, T/T, D/D, M/T, promissory note, or cash.

(10) Means of transportation. This refers to the means of transportation when the exported goods stand off, for instance, seaway, airway, roadway, railway, postal, or multi-mode transports.

(11) Marks & numbers, and number of packages. This box refers to the shipping marks & numbers on the packing of exported goods, and the number of the outer packaging.

(12) Description of commodity and commodity number. This box requires filling in the detailed and standard description and code of goods listed on the export license supervision goods directory publicized by the Ministry of Commerce of People's Republic of China.

(13) Specification. This box covers the detailed quality specification of goods to be exported.

(14) Unit. The unit here refers to the measurement unit complying with the stipulations under the Harmonized Commodity Classification System (H. S. ).

(15) Quantity. The box of quantity refers to the quantity of goods being granted to export by the export license. The value of this figure is allowed to remain one decimal digit, and the round principle applied when necessary. In the case of the measurement unit "one lot", the quantity should be "1".

(16) Unit price. The box of unit price refers to the unit price in compliance with the measurement unit in item (14). In the case of the measurement unit "one lot", the total amount should be filled in this item.

(17) Amount. This box requires filling the total value of goods to be exported and the money of account as well.

(18) Amount in USD. This box refers to the equivalent value of exported goods in USD, which may be converted at a prevailing or a pre-agreed foreign exchange rate.

(19) Total. This box refers to the sum of the above mentioned items when necessary.

(20) Supplementary details. This box refers to all matters not mentioned above.

(21) Issuing authority's stamp and signature date. After examination and assurance of information accuracy, it is for the license issuing authority stamp on the export license, the signature of the qualified person, and the signature date.

### 8.1.5  Specimens

A specimen of a general export license (in both Chinese and English) of the People's Republic of China is enclosed in the part of appendix in this chapter (Specimen 4).

In addition, specimens of China's export license of textile products exported to EU, U. S. A. , and Canada are also given in the appendix of this chapter (Specimen 5~7).

## 8.2  Certificate of Origin

### 8.2.1  Definition

A certificate of origin (often abbreviated as CO or COO), also known as declaration of origin, is a document certifying a shipment's country of origin. It is used between members of a trading block or where special privileges are granted to goods produced in certain countries. certificate of origin is usually issued by a trade promotion office, or a chamber of commerce in the exporting country. [1]

A certificate of origin traditionally states from what country the shipped goods originate, but "originate" in a CO does not mean the country the goods are shipped from, but the country where the goods are actually made. This raises a definition problem in cases where less than 100% of the raw materials and processes and added value are all from one single country. A common practice is that, if more than 50% of the value of sales price of the goods originates from one country, that country is regarded as the country of origin (then the "national content" is more than 50%). In various international agreements, other percentages of national content are acceptable. [2]

### 8.2.2  Functions

Certificate of origin is usually required by countries that do not use customs invoice or consular invoice. It is used to serve the following purposes:

● To act as one of the support documents at the time of importation, and to enable the buyers to process their importation of the goods.

● To classify the goods in the customs regulations of the importing country, thus defining how much duty shall be paid and permitting preferential import duties where appropriate.

● To evidence a shipment's country of origin for import quota purposes.

● To evidence a shipment's country of origin for statistical purposes.

● To evidence a shipment's country of origin for health regulations (especially for food shipments).

● To act as a support document for goods delivery, payment settlement and claims settlement.

### 8.2.3  Application

In practice, the following procedures may be involved when applying for a certificate of origin.

---

[1]  http://www. businessdictionary. com/definition/certificate-of-origin. html.

[2]  http://en. wikipedia. org/wiki/Certificate_of_origin.

(1) Before concluding a transaction, the exporter and importer should always clarify whether a CO is required, and if so, agree on exactly the form and content of the CO.

(2) Exporters should learn who are qualified to issue certificate of origin of the items they are planning to export.

A certificate of origin may be an informal document or a formal one. An informal certificate of origin is usually issued by the exporter or the manufacturer, while a formal certificate of origin is usually confirmed by an official body in the exporting country, such as the chamber of commerce and the bureau of inspection, etc.

In practice, the importing country may often require a formal certificate of origin. In China, this certificate is generally issued by the Import and Export Commodity Inspection Bureau, or the China Council for Promotion of International Trade (CCPIT).

(3) When a formal certificate of origin is required, the exporter can fill in the certificate of origin application form accordingly, and provide necessary documents. Two specimens of application form for export license of the People's Republic of China is given in the appendix part of this chapter (Specimen 8~9).

(4) If exporters apply for CO electronically, relevant documents may not be required, and the following procedures are involved.

● Login www. co. ccpit. org, the specific website of China Council for Promotion of International Trade from which to apply for a CO.

● Register if the first time to login the website.

● Fill in the application form, particularly the items with " * " are mandatory to fill in.

● After being examined by the CCPIT, you may obtain your username and password.

● Login the navigation interface with username and password to start making out a CO at ease.

● Save your CO, simultaneously the system will automatically check the contents you have prepared and remind you of correction if necessary.

● Preview the CO and invoice for assurance of information accuracy, then send the document to the CCPIT.

● Receive return receipt from CCPIT after its few-second automatic auditing.

● Get the printed-out CO from CCPIT with commercial invoice and other required documents accompanied.

● A CO can be corrected and renewed, if necessary, through the same route of applying for a new CO.

The detailed guideline of applying for a CO is enclosed in the appendix part of this chapter (Internet flowchart 2).

## 8.2.4  Contents

A typical certificate of origin usually contains the nature, quantity, value of the goods and place of manufacturing. There is no particular format existing internationally. It may cover the following items in varied boxes:

(1) Certificate number. The certificate will be invalid if the column is blank.

(2) Exporter. It is the beneficiary of relevant L/C. The exporter's detailed address is required, including doorplate number, street, city and country.

(3) Consignee. It is usually the buyer or the notify party of the B/L. If it is required to be blank, "to order" is usually marked here.

(4) Means of transportation and route. The port of shipment and destination, terms of shipment are to be made out. If transshipment is allowed, the place of transshipment is marked. The following is an example.

FROM QINGDAO TO ROTTERDAM VIA HONG KONG BY VESSEL

(5) Country / Region of destination. It refers to the country or region in which the goods arrive, the middle businessman is not mentioned.

(6) For certifying authority use only. It is usually kept blank. The content is made out by the issuing organization according to the concrete condition.

(7) Marks and numbers. It is to be made out according to the invoice, the phrases "as per invoice No. ×××" or "As per B/L No. ×××" are not allowed. "N/M" is filled in where there is no mark.

(8) Number and kind of packages/description of goods. e. g. :

ONE HUNDRED AND FIFTY (150) CARTONS OF MEN's T/C PRINTED JACKET SIXTY-SEVEN (67) CARTONS OF BOY's T/C PRINTED JACKET, OR

150 CARTONS (ONE HUNDRED AND FIFTY CARTONS ONLY) OF MEN's T/C PRINTED JACKET 67 CARTONS (SIXTY-SEVEN CARTONS ONLY) OF BOY's T/C PRINTED JACKET

(9) H. S. Code. This part should be kept in conformity with customs declaration.

(10) Quantity. The quantity and measurement are required to be printed, for example: 100 sets N. W. 1, 000 MT or 1,000 MT (N. W. )

(11) Number and date of invoice. It is to be in conformity with the invoice.

(12) Declaration by the exporter. The issuing place and date are printed here with the exporter's stamp and signature. The date shall not be later than the date of B/L or earlier than the date of invoice.

(13) Certification. The issuing place and date are required. The issuer should sign manually with seal.

(14) For official use, stamp "ISSUED RETROSPECTIVELY" (in red); if CO is lost or stolen, then stamp as "THIS CERTIFICATE IS IN REPLACEMENT OF CERTIFICATE OF ORIGIN NO. ××× DATED ××× WHICH IS CANCELLED" (in red).

(15) Item number.

(16) Origin criterion. As for alternative criterion of origin, please refer to "Guide to Origin Criteria for Schemes of Preferences and Free Trade Agreements". [1]

In China, two kinds of Certificate of Origin are generally adopted: Certificate of Origin issued by the CIQ (the China Exit and Entry Inspection and Quarantine Bureau) or the CCPIT (the China Council for the Promotion of International Trade) and the Generalized System of Preference Certificate of Origin Form A (GSP Form A) issued by the CIQ. The GSP Form A can be used to get preferential import duties in many countries, such as New Zealand, Canada, Japan, EU members, etc.

### 8.2.5  Specimens

Several samples of certificates of origin of People's Republic of China are given in the appendix of this chapter, covering:

- 2 general CO (Specimen 10~11).
- 1 certificate of GSP Form A (Specimen 12).
- 1 CO of Textile Products exported to EU (Specimen 13).
- 1 CO under Asia-Pacific Trade Agreement (Specimen 14).

### 8.2.6  New changes

(1) The Emergence of RCEP Certificate of Origin. The Regional Comprehensive Economic Partnership (RCEP), is by far the world's largest trading bloc, comprises 15 Asia-Pacific countries (10 member states of the Association of Southeast Asian Nations (ASEAN), China, Japan, the Republic of Korea, Australia, and New Zealand), and covers about 30 percent of the world's population and 30 percent of global economic and trade volume. The RCEP agreement involves various areas such as tariff reductions, trade facilitation, and the opening up of services and investment, highlighting the importance of multilateralism and an open world economy.

Since the RCEP pact came into effecton January 1, 2022, China remains committed to high-quality RCEP implementation to promote regional economic integration. Undoubtedly, the RCEP serves as a gateway allowing other member countries to benefit from China's development opportunities. "It has helped member countries to boost post pandemic recovery and sustainable long-term economic growth, contributing to enhancing regional peace, stability, harmony, development and prosperity". [2] Moreover, RCEP could offer individual exporter double benefits:

---

[1]  www. customs. gov. sg/NR/rdonlyres/B5C01C21-1B57-4E1B-B766-18F7C4170E1B/19101/ROOCrit3. doc.

[2]  RCEP fuels regional growth amid economic recovery, challenges-Opinion-Chinadaily. com. cn.

preferential tax rates and approved exporter policy.

With the full implementation of RCEP in 15 member countries, the RCEP certificate of origin is increasingly welcomed by more and more enterprises, since the certificates will grant companies tariff reductions. For example, Seduno, Ningbo's first RCEP-approved exporter, has leveraged 3,649 RCEP certificates of origin since 2022. [1] Just in November of 2023, CCPIT branches issued 19,834 RCEP Certificates of Origin nationwide, up 20.83 percent year-on-year. It is expected to reduce tariffs by \$9 million on Chinese product exports to RCEP member countries[2]. Another typical example is Qingdao, the coastal city in East China's Shandong province, issued 112,000 certificates of origin under the RCEP agreement in 2023, a year-on-year increase of 35.3 percent and the most in the country. The certificates are expected to reduce tariffs by nearly 300 million Chinese yuan for Chinese products in RCEP importing countries. The policy of tariff reductions under RCEP has continued to pay dividends and further enhance the competitiveness of Chinese enterprises in exporting products. The tariff reductions also strengthen the resilience of regional industrial and supply chains and are an important force in stabilizing the foundation of China's foreign trade.

On November 23, 2021, the General Administration of Customs issued Order No. 255, announcing the "Measures for the Administration of the Origin of Import and Export Goods under the Regional Comprehensive Economic Partnership Agreement of the People's Republic of China Customs" (hereinafter referred to as the "Measures")[3], which came into effect on January 1, 2022. The "Measures" covers the following points:

- Application Conditions for RCEP Certificate of Origin
- Application Materials for RCEP Certificate of Origin
- Application Process for RCEP Certificate of Origin
- Analysis of RCEP Rules of Origin
- Reissue and Correction of RCEP Certificate of Origin

(2) The suspension of GSP Certificate of Origin. In 2021, the General Administration of Customs made two announcements regarding the suspension of the signing of the Generalized System of Preferences Certificate of Origin.

The Generalized System of Preferences, abbreviated as GSP, is ageneralized, non-discriminatory, and non-reciprocal system of tariff preferences granted by developed countries to developing countries and regions for exporting manufactured and semifinished products. The Generalized System of Preferences (GSP) was born in 1968 and has been implemented since

---

[1] Zhejiang's new-round action plan to foster MNCs – Chinadaily. com. cn.

[2] https://www.chinadaily.com.cn/a/202312/28/WS658ccd6aa31040ac301a9e54.html.

[3] 政策解读:RCEP 出口原产地签证指南 (anycase.cn).

1971. It aims to increase the export benefits of developing countries, promote their industrialization, and accelerate their economic growth rate.

The GSP Form A is a preferential certificate of origin issued by an authorized agency of the grantee country in accordance with the rules of origin and relevant requirements of the GSP granting country. It is an official certification document for export products to enjoy the tariff preferences of the GSP granting country. The certificate format follows the GSP (Combined Declaration and Certification) Form A, which is printed by the grantee country in accordance with the unified format specified by the United Nations Conference on Trade and Development (UNCTAD) Special Committee on Preferential Issues and filled out and issued in accordance with the relevant regulations of the granting country. In China, customs authority is the only visa authority for the certificate of origin under the Generalized System of Preferences.

There are 41 granting countries, including 28 EU countries [France, U. K. (post Brexit), Ireland, Germany, Denmark, Italy, Belgium, Netherlands, Luxembourg, Greece, Spain, Portugal, Austria, Sweden, Finland, Czech Republic, Slovakia, Poland, Estonia, Latvia, Slovenia, Cyprus, Lithuania, Malta, Hungary; adding Romania, Bulgaria, Croatia], Switzerland, Norway, Japan, the United States, Canada, Australia, New Zealand, Russia, Ukraine, Belarus, Kazakhstan, Türkiye, Liechtenstein. While there are 170 grantee developing countries and regions, including China.

Since the implementation of the Generalized System of Preferences (GSP) in 1978, among the 41 granting countries mentioned above, 40 countries, excluding the United States, have given China preferential tariff treatment under the GSP. China has also actively utilized the Generalized System of Preferences to expand exports to developed countries.

With the continuous improvement of China's economy and the people' living standards, China is no longer a low-income or middle-income economy (World Bank standards, per capita GNI less than $4,095, 2020). For this reason, several granting countries such as the European Union have announced in recent years the cancellation of their preferential treatment for China. In other words, China has gradually "graduated" from the preferential treatment system of various developed economies.

As of now, only Norway, New Zealand, and Australia are the countries that still retain the GSP treatment for China. Enterprises can still apply for the GSP certificate for goods exported to these three countries.

At the enterprise level, China's exporters are supposed to communicate and explain to relevant foreign customers duly, in order to help them to understand the changes in trade costs caused by no longer enjoying preferential treatment, and make corresponding adjustments.

## 8.3 Certificate of Inspection

### 8.3.1 Definition

An inspection certificate, called certificate of inspection, or inspection report, is a statement issued and signed by the appropriate authority, evidencing that the goods have been inspected and what the results of such inspection are.

It is usually required for import of industrial equipment, meat products, and perishable merchandise, to certify that the item meets the required specifications and was in good condition and correct quantity when it left the port of departure. [1]

### 8.3.2 Functions

An inspection certificate may play the following important roles in practice of international trade.

● To evidence the quality, quantity, weight, physical and technical specifications scientifically.

● To support the payment settlement.

● To support the customs clearing.

● To support the trade dispute settlement.

● To protect the human, animal and plants from infectious disease.

● To certify the compliance of goods delivered with terms and conditions of relevant S/C and L/C.

### 8.3.3 Types

In practice, the issuer of an inspection certificate may be a governmental organization such as the CIQ or the China Certification & Inspection (Group) Co., Ltd. (CCIC) in China, a non-governmental organization such as authentic surveyor, sworn measurer, the manufacturer of the goods, or the user or importer of the goods.

The most often used inspection certificates issued by national inspection organizations in China include:

● Inspection certificate of quality.

● Inspection certificate of quantity.

● Inspection certificate of weight.

● Certificate of value.

● Certificate of origin.

● Health and sanitary inspection certificate.

● Disinfection inspection certificate.

---

[1]  http://www. businessdictionary. com/definition/certificate-of-inspection. html.

- Inspection certificate of temperature.
- Veterinary inspection certificate.
- Inspection certificate on damaged cargo.

World-widely speaking, the following four types of inspection certificate deserve our much attention.

(1) Health, veterinary and sanitary certificates. These certificates are used where livestock, hide, foodstuffs, agricultural goods or some packing materials are exported. They are signed by the health authorities of the exporting country, certifying that the goods are free of disease, e. g. mad cow disease, [1] and etc.

(2) Legalized invoices. These invoices are authorized by the consulate representing the importer's country or the local Chamber of Commerce in the exporter's country. The purpose of this invoice is to give the importing country an official record of the transaction. [2]

(3) Third party inspection certificates. These certificates are issued by recognized independent third parties declaring the result of an examination of the goods exported. The importer may call for such an examination of the goods before shipment to protect him/her from paying for sub-standard goods. [3]

(4) Weight certificates. Weight certificates give details of the gross or net weights of goods. These documents are used for goods not packed in boxes or containers, e. g. wheat, grain, corn, etc. These are important where loss of weight may occur through evaporation or some other factors. A weight certificate may be issued by the exporter or a public weigher, or an independent weigher for a fee. [4]

## 8.3.4 Contents

When preparing and examining an inspection certificate, the involved parties should consider the following issues with great care:

- They should be made out carefully and can not be modified willfully, to guarantee that they look clean and correct apparently.
- The date of inspection certificate should be earlier than the date of transportation documents and later than that of the invoice or as the same.
- The certificate category should be complied with the stipulation of L/C.
- The specification, quality and quantity should be complied with the requirement of the invoice.

---

[1]  http://www.fnb.co.za/corporate/international/imports/.
[2]  http://www.fnb.co.za/corporate/international/imports/.
[3]  ditto.
[4]  ditto.

● The certificate is issued usually by the official organization with reasonable charges.

### 8.3.5 Specimen

In order to obtain an inspection certificate, the trader should first fill in an application form for inspection. A sample application form for import inspection is given in the appendix of this chapter (Specimen 15).

Two samples of certificates of inspection are given in the appendix of this chapter, covering:

● 1 inspection certificate of quality issued by Entry-Exit Inspection and Quarantine of the People's Republic of China (Specimen 16).

● 1 certificate of quantity and weight issued by SGS (Specimen 17).

## 8.4 Customs Declaration Form

Customs declaration, also known as customs entry, duty entry, or just entry, refers to the declaration of information on imported or exported goods, prepared by a customs broker on a prescribed form called Entry Form or Duty Entry Form, and submitted to the customs. It states the customs classification number, country of origin, description, quantity, and CIF value of the goods, and the estimated amount of duty to be paid. Upon examination by a customs officer, if the entry is verified as a correct or "perfect entry", the goods in question are released (on payment of duty and other charges, if any) to the importer, or are allowed to be exported. [1]

### 8.4.1 Definition

Customs declaration form is a document prepared by an exporter before shipment and used to apply to the customs for declaration of the exported goods. The customs officer will sign on the customs declaration form and release the goods if the goods meet the requirements.

The customs declaration form is usually in different colors. Taking China's customs declaration form as an example, the white one is made out for general trade while the pink one is for processing trade. However, the contents of these documents are quite similar.

To be noted, not anyone can apply for customs declaration. The person asking for declaration should be qualified, that is, he/she should have the certificate of customs declaration, which can be obtained by passing the examination held by the General Administration of Customs of the P. R. C.

### 8.4.2 Contents

Practically, customs declaration form is one of the most important and complicated documents. In order to make out a sound customs declaration form and facilitate the customs declaration procedures, one should firstly get familiar with the main contents of a typical customs declaration form, and secondly keep in touch with the latest requirements by the China's General

---

[1] http://www. businessdictionary. com/definition/customs-entry. html.

Administration of Customs (CGAC).

The CGAC made the Announcement No. (2016) 20 on March 24, 2016, and made it into effect on March 30, 2016, since then the Announcement has been providing detailed guidance on preparing a qualified customs declaration form[1].

Detailed items covered in a typical customs declaration form are discussed as follows.

(1) Pre-record No. This number is auto-generated by the customs' computer system while the exporter is applying to customs.

(2) Number of Customs. The number of customs is either auto-generated by the computer system, or assigned by the customs officer.

The unique number of each customs declaration form consists of 18 characters, among which the 1-4 digits are the customs code (refer to Customs Code Table[2]), the 5-8 digits indicate the year of the solar calendar, the 9th character indicates the type of transaction/customs declaration (in general customs declaration, "1" for import, "0" for export; while in centralized declaration, "I" for import and "E"), and the remaining 9 digits are serial numbers.

(3) Consignor. It refers to the name of a company who signs and executes the S/C (generally refers to the exporter), and the code for the company (either an 18-digit uniform social credit code, or a 10-digit customs registration code).

In case that the contracting party differs from the executive party, the consignor should be the executive party; in case those two companies have mutual agent relationship in customs declaration, the consignor should be the principal exporting company.

(4) Port of Export. It usually refers to the name and code of the customs of the final port of export. When transferring the bonded goods across the customs zones, the port of export refers to the name of the departure port and its customs code. When transferring the deep processing goods for processing trade across the customs zones, the port of export indicates the name of the transferring-out port and its customs code. When transferring the bonded goods across the special customs surveillance zones or areas, the port of export indicates the name of the receiving port and its customs code. And for those goods without actual entry and exit, the port of export refers to the name of the declaring customs and its customs code.

(5) Date of Export. It refers to the customs declaring date of the carrying means of exported goods. It is only used in printing a customs declaration for certificate, but not required in applying a customs declaration.

For those goods without actual entry and exit, the date of export on customs declaration form refers to the customs authority's recording date of the relevant customs declaration.

---

[1]    http://www.customs.gov.cn/publish/portal0/tab49564/info790113.htm.

[2]    http://www.customs.gov.cn/default.aspx? tabid=9410.

The date of export is an 8-digit-number, ordering as YYYY/MM/DD.

(6) Date of Application. It is the date on which the customs authority records the customs declaration application from a consignor or from an entrusted customs broker. If a customs declaration is applied electronically, the date of application is to be recorded automatically by the computer system of the customs authority. If a customs declaration is applied in writing, the date of application is to be deemed as the date of receiving and recording the paper customs declaration by the customs authority.

The date of application is also an 8-digit-number, ordering as YYYY/MM/DD. And it is not required for a consignor in applying a customs clearance.

(7) Producer/Seller. The producer/seller indicates the name of domestic producer and/or seller of the exported goods, including those exporters who export independently and those who entrust other trading companies to export. The name of the producer/seller should be filled in CHINESE character.

A unique code must be accompanied with the name of the domestic producer/seller. Practically, the code may be an 18-digit uniform social credit code for a legal person company or other entities, be a 10-digit customs registration code for the producer/seller, or a 9-digit organization code certificate (OCC). And if there is no OCC for the producer/seller, a mark "NO" is required to insert.

For the goods supervised by the Manual of Processing Trade, the name of the producer/seller should be consistent with that of the processing trade company listed on the Manual; for the goods granted some tax deduction or exemption, the name of the producer/seller should be consistent with that of the tax-preference applicants who are supported by duty-free certificate of exported goods.

(8) Mode of Transportation. Mode of transportation may be the actual mode of transportation, which is typed by the means of conveyance, such as water, air, road, rail, etc. ; or the special mode of transportation required by the customs authority when goods are transported domestically and involved in no actual entry-exit.

Specific code for different modes of transportation are summarized as the table 8. 1 below.

**Table 8. 1 Code for Mode of Transportation**

| Code | Mode of Transportation | Code | Mode of transportation |
| --- | --- | --- | --- |
| 0 | Non-bonded area | 8 | Bonded warehouse |
| 1 | Supervised warehouse | 9 | Others |
| 2 | Water | H | Special border customs |
| 3 | Rail | T | Comprehensive experimental community |
| 4 | Road | W | Logistics center |
| 5 | Air | X | Logistics park |

续表

| Code | Mode of Transportation | Code | Mode of transportation |
|------|------------------------|------|------------------------|
| 6 | Mail | Y | Bonded port area |
| 7 | Bonded area | Z | Export processing zone |

Source: http://www. customs. gov. cn/publish/portal0/tab9410.

(9) Name of Transportation Tool. It refers to the name of departure tool of transportation and its reference number (for example, vessel and voyage number for seaway, the number of train for railway and the number of flight for airway).

Detailed requirements are summarized as the table 8. 2 below.

**Table 8. 2  Name of Transportation Tool under Different Modes of Transportation**

| Mode of Customs Declaration | Mode of Transportation | | Name of Transportation Tool |
|---|---|---|---|
| Direct Declaration or under Regionally Integrated Customs Declaration | Water | | The official number of the carrying vessel, or its name in English |
| | Road | | Domestic license number of the carrying truck before issuing a roadway bill; not required after a roadway bill is issued |
| | Rail | | Number of the railway carriage, or number of the delivery receipt |
| | Air | | Number of the flight |
| | Mail | | Number of the postal parcel |
| | Others | | Detailed mode of transport, e. g. pipeline, pack animals |
| Trans-Customs Declaration | Water | Non-transit | @ 16-digit pre-record number of the application for customs transfer (or a 13-digit number of cargo list) |
| | | Transit | when more than one customs declaration form transferred via one customs declaration form @ transshipped cargo and any of the following: Inland Waterway: Name of the lighter Inland Railway: 4-digit Code for Competent Customs+Name of the train Inland Roadway: 4-digit Code for Competent Customs+Name of Truck |
| | Rail | | @ 16-digit pre-record number of the application for customs transfer (ora 13-digit number of cargo list); @ when more than one customs declaration form transferred via one customs declaration form |
| | Air | | @ 16-digit pre-record number of the application for customs transfer (or 13-digit number of cargo list); @ when more than one customs declaration form transferred via one customs declaration form |
| | Others | | @ 16-digit pre-record number of the application for customs transfer (or 13-digit number of cargo list) |

续表

| Mode of Customs Declaration | Mode of Transportation | Name of Transportation Tool |
|---|---|---|
| Centralized Declaration | | Centralized Declaration |
| No Actual Entry-Exit | | Exempted from Declaration |

(10) Voyage Number. It indicates the voyage number of the means of conveyance. Detailed requirements are summarized as the table 8.3 below.

**Table 8.3   Number of Voyage under different Modes of Transportation**

| Mode of Customs Declaration | Mode of Transportation | | Number of Voyage |
|---|---|---|---|
| Direct Declaration or under Regionally Integrated Customs Declaration | Water | | Voyage No. of the carrying vessel |
| | Road | | An 8-digit date of departure as YYYY/MM/DD before issuing a roadway bill; No. of batches of transported cargoes |
| | Rail | | Departure date of Train |
| | Air | | Free from reporting |
| | Mail | | Departure date of transportation tool |
| | Others | | Free from reporting |
| Trans-Customs Declaration | Water | Non-transit | Free from reporting |
| | | Transit | Voyage No. of Lighters; An 8-digit Departure Date: YYYY/MM/DD An 8-digit Departure Date: YYYY/MM/DD |
| | Rail | | Free of reporting when exported via lift-sharing, LCL |
| | Air | | Free from reporting |
| | Others | | Free from reporting |
| Centralized Declaration | | | Free from reporting |
| No Actual Entry-Exit | | | Free from reporting |

(11) Number of Delivery/Shipping Document. It refers to number of transportation document. Such as B/L No. for sea, flight bill No. for air and receipt No. for road, etc.

Usually, one customs declaration form can only cover one B/L or one other shipping document. When more than one Bs/L or shipping documents involved in one shipment, they should be reported under separate customs declaration form. Specific requirements on reporting the delivery numbers are as follows.

**Table 8.4  Delivery/Shipping Document Number**

| Mode of Customs Declaration | Mode of Transportation | | Delivery Number |
|---|---|---|---|
| Direct Declaration or Under Regionally Integrated Customs Declaration | Water | | Ref. No. of B/L; <br> Ref. No. of B/L * Ref. No. of House B/L |
| | Road | | Free from reporting before issuing the Roadway Bill; <br> Ref. No. of Master Bill after issuing the Roadway Bill |
| | Rail | | Ref. No. of Railway Bill |
| | Air | | Ref. No. of Master bill "-" Ref. No. of House Bill; <br> Ref. No. of Master Bill |
| | Mail | | Ref. No. of Postal Parcel |
| | Others | | Free from reporting |
| Trans-Customs Declaration | Water | Non-transit | Free from reporting |
| | | Transit | No. of B/L |
| | Rail | | Free from reporting |
| | Air | | Free from reporting |
| | Others | | Free from reporting |
| Centralized Declaration | | | Duration of Importing and Exporting <br> YYYY/MM/DD-YYYY/MM/DD |
| No Actual Entry-Exit | | | Free from reporting |

(12) Name of Declarer. For self-declaration companies, it refers to the name and code of the exporting company; for agent-declaration companies, it refers to the name and code of the customs broker.

The code may be an 18-digit uniform social credit code, or a 10-digit customs registration code.

This box also includes signatures of individual customs clearance officer and the declaring company.

(13) Mode of Supervision. It refers to a 4-digit mode for specific mode of trade. For instance, "0110" stands for "general trade", "0130" stands for "barter trade", and "1523" for "leasing trade". There are 95 codes in all for corresponding 95 modes of trade, and Table 8.5 below delivers the respective customs code for selected 15 modes of trade.

**Table 8.5  Customs Code for Selected Modes of Trade**

| Customs Code | Mode of Trade |
|---|---|
| 0110 | General Trade |

| Customs Code | Mode of Trade |
| --- | --- |
| 0130 | Barter Trade |
| 0214 | Processing Supplied Material |
| 0255 | Deep Processing Supplied Material |
| 0513 | Compensation Trade |
| 1215 | Bonded Factory |
| 1233 | Bonded Warehouse Cargoes |
| 1523 | Leasing Trade |
| 1616 | Sales on Consignment |
| 1741 | Duty-free Goods |
| 1831 | Duty-free Foreign Exchange Products |
| 3422 | Exports under Overseas Contracting Projects |
| 3612 | Donations |
| 3910 | Military Equipments |
| 4019 | Small-scaled Border Trade |

Source: http://www. customs. gov. cn/default. aspx? tabid = 9410.

(14) Types of tax. According to "the Customs Tax Types", traded goods may be taxed generally or free of tax. Usually, the type of tax (a 3-digit code) in brief style is filled in here[1]. For instance, "101" stands for "general tax", "118" for "tax on finished vehicle", and "119" for "parts and components of vehicle". There are 45 types of tax in total, and table 8. 6 below indicates selected types of tax and their respective codes.

**Table 8. 6   Customs Code for Selected Types of Tax**

| Code | Type of Tax |
| --- | --- |
| 101 | General Tax |
| 118 | Finished Vehicles |
| 119 | Parts and Components of Vehicles |
| 201 | Non-reimbursable Assistance |
| 301 | Special Area |
| 307 | Bonded Area |
| 401 | Scientific and Educational Supplies |
| 403 | Technical Innovation |
| 408 | Material Technological Equipment |

---

[1]  http://www. customs. gov. cn/publish/portal0/tab9410.

| Code | Type of Tax |
|------|-------------|
| 412 | Infrastructure |
| 501 | Equipment for Processing Trade |
| 502 | Processing with Provided Materials |
| 503 | Processing with Imported Materials |
| 506 | Small-scaled Border Trade |
| 601 | Equity Joint Venture |
| 602 | Contractual Joint Venture |
| 603 | Wholly-owned Subsidiary |
| 997 | Free Trade Agreement |
| 999 | Exceptional Tax Exemption |

(15) Record number for checking. It refers to the number of "Register Manual" or the number of "Certificate of Paid or Free Tax".

(16) Trading Countries/Regions. It refers to the customs code for relevant country/region and its name in CHINESE character. There are 243 customs codes for respective countries/regions, and Table 8. 7 below indicates the first 10 countries/regions.

**Table 8. 7    Customs Code for Selected Countries/Regions**

| Code | Abbreviated Name in English |
|------|------------------------------|
| 101 | Afghanistan |
| 102 | Bahrian |
| 103 | Bangladesh |
| 104 | Bhutan |
| 105 | Brunei |
| 106 | Myanmar |
| 107 | Cambodia |
| 108 | Cyprus |
| 109 | Korea, DPR |
| 110 | Hong Kong, China |

Source:http://www. customs. gov. cn/publish/portal0/tab9410.

If there is no actual entry/exit, China territory and the code "142" should be filled in this box.

(17) Departure/Arrival Country/Region. It refers to the customs code for relevant country/region and its name in CHINESE character.

When goods were transported directly from the exporting country to the importing country, the departure country/region refers to the country/region where goods were loaded/shipped, and the arrival country/region refers to the destination country/region.

When goods were transshipped via a third country/region, and business transaction occurred in transit, the departure country/region would be the transshipping country/region; when goods were transshipped via a third country/region, and no business transaction occurred in transit, the departure country/region would be the original country/region from which cargoes were loaded and shipped.

If there is no actual entry/exit, China territory and the code "142" should be filled in this box.

(18) Port of Loading/Discharge. It refers to the customs code for port and its name in CHINESE character. If there is neither customs code nor name for a port, the customs code for and the name of the correspondent country should be inserted here.

Port of loading refers to the last port abroad before goods' arrival at Chinese customs.

Port of discharge refers to the final port of destination to which goods are to be transported; and if port of discharge is unpredictable, one should make sure the possible port of discharge to his/her best ability and fill it in this box.

If there is no actual entry/exit, China territory and the code "142" should be inserted here.

(19) Domestic Place of Destination/Origin. It refers to the customs code for respective domestic territory and its name in CHINESE character.

Domestic place of destination refers to the place where the imported goods are to be consumed, used or processed. If it is not easy to determine the place of destination, one should fill the pre-advised place where the cargoes are to be received.

Domestic sourcing place should be the original place of production or original place of departure. If there exist difficulties in determining the sourcing place, one should fill in the original place of departure.

(20) Terms of Price. Fill in the customs code of price terms stipulated in "Customs Codes for Trade Terms". The codes for different price terms are listed in table 8. 8 below.

**Table 8. 8　Customs Code for Trade Term**

| Code for Trade Term | Trade Term |
| --- | --- |
| 1 | CIF |
| 2 | C&F |
| 3 | FOB |
| 4 | C&I |
| 5 | Market price |

Source: http://www.customs.gov.cn/tabid/5469/ctl/CscxListView/mid/17784/Default.aspx?

If there is no actual entry/exit, CIF is to be filled in importing customs clearance forms, and FOB in exporting customs clearance forms.

(21) Freight. The freight refers to the charges paid to the shipping company for transportation, including the foreign currency of account.

To be noted, "1", "2" and "3" are used to stand for freight rate, unit freight and total-freight respectively. And three-digit-codes are used to stand for foreign currencies, such as 502 (USD), 110(HKD), 116(JPY), 303(GBP), 300(EUD), 142(CNY)①.

Accordingly, 5% freight should be written as 5/1; unit freight of USD 24 is 502/24/2; and total freight of USD 7,000 is 502/700/3.

(22) Insurance Premium. It refers to the premium paid by the exporter for insurance covering the contracted goods on CIF or CIP trade terms. In addition, the type of foreign currency should be indicated.

Insurance premium may be filled as total insurance or premium rate, and "1" indicates premium rate, "3" indicates total insurance premium, and three-digit-codes are used to stand for foreign currencies.

(23) Additional Expenses. It refers to charges other than the main carriage and the insurance premium, and it is in terms of CNY.

Additional expenses may be filled as total expenses, or as rate of expense. "1" is the customs code for rate of expenses, and "3" for total additional expenses.

(24) Contract Number. Number of sales/purchase contract/agreements or order should be inserted here. It is free from reporting if there is no existence of business transaction.

(25) Number of Packages. It refers to the total number of outer packages of the traded goods. If the manifest is numbered in containers, then the container No. should be filled; if the goods are packed in pallet, then the pallet No. should be filled. If the goods are nude ones, then the code "1" should be filled, and the code "0" is in no way to be filled in this box.

(26) Type of Package. The customs code for the actual type of outer packing(carton, bale, drum, case) should be filled in this box.

(27) Gross Weight. It refers to the gross weight including the tare in kg. If the gross weight is less than 1 kg. , the code "1" should be filled in this box.

(28) Net Weight. It refers to the net weight excluding the tare in kg. If the net weight is less than 1 kg. , the code "1" should be filled in this box.

(29) Container Number. It refers to the number of containers (includingless than container load, LCL) for imported/exported goods. One record should be made for one container, indica-

---

① As for further codes of foreign currency, please refer to http://www.customs.gov.cn/tabid/5469/ctl/CscxListView/mid/17784/Default.aspx? ContainerSrc=[G].

ting its global unique reference no. , its size, and its own weight. And the code "0" is for non-containerized goods.

(30) Attached Documents. In addition to the customs declaration form, there may be some documents attached, such as copy S/C, Invoice, Packing List, etc.

(31) Number of Item and Commodity. It refers to a 10-digit code. The first 8 digits are the tariff number stipulated in the Commodity Classification for China Customs Statistics, while the last 2 digits additional numbers are required by the customs regulatory authority.

(32) Marks, Numbers and Remarks. This column includes:

①Characters and numbers other than graphs in shipping marks.

②Name of importing and exporting company entrusted by wholly-owned foreign subsidiary to import capital equipment.

③Related records, related customs declaration form, and other relevant code, depending on specific cases.

(33) Number, Specification and Model of Item/Commodity. It consists of two boxes and two lines. The first line records the normal name of commodity in Chinese character, while the second line records its specification and model.

(34) Quantity and Unit. It is to be recorded and printed in three lines.

The first line records quantities and units of the first legal measurement units stipulated in the Commodity Classification for China Customs Statistics. The second line should record the second measurement units if any, and leave it blank if no such second measurement units. The contracting measurement units and quantities should be filled and printed on the third line. It may involve several special requirements when "kg" is used as the legal measurement units.

(35) Country/Territory of Origin. It refers to the customs code (refers to table 8.7 and the hype-link site) for relevant country and its name.

When record the country of origin, the Rules of Origin for Import and Export Goods of the P. R. C. , the Regulations on Material Transformation Criteria in Implementing Non-preferential Rules of Origin of the CGAC, and the related regulations on managing varied preferential trade agreements may all be used to determine the country/place of origin. The code "701" is to be used for the "unknown country" if the country of origin for imported goods cannot be assured.

(36) Final Country/Place of Destination. It refers to the customs code for respective country/territory of destination and its name.

The final country/place of destination is the place where the imported goods are to be consumed, used or processed.

For example, if the goods exported directly to Geneva, then the final destination country should be Geneva; if the goods exported to Geneva and transshipped via Antwerp, then the final destination country should also be Geneva; in the case of entrepot trade by Hong Kong and the final destination country cannot be foreseen, Hong Kong may be filled in as the final destination region; and in the case of exporting transaction based on "optional ports", the first optional port may be recorded as the final destination country/region.

(37) Unit Price. It refers to the terms of unit price stipulated in the underlying sales contract. For instance, USD 600.00/MT CIF Rotterdam. Value of goods traded should be recorded in the case of no available actual transacted price.

(38) Total Value. It records the total value of traded goods under one customs clearance form. The volume of goods should be filled in this box in the case of no available actual transacted price.

(39) Name and Code of Currency. It records the customs code for relevant currency and its name. If the actual accounting currency is not listed on the table of customs code for currencies[1], one should convert the currency into the listed currency at the current rate of exchange, and then records the customs code for the converted currency.

(40) Tax Exemption. It refers to the customs code for the method of tax exemption for all items listed on the customs declaration form, supporting by related regulations and the Tax Exemption Certificate issued by the customs authority.

The customs declaring company of cargoes for processing trade should fill in the box according to the recorded stipulations in the Manual of Processing Trade. If "Cash Deposits" of "Letter of Guarantee" are recorded in the Manual, "Tax Free" should be inserted in the box.

(41) Special Relation Confirmation. According to the Methods in Determining the Customs' Dutiable Value of Import and Export Goods, this box should report whether there are special relations between the seller and the buyer in the relevant import and export transaction. The mark "YES" should be inserted here if any of the following requirements are met:

- the seller and the buyer are two members of one family.
- the seller and the buyer are mutual senior officials or directors of business.
- one party is directly/indirectly controlled by another party.
- the buyer and the seller are both directly/indirectly controlled by a third party.
- a third party is directly/indirectly controlled by both the seller and the buyer.
- one party directly/indirectly owns, controls or holds 5% or more of another party's voting shares.
- one party is the employee, chief official or director of another party.
- they are two members of a partnership.

In addition, special relations also exist when they have mutual business relations, for instance, one party acts as an agent, sole distributor or assignee of another party, and the code

---

[1]  http://www.customs.gov.cn/publish/portal0/tab9410.

"YES" should be inserted here.

(42) Identifying Effects of Special Relations on Pricing. According to the Methods of Determining the Customs' Dutiable Value of Import and Export Goods (Article 17), the column reports and confirms whether the special relation between the seller and the buyer has affected the transaction price. The mark "YES" should be inserted here if the taxpayer cannot evidence that the transacted price is the same as or similar to the arm's length price at which the same or similar goods were sold to its domestic buyers; or to the dutiable price deducted from the transaction price according to the Methods; or is the same as or similar to dutiable price calculated and evaluated on the basis of the Methods. Otherwise, the mark "NO" should be filled in the box.

(43) Confirming the Payment of Royalty. According to the Methods of Determining the Customs' Dutiable Value of Import and Export Goods (Article 13), the box reports and confirms whether the buyer has directly/indirectly paid the seller royalty. The mark "YES" should be inserted her if the buyer under an import transaction has directly/indirectly paid the seller royalties, and "NO" if no royalties has ever paid.

(44) Number of Version. It is only applicable to an export customs clearance form under a processing trade. The number should be consistent with the record version in the Manual of Processing Trade.

(45) Article Number. This is also applicable to an export customs clearance form under a processing trade. The number can be got from the registered information of the Manual of Processing Trade, or against with an exports customs clearance form.

(46) Data-entry Staff. This column records the name of the data-entry staff.

(47) Data-entry Unit. This column records the name of the data-entry company.

(48) Customs Annotation and Signature. The customs official can make his/her signature here to annotate the operation of the customs clearance.

It is worth noting that the half-width non-Chinese characters should be used when punctuations as "<>" "," "-" ":", etc. and figures are used in preparing a customs clearance form.

### 8.4.3  Specimens

Three samples of customs declaration forms are given in the appendix of this chapter, namely:

- 1 customs declaration form of the People's Republic of China (in Chinese) (Specimen 18~19).

- 1 customs declaration form of the People's Republic of China (in both English and Chinese) (Specimen 20).

- 1 customs declaration form for Exhibits CHINA-ASEAN EXPO (Specimen 21).

## 8.5　Import License

Many countries use import license and foreign exchange authorization system to restrict imports. Importers have to present pro forma invoices to their licensing authorities or to their central banks, or sometimes to both to apply for the license. If the planned importation is legal and meets current requirements, the license will be issued. Therefore, exporters should not ship the goods to the importers who need licenses until the licenses are actually in hand.

### 8.5.1　Definition

An import license is a document issued by a national government authorizing the importation of certain goods into its territory. Import licenses are considered to be non-tariff barriers (NTBs) to trade when used as a way to discriminate against another country's goods in order to protect a domestic industry from foreign competition. Each license specifies the volume of imports allowed, and the total volume allowed should not exceed the quota. Licenses can be sold to importing companies at a competitive price, or simply a fee. However, it is argued that this allocation method provides incentives for political lobbying and bribery. ①

### 8.5.2　Functions

As a permit that allows an importer to bring in a specified quantity of certain goods during a specified period ( usually one year ), import licenses may be used to serve the following functions. ②

● To act as means of restricting outflow of foreign currency and to improve a country's balance of payments position.

● To control entry of dangerous items such as explosives, firearms, and certain substances.

● To protect the domestic industry from foreign competition.

### 8.5.3　Types

Import licensing in China can be divided into three categories:

(1) Import license administration. Import license administration is applicable to all the products subject to import restriction, including chemicals that may be used for military weapons, toxicant or drugs as well as ozone depleting materials.

(2) Automatic import licensing. Automatic import licensing is applicable to products free from import restriction, but the importation of which needs monitoring, including poultry, vegetable oil, wine, tobacco, asbestos, copper ore and concentrates, coal, terephthalic acid, plas-

---

① http://en. wikipedia. org/wiki/Import_license.

② http://www. businessdictionary. com/definition/import-license. html.

tic raw material, natural rubber, synthetic rubber, waste paper, synthetic fiber cloth, cellulose diacetate filament tow, copper, aluminum, mechanic and electrical products, iron ore, crude oil, processed oil, alumina, chemical fertilizer, pesticide, sliced or chipped polyester, automobile tyre, terylene, steel and steel billet.

(3) Import tariff rate quota administration. Import tariff rate quota administration is applicable to grain, cotton, sugar, wool, wool top and chemical fertilizer.

## 8.5.4 Documentation and Other Requirements for Application for License

For information required to be provided in the application for import license, please refer to the Measures on Administration of Import License for Goods published on December 10, 2004 in MOFCOM Decree No. 27 of 2004.

For information required to be provided in the application for automatic import license, please refer to the Measures on Administration of Automatic Import Licensing for Goods published on November 10, 2004 in MOFCOM and GCA Joint Decree No. 26 of 2004.

For information required to be provided in the application for tariff rate quota for importation of agricultural products, please refer to the Quantities, Application Conditions and Allocation Methods of Tariff Rate Quota for Importation of Grain and Cotton of 2006 published on September 30, 2005 in NDRC's Announcement No. 58 of 2005, the Application and Allocation Methods of Tariff Rate Quota for Importation of Sugar of 2006 was published on September 26, 2005 in MOFCOM's Announcement No. 64 of 2005, and the Implementing Rules on the Administration of Tariff Rate Quota for Importation of Wool and Wool Tops of 2006 published on September 26, 2005 in MOFCOM's Announcement No. 65 of 2005.

For information required to be provided in the application for tariff rate quota for importation of fertilizers, please refer to the Quantities, Allocation Principles and Application Procedures of Tariff Rate Quota for Importation of Fertilizers of 2006 published on September 29, 2005 in MOFCOM's Announcement No. 67 of 2005.

For documents required to be provided in the actual importation of products under import license administration, please refer to the Measures on Administration of Import License for Goods published on December 10, 2004 in MOFCOM Decree No. 27 of 2004.

For documents required to be provided in the actual importation of products under automatic import licensing, please refer to the Measures on Administration of Automatic Import Licensing for Goods published on November 10, 2004 in MOFCOM and GCA Joint Decree No. 26 of 2004.

For documents required to be provided in actual importation of products under import tariff rate quota administration of agricultural products, please refer to the Interim Measures on Administration of Tariff Rate Quota for Importation of Agricultural Products published on September 27, 2003 in MOFCOM and NDRC Joint Decree No. 4 of 2003.

For documents required to be provided in actual importation of products under import tariff rate quota administration of fertilizers, please refer to the Interim Measures on Administration of Tariff Rate Quota for Importation of Fertilizers published on January 15, 2002 in Decree No. 27 of 2002 of the former State Economic and Trade Commission and GCA.

There is no licensing fees or administrative charges. And there is no deposit or advance payment requirement associated with the issue of licenses.

### 8.5.5 Conditions of Licensing

An import license is valid throughout the whole calendar year, and no other limitation is attached. The validity period for a license can be extended once, but no longer than 3 months.

The validity period for an automatic import license is six months, and the license is valid only in the calendar year when it is issued. However, if the holder needs to have the validity period of the license extended in case of uncompleted importation or business contract, he has to apply to the former license issuing body again.

The validity period for the import tariff rate quota is one calendar year.

For the TRQ holder for grain, cotton and sugar, a TRQ warrant, which should be provided during customs clearance, is valid throughout the whole calendar year. The TRQ holder is entitled to demand an extension for the warrant from the competent authority if the original warrant expired in case of uncompleted importation or business contract, but the validity period of the warrant should not exceed the end of February of the next calendar year.

For the TRQ holder for wool and wool top, the TRQ warrant is valid for six months within the calendar year. However, the TRQ holder is entitled to demand an extension for warrant from the competent authority if the original warrant expired in case of uncompleted importation or business contract. The validity period of the warrant should not exceed the end of February of the next calendar year.

For the TRQ holder for chemical fertilizer, the TRQ warrant is valid for six months. However, the TRQ holder is entitled to demand an extension for the warrant from the competent authority if the original warrant expired in case of uncompleted importation. The extension should not exceed the validity period of the Tariff Rate Quota.

For products under import tariff rate quota administration, the TRQ holders should annually return, for reallocation, the unfilled tariff rate quota of the calendar year within the scheduled time limit. To ensure that the allocated tariff rate quota are used for importation, for the TRQ holders who do not fully use tariff rate quota for the year and do not return the unfilled tariff rate quota within the scheduled time limit, their next year quantity of tariff rate quota will be reduced accordingly.

For the products under import license administration and automatic import licensing, non-utilization or utilizing a portion of license will not be punished.

The 3 categories of licenses listed above are not transferable. And there are no other conditions attached to the issue of a license.

### 8.5.6 Other Procedural Requirements

For products included in the catalogue of products subject to statutory inspection, an inspection and quarantine certificate issued by quality supervision, inspection and quarantine authorities should be provided prior to importation.

For products under automatic import licensing, the bank will provide foreign exchange to applicants with an automatic import license.

For products under import license administration and import tariff rate quota administration, foreign exchange will be provided pursuant to relevant regulations of the State Administration of Foreign Exchange.

Generally foreign exchange is available to cover licenses issued. [1]

### 8.5.7 Contents and Specimens

An import license in China mainly covers such items as: name and address of importer; name and address of consignee; number of import license; import license expiry date; terms of trade; terms of foreign exchange; place of clearance; country/region of exportation; country/region of origin; use of goods; description of goods and code of goods; specification; unit; quantity; unit price; amount; amount in USD; total; supplementary details; issuing authority's stamp and signature; license date.

Guidelines for filling in an import license are quite similar to that of official documents discussed above.

A sample of application form for import license of the People's Republic of China (Specimen 22) and a sample of import license of the People's Republic of China (Specimen 23) are given in the appendix of this chapter.

---

[1] http://www.export.gov/china/exporting_to_china/China_WTO_Import_Licensing.pdf.

# Questions and Problems

## I. Make out a certificate of origin based on the particulars below：

<table>
<tr>
<td colspan="4" align="center">销售合同<br>**SALES CONTRACT**</td>
</tr>
<tr>
<td rowspan="2">卖方 SELLER：</td>
<td rowspan="2">KKK TRADING CO., LTD.<br>HUARONG MANSION RM2901 NO. 85 GUANJIAQIAO,<br>NANJING 210005, CHINA<br>TEL：0086-25-4715004　FAX：0086-25-4711363</td>
<td>编号 NO.：</td>
<td>NEO20240116</td>
</tr>
<tr>
<td>日期 DATE：</td>
<td>Nov. 8, 2023</td>
</tr>
<tr>
<td rowspan="2">买方<br>BUYER：</td>
<td rowspan="2">NEO GENERAL TRADING CO.<br>P. O. BOX 99552, RIYADH 22766, KSA<br>TEL：00966-1-4659220 FAX：00966-1-4659213</td>
<td>地点 SIGNED IN：</td>
<td>SHANGHAI, CHINA</td>
</tr>
<tr>
<td></td>
<td></td>
</tr>
<tr>
<td colspan="4">买卖双方同意以下条款达成交易：<br>This contract is made by and agreed between the BUYER and SELLER , in accordance with the terms and conditions stipulated below</td>
</tr>
<tr>
<td align="center">1. 品名及规格<br>Commodity & Specification</td>
<td align="center">2. 数量<br>Quantity</td>
<td align="center">3. 单价及价格条款<br>Unit Price & Trade Terms</td>
<td align="center">4. 金额<br>Amount</td>
</tr>
<tr>
<td></td>
<td></td>
<td colspan="2" align="right">CFR DAMMAM PORT, SAUDI ARABIA</td>
</tr>
<tr>
<td>ABOUT 1,700 CARTONS CANNED MUSH-ROOMS PIECES & STEMS 24 TINS X 227 GRAMS NET WEIGHT (G. W. 425 GRAMS) AT USD 7.80 PER CARTON.<br>ROSE BRAND.</td>
<td>1,700 CARTONS</td>
<td>USD 7.80</td>
<td>USD 13,260.00</td>
</tr>
<tr>
<td align="right">Total：</td>
<td>1,700 CARTONS</td>
<td></td>
<td>USD 13,260.00</td>
</tr>
<tr>
<td align="center">允许<br>With</td>
<td colspan="3">溢短装，由卖方决定<br>More or less of shipment allowed at the sellers' option</td>
</tr>
<tr>
<td>5. 总值<br>Total Value</td>
<td colspan="3">USD THIRTEEN THOUSAND TWO HUNDRED AND SIXTY ONLY</td>
</tr>
<tr>
<td>6. 包装<br>Packing</td>
<td colspan="3">EXPORTED BROWN CARTON</td>
</tr>
<tr>
<td>7. 唛头<br>Shipping Marks</td>
<td colspan="3">ROSE BRAND<br>178/2023<br>RIYADH</td>
</tr>
<tr>
<td>8. 装运期及运输方式<br>Time of Shipment & means of Transportation</td>
<td colspan="3">Not Later Than JAN. 15, 2024 BY VESSEL</td>
</tr>
</table>

续表

| 9. 装运港及目的地<br>Port of Loading & Destination | From : SHANGHAI PORT, CHINA<br>To : DAMMAM PORT, SAUDI ARABIA |
|---|---|
| 10. 保险<br>Insurance | TO BE COVERED BY THE BUYER |
| 11. 付款方式<br>Terms of Payment | The Buyers shall open through a bank acceptable to the Seller an Irrevocable Letter of Credit payable at sight of reach the seller 30 days before the month of shipment, valid for negotiation in China until the 15th day after the date of shipment |
| 12. 备注<br>Remarks | |

| The Buyer | The Seller |
|---|---|
| NEO GENERAL TRADING CO. | KKK TRADING CO. , LTD. |
| ( signature ) | ( signature ) |

| **MT S700** | **ISSUE OF A DOCUMENTARY CREDIT** | |
|---|---|---|
| | | PAGE<br>00001 |
| APPLICATION HEADER | | RJHISARIAXXX<br>∗ ALRAJHI BANKING AND INVESTMENT<br>∗ CORPORATION<br>∗ RIYADH<br>∗ ( HEAD OFFICE ) |
| SEQUENCE OF TOTAL | ∗ 27 | 1 / 1 |
| FORM OF DOC. CREDIT | ∗ 40 A | IRREVOCABLE |
| DOC. CREDIT NUMBER | ∗ 20 | 0011LC123756 |
| DATE OF ISSUE | 31 C | 231202 |
| APPLICABLE RULES | 40 E | UCP LATEST VERSION |
| DATE/PLACE EXP. | ∗ 31 D | DATE 240130 PLACE CHINA |
| APPLICANT | ∗ 50 | NEO GENERAL TRADING CO.<br>P. O. BOX 99552, RIYADH 22766, KSA<br>TEL: 00966-1-4659220　FAX: 00966-1-4659213 |
| BENEFICIARY | ∗ 59 | KKK TRADING CO. , LTD.<br>HUARONG MANSION RM2901 NO. 85 GUANJIAQIAO, NANJING 210005, CHINA<br>TEL: 0086-25-4715004　FAX: 0086-25-4711363 |
| AMOUNT | ∗ 32 B | CURRENCY USD AMOUNT 13,260 |

| | | |
|---|---|---|
| PERCENTAGE CREDIT AMOUNT TOLERANCE | 39 A | 10/10 |
| AVAILABLE WITH/BY | *41 D | ANY BANK IN CHINA, BY NEGOTIATION |
| DRAFTS AT . . . | 42 C | SIGHT |
| DRAWEE | 42 A | RJHISARI |
| | | * ALRAJHI BANKING AND INVESTMENT<br>* CORPORATION<br>* RIYADH<br>* (HEAD OFFICE) |
| PARTIAL SHIPMTS | 43 P | NOT ALLOWED |
| TRANSSHIPMENT | 43 T | NOT ALLOWED |
| PORT OF LOADING | 44 E | CHINESE MAIN PORT, CHINA |
| PORT OF DISCHARGE | 44 F | DAMMAM PORT, SAUDI ARABIA |
| LATEST SHIPMENT | 44 C | 240115 |
| GOODS DESCRIPTION | 45 A | |
| | | ABOUT 1,700 CARTONS CANNED MUSHROOMS PIECES & STEMS 24 TINS X 227 GRAMS NET WEIGHT (G. W. 425 GRAMS) AT USD 7. 80 PER CARTON. ROSE BRAND. |
| DOCUMENTS REQUIRED: | 46 A | |
| | | + SIGNED COMMERCIAL INVOICE IN TRIPLICATE ORIGINAL AND MUST SHOW BREAK DOWN OF THE AMOUNT AS FOLLOWS: FOB VALUE, FREIGHT CHARGES AND TOTAL AMOUNT C AND F. |
| | | + FULL SET CLEAN ON BOARD BILL OF LADING MADE OUT TO THE ORDER OF ALRAJHI BANKING AND INVESTMENT CORP, MARKED FREIGHT PREPAID AND NOTIFY APPLICANT, INDICATING THE FULL NAME, ADDRESS AND TEL NO. OF THE CARRYING VESSEL'S AGENT AT THE PORT OF DISCHARGE. |
| | | + PACKING LIST IN ONE ORIGINAL PLUS 5 COPIES, ALL OF WHICH MUST BE MANUALLY SIGNED. |
| | | + INSPECTION (HEALTH) CERTIFICATE FROM C. I. Q. (ENTRY-EXIT INSPECTION AND QUARANTINE OF THE PEOPLES REP. OF CHINA) STATING<br>GOODS ARE FIT FOR HUMAN BEING. |

续表

| | | |
|---|---|---|
| | | + CERTIFICATE OF ORIGIN DULY CERTIFIED BY C. C. P. I. T. STATING THE NAME OF THE MANUFACTURERS OF PRODUCERS AND THAT GOODS EXPORTED ARE WHOLLY OF CHINESE ORIGIN. |
| | | + THE PRODUCTION DATE OF THE GOODS NOT TO BE EARLIER THAN HALF MONTH AT TIME OF SHIPMENT. BENEFICIARY MUST CERTIFY THE SAME. |
| | | + SHIPMENT TO BE EFFECTED BY CONTAINER AND BY REGULARE LINE. SHIPMENT COMPANY'S CERTIFICATE TO THIS EFFECT SHOULD ACCOMPANY THE DOCUMENTS. |
| ADDITIONAL CONDITION | 47 A | |
| | | A DISCREPANCY FEE OF USD 50. 00 WILL BE IMPOSED ON EACH SET OF DOCUMENTS PRESENTED FOR NEGOTIATION UNDER THIS L/C WITH DISCREPANCY. THE FEE WILL BE DEDUCTED FROM THE BILL AMOUNT. PAYMENT UNDER THE GOODS WAS APPROVED BY SAUDI GOVERNMENT LAB. |
| CHARGES | 71 B | ALL CHARGES AND COMMISSIONS OUTSIDE KSA ON BENEFICIARIES' ACCOUNT INCLUDING REIMBURSING, BANK COMMISSION, DISCREPANCY FEE (IF ANY) AND COURIER CHARGES. |
| CONFIRMAT INSTR | *49 | WITHOUT |
| REIMBURS. BANK | 53 D | ALRAJHI BANKING AND INVESTMENT CORP RIYADH (HEAD OFFICE) |
| INS PAYING BANK | 78 | |
| | | DOCUMENTS TO BE DESPATCHED IN ONE LOT BY COURIER. ALL CORRESPONDENCE TO BE SENT TO ALRAJHI BANKING AND INVESTMENT COPRORATION RIYADH (HEAD OFFICE) |
| SEND REC INFO | 72 | REIMBURSEMENT IS SUBJECT TO ICC URR 525 |

## Other particulars:

  √PACKING: 1,750 CTNS

  √SIZE OF CARTON:20CM×25CM×30CM

  √3. INVOICE NO: 2023SDT001　　INVOICE DATE: DEC. 13, 2023

√SHIPPING MARKS:

      ROSE BRAND

      178/2023

      RIYADH

√FREIGHT: USD 1,000.00

√SHIPPED IN 1×20' FCL

√DATE OF SHIPMENT: DEC. 26, 2023

| ORIGINAL | |
|---|---|
| 1. Exporter | Certificate No. |
| 2. Consignee | **CERTIFICATE OF ORIGIN OF THE PEOPLE'S REPUBLIC OF CHINA** |
| 3. Means of transport and route | 5. For certifying authority use only |
| 4. Country / region of destination | |

| 6. Marks and numbers | 7. Number and kind of packages; description of goods | 8. H. S. Code | 9. Quantity | 10. Number and date of invoices |
|---|---|---|---|---|
| | | | | |

续表

**********************************

| 11. Declaration by the exporter | 12. Certification |
|---|---|
| The undersigned hereby declares that the above details and statements are correct, that all the goods were produced in China and that they comply with the Rules of Origin of the People's Republic of China.<br><br><br><br>( signature )<br><br><br><br>------------------------------------ <br>----------- <br>Place and date, signature and stamp of authorized signatory | It is hereby certified that the declaration by the exporter is correct.<br><br><br><br><br><br><br><br><br><br>------------------------------------ <br>----------- <br>Place and date, signature and stamp of certifying authority |

## II. Make out a customs declaration according to the sales contract and letter of credit in problem I, and the relevant information below.

√这是一笔出口到沙特阿拉伯的食品业务,由于要从上海出运,因此 KKK 国际贸易公司委托上海凯通国际货运代理有限公司代理报关。到目前为止,KKK 国际贸易公司已经拿到了出口收汇核销单和商检换证凭单。现在,请你根据上述单据,配齐出口报关所需的全套单证寄往上海。

√KKK 国际贸易公司委托上海凯通国际货运代理有限公司代理报关,公司资料如下所列:

地址:南京市管家桥 85 号华荣大厦 2901 室

邮编:210005

联系电话:025-4715004

公司十位编码:73314337-5

公司海关代码:3201003830

税务登记号码:320102200618388

√报关单预录入编号:DS9110008

√出运日期:2024-04-06

√此份报关单是给报关行或代理公司委托报关之用,报关单上的海关编码、报关单填制日期可空着不写。

## 中华人民共和国海关出口货物报关单

| 预录入编号： | | 海关编号： | | |
|---|---|---|---|---|

| 出口口岸 | | 备案号 | | 出口日期 | 申报日期 |
|---|---|---|---|---|---|
| | | | | | |

| 经营单位 | | 运输方式 | 运输工具名称 | | 提运单号 |
|---|---|---|---|---|---|
| | | | | | |

| 发货单位 | | 贸易方式 | 征免性质 | | 结汇方式 |
|---|---|---|---|---|---|
| | | | | | |

| 许可证号 | | 运抵国（地区） | 指运港 | | 境内货源地 |
|---|---|---|---|---|---|
| | | | | | |

| 批准文号 | | 成交方式 | 运费 | 保费 | 杂费 |
|---|---|---|---|---|---|
| | | | | | |

| | | 件数 | 包装种类 | 毛重(公斤) | 净重(公斤) |
|---|---|---|---|---|---|
| | | | | | |

| 集装箱号 | | 随附单据 | | 生产厂家 |
|---|---|---|---|---|
| | | | | |

标记唛码及备注

| 项号 | 商品编号 | 商品名称、规格型号 | 数量及单位 | 最终目的国/地区 | 单价 | 总价 | 币制 | 征免 |
|---|---|---|---|---|---|---|---|---|
| | | | | | | | | |

税费征收情况

| 录入员 | 录入单位 | 兹声明以上申报无讹并承担法律责任 | 海关审单批注及放行日期(签章) | |
|---|---|---|---|---|
| | | | 审单 | 审价 |
| 报关员 | | 申报单位(签章) | 征税 | 统计 |
| 单位地址 | | | 查验 | 放行 |

| 邮编 | | 电话 | | 填制日期 | | |
|---|---|---|---|---|---|---|

# Appendix

**Specimen 1**

Export License Application Form①
中华人民共和国出口许可证申请表

| 1. 出口商：　　　　代码：<br><br>领证人姓名：　　电话： | 3. 出口许可证号： | | |
| --- | --- | --- | --- |
| 2. 发货人：　　　　代码： | 4. 出口许可证有效截止日期：<br>　　　　　　　　　　　年　　月　　日 | | |
| 5. 贸易方式： | 8. 进口国（地区）： | | |
| 6. 合同号： | 9. 付款方式： | | |
| 7. 报关口岸： | 10. 运输方式： | | |
| 11. 商品名称：　　　　　　　　　商品编码： | | | |

| 12. 规格、等级 | 13. 单位 | 14. 数量 | 15. 单价（币别） | 16. 总值（币别） | 17. 总值折美元 |
| --- | --- | --- | --- | --- | --- |
|  |  |  |  |  |  |
|  |  |  |  |  |  |
|  |  |  |  |  |  |
| 18. 总　计 |  |  |  |  |  |

| 19. 备　注<br>　　　申请单位盖章<br><br><br>申领日期： | 20. 签证机构审批（初审）：<br><br><br>　　　　　　　　　　　　经办人：<br>终审： |
| --- | --- |

填表说明：1. 本表应用正楷逐项填写清楚, 不得涂改、遗漏, 否则无效；
　　　　　2. 本表内容需打印多份许可证的, 请在备注栏内注明。

① http://www.licence.org.cn/Web/xgxz/sqb/biaoge/ck/出口许可证申请表.doc.

**Specimen 2**

Application Form for Export License/Certificate of Origin of Textiles Exported to EU①
输欧盟纺织品出口许可证/产地证申请表

| | | |
|---|---|---|
| 1 Exporter（EID, name, full address, country）3200134788888<br>JIANG SU JINGPU EXP. & IMP. LTD<br>30 ,BEIJING XI ROAD ,NANJING,JIANGSU | 2 申请表号 | |
| | 3 许可证号 | |
| | 4 产地证号 | |
| 5 Consignee（name, full address, country）<br>SAURO SRL<br>VIA GORD BEL 44/2<br>59111 PRATO PO ITALY | （Textile products） | |
| | 6 Category number 4 | |
| | 7 Country of origin<br>**CHINA** | 8 Country of destination<br>**ITALY** |
| 9 Place and date of shipment<br>FROM NANJING TO LA SPEZIA PORT ITALY BY SEA/AIR IN SEP/OCT 2024 | 10 Supplementary details | |
| 11 DESCRIPTION OF GOODS | 12 Quantity（单位） | 13 FOB Value（币别） |
| 1）T-SHIRT | 1 000 | 30 000 |
| 2）H. S. CODE：6105200029 | | |
| 14 Marks<br>N/M | | |
| | 15 MID CODE<br>CNCHAGENWUX | |
| | 16 童装标志：□是　　□否 | |
| 联系人：王芳<br>联系电话：025-88888888<br>申请日期：2024-10-18 | 签证机构审批： | |
| 申请单位盖章 | 经办人： | |

商务部配额许可证事务局　监制

---

① http://www.jsdoftec.gov.cn/downloadcss/16.doc.

**Flow Chart 1**

Internet Applying for Imp/Exp Licenses①
进出口许可证网上申领流程图

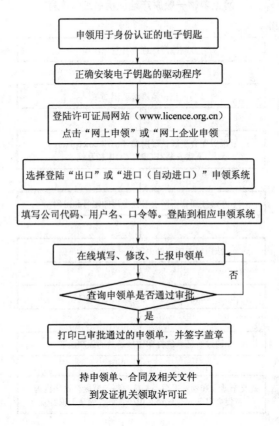

① http://www.licence.org.cn/Web/bszn/9.htm.

**Flow Chart 2**

Internet Applying for Certificate of Origin[1]
Web EDI−CCPIT
网上申领一般原产地证明书工作流程

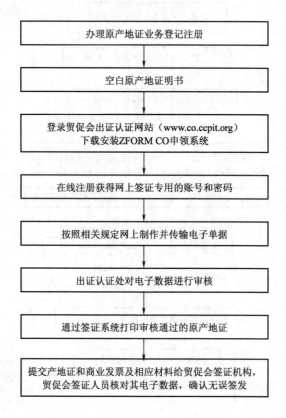

办理原产地证业务登记注册

空白原产地证明书

登录贸促会出证认证网站（www.co.ccpit.org）
下载安装ZFORM CO申领系统

在线注册获得网上签证专用的账号和密码

按照相关规定网上制作并传输电子单据

出证认证处对电子数据进行审核

通过签证系统打印审核通过的原产地证

提交产地证和商业发票及相应材料给贸促会签证机构，
贸促会签证人员核对其电子数据，确认无误签发

---

[1]  http://www.ccpitgx.org/spe_show.asp? id=1409&CataID=64.

**Specimen 3**

Application Form for GFACA Certificate①
进出口许可证企业电子钥匙申请表

---

用户基本信息

★ 企业名称：_____

★ 企业代码：_____（13 位进出口企业编码）

★ 企业类型：□内资企业　　□外资企业

★ 登录许可证申领系统的用户名：_____（大写的英文或拼音,不超过 8 位）

★ 申请者姓名：_____性　别：□ 男　　□ 女

★ 证件名称：□身份证 □军官证 □士兵证 □护照 □其他　备注信息_____

★ 证件号码：_____

★ 户口所在地：_____国_____省(市)_____

★ 电子信箱：_____

**联系方式**

★ 联系地址：_____

★ 邮政编码：_____ 联系电话：_____

　移动电话：_____ 移动电话：_____

　工作单位：_____ 职务：_____

　工作地址_____

**本人在此郑重声明:** 表内所填内容完全属实,接受据此颁发的数字证书,保证遵守所附责任书中所明确的职责,并承担相关法律责任。

请人签名盖章：_____　日期：_____年___月___日

**审批受理点盖章处**

经办人：_____　　　　　日期：_____年___月___日

---

（注:请用正楷字填写,带★号选项为必填项）

---

① http://www.licence.org.cn/Web/xgxz/sqb/biaoge/qt/网上申领电子钥匙申请表.doc.

**Specimen 4**

**China's General Export License**①

| 1. 申领许可证单位　　编码<br>Exporter | 3. 出口许可证编号<br>License No. | | | | |
|---|---|---|---|---|---|
| 2. 发货单位<br>Consignor | 4. 许可证有效期<br>Validity | | | | |
| 5. 贸易方式<br>Terms of trade | 8. 输往国家(地区)<br>Country of destination | | | | |
| 6. 合同号<br>Contract No. | 9. 收款方式<br>Terms of payment | | | | |
| 7. 出运口岸<br>Port of shipment | 10. 运输方式<br>Means of transport | | | | |
| 11. 唛头/包装件数<br>Marks & numbers/number of packages | | | | | |
| 12. 商品名称　　　　　　商品编码<br>Description of commodity　　　Commodity No. | | | | | |
| 13. 商品规格、型号<br>Specification | 14. 单位<br>Unit | 15. 数量<br>Quantity | 16. 单价<br>Unit price | 17. 总值<br>Amount | 18. 总值折美元<br>Amount in USD |
| | | | | | |
| | | | | | |
| | | | | | |
| | | | | | |
| | | | | | |
| | | | | | |
| 19. 总计<br>　Total | | | | | |
| 20. 备注<br>Supplementary | 21. 发证机关盖章<br>Issuing Authority's Stamp<br>发证日期<br>Signature Date | | | | |

---

① http://www.sxdofcom.gov.cn/Files.

**Specimen 5**

China's Export License of Textiles to EU①

| 1. Export(EID, name, full address, country) | copy | | 2. License No. |
|---|---|---|---|
| | 3. Quota year | | 4. Category number |
| 5. Consignee(name, full address, county) | **EXPORT LICENSE**<br>(Textile products) | | |
| | 6. Country of origin | | 7. Country of destination |
| 8. Place and date of shipment−Means of transport | 9. Supplementary details | | |
| 10. Marks and number−number and kind of packages−DESCRIPTION OF GOODS | 11. Quantity | | 12. FOB Value |
| 13. M. I. D. CNXXXGARSHE | | | |
| 14. Exporter's stamp and signature<br>加盖公司进出口业务章(中英文)<br>和公司法人签字(章) | 15. Issuing authorities' stamp and signature | | |

---

① http://www.sxdofcom.gov.cn/Files.

**Specimen 6**

China's Export License of Textiles to U. S. A. ①

| 1. Exporter(EID, name & address)<br><br>4403×××××××29<br><br>SHENZHEN ×××× TRADING CO. , LTD.<br><br>RM ××, ××× BLDG. , ××× STREET,<br>SHENZHEN, CHINA | 2. License No. 800001 | |
|---|---|---|
| | 3. Agreement year<br>2024 | 4. Category No. 647 |
| | 5. Invoice No. | |
| 6. Consignee (name & address)<br><br>ABC INC.<br>ABC STREET LA U. S. A. | 7. Place & time of shipment, destination<br>FROM CHINA TO LA U. S. A.<br>BY SEA/AIR IN NOV/DEC, 2024. | |
| | 8. value of FOB Chinese port USD 1,000.00 | |

| 9. Marks & number-number of package-DESCRIPTION OF GOODS<br>N / M　　MEN's 100% POLYESTER WOVEN PANTS | 10. Quantity<br><br>* 10DOZ *<br><br><br>TOTAL:TEN DOZ ONLY.<br><br><br>TOTAL:10.00 * DOZ | 11. unit price<br>FOB<br><br>USD/DOZ<br>100.00 | 12. Amount<br><br>CHINA<br>USD<br>1,000.00 |
|---|---|---|---|
| M. I. D. NAME:XXXXXX GARMENT FACTORY OF SHENZHEN<br>ADDR:XXX IND. ZONE, SHENZHEN, CHINA<br>CITY:SHENZHEN | | | |

| 13. M. I. D. | CNXXXGARSHE | | |
|---|---|---|---|

| 14. Exporter's stamp and signature<br>加盖公司进出口业务章(中英文)<br>和公司法人签字(章)<br><br><br><br><br>Date Nov 11, 2024 | 15. Issuing authorities' stamp and signature |
|---|---|

① http://www. sxdofcom. gov. cn/Files.

**Specimen 7**

China's Export License of Textiles to Canada①

| 1. Exporter(EID, name & address) | **COPY** | | 2. No. | |
| --- | --- | --- | --- | --- |
| | 3. Quota year | | 4. Category number | |
| 5. Consignee (name, full address, country) | **EXPORT LICENSE**<br>(**Textile products**) | | | |
| | 6. Country of origin<br>**CHINA** | | 7. Country of destination<br>**CANADA** | |
| 8. Place and date of shipment – Means of transport | 9. Supplementary details | | | |
| 10. Marks & numbers – Number and kind of package – DESCRIPTION OF GOODS | | 11. Quantity | | 12. FOB Value |
| 13. CERTIFICATION BY THE COMPETENT AUTHORITY<br><br><br><br><br>(Signature)<br>(Stamp–Cachet) | | | | |
| 14. Competent authority(name, full address, country) | | | | |

---

① http://www.sxdofcom.gov.cn/Files.

**Specimen 8**

Application for GSP Form A①
## 普惠制产地证明书申请书

申请单位(盖章):＿＿＿＿＿＿＿＿＿  证书号:＿＿＿＿＿

申请人郑重声明＿＿＿＿＿＿＿＿＿  注册号: A099

本人被正式授权代表本企业办理和签署本申请书。

本申请书及普惠制产地证格式 A 所列内容正确无误,如发现弄虚作假,冒充格式 A 所列货物,擅改证书,自愿接受签证机关的处罚及负法律责任。现将有关情况申报如下:

| 生产单位 | | | 生产单位联系人电话 | |
|---|---|---|---|---|
| 商品名称(中英文) | | | H.S. 税目号<br>(以六位数码计) | |
| 商品(FOB)总值(以美元计) | | | 发票号 | |
| 最终销售国 | | 证书种类划"/" | 加急证书 | 普通证书 |
| 货物拟出运日期 | | | | |

| 贸易方式和企业性质(请在适用处划"/") | | | | | | | |
|---|---|---|---|---|---|---|---|
| 正常贸易.C | 来料加工.L | 补偿贸易.B | 中外合资.H | 中外合作.Z | 外商独资.D | 零售.Y | 展卖.M |
| | | | | | | | |

| 包装数量或毛重或其他数量 |
|---|
| |

原产地标准:

本项商品系在中国生产,完全符合该给惠国给惠方案规定,其原产地情况符合以下 第　　条。

(1)"P"(完全国产,未使用任何进口原材料);

(2)"W"其 H.S 税号为(含进口成分);

(3)"F"(对加拿大出口产品,其进口成分不超过产品出厂价值的40%)。

本批产品系:1.直接运输从＿＿＿＿＿＿到＿＿＿＿＿＿.

　　　　　　2.转圈运输从＿＿＿＿＿＿ 中转国(地区)＿＿＿＿到＿＿＿＿.

申请人说明

　　　　　　　　　　　　　　　　领证人(签名)

　　　　　　　　　　　　　　　　电　话:

　　　　　　　　　　　　　　　　日期　年　月　日

现提交中国出口商业发票副本一份,普惠制产地证明书格式A(FORM A)一正二副,以及其他附件　份,请予审核签证。

注:凡含有进口成分的商品,必须按要求提交《含进口成分受惠商品成本明细单》。

签证人:

---

① www2. ziq. gov. cn/dqj/taizhou/cdz/ph%5B1%5D. doc.

**Specimen 9**

Application for General CO/Assembly with Provided Components①

一般原产地证明书/加工装配证明书

## 申　请　书

申请单位注册号：　　　　　　　　　证书号：

申请人郑重声明：

　　本人被正式授权代表本企业办理和签署本申请书。

　　本申请书及一般原产地证明书/加工装配证明书所列内容正确无误，如发现弄虚作假、冒充证书所列货物、擅改证书，本人愿按中华人民共和国出口货物原产地规则的有关规定接受处罚。现将有关情况申报如下：

| 企业名称 | | 发票号 | | |
|---|---|---|---|---|
| 商品名称 | | **H. S.** 编码（六位数） | | |
| 商品 **FOB** 总值（以美元计） | | 最终目的地国家/地区 | | |
| 拟出运日期 | | 转口国（地区） | | |
| 贸易方式和企业性质（请在适用处划"/"） | | | | |
| 一般贸易 | | 三来一补 | | 其他贸易方式 |
| 国营企业 | 三资企业 | 国营企业 | 三资企业 | 国营企业 | 三资企业 |
| | | | | | |
| 包装数量或毛重或其他数量 | | | | |
| 证书种类（划"/"） | | 一般原产地证明书 | | 加工装配证明书 |

　　现提交中国出口货物商业发票副本一份，一般原产地证明书/加工装配证明书一正三副，以及其他附件＿＿＿份，请予审核签证。


　　申请单位盖章

　　　　　　　　　　　　　　　　　　　　　　　　　　申领人（签名）

　　　　　　　　　　　　　　　　　　　　　　　　　　电　话：

　　　　　　　　　　　　　　　　　　　　　　　　　　日　期：年 月 日

---

①　www2. ziq. gov. cn/dqj/taizhou/cdz/ph%5B1%5D. doc.

**Specimen 10**

## Certificate of Origin of PRC

| 1. Exporter<br>SHANDONG OCEANCHEM IMP & EXP CORPORATION<br>5, WQ ROAD, WEIFANG, 261000 CHINA | Certificate No. 099897879<br>CERTIFICATE OF ORIGIN<br>OF<br>THE PEOPLE's<br>REPUBLIC OF CHINA |
|---|---|
| 2. Consignee<br>DHT TRADE CO., LTD.<br>105 BROAD ST., ROTTERDAM, HOLLAND | |
| 3. Means of transport and route<br>SHIPMENT FROM QINGDAO, CHINA TO<br>ROTTERDAM, HOLLAND PER VESSEL | 5. For certifying authority use only |
| 4. Country/region of destination<br>HOLLAND | |

| 6. Marks and number | 7. Number and kind of packages; description of goods | 8. H. S. | 9. Quantity | 10. Number and date of invoices |
|---|---|---|---|---|
| 1101/<br>ANAN<br>69<br>* * * * * | 160 ( ONE HUNDRED AND SIXTY )<br>DRUMS OF CALCIUM METAL<br>* * * * * * * * * * * * * * | 280501 | G. W.<br>24,000KGS<br>* * * * * * * * | SFZ230333<br>AUG. 15, 2024<br>* * * * * * * * * |

| 11. Declaration by the exporter | 12. Certification |
|---|---|
| The undersigned hereby declares that the above details and statements are correct, that all the goods were produced in China and that they comply with the Rules of Origin of the People's Republic of China.<br>WEIFANG, CHINA AUG. 17, 2024　牛劲<br>Place and date, signature of authorized signatory | It is hereby certified that the declaration by the exporter is correct.<br><br><br><br>WEIFANG, CHINA AUG. 17, 2024　刘蒙<br>Place and date, signature of authorized signatory |

**Specimen 11**

## China's General Certificate of Origin[①]

| 1. Exporter (full name and address)<br>出口商(姓名、地址)<br><br>2. Consignee(full name, address, country)<br>收货人(姓名、地址、国家) | | | Certificate No. 0503280<br>证明书编号：<br>CERTIFICATE OF ORIGIN OF THE PEOPLE'S REPUB-<br>LIC OF CHINA<br>中华人民共和国原产地证明 | |
| --- | --- | --- | --- | --- |
| 3. Means of transport and route<br>运输方式和路线<br>4. Destination port<br>目的港 | | | 5. For certifying authority use only<br>核证当局专用栏 | |
| 6. Marks and numbers of pack-ages<br>包装标记和件数 | 7. Description of goods, number and kind of pack-ages<br>货物名称、件数和包装种类 | 8. H. S. Code<br>H.S 编码 | 9. Quantity or weight<br>数量或重量 | 10. Number and date of in-voices<br>发票编号和日期 |
| 11. Declaration by the exporter<br>The undersigned hereby declares that the above details and statements are correct; that all the goods were produced in China and that they comply with the Rules of Origin of the People's Republic of China.<br>出口商声明<br>以下签名者特此声明：上述细节及陈述均确凿无误,保证所有产品均为中国制造,且符合中华人民共和国原产地原则。 | | | 12. Certification<br>It is hereby certified that the declaration by the exporter is correct.<br>证明<br>兹证明出口商的声明确凿无误。 | |
| Place and date, signature and stamp of authorized signatory<br>地址、日期以及业经授权的签署者的签名和印章 | | | Place and date, signature and stamp of authorized signatory<br>地址、日期以及业经授权的签署者的签名和印章 | |

---

① www2. sdwfvc. cn/jpkc/swyyhd/html/JIAOAN/unit13. doc.

**Specimen 12**

## Certificate of GSP Form A①

| 1. Exporter (full name, address, country)<br><br>AQ FOODSTUFF IMPORT AND EXPORT CO., LTD.<br>65, NO. 2 ROAD, ANQIU, SHANDONG, 261000 CHINA | Certificate No. SG200709157879<br><br>GENERALIZED SYSTEM OF PREFERENCES<br>CERTIFICATE OF ORIGIN<br>(Combined declaration and certificate)<br>FORM A |
|---|---|
| 2. Consignee (full name, address, country)<br><br>ABC TRADE CO., LTD.<br>119 MUSIC ST., ROTTERDAM HOLLAND | Issued by THE PEOPLE's<br>REPUBLIC OF CHINA<br>(Country)<br>See Notes, Overleaf |
| 3. Means of transport and route<br>SHIPMENT FROM QINGDAO, CHINA TO<br>ROTTERDAM, HOLLAND PER VESSEL | 4. For official use |

| 5. Item number | 6. Marks and numbers of packages | 7. Description of goods; Number and kind of packages | 8. Origin criterion (see Notes overleaf) | 9. Gross weight or other quantity | 10. Number and date of invoices |
|---|---|---|---|---|---|
| 1<br>* * * * * | | 596 (FIVE HUNDRED AND NINETY SIX ONTY) DRUMS OF PICKLED BURDOCK<br>* * * * * * * *<br>* * * * * * * * | "P"<br>* * * * * * * * | G. W.<br>21,045KGS<br>* * * * * * *<br>* * * * | 36XH321<br>SEP 20,2024<br>* * * * * * *<br>* * * * * |

| 11. Certification<br>    It is hereby certified, on the basis of control carried out, that the declaration by the exporter is correct.<br><br><br><br><br>WEIFANG, CHINA SEP 21, 2024<br>Place and date, signature of authorized signatory | 12. Declaration by the exporter<br>    The undersigned hereby declares that the above details and statements are correct; that all the goods were produced in CHINA<br>(county)<br>and that they comply with the origin requirements specified for those goods in the Generalized System of Preferences for goods exported to HOLLAND<br>(importing country)<br>WEIFANG CHINA SEP 20, 2024<br>Place and date, signature of authorized signatory |
|---|---|

① www2.sdwfvc.cn/jpkc/swyyhd/html/JIAOAN/unit13.doc.

**Specimen 13**

## CO of Textile Products Exported to EU
## 输欧盟纺织品产地证

| 1. Exporter(EID, name & address)<br>4403XXXXXXX29<br>SHENZHEN XXXX TRADING CO., LTD.<br>RM XX, XXX BLDG., XXX STREET,<br>SHENZHEN, CHINA | COPY | 2. No. CN DE<br>44800001 | |
|---|---|---|---|
| | 3. Quota year<br>2024 | 4. Category number<br>27 | |
| 5. Consignee (name, full address, country)<br>ABC INC.<br>ABC STREET, ABC CITY<br>GERMANY | **CERTIFICATE OF ORIGIN**<br>(Textile products)<br>CERTIFICAT D'ORIGINE<br>(Produits textiles) | | |
| | 6. Country of origin<br>CHINA | 7. Country of destination<br>F. R. G. | |
| 8. Place and date of shipment – Means of transport<br>FROM CHINA TO GERMANY<br>VIA HONG KONG BY SEA/AIR IN NOV/DEC. 2024. | 9. Supplementary details | | |
| 10. Marks & numbers – Number and kind of package – DESCRIPTION OF GOODS<br>10 CTNS<br>P/O NO.<br>STYLE NO. LADIES' 100% COTTON WOVEN SKIRTSC/NO.<br>MADE IN CHINA H. S. CODE: 6204 5200 00 | 11. Quantity(1)<br>* 100PCS *<br>(50KGS) | 12. FOB Value(2) | |
| | TOTAL: ONE HUNDRED PCS ONLY. | | |
| M. I. D. NAME: XXXXXX GARMENT FACTORY OF SHENZHEN<br>    ADDR: XXX IND. ZONE, SHENZHEN, CHINA<br>    CITY: SHENZHEN<br>    CODE: CNXXX GARSHE<br>TOTAL: 1,000.00 USD | * *100.00 * PCS | | |
| 13. CERTIFICATION BY THE COMPETENT AUTHORITY | | | |
| 14. Competent authority(name, full address, country)<br>SHENZHEN BUREAU OF FOREIGN<br>TRADE & ECONOMIC COOPERATION<br>1023 Shangbu Zhong Rd., 2nd Govt.<br>Bldg., Shenzhen 518006, China | At-A SHENZHEN      on-le<br><br>(Signature)<br>(Stamp-Cachet) | | |

**Specimen 14**

## CERTIFICATE OF ORIGIN①
### Asia–Pacific Trade Agreement
（Combined declaration and certificate）

| 1. Goods consigned from: <br>（Exporter's business name, address, country） | Reference No. <br><br> Issued in ...... <br> （Country） |
|---|---|
| 2. Goods consigned to: <br>（Consignee's name, address, country） | 3. For official use |
| 4. Means of transport and route: | |

| 5. Tariff item number: | 6. Marks and number of Packages: | 7. Number and kind of packages/ description of goods: | 8. Origin criterion （see notes over-leaf） | 9. Gross weight or other quantity: | 10. Number and date of invoices: |
|---|---|---|---|---|---|
| | | | | | |

| 11. Declaration by the exporter : <br>The undersigned hereby declares that the above details and statements are correct: that all the goods were produced in <br><br> .................................. <br> （Country） <br> and that they comply with the origin requirements specified for these goods in the Asia–Pacific Trade Agreement for goods exported to <br><br> .................................. <br> （Importing Country） <br><br> .................................. <br> Place and date, signature of authorized Signatory | 12. Certificate <br>　　It is hereby certified on the basis of control carried out, that the declaration by the exporter is correct. <br><br><br><br><br><br><br><br> .................................. <br> Place and date, signature and stamp of certifying authority |

---

① http://www.sz.gov.cn/mygyj/xgwd/bgxz/200810/P020081009372558959949.doc.

Specimen 15

## 中华人民共和国出入境检验检疫
## 入境货物报检单①

报检单位(加盖公章)：　　　　　　　　　　　　　　　　编号 ＿＿＿＿＿

报检单位登记号：　　　联系人：　　　电话：　　　　　报检日期：＿＿年＿＿月＿＿日

| 发　货　人 | (中文) | | | | | |
|---|---|---|---|---|---|---|
| | (外文) | | | | | |
| 收　货　人 | (中文) | | | | | |
| | (外文) | | | | | |
| 货物名称(中/外文) | H. S. 编码 | 产地 | 数/重量 | | 货物总值 | 包装种类及数量 |
| | | | | | | |
| 运输工具名称号码 | | 贸易方式 | | 货物存放地点 | | |
| 合同号 | | 信用证号 | | 用　途 | | |
| 到货日期 | | | | | | |
| 起运地 | | | | | | |
| 集装箱规格、数量及号码 | | | | | | |
| 合同、信用证订立的检验检疫条款或特殊要求 | | 标记及号码 | | 随附单据(划"√"或补填) | | |
| 需要单证名称(划"√"或补填) | | | | 检验检疫费 | | |
| 品质证书<br>重量证书<br>兽医卫生证书<br>健康证书<br>卫生证书<br>动物卫生证书 | | 植物检疫证书 | | 总金额<br>(人民币元) | | |
| | | | | 计费人 | | |
| | | | | 收费人 | | |
| 报检人郑重声明：<br>1 本人被授权报检。<br>2 上列填写内容正确属实,货物无伪造或冒用他人的厂名、标志、认证标志,并承担货物质量责任。<br>签名：＿＿＿＿＿ | | | | 领取证单 | | |
| | | | | 日期 | | |
| | | | | 签名 | | |

---

① www. dhp. gov. cn/lists/GuideForInvestment/BGDT/bscx/jyjyj/uploads/中华人民共和国出入境检验检疫出境货物报检单. doc.

**Specimen 16**

**Inspection Certificate of Quality①**

**商品质量检验证书**

中华人民共和国出入境检验检疫

ENTRY-EXIT INSPECTION AND QUARANTINE

OF THE PEOPLE's REPUBLIC OF CHINA

编号 NO. :

QUALITY AND

MICROBIOLOGICAL INSPECTION

发货人＿＿＿＿＿＿

Consignor＿＿＿＿＿＿＿＿＿＿

收货人＿＿＿＿＿＿

Consignee＿＿＿＿＿＿＿＿＿＿＿＿

品名                                        标记及号码

Description of Goods＿＿＿＿＿＿             Marks & No.

报检数量/重量

Quantity / Weight Declared＿＿＿＿＿＿＿

Number and Type of Packages＿＿＿＿＿＿

运输工具

Means of Conveyance＿＿＿＿＿＿＿

检验结果

RESULTS OF INSPECTION

签证地点 Place of Issue＿＿＿＿＿＿            签证日期 Date of Issue＿＿＿＿＿＿

授权签字人 Authorized Officer＿＿＿＿＿＿      签名 Signature＿＿＿＿＿＿

我们已尽所知和最大能力实施上述检验,不能因我们签发本证书而免除卖方或其他方面根据合同和法律所承担的产品质量责任和其他责任。All inspections are carried out conscientiously to the best of our knowledge and ability. This certificate does not in any respect absolve the seller and other related parties from his contractual and legal obligations especially when product quality is concerned.

[cl-1(2007.1)]

---

① www2. sdwfvc. cn/jpkc/swyyhd/html/JIAOAN/unit13. doc.

**Specimen 17**

Certificate of Quantity and Weight Issued by SGS①

SGS Canada Inc.

50-655 West Kent Avenue N.

Vancouver, British Columbia

Canada V6P 6T7

Tel: (604)324-1166

Fax: (604)324-1177

Certificate No. :

Certificate of Quantity and Weight:

COMMODITY:

QUANTITY:

WEIGHT:

LOADED TO THE VESSEL:

TERMINAL:

STOWAGE:

LOADED ON BOARD:

PORT OF DESTINATION:

REFERENCE NO. :

PACKING CONDITIONS:

THIS IS TO CERTIFY

THIS SHIPMENT, BEING PART OF THE TOTAL LOADED, REPRESENTS:

SGS Canada Inc.

This certificate is issued by the Company under its General Conditions for Inspection and Testing Services, printed overleaf. The issuance of this Certificate does not exonerate buyers or sellers from exercising all their rights and discharging all their liabilities under the Contract of Sale. Stipulations to the contrary are not binding on the Company. The company's responsibility more than ten times the amount of the fees or commission. Except by special arrangement, samples, if drawn, will not be retained by the Company for more than three months.

---

① www2. sdwfvc. cn/jpkc/swyyhd/html/JIAOAN/unit13. doc.

**Specimen 18**

## 中华人民共和国海关出口货物报关单(2016年新版)

预录人编号：　　　　　　　　海关编号：

| 收发货人 | | 出口口岸 | 出口日期 | 申报日期 |
|---|---|---|---|---|
| 生产销售单位 | | 运输方式 | 运输工具名称 | 提运单号 |
| 申报单位 | | 监管方式 | 征免性质 | 备案号 |
| 贸易国(地区) | 运抵国(地区) | | 指运港 | 境内货源地 |
| 许可证号 | 成交方式 | 运费 | 保费 | 杂费 |
| 合同协议号 | 件数 | 包装种类 | 毛重(千克) | 净重(千克) |
| 集装箱号 | 随附单证 | | | |

标记唛码及备注

| 项号 | 商品编号 | 商品名称、规格型号 | 数量及单位 | 最终目的国(地区) | 单价 | 总价审单币制 | 征免 |
|---|---|---|---|---|---|---|---|
| | | | | | | | |
| | | | | | | | |
| | | | | | | | |

特殊关系确认：　　　　　　　　价格影响确认：　　　　　　　　支付特权使用费确认：

| 录入员录入单位 | 兹声明以上内容承担如实申报、依法纳税之法律责任 | 海关批注及签章 |
|---|---|---|
| 报关人员 | 申请单位(签章) | |

**Specimen 19**

### 中华人民共和国海关出口货物报关单

预录入编号：　　　　　　　海关编号：

| 出口口岸 | 备案号 | | 出口日期 | | 申报日期 |
|---|---|---|---|---|---|
| 经营单位 | 运输方式 | | 运输工具名称 | | 提运单号 |
| 发货单位 | 贸易方式 | | 征免性质 | | 结汇方式 |
| 许可证号 | 运抵国(地区) | | 指运港 | | 境内货源地 |
| 批准文号 | 成交方式 | 运费 | 保费 | | 杂费 |
| 合同协议号 | 件数 | | 包装种类 | 毛重(公斤) | 净重(公斤) |
| 集装箱号 | 随附单据 | | | 生产厂家 | |

标记唛码及备注

| 项号　商品编号　商品名称、规格型号　数量及单位　最终目的国(地区)单价　总价　币制　征免 |
|---|
| |

税费征收情况

| 录入员　录入单位 | 兹声明以上申报无讹并承担法律责任 | 海关审单批注及放行日期(签章) |
|---|---|---|
| 报关员 | 申报单位(签章) | 审单　　　　审价 |
| | | 征税　　　　统计 |
| 单位地址：<br><br>邮编： | 电话：　　　填制日期： | 查验　　　　放行 |

**Specimen 20**

Customs Declaration Form

## 中华人民共和国海关出口货物报关单

预录入编号：002112115                                     海关编号：151088777

| 出口口岸 | 备案号 | | 出口日期 | 申报日期 |
|---|---|---|---|---|
| 经营单位<br><br>潍坊市进出口贸易公司<br>（411110530） | 运输方式<br><br>海运（2） | | 运输工具名称<br><br>HAIHE V.1 | 提运单号<br><br>K2134569 |
| 发货单位<br><br>潍坊市进出口贸易公司<br>（911110530） | 贸易方式<br><br>一般贸易（0110） | | 征免性质<br><br>一般征税 | 结汇方式<br><br>信用证（6） |
| 许可证号 | 运抵国（地区）<br><br>荷属安的列斯（XXX） | | 指运港<br><br>库拉索（XXX） | 境内货源地<br><br>广州（XXX） |
| 批准文号<br><br>4202010530 | 成交方式<br><br>CFR（2） | 运费<br><br>110/10000/3 | 保费<br><br>0.00 | 杂费<br><br>0.00 |
| 合同协议号<br><br>QIMEX07072 | 件数<br><br>200 | 包装种类<br><br>纸箱 | 毛重（公斤）<br><br>6,000 | 净重（公斤）<br><br>5,600 |
| 集装箱号<br><br>SN256788 | 随附单据<br><br>核销单、发票、装箱单、出境通关单 | | 生产厂家 | |
| 标记唛头及备注：N/M | | | | |

| 项号  商品编号 | 商品名称、规格型号 | 数量及单位 | 最终目的国（地区） | 单位  总价  币制  征免 |
|---|---|---|---|---|
| 62034200 | 男童石磨牛仔<br>BOYS STONEWASH JEANS | CFR | 荷属安的列斯（XXX） | HKD |
| | SIZE：2-8 | 40.00 DOZ | HKD 233.00/DOZ | HKD 9,320.00 |
| | SIZE：6-16 | 760.00 DOZ | HKD 293.00/DOZ | HKD 222,680.00 |

TOTAL：800 DOZ          HKD 232,000.00

FOR：HKD 222,000.00          MEAS：15.5 CUM

FREIGHT PREPAID

税费征收情况

| 录入员  录入单位  兹声明以上申报无讹并承担法律责任<br><br>报关员<br><br>申报单位（签章）<br><br>单位地址：胜利东街 17 号潍坊市进出口贸易公司<br><br>邮编 261031 电话：8881766 填制日期 NOV 20, 2024 | 海关审单批注及放行日期（签章）<br><br>审单          审价<br><br>征税          统计<br><br>查验          放行 |
|---|---|

**Specimen 21**

CHINA—ASEAN EXPO.

CUSTOMS DECLARATION FORM FOR EXHIBITS PACKING LIST & INVOICE①

SHIPPING MARK：  MEANS OF TRANSPORT：

唛 头：  运输方式：

PORT OF IMPORT：  PAGE NO. ：

入境口岸：  第 页

| Exhibitor/Country 展出者/国别 | | | | Country of Origin 原产国 | | HALL NO. ： 展厅号： | | | | BOOTH NO. ： 展台号： |
|---|---|---|---|---|---|---|---|---|---|---|
| Case order No. | Length ＊ Width ＊ Height ＊ （CM） 长＊宽＊高 | Weight （KGS） 重量 | | Description of goods 货物描述 | | | Quantity 数 量 | CIF Value 到岸价 | | R. 复运出口 To Be Returned G. 赠送 Given Away C. 消耗 Consumed A. 放弃 Abandoned S. 销售 Sold |
| | | Gross 毛重 | Net 净重 | Eng-lish 英文 | Chi-nese 中文 | H.S. NO. ： 商品编码 | | Unit Price 单价 | Total Value 总价 | |
| | | | | | | | | | | |
| | | | | | | | | | | |
| | | | | | | | | | | |
| | | | | | | | | | | |
| | | | | | | | | | | |
| | | | | | | | | | | |
| | | | | | | | | | | |
| | | | | | | | | | | |
| | | | | | | | | | | |
| 海关记录： Customs Remarks： | | | | | | | | | | |

APPLICANT：SIGNATURE OF RESPONSIBLE PERSON   DATE OF APPLICATION

申请单位：  负责人签名：  申请日期：

---

① eng. caexpo. org/download/CUSTOMS_DECLARATION_FORM. doc.

**Specimen 22**

Application Form for Import License of P. R. C.
### 中华人民共和国进口货物许可证申请表

| 1. 我国对外成交单位及编码<br>（成交单位或指标单位盖章） | 3. 进口许可证编号： |
|---|---|
| | 4. 许可证有效期：<br>至 ____ 年 ___ 月 ___ 日止 |
| 2. 收货单位： | |
| 5. 贸易方式： | 8. 进口国别. (地区)： |
| 6. 外汇来源： | 9. 商品原产地： |
| 7. 到货口岸： | 10. 商品用途： |

| 11. 商品名称： | | | 商品编码 | | |
|---|---|---|---|---|---|
| 12.商品规格、型号 | 13.单位 | 14.数量 | 15. 单价<br>（币制） | 16.总值 | 17. 总值折美元 |
| | | | | | |
| 18. 总计 | | | | | |

| 填表须知：1. 本申请表一式两联，由领证人填写，未经盖章本表无效，申领许可证时两联均需交给发证机关。<br>2. "商品名称"栏，每份申请表只能填写一种商品，或同一品种不同型号的商品。<br>3. 商品用途：指自用、生产用、内销、维修、样品、外销。<br>4. 外汇来源：指中央、留成、贷款、外资、调剂、劳务、赠送、索赔、无偿援助、不支付外汇。<br>5. 贸易方式：指一般、易货、国际租赁、华侨捐赠、友好赠送、经贸往来赠送、外商投资企业进口、补偿贸易、进料加工、对销、国际招标、国际援助、劳务补偿、来料加工、国际贷款、其他贸易。 | 领证人姓名：<br><br>领证人驻京电话：<br><br>下次联系日期： |
|---|---|

**Specimen 23**

## 中 华 人 民 共 和 国 进 口 许 可 证①

Import License of the People's Republic of China

| 1. 进口商：<br>Importer | 3. 进口许可证号：<br>Import license no. |
|---|---|
| 2. 收货人：<br>Consignee | 4. 进口许可证有效截止日期：<br>Import license expiry date |
| 5. 贸易方式：<br>Terms of trade | 8. 出口国(地区)：<br>Country/region of exportation |
| 6. 外汇来源：<br>Terms of foreign exchange | 9. 原产国(地区)：<br>Country/region of origin |
| 7. 报关口岸：<br>Place of clearance | 10. 商品用途：<br>Use of goods |

| 11. 商品名称：<br>Description of goods | | | 商品编码：<br>Code of goods | | |
|---|---|---|---|---|---|
| 12. 规格型号<br>Specification | 13. 单位<br>Unit | 14. 数量<br>Quantity | 15. 单价<br>Unit price | 16. 总值<br>Amount | 17. 总值折美元<br>Amount in USD |
| | | | | | |
| | | | | | |
| 18. 总计 Total | | | | | |

| 19. 备注<br>Supplementary details | 20. 发证机关签章：<br>Issuing authority s stamp & signature |
|---|---|
| | 21. 发证日期：<br>License date |

---

① http://tguide. ec. com. cn/article/myxy/myzncydj/200606/621943_1. html.

# Chapter 9　Improving International Trade Documentation

## 【本章提要】

鉴于外贸制单的专业性、复杂性和非标准性,外贸制单和审单都是费时费力的工作。外贸制单工作中的任何细微疏漏,都有可能增加交易成本,甚至阻碍整个国际交易的顺利进行。因此,改进和完善外贸制单势在必行。令人欣慰的是,包括联合国在内的许多国际组织已经做出实质性的努力,外贸制单工作也因此出现了简单化、标准化、协调化和自动化的改进趋势。未来要进一步完善外贸制单工作,更需要各国的进出口商、贸易促进机构和国际组织等方面的共同努力。

According to the UNCTAD's statistics, international businesses, traders, and transport operators have to deal with numerous documents and forms (up to 40 originals), often containing redundant and repetitive data and information (200 data elements on average). These documents, frequently not standardized, are complex and cumbersome for traders to complete and for authorities to verify. Excessive paperwork takes time for import/export and transit procedures and formalities and results in the employment of more human resources in government and the private sector. This invites errors in submissions and malfeasance, raises trade transactions costs, and slows down trade flows[1]. It is thus necessary to improve the international trade documentation.

The WTO has recently made a great progress in this aspect.

The WTO's Director-General announced on Feb. 22, 2017 that the Trade Facilitation Agreement has entered into force after two thirds of members completed their domestic ratification process.

The landmark covenant, which opened for ratification in 2014, seeks to facilitate the movement, release and clearance of goods across international customs.

According to estimates, the full implementation of the treaty could decrease global trade costs by as much as 14.3 percent.

This is of particular significance for developing and least developed countries which typically have to contend with higher levels of trade costs.

---

[1]　http://www.unescap.org/tid/publication/chap4_2224.pdf, improving trade documentation for details.

"It will help these countries to diversify their trade. Developing countries could increase the number of products they export by 20 percent, while LDCs could see an increase of up to 35 percent," Azevedo explained.

"In addition, developing countries could enter a third more foreign markets on average, while LDCs could access 60 percent more, making these countries less vulnerable to external economic shocks," he added.

The cumulative ramifications of the TFA are also very promising; with experts estimating that the full implementation of the agreement could boost global trade by as much as 1 trillion U. S. dollars per year.

According to estimates, the TFA is expected to add 2. 7 percentage points per year to world trade growth, and over half a percentage point per year to world GDP growth by 2030.

"This impact would be greater than the elimination of all existing tariffs around the world," Azevedo highlighted.

"The Trade Facilitation Agreement is the biggest reform of global trade this century," he added.

In December 2013, WTO members concluded negotiations on a Trade Facilitation Agreement at the Bali Ministerial Conference, as part of a wider "Bali Package".

It is the first multilateral agreement to be reached since the organization came into being over the past 20 years. [1]

To sum up, the latest decades witnessed several noticeable trends in improving trade documentation.

# 9.1 Simplification

Simplification is the process of eliminating all redundancies and repetitions in formalities, processes and procedures. Simplified trade documents and procedures aligned to international standards will expedite trade transactions as they provide a common basis for similar measures applied by different countries and regions. Simplification is consistent with the WTO's "recognize the need for minimizing the incidence and complexity of import and export formalities and for decreasing and simplifying import and export document requirements" [2].

Specifically, trade documents simplification will inevitably save time and costs. The reasons can be listed as: fewer documents and forms are easier to deal with; reduced time, money, and human resources can lower total transaction costs; harmonized data elements can facilitate document transmission between countries and remove language barriers; entered-only-once

---

[1] Source: From: http://www.hxen.com/englishnews/world/2017-02-23/459768.html.
[2] GATT Article VIII (1).

data can ease the reproduction and reduce chances of mistakes; administrative controls can be improved; and thus the transition to automation and electronic documents submission becomes swifter and smoother.

Over the past 40 years, many efforts have been made by the United Nations (UN) to move towards simplified and standardized trade documentation. As a first step, UN/CEFACT① recommends that all participants in international trade should limit request for original or copies of trade documents②. Other initiatives are UNLK③, UNTDED④, UN/EDIFACT⑤, and UNeDocs⑥, etc. Among those, the United Nations Layout Key for Trade Documents (UNLK; ISO 6422) is the most widely used international standard for trade documents.

## 9.2 Standardization

Documents simplifications do save time and money, however, too much or too less simplification may result in ambiguity and misunderstanding, which definitely violates the initial purpose of documents simplification and trade facilitation. It is of practical significance to standardize the rules of documents simplification, that is, the standardization.

Standardization is the process of developing internationally agreed formats for practices and procedures, documents and information. Where such standards are adopted, the importers and exporters will not only be able to communicate better among themselves and with the authorities in their country, but also with parties in other countries. As for trade documents, they may be standardized in both physical format and information items and data.

(1) Physical format standardization. The UNLK, the most widely used standard for the

---

① the United Nations Centre for Trade Facilitation and Electronic Business.

② Recommendation No. 12.

③ UNLK (the UN Layout Key) was first adopted in 1963 and became UNECE recommendation No. 1 in 1978. It organizes coded information (address, buyer, seller, documentation requirements for certain products, etc) in a box format in fixed locations on a document (the so called "Aligned Paper Documents"). UNLK is essentially a master layout design from which other trade documents (administrative, commercial) can be derived, and thus it can be used for creating international and national layout keys and standard forms and visual display in automated data processing applications.

④ UNTDED (the UN Trade Data Elements Directory) was published jointly by the ISO and UNECE, contains the building blocks, codes and definitions.

⑤ UN/EDIFACT (the UN Electronic Data Interchange for Administration, Commerce and Transport) was approved as an ISO standard and became UNECE Recommendation No. 25 in 1987. It comprises internationally agreed standards, directories and guidelines for the electronic interchange of structured trade data between independent computerized information systems.

⑥ UNeDocs (the United Nations electronic Trade Documents) is a project set up by the UNECE in 2000. Using the latest internet technologies and standards, the project combines paper and electronic options, since some governments and traders are likely to have to rely on paper trade documentation for some time to come. Users benefit from data security, signature authentication, mobile access to secured information and the exchange of advance information of trade data for security or goods clearing purposes.

physical format and size of documents, does provide an ensuring compatibility between different paper formats and sizes. Using the UNLK ensures that the same information and data are found in the same place on all documents, and the same format is used regardless of the size of paper. For example, between A4 used in Europe and the legal size used in the United States, one document is being printed. It also prescribes the size of boxes, margin, spacing and other requirements, which are vital for physical document layout[1].

(2) Contents standardization. In addition to the standardized format, some information items and data contained in the UNLK are also standardized based on the following international standards[2].

● Code for the representation names of countries (ISO 3166) — usually two digit Alpha codes. For example: AU for Australia, CN for China, VN for Viet Nam, GB for United Kingdom, etc.

● Numerical representation of dates, time and periods of time (ISO 8601:2000). For example, July 30, 2024 can be written as 2024-07-30 or 24-07-30.

● Alphabetic code for the representation of currencies (ISO 4217). For example, CNY for Chinese Yuan, USD for United States Dollars, HKD for Hong Kong Dollar, etc.

● UN/LOCODE—port of shipment code with five digit Alpha code. The first two digits identify country and the last three digits identify location of the port. For example: CNSHA for Shanghai, JPNGS for Nagasaki, GBSOU for Southampton, etc.

● INCOTERMS—are common list of trade terms used for international trade and developed by the International Chamber of Commerce (ICC). The purpose is to establish a set of international rules for interpretation of trade terms. For example: EXW Ex works, CFR Cost and Freight, CIF Cost, Insurance and Freight, FOB Free on Board, etc.

● Codes for mode of transport—standard codes depicting mode of transport. For example: Sea 1, Rail 2, Road 3, and Air 4.

## 9.3　Harmonization

Harmonization is the alignment of national formalities, procedures, operations and documents with international conventions, standards, and practices. This will make it easer to complete forms and procedures. With existing international standards and practices, the effectiveness and speed of regional harmonization efforts will increase significantly.

---

① www. sitpro. org. uk/documents/index. html for SITPRO. A complete toolkit for the design of UNLK aligned trade documents is also available at www. unedocs. org.

② www. unece. org/cefact/recommendations/rec_index. htm.

As mentioned above, UNLK is the most widely used international standard for trade documents. On the basis of the UNLK, aligned series of trade documents and forms can be designed, which means that documents can be copied from one format to another without loosing information.

One typical example is SITPRO, the U. K. 's trade facilitation body, which involves in the development of the U. K. Aligned Series of Export documents, maintains those documents and licenses a network of approved suppliers to produce and supply the standard forms, computer software and laser systems to create them. This series now contains about 70 standard commercial, transportation, banking, insurance and other official forms[1].

There are some other examples of international sectoral documents based on the UNLK.

Regulatory documents:

- Single Administrative Document (SAD, European Union).
- Phytosanitary Certificate (Plant Protection Convention).
- Certificate of Origin (WCO Kyoto Convention).
- GSP Certificate (UNCTAD) .
- Dangerous Goods Declaration (UNECE).
- Dispatch Note for Post parcels (World Post Convention).

Transport documents:

- Standard Bill of Lading (International Chamber of Shipping).
- Freight Forwarding Instructions (FIATA).
- International Road Consignment Note (CMR).
- International Rail Consignment Note (CIM).
- Universal Air Waybill (IATA).
- The IMO Standardized Forms (FAL 1–7).

Furthermore, regular consultation and feedback between the government and the private sector is required to ensure that the simplification, standardization and harmonization efforts undertaken by the administration are consistent with the needs of the end-user of the trade administrative system and to ensure that any change to the procedures is beneficial to all parties.

## 9.4 Automation

The drastic increase in international trade volume over the latest decades makes a great challenge for the slow-speeded traditional paper-based system. Some established trade experiences indicate that effective electronic and automated trade systems can increase transaction speed and make the regulatory system more transparent and predictable. For instance, e-pay-

---

[1] www. sitpro. org. uk/documents/index. html.

ment systems allow traders to pay customs duties or settle trade transactions in seconds rather than hours or days; and electronic trade document systems allow them to apply and obtain the necessary papers in minutes rather than days or weeks. This results in productivity improvements.

One of successive examples is Singapore's TradeNet. Relevant statistics indicate that TradeNet reduced trade documentation processing costs by 20 percent or more. These cost-savings accrued not only to the users of TradeNet from the private sector, but also from government agencies.

Instead of filling out more than 20 paper forms in the past, users of TradeNet now were required to fill out only one single online form. This greatly eliminated the use of clerks or couriers to transport trade documents to various agencies, and led to significant savings in time and money. Staff no longer needed to stand in lines and wait for documents to be cleared. Faster turnaround made it possible to better organize shipments and overall productivity. Several freight forwarders reported savings of 25 ~ 35 percent in handling trade documentation as TradeNet operates 24 hours a day and 7 days a week as opposed to using agencies that open only during normal office hours of business days.

Benefits also accrued to government agencies using the system. Customs moved from a system of post-approval of applications to pre-approval, and Customs duties are now pre-paid through electronic means and Customs receive payments faster. The ETDS also enabled faster compilation of more accurate and complete external trade statistics as the data from the documents need not be re-keyed in by the Government agencies to compile the trade statistics. Such accurate statistics will not only serve the private sector better by providing them with timely trade statistics for market analyses and marketing policy formulation, but also help the Government agencies for trade policy, trade surveillance and trade monitoring.

It is obvious that, the development of electronic trading system, which allows for paperless trading, is the ultimate step in improving the paper flow. However, aligned trade documents are the first step towards electronic documents submission and Customs automation. An electronic trade documentation and processing system can be successful only when the trade documents and related procedure have already been simplified, standardized and harmonized as explained earlier. Accordingly, the ECE[1] and some international organization have developed standards for the exchange of electronic trade documents, (e. g. EDIFACT and ebXML). Those standards have been widely adopted and should be used to develop any trade-related electronic sys-

---

① Abbreviation for Economic Commission for Europe.

tem to allow cross-border exchange of information.

## 9.5　Implementation Requirements

To implement the system of Trade documents simplification, standardization, harmonization and automation, there should be a clearly and reasonably planned project of trade documentation simplification, a sufficient financial budget for potential costs, and a close eye on the prevailing practice of international trade.

(1) Key steps for project of trade documentation simplification. Before introducing simplified trade documentation, it is essential to set up a project team, consisting of officials from Customs, trade agencies and industry/external private agents, as well as some specialized international trade experts. The function of this team is to make an inventory of existing regulations, procedures formalities and forms. A project team set up for this purpose by scanning current trade practices, related statutes and the required documents from the beginning to the end of a trade transaction[1]. The key steps are as follows.

- Set up project team responsible for stocktaking and analysis of existing trade procedures and requisite formalities and documentation.

- Ensure active involvement and input from private traders, manufacturers, transport operators, agents, insurers and forwarders, including their commercial and documentation practices and information technology capabilities.

- Assemble and compare trade rules, statutory requirements and administrative rulings with Customs procedures and requisite documentation.

- Draw up flowcharts/matrices noting procedures and related formalities, documents and forms.

- Select one type of trade operation, such as importing essential manufacturing inputs or exporting products vital for the local economy, and trace all necessary steps from licensing requirements, manufacturers need to government agencies and customs formalities involved to border entry/exit, including official/client interactions, manual verification and the average time it takes to complete the procedure.

- Eliminate unnecessary steps and formalities and simplify the process and documentation requirements on the basis of available UN guidelines and proven international documentation standards and data requirements as elaborated below.

- Initiate a public relations campaign to inform stakeholders of new procedures and

---

[1]　UNCTAD Trust Fund for Trade Facilitation Negotiations Technical Notes 1, 2, 6, 11, 16 and 20, b.

planned legislation.

- Enact statutes or amendments related to new procedures and documentation requirements.

- Publish and make new documents and procedural requirements widely available.

(2) Financial budgets for potential costs . The effective performance of the above project
will definitely involve significant costs in the following cases:

- Computers and specialized software acquisition. Initial costs might involve the acquisition of computers and specialized software for the digitization of existing rules and documents to
facilitate review and assessment of current trade formalities and documentation requirements.

- New formats of aligned documents introduction. Administrative changes implied by
simplification and standardization of trade documents might involve one-time costs related to introduction of the new formats of aligned documents. The costs would involve hiring experts and training
staff in the production of the national sets of aligned trade documents and operating computer software. But once the new document formats are in place, the additional costs should be minimal.

For developing and least-developed countries and SMEs worldwide, the Trade Documents Toolkits, developed by the UN Regional Commissions, is definitely a reasonable and low-cost alternative. They contain an electronic toolkit for the development of write-enabled paper documents, a
handbook and sample document forms, and a library of resources for the alignment of trade documents. To put the toolkits to practical use, it is necessary to carry out analysis of existing procedures and related documents with a view to rationalizing or complementing them, particularly in
least-developed countries; and then to request some technical assistance from the Commission, from
which Customs officials as well as users of aligned trade documents should benefit.

(3) Following the Latest Documentary Practices. In addition to the initiatives launched by
the UN and similar organizations, a considerable simplification of documentary practices has
been achieved in recent years. For instance, Bills of lading are frequently replaced by non-
negotiable documents similar to those used for other modes of transport than carriage by sea.
Non-negotiable documents are quite satisfactory except where the buyer wishes to sell the goods
in transit by surrendering a paper document to the new buyer. In order to make this possible,
the obligation of the seller to provide a bill of lading under CFR and CIF must be retained.
However, when the contracting parties know that the buyer does not contemplate selling the
goods in transit, they may agree to relieve the seller from the obligation of providing a bill of
lading, or, alternatively, CPT and CIP may be used where there is no requirement to provide a
bill of lading.

# References

[1] David P, Stewart R. International Logistics: the Management of International Trade Operations[M]. 2nd Edition. Beijing: Tsinghua University Press, 2007.

[2] Marshall C. Mastering International Trade[M]. Great Britain: PALGRAVE, 2003.

[3] Bisnop E. Finance of International Trade[M]. Great Britain: ELSEVIER, 2004.

[4] Whitehead G. Elements of International Trade and Payment[M]. Cambridge: Woodhead-Faulkner, 1983.

[5] Plamer H. International Trade and Pre-trade Finance [M]. England: Euromoney Books.

[6] Bergamin J. Payment Techniques in Trade Finance[M]. ING BARINGS, 1999-04/05:13-15..

[7] Collins Essential English Dictionary [M]. 2nd Edition. HarperCollins Publishers 2004, 2006.

[8] Hinkelman E H. Longman Dictionary of International Trade[M]. Longman and China Renmin University Press, 2000.

[9] Laryea, Emmanuel T. Demateralisation of Insurance Documents in International Trade Transactions: A Need for Legislative Reform[J]. The University of New South Wales Law Journal, 2000, 23 (1):78-104.

[10] UNCTAD secretariat. The Use of Transport Documents in International Trade[D]. UNCTAD/SDTE/TLB/2003/3.

[11] http://www. unescap. org/tid/publication/chap4_2224. pdf, improving trade documentation.

[12] UNCTAD. Trust Fund for Trade Facilitation Negotiations Technical Note No. 13. Simplification of Trade Documentation using International Standards.

[13] The United Nations Commission on International Trade Law (UNCITRAL). Convention on Contracts for the International Sale of Goods (1980).

[14] Uniform Rules for Documentary Collections, ICC Publication No. 522.

[15] Uniform Customs and Practices for Documentary Credits, ICC Publication No. 600.

[16] International Rules for Interpretation of Trade Terms, ICC Publication No. 456.

[17] Incoterms® 2010(The Incoterms rules or International Commercial Terms2010).

[18] Incoterms® 2020 (ICC rules for the use of domestic and international trade terms).

[19] ISBP for UCP 600 (ICC Publication No. 681,745,821).

[20] U. K. Bill of Exchange Act 1882, and supplementary version 1957.

[21] The United Nations Commission on International Trade Law (UNCITRAL). Convention on International Bills of Exchange and International Promissory Notes of 1988.

[22] Negotiable Instrument law of People's Republic of China (2004 Revision).

[23] UCC (Uniform Commercial Code) 1952.

[24] http://www. thefreedictionary. com/.

[25] http://en. wikipedia. org/.

[26] http://www. businessdictionary. com/.

[27] http://www. lectlaw. com/ .

[28] http://dictionary. die. net/ .

[29] http://www. teachmefinance. com/.

[30] http://www. unzco. com/ .

[31] http://www. uncitral. org/ .

[32] http://www. sitpro. org. uk/ .

[33] http://www. iccwbo. org/ .

[34] http://resources. alibaba. com/ .

[35] http://www. oecd. org/ .

[36] http://www. unece. org/ .

[37] http://www. iata. org/ .

[38] http://www. free-logistics. com/ .

[39] http://www. exporthelp. co. za/ .

[40] http://www. cargolaw. com/.

[41] http://business-heaven. blogspot. com/ .

[42] http://www. investorwords. com/ .

[43] http://www. economist. com/ .

[44] http://www. dhl-usa. com/ .

[45] http://www. licence. org. cn/ .

[46] https://www. fnb. co. za/ .

[47] http://www. banking. about. com/ .

[48] http://www. legal-explanations. com/ .

[49] http://wmdz. jp. zfc. edu. cn/Practice. aspx .

[50] http://jpk. niit. edu. cn/gs/h2. html.

[51] http://guomaoren. com/.

[52] http://mep128. mofcom. gov. cn/mep/wmzs/dzzs/dzzz/48991. asp.

[53] 广银芳,等. 外贸单证制作实务[M]. 北京:清华大学出版社,2007.

[54] 王丽丽. 国际贸易单证理论与实训[M]. 北京:北京大学出版社,2007.

［55］余世明. 国际商务单证实务［M］. 广州:暨南大学出版社,2007.

［56］刘启萍,周树玲.外贸英文制单［M］. 2 版. 北京:对外经济贸易大学出版社,2006.

［57］苏定东,王群飞.国际贸易单证实务［M］.北京:北京大学出版社,2006.

［58］姚新超.国际贸易惯例与规则实务［M］.北京:对外经济贸易大学出版社,2012.

［59］卓乃坚. 国际贸易支付与结算及其单证实务［M］. 上海:东华大学出版社,2005.

［60］赵薇. 国际结算-国际贸易融资支付方法［M］. 南京:东南大学出版社,2008.

［61］余世明,冼燕华.国际商务模拟实习教程［M］.广州:暨南大学出版社,2004.

［62］中国国际商会/国际商会中国国家委员会. 国际贸易术语解释通则 2020(中英版)［M］. 北京:对外经济贸易大学出版社,2020.

# Key to Questions and Problems

## Chapter 1   Overview

I . Choose the best answer to fill in the blank.

1~4: B, A, C, B

5~8: A, C, C, C

## Chapter 2   International Contract of Sale

I . Choose the best answer to fill in the blank.

1~5: B, D, D, A, C

6~10: D, A, B, D, C

11~15: A, D, D, A, D

II . Case analysis.

1. Yes. Lee could reject Dee's so-called acceptance.

According to the UNCISG, a reply to an offer which purports to be an acceptance but contains material alterations (here refer to the lower price) is a rejection of the offer and constitutes a counter-offer, which can be deemed as a new offer.

In this case, Dee Inc. made a material change on the price, so this was a counter-offer, which caused the initial offer to be invalid.

2. According to the UNCISG, an alteration on time of shipment is deemed as a material alteration and constitutes a counter-offer.

In this case, Company X can deal with company Y as follows:

√Informs Company Y that the initial offer has been invalid because of being counter-offered by Company X.

√Make a new offer with a higher price.

√Accept Company Y's counter-offer if Company X is willing to do so.

## III. Fill in the blank form contact in English with the following particulars.

### CONTRACT No. AC4789

**Sellers**: Beijing Light Industrial Products Import and Export Corporation

**Buyers**: Trading Company , New York

The undersigned Sellers and Buyers have agreed to close the following transaction according to the terms and conditions stipulated below:

**Commodity**: "YONGJIU" Brand Bicycle

**Specifications**: Model YE110

**Quantity**: 1,000 Bicycles

**Unit Price**: At USD 100 each CIF New York

**Total Value**: USD 100,000 ( Say United States Dollars One Hundred Thousand Only)

**Packing**: In wooden cases

**Shipping Mark**: At Sellers' option

**Insurance**: To be covered by the Sellers for 110% of the invoice value against All Risks and War Risk as per CIC dated 1st January, 1981.

**Time of Shipment**: To be effected not later than 31st March, 2024, not allowing partial shipments and transshipment.

**Port of Shipment**: China Port

**Port of Destination**: New York

**Terms of Payment**: By irrevocable L/C at sight to reach the Sellers a month prior to the time of shipment and remain valid for negotiation in China until the 15th day after the final date of shipment.

The sellers                                                    The buyers


Beijing Light Industrial Products
Import and Export Corporation                      Trading Company , New York


Done and signed in Beijing on this____ day of_____ , 20_____.

330

## IV. Calculations and sales contract drafting.

1. USD 2,349

2. USD 44,631

3. Fill in the following blank form sales contract.

<table>
<tr>
<td colspan="4" align="center">销售合同<br>**SALES CONTRACT**</td>
</tr>
<tr>
<td>卖方 SELLER：</td>
<td>DESHENG TRADING CO. ,LTD.<br>29TH FLOOR KINGSTAR MANSION,<br>623 JINLIN RD. , SHANGHAI CHINA</td>
<td colspan="2">编号 NO. ：<br>日期 DATE：<br>地点 SIGNED IN：</td>
</tr>
<tr>
<td>买方<br>BUYER：</td>
<td>NFO GENERAL TRADING CO.<br># 362 JALAN STREET, TORONTO,<br>CANADA</td>
<td colspan="2"></td>
</tr>
<tr>
<td colspan="4">买卖双方同意以下条款达成交易：<br>    This contract is made by and agreed between the BUYER and SELLER, in accordance with the terms and conditions stipulated below.</td>
</tr>
<tr>
<td align="center">1. 品名及规格<br>Commodity & Specification</td>
<td align="center">2. 数量<br>Quantity</td>
<td align="center">3. 单价及价格条款<br>Unit Price & Trade Terms</td>
<td align="center">4. 金额<br>Amount</td>
</tr>
<tr>
<td>CHINESE CERAMIC DINNERWARE<br>DS1511 30-Piece Dinnerware and Tea Set<br>DS220120-Piece Dinnerware Set<br>DS450445-Piece Dinnerware Set<br>DS512095-Piece Dinnerware Set</td>
<td align="center"><br>542<br>800<br>443<br>254</td>
<td align="center">CIF5% TORONTO<br>USD 23.50/SET<br>USD 20.40/SET<br>USD 23.20/SET<br>USD 30.10/SET</td>
<td align="right"><br>USD 12,737<br>16,320<br>10,277.6<br>7,645.4</td>
</tr>
<tr>
<td align="right">Total</td>
<td align="center">2,039</td>
<td></td>
<td align="right">USD 46,980</td>
</tr>
<tr>
<td colspan="2" align="center">允许       10%<br>With</td>
<td colspan="2">溢短装,由卖方决定<br>More or less of shipment allowed at the sellers' option</td>
</tr>
<tr>
<td>5. 总值<br>Total Value</td>
<td colspan="3">SAY UNITED STATES DOLLARS FORTY-SIX THOUSAND NINE HUNDRED AND EIGHTY ONLY</td>
</tr>
<tr>
<td>6. 包装<br>Packing</td>
<td colspan="3">PACKED IN CARTONS.<br>DS2201：2 SETS TO A CARTON<br>DS1151,DS4504,DS5120：ONE SET TO A CARTON<br>TOTAL PACKAGES：1,639 CARTONS</td>
</tr>
</table>

| 7. 唛头<br>Shipping Marks | AT BUYER's OPTION BEFORE GOODS TO BE SHIPPED |
|---|---|
| 8. 装运期及运输方式<br>Time of Shipment & means of Transportation | Time of shipment & means of transportation |
| 9. 装运港及目的地<br>Port of loading & destination | Port of Loading & Destination |
| 10. 保险<br>Insurance | TO BE EFFECTED BY THE SELLER FOR 110% OF CONTRACTED CIF VALUE, AGAINST WPA, BREAKAGES AND DAMAGES, AND WAR RISKS OF C. I. C DATED 1981-01-01. |
| 11. 付款方式<br>Terms of Payment | IRREVOCABLE LETTER OF CREDIT PAYABLE BY DRAFT AT SIGHT, TO REACH THE SELLER BEFORE APRIL 5 AND TO REMAIN VALID FOR NEGOTIATION IN CHINA UNTIL 15 DAYS AFTER THE TIME OF SHIPMENT. |
| 12. 备注<br>Remarks | |

| The Buyer<br>NFO GENERAL TRADING CO.<br>（signature） | The Seller<br>DESHENG TRADING CO. , LTD.<br>（signature） |
|---|---|

## Chapter 3　Documentary Letter of Credit

Ⅰ. Choose the best answer to fill in the blank.

　　1~5:A, B, D, A, C

　　6~10:A, A, D, B, D

Ⅱ. True（T）or false（F）.

　　1~5: F, F, T, T, T

　　6~10: T, F, T, T, T

　　11~15: T, T, F, F, T

## III. Fill in the blank form L/C application according to the following contract.

### IRREVOCABLE DOCUMENTARY CREDIT APPLICATION

TO: BANK OF New York                                                                 Date:

| | |
|---|---|
| Beneficiary (full name and address)<br><br>Jiahe Trading Company, 60 Niujie Road, Beijing, China | L/C No.<br>Ex-Card No.<br>Contract No. AC4789 |
| | Date and place of expiry of the credit<br>remain valid for negotiation in China until the 15th day after<br>the final date of shipment |

| Partial shipments | Transshipment | |
|---|---|---|
| ☒ allowed<br>☐ not allowed | ☐ allowed<br>☒ not allowed | ☐ Issue by airmail<br>☐ With brief advice by teletransmission<br>☐ Issue by express delivery<br>☒ Issue by SWIFT |

| | |
|---|---|
| Loading on board/dispatch/taking in charge at/<br>from China Port<br>Not later than 31st March, 2024<br>for transportation to New York | Amount (both in figures and words)<br>USD 100,000 ( Say United States Dollars One Hundred<br>Thousand Only) |

| | |
|---|---|
| Description of goods:<br>1,000 "YONGJIU" Brand Bicycle Model YE110 at USD<br>100 each CIF New York | Credit available with<br>☒ by sight payment      ☐ by acceptance<br>☐ by negotiation      ☐ by deferred payment at<br>against the documents detailed herein<br>☐ and beneficiary's draft for  % of the invoice value<br>At Beijing, China<br>on or before April 15, 2024 |
| Packing: In wooden cases | ☐ FOB    ☐ CFR    ☒ CIF    ☐ or other terms |

Documents required: (marked with x)

    1. ( ✕ ) Signed Commercial Invoice in FIVE copies indicating invoice no., contract no.

    2. ( ✕ ) Full set of clean on board ocean Bills of Lading made out to order and blank endorsed, marked "freight (  ) to collect / ( ✕ ) prepaid (  ) showing freight amount" notifying

    3. (  ) Air Waybills showing "freight (  ) to collect / (  ) prepaid (  ) indicating freight amount" and consigned to_____

4. (　) Memorandum issued by＿＿＿＿consigned to＿＿＿＿

5. (×) Insurance Policy / Certificate in copies for 110% of the invoice value showing claims payable in China in currency of the draft, blank endorsed, covering (×) Ocean Marine Transportation / (　) Air Transportation / (　) Over Land Transportation(　)All Risks, War Risks.

6. (×) Packing List / Weight Memo in FOUR copies indicating quantity / gross and net weights of each package and packing conditions as called for by the L/C.

7. (　) Certificate of Quantity / Weight in＿copies issued an independent surveyor at the loading port, indicating the actual surveyed quantity / weight of shipped goods as well as the packing condition.

8. (×) Certificate of Quality in THREE copies issued by (　) manufacturer / (×) public recognized surveyor / (　)

9. (×) Beneficiary's certified copy of FAX dispatched to the accountee with ＿3＿ days after shipment advising (×) name of vessel / (×) date, quantity, weight and value of shipment.

10. (　) Beneficiary's Certificate certifying that extra copies of the documents have been dispatched according to the contract terms.

11. (　) Shipping Company's Certificate attesting that the carrying vessel is chartered or booked by accountee or their shipping agents：

12. (×) Other documents, if any：

(×) a) Certificate of Origin in TEREE copies issued by authorized institution.

(　) b) Certificate of Health in＿copies issued by authorized institution.

Additional instructions：

1. (×) All banking charges outside the opening bank are for beneficiary's account.

2. (×) Documents must be presented with ＿15＿ days after the date of issuance of the transport documents but within the validity of this credit.

3. (×) Third party as shipper is not acceptable. Short Form / Blank Back B/L is not acceptable.

4. (　) Both quantity and amount＿% more or less are allowed.

5. (　) prepaid freight drawn in excess of L/C amount is acceptable against presentation of original charges voucher issued by Shipping Co. / Air line / or it's agent.

6. (×) All documents to be forwarded in one cover, unless otherwise stated above.

7. (　) Other terms, if any：

Advising bank：Bank of China, Beijing Branch

Account No.：with (name of bank)Bank of New York, New York

Transacted by：Applicant(name, signature of authorized person)

Telephone No.：(with seal)

# IV. Issue a documentary credit by SWIFT according to the application in problem III above.

## Issue of a Documentary Credit

| | | |
|---|---|---|
| Issuing Bank | | BKNYXXXX SESSION: 000 ISN: 000000<br>BANK OF NEW YORK<br>One Wall Street, New York, NY 10286 United States |
| Destination Bank | | XXXXXXXX<br>BANK OF CHINA, BEIJING BRANCH<br>2 CHAOYANGMEN NEIDAJIE, BEIJING, CHINA |
| Type of Documentary Credit | 40A | IRREVOCABLE |
| Letter of Credit Number | 20 | NYC–102156 |
| Date of Issue | 31G | 240215 |
| Date and Place of Expiry | 31D | 240415 CHINA |
| Applicant Bank | 51D | NEW YORK BANK , NEW YORK |
| Applicant | 50 | GLOBAL TRADING COMPANY, 30 FIFTH AVENUE, NEW YORK, USA |
| Beneficiary | 59 | JIAHE INTER TRADING CO. , 60, NIUJIE ROAD, BEIJING, CHINA |
| Currency Code, Amount | 32B | USD 100,000 |
| Available with. . . by. . . | 41D | ANY BANK BY NEGOTIATION |
| Drafts at | 42C | AT SIGHT |
| Drawee | 42D | NEW YORK BANK , NEWYORK |
| Partial Shipments | 43P | NOT ALLOWED |
| Transshipment | 43T | NOT ALLOWED |
| Shipping on Board/Dispatch/Packing in Charge at/ from | 44A | |
| Transportation to | 44B | NEW YORK |
| Latest Date of Shipment | 44C | 240331 |

Description of Goods or Services: 45A

1,000 YONGJIU BRAND BICYCLE

Model YE110

CIF NEW YORK

CHINA ORIGIN

Documents Required: 46A

1. SIGNED COMMERCIAL INVOICE IN 5 COPIES.

2. FULL SET OF CLEAN ON BOARD OCEAN BILLS OF LADING MADE OUT TO ORDER AND BLANK ENDORSED, MARKED"FREIGHT PREPAID"NOTIFYING ACCOUNTEE.

3. PACKING LIST/WEIGHT MEMO IN 4 COPIES INDICATING QUANTITY/GROSS AND NET WEIGHTS OF EACH PACKAGE AND PACKING CONDITIONS AS CALLED FOR BY THE L/C.

4. CERTIFICATE OF QUALITY IN 3 COPIES ISSUED BY PUBLIC RECOGNIZED SURVEYOR.

5. BENEFICIARY'S CERTIFIED COPY OF FAX DISPATCHED TO THE ACCOUNTEE WITH 3 DAYS AFTER SHIPMENT ADVISING NAME OF VESSEL, DATE, QUANTITY, WEIGHT, VALUE OF SHIPMENT, L/C NUMBER AND CONTRACT NUMBER.

6. CERTIFICATE OF ORIGIN IN 3 COPIES ISSUED BY AUTHORIZED INSTITUTION.

7. CERTIFICATE OF HEALTH IN 3 COPIES ISSUED BY AUTHORIZED INSTITUTION.

ADDITIONAL INSTRUCTIONS: 47A

1. CHARTER PARTY B/L AND THIRD PARTY DOCUMENTS ARE ACCEPTABLE.

2. SHIPMENT PRIOR TO L/C ISSUING DATE IS ACCEPTABLE.

3. BOTH QUANTITY AND AMOUNT 10 PERCENT MORE OR LESS ARE ALLOWED.

| Charges | 71B | ALL BANKING CHARGES OUTSIDE THE OPENNING BANK ARE FOR BENEFICIARY'S ACCOUNT. |
| --- | --- | --- |
| Period for Presentation | 48 | DOCUMENTS MUST BE PRESENTED WITHIN 15 DAYS AFTER THE DATE OF ISSUANCE OF THE TRANSPORT DOCUMENTS BUT WITHIN THE VALIDITY OF THE CREDIT. |
| Confirmation Instructions | 49 | WITHOUT |

Instructions to the Paying/Accepting/Negotiating Bank: 78

1. ALL DOCUMENTS TO BE FORWARDED IN ONE COVER, UNLESS OTHERWISE STATED ABOVE.

2. DISCREPANT DOCUMENT FEE OF USD 50.00 OR EQUAL CURRENCY WILL BE DEDUCTED FROM DRAWING IF DOCUMENTS WITH DISCREPANCIES ARE ACCEPTED.

| "Advising Through" Bank | 57A | BANK OF CHINA, BEIJING BRANCH 2 CHAOYANGMEN NEIDAJIE BEIJING, CHINA TEL:010-8512XXXX |
| --- | --- | --- |

******** other wordings between banks are omitted ********

**V.** Examine the following L/C with the following contract to see whether the stipulations in the L/C are exactly the same as those in the contract. If not, please make necessary amendments.

| Item | Wrong | Correct |
|---|---|---|
| S/C No. | 95/4527 | 95/3527 |
| Drawee of the draft | Messrs. Macdnoald & Evans Co. | The First National City Bank New York, USA |
| Credit amount | USD 60,700 (SAY US DOLLARS SIXTY THOUSAND SEVEN HUNDRED ONLY) | USD 56,000 (Say US Dollars Fifty Six Thousand Only) |
| Type of packing | wooden cases | reinforced cardboard box |
| Port of destination | Boston | New York |
| Transshipment | allowed | prohibited |
| Tenor of payment | at 30 days after sight | at sight |
| Time of shipment | on or before 10 July, 2024 | in July, 2024 |

# Chapter 4　Delivery Documents

**I. True (T) or false (F).**

　　1~5: T, T, T, F, T

　　6~10: T, T, T, T, F

　　11~15: T, F, F, T, F

**II. Translate the following into Chinese.**

| In Duplicate | 2−Fold | 一式二份 |
|---|---|---|
| In Triplicate | 3−Fold | 一式三份 |
| In Quadruplicate | 4−Fold | 一式四份 |
| In Quintuplicate | 5−Fold | 一式五份 |
| In Sextuplicate | 6−Fold | 一式六份 |
| In Septuplicate | 7−Fold | 一式七份 |
| In Octuplicate | 8−Fold | 一式八份 |
| In Nonuplicate | 9−Fold | 一式九份 |
| In Decuplicate | 10−Fold | 一式十份 |

Ⅲ. **Examine the following items of commercial invoices presented by the beneficiary, and determine whether they are acceptable ( √ ) , or not acceptable ( ✗ ) ?**

| Letter of Credit | Documents | | acceptable |
|---|---|---|---|
| | Type | Items | /not acceptable |
| Commercial Invoice | I | Without signature of beneficiary | ✓ |
| 5,000 bags bombazine | N | 4,950 bags bombazine | ✗ |
| 5,000 Metric Ton peanut oil | V O | 4,692 Metric Ton peanut oil | ✗ |
| Amount: USD 100,000.00 | I C | USD 110,000.00 (B/E value: USD 110,000.00) | ✗ |
| Amount: USD 100,000.00 | E | USD 110,000.00 (B/E value: USD 100,000.00) | ✓ |
| CIFC5 Hong Kong USD 145,935.00 | | USD 137,638.25 (Total Amount) | ✗ |
| CIF Hong Kong 147,550.00 Freight fee: HKD 10,560.00 Insurance fee: HKD 140.00 | | CIF Hong Kong HKD 147.550.00 Less F HKD 10,560.00 Less I HKD 140.00 FOB HKD 136,850.00 | ✓ |

Ⅳ. **Make a commercial invoice based on the particulars given below.**

| ZHEJIANG ANIMAL BY-PRODUCTS IMP. & EXP. CORPORATION 76 WULIN RD, HANGZHOU, CHINA | | | | | |
|---|---|---|---|---|---|
| **COMMERCIAL INVOICE** | | | | | |
| To: | WOODLAND LIMITED 450 CASTLE PEAK ROAD, KIN. , HONG KONG, CHINA | Invoice No. : | | | |
| | | Invoice Date: | | | |
| | | S/C No. : | 24ZA16IA0019 | | |
| | | S/C Date | MAR. 13, 2024 | | |
| From: | SHANGHAI PORT, CHINA | To: | HONGKONG | | |
| L/C No. : | 281-12-6222571 | Issued By: | HSBC, HONGKONG. | | |
| Date of Issue: | APRIL. 2, 2024 | | | | |
| Marks and Numbers | Number and kind of package description of goods | Quantity | | Unit Price | Amount |

续表

| Z. J. A. B HONGKONG 24ZA16IA0019 C/NO. 1-850 | PACKING IN CARTONS OF 50 PCS EACH. STYLE NO. ZEAPEL01 ZEAPEL02 ZEAPEL04 ZEAPEL05 | 7,000PCS 5,00PCS 5,000PCS 30,000PCS | CIFC5 HONGKONG AS PER INCO-TERMS 2020 USD 0.345/PC USD 0.65/PC USD 1.10/PC USD 0.31/PC | USD 2,415.00 USD 325.00 USD 5,500.00 USD 9,300.00 |
|---|---|---|---|---|
| | TOTAL: | 42,500 PIECES | | USD 17,540.00 |
| SAY TOTAL: | U. S. DOLLARS SEVENTEEN THOUSAND FIVE HUNDRED AND FORTY ONLY. | | | |
| | ZHEJIANG ANIMAL BY-PRODUCTS IMP. & EXP. CORPORATION | | | |

## V. Make a packing list based on the particulars given below.

**COFCO NINGBO CEREALS AND OILS CO. , LTD.**

**PACKING LIST**

| To: | F - I - T FRANCE INTERNATIONAL TRADE 24 AVENUE HENRI FREVILLE 352006 | Invoice No. : | 2024-02-01 | | | |
|---|---|---|---|---|---|---|
| | | Invoice Date: | FEB. 1,2024 | | | |
| | | S/C No. : | | | | |
| | | S/C Date: | | | | |
| From: | SHANGHAI, CHINA | To: | ROTTERDAM NETHERA-LANDS | | | |
| Letter of Credit No. : | 3/0146/35 | Date of Shipment: | FEB. 28,2024 | | | |
| Date of Issue: | FEB. 10,2024 | | | | | |
| Marks and Numbers | Number and kind of package Description of goods | Quantity | Package | G. W | N. W | Meas. |
| N/M | LADIES' JACKETS STYTLE NO. 70019 PO NO. D42067 70016 PO NO. D42067 70094 PO NO. D42067 | 160PCS 320PCS 320PCS | 25CARTONS 50CARTONS 50CARTONS | 230KGS 420KGS 420KGS | 150KGS 300KGS 300KGS | 1.500CBM 3.000CBM 3.000CBM |
| | TOTAL: | 125CARTONS | | 1,070KGS | 750KGS | 7.500M$^3$ |
| SAY TOTAL: | ONE HUNDRED AND TWENTY-FIVE CARTONS ONLY. | | | | | |
| | COFCO NINGBO CEREALS AND OILS CO. , LTD. | | | | | |

# Chapter 5   Transport Documents

**I. Choose the best answer to fill in the blank.**

   1~5: B, B, D, A, A

   6~10: C, B, C, B, B

**II. True (T) or false (F).**

   1~5: T, F, T, T, T

   6~10: T, F, T, T, T

**III. Practical Application.**

   1. Fill in the blank form bill of lading according to the particulars below:

| | |
|---|---|
| Shipper<br>ZHEJIANG LIGHT INDUSTRIAL PRODUCTS IMPORT AND EXPORT CORPORATION | B/L NO. CJ2651<br><br>**PIL**<br><br>**PACIFIC INTERNATION LINES (PTE) LTD**<br>(Incorporated in Singapore)<br>**COMBINED TRANSPORT BILL OF LADING** |
| Consignee<br>TO ORDER OF SHIPPER | Received in apparent good order and condition except as otherwise noted the total number of container or other packages or units enumerated below for transportation from the place of receipt to the place of delivery subject to the terms hereof. One of the signed Bills of Lading must be surrendered duly endorsed in exchange for the Goods or delivery order. On presentation of this document (duly) Endorsed to the Carrier by or on behalf |
| Notify Party<br>ABC TRADING CO., KARACHI | of the Holder, the rights and liabilities arising in accordance with the terms hereof shall (without prejudice to any rule of common law or statute rendering them binding on the Merchant) become binding in all respects between the Carrier and the Holder as though the contract evidenced hereby had been made between them.<br>**SEE TERMS ON ORIGINAL B/L** |

| Vessel and Voyage Number<br>CHANGJIANG V. 231 | Port of Loading<br>NINGBO | Port of Discharge |
|---|---|---|
| Place of Receipt<br>KARACHI | Place of Delivery | Number of Original Bs/L<br>CJ2651 |

| PARTICULARS AS DECLARED BY SHIPPER – CARRIER NOT RESPONSIBLE | | | |
|---|---|---|---|
| Container Nos/Seal Nos.<br>Marks and/Numbers | No. of Container / Packages /<br>Description of Goods | Gross Weight<br>(Kilos) | Measurement<br>(cu–meters) |

续表

| ADH "GOLD ELEPHANT" BRAND WATCH 1-40CTN | "GOLD ELEPHANT" BRAND WATCH QUANTITY OF GOODS: 1,000PCS; PACKING IN 40 CTNS | 640 | 12 |
|---|---|---|---|
| FREIGHT & CHARGES FREIGHT PREPAID | Number of Containers/Packages (in words) FORTY CATONS ONLY | | |
| | Shipped on Board Date: SEP 15, 2024 | | |
| | Place and Date of Issue: NINGBO, CHINA; SEP 5, 2024 | | |
| | In Witness Whereof this number of Original Bills of Lading stated Above all of the tenor and date one of which being accomplished the others to stand void. B/L(3COPIES) for PACIFIC INTERNATIONAL LINES (PTE) LTD as Carrier | | |

2. Fill in the blank form bill of lading according to the particulars below:

| Shipper ZHEJIANG LIGHT INDUSTRIAL PRODUCTS IMPORT AND EXPORT CORPORATION | B/L NO. YB5008 |
|---|---|
| | **PIL** PACIFIC INTERNATION LINES (PTE) LTD (Incorporated in Singapore) |
| Consignee TO ORDER OF APPLICANT | **COMBINED TRANSPORT BILL OF LADING** Received in apparent good order and condition except as otherwise noted the total number of container or other packages or units enumerated below for transportation from the place of receipt to the place of delivery subject to the terms hereof. One of the signed Bills of Lading must be surrendered duly endorsed in exchange for the Goods or delivery |
| Notify Party BLUE SKY HOLDINGS LTD. HONGKONG | order. On presentation of this document (duly) Endorsed to the Carrier by or on behalf of the Holder, the rights and liabilities arising in accordance with the terms hereof shall (without prejudice to any rule of common law or statute rendering them binding on the Merchant) become binding in all respects between the Carrier and the Holder as though the contract evidenced hereby had been made between them. **SEE TERMS ON ORIGINAL B/L** |

续表

| Vessel and Voyage Number<br>SUNFENG V. 188 | Port of Loading<br>SHANGHAI, CHINA | Port of Discharge | |
|---|---|---|---|
| Place of Receipt<br>HAMBURG | Place of Delivery | Number of Original Bs/L<br>YB5008 | |

| PARTICULARS AS DECLARED BY SHIPPER – CARRIER NOT RESPONSIBLE | | | |
|---|---|---|---|
| Container Nos/Seal Nos.<br>Marks and/Numbers | No. of Container / Packages /<br>Description of Goods | Gross Weight<br>(Kilos) | Measurement<br>(cu-metres) |
| BLUE SKY<br>TOYS<br>1–200CTNS<br>L/C NO. LC–515 | GVDU2041118/SEAL 21281<br>TOTAL PACKED IN 200 CAR-<br>TONS<br>TOYS    DETAILS AS PER OR-<br>DER<br>NO. P01009 FOB SHANGHAI | 4,200 | 17.2 |

| FREIGHT & CHARGES<br>FREIGHT COLLECT | Number of Containers/Packages (in words)<br>GVDU2041118/SEAL 21281/TWO HUNDRED CARTONS ONLY |
|---|---|
| | Shipped on Board Date:<br>FEB. 28,2024 |
| | Place and Date of Issue:<br>SHANHAI,CHINA; FEB. 22,2024 |
| | In Witness Whereof this number of Original Bills of Lading stated<br>Above all of the tenor and date one of which being accomplished<br>the others to stand void.<br>B/L(3COPIES) |
| | for PACIFIC INTERNATIONAL LINES (PTE) LTD as Carrier |

# Chapter 6    Insurance Documents

Ⅰ. True (T) or false (F).

   1~6: T, F, T, T, T, F

Ⅱ. Choose the best answer to fill in the blank.

   1~6: C, B, D, C, ABCD, AB

**III. Calculation questions.**

1.

(1) Insurance premium

= CIF×110%×insurance premium rate = USD 9,000×110%×1% = USD 99.00

(2) Value of remedy

= insured amount×damage percentage

= USD 9,000×110%×10%

= USD 990

(3) Value of remedy

= insurable amount×damage percentage

= USD 9,000×110%×(10%−5%)

= USD 495

2.

(1) Total CIF based Invoice Value

= Unit Price ×Quantity

= 2.0×50,000

= USD 100,000

(2) Payable Insurance Premium

= Insurable Amount ×Insurance Premium Rate

= 100,000×110%×(0.4% + 0.6%)

= USD 1,100

(3) FOB based invoice value in USD

= Net Export Income in USD

= 100,000−5,000−1,100

= USD93,900

(4) Net Export Income in CNY

= Buying Exchange Rate of USD ×Net Export Income in USD

= 6.1193×93,900

= CNY574,602.27

**IV. Practical application.**

1. Answer questions based on the insurance policy below:

(1) Invoice No.: INV52148

(2) The Seller: NANJING FOREIGN TRADE IMP. AND EXP. CORP.

318 TIANSHI ROAD NANJING, CHINA

(3) Commodity: LADIES LYCRA LONG PANT

(4) Quantity: 2,400PCS

(5) Unit Price：USD 2/PCS CIF LONDON

(6) Total Invoice Value：FOUR THOUSAND EIGHT HUNDRED UNITED STATES DOLLARS

(7) Packing：PACKED IN SEAWORTH CARTONS, TWO PCS IN ONE CARTON

(8) Shipping Mark：

CBD

LONDON

NOS1-200

(9) Insurance：TO BE EFFECTED BY THE SELLER FOR 110% OF INVOICE VALUE AGAINST ICC(A) AND WAR RISKS SUBJECT TO ICC DATED 2009-01-01.

(10) Time of Shipment：ON OR BEFORE OCT. 20, 2024.

(11) Port of Shipment：NANJING

(12) Port of Destination：LONDON

(13) No. and Date of the insurance policy：OCT. 19, 2024

(14) Place of claims payable in：NANJING (IN USD)

2. Fill in the blank form insurance policy according to the particulars below：

# 中保财产保险有限公司

## The People's Insurance (Property) Company of China, Ltd

| 发票号码<br>Invoice No. | KW-030419 | 保险单号次<br>Policy No. | KC03-85362 |
| --- | --- | --- | --- |

## 海洋货物运输保险单

## MARINE CARGO TRANSPORTATIONINSURANCE POLICY

| 被保险人：<br>Insured： | G. M. G. HARDWEAR & TOOLS IMP & EXP CO. LTD.<br>726 DONGFENG EAST STREET, GUANGZHOU, CHINA |
| --- | --- |

中保财产保险有限公司(以下简称本公司)根据被保险人的要求,及其所缴付约定的保险费,按照本保险单承担险别和背面所载条款与下列特别条款承保下列货物运输保险,特签发本保险单。

This policy of Insurance witnesses that the People's Insurance (Property) Company of China, Ltd. (hereinafter called "The Company"), at the request of the Insured and in consideration of the agreed premium paid by the Insured, undertakes to insure the under mentioned goods in transportation subject to conditions of the Policy as per the Clauses printed overleaf and other special clauses attached hereon.

| 保险货物项目<br>Descriptions of Goods | 包装单位数量<br>Packing Unit Quantity | 保险金额<br>Amount Insured |
| --- | --- | --- |
| HANDLE TOOLS | 350CTNS(42,000PCS) | USD 51,150.00 |

| 承保险别<br>Conditions | 货物标记<br>Marks of Goods |
| --- | --- |
| | |

续表

| ICC(A)and WAR RISKS | | | ZELLERS CANADA/VANCOUVER/ NOS1-350 | | |
|---|---|---|---|---|---|
| 总保险金额：<br>Total Amount Insured： | UNITED STATES DOLLARS FIFTY-ONE THOUSAND ONE HUNDRED AND FIFTY ONLY | | | | |
| 保费<br>Premium | AS ARRANGED | 载运输工具<br>Per conveyance S. S | CHAOHE/ZIM<br>CANADA V. 44E | 开航日期<br>Slg. on or abt | 2024-04-19 |
| 起运港<br>Form | GUANGZHOU | 目的港<br>To | VANCOUVER | | |

所保货物,如发生本保险单项下可能引起索赔的损失或损坏,应立即通知本公司下述代理人查勘。如有索赔,应向本公司提交保险单正本(本保险单共有2份正本)及有关文件。如一份正本已用于索赔,其余正本则自动失效。

In the event of loss or damage which may result in acclaim under this Policy, immediate notice must be given to the Company's Agent as mentioned here under. Claims, if any, one of the Original Policy which has been issued in    TWO    original (s) together with the relevant documents shall be surrendered to the Company. If one of the Original Policy has been accomplished, the others to be void.

| 赔款偿付地点<br>Claim payable at | VANCOUVER | | |
|---|---|---|---|
| 日期<br>Date | 2024-04-18 | 在<br>at | GUANGZHOU（IN USD） |
| 地址：<br>Address： | XXXXXXXXX,GUANGZHOU,CHINA | | |

# Chapter 7   Payment Documents

## I . True or False：

1~5：T, F, F, T, T

6~10：T, T, T, T, T

11~15：F, T, F, F, F

16~20：T, T, T, T, T

## II . Best Choice：

1~5：A,C, A, B, C

6~10：D, C, B, C, D

## Ⅲ. Practical Application.

1.

---

### BILL OF EXCHANGE

凭
Drawn Under — COMMERCIAL BANK OF KUWAIT

不可撤销信用证 18/1234-B/128
Irrevocable    L/C   No.

日期
Date    JUNE 2,2024

支取 Payable
With interest    @    %    按    息    付款

号码
No.   12469

汇票金额
Exchange for   USD 19,458.20

杭州
Hangzhou     JULY 16,2024

见票
at    SIGHT

日后（本汇票之副本未付）付交
sight of this FIRST of Exchange (Second of
Exchange Being unpaid)

Pay to the order of    ZHEJIANG CHEMICALS IMPORT & EXPORT CORPORATION

金额
the sum of    U. S. DOLLARS NINTEEN THOUSAND FOUR HUNDREDAND FIFTY EIGHT AND TWENTY CENTS ONLY

此致
To    COMMERCIAL BANK OF KUWAIT

ZHEJIANG CHEMICALS IMPORT &
EXPORT CORPORATION

签字

---

2.

---

### BILL OF EXCHANGE

凭
Drawn Under — ISREAL DISCOUNT BANK OF NEW YORK,
NEW YORK BRANCH

不可撤销信用证 A-12B-34C
Irrevocable    L/C   No.

日期
Date    NOV. 11,2024

支取
Payable With interest    @    %    按    息    付款

号码
No.   12346

汇票金额
Exchange for   USD 5,390.00

杭州
Hangzhou     DEC. 24,2024

见票
at    SIGHT

日后（本汇票之副本未付）付交
sight of this FIRST of Exchange (Second of
Exchange Being unpaid)

---

| Pay to the order of | ZHEJIANG TEXITILES IMPORT & EXPORT CORPORATION | |
|---|---|---|
| 金额<br>the sum of | U. S. DOLLARS FIVE THOUSAND THREE HUNDRED AND NINTY ONLY | |
| 此致<br>To | ISREAL DISCOUNT BANK OF NEW YORK, NEW YORK BRANCH | ZHEJIANG TEXITILES IMPORT & EXPORT CORPORATION<br><br>签字 |

3.

## BILL OF EXCHANGE

No.   81609D3030

For   USD 738,000.00    2024-12-24, SEOUL, KOREA.

   ( amount in figure )     ( place and date of issue )

At  120 DAYS AFTER THE DATE OF SHIPMENT   sight of this FIRST Bill of exchange (SECOND being unpaid)

pay to  BANK OF CHINA SEOUL BRANCH, SEOUL   or order the sum of

UNITED STATES DOLLARS SEVEN HUNDRED AND THIRTY-EIGHT THOUSAND ONLY

       ( amount in words )

Value received for  630CARTONS  of  CANNED LITCHIS

     ( quantity )    ( name of commodity )

Drawn under  BANK OF CHINA SHANDONG BRANCH

L/C No.  810080000797  dated   2024-11-07

    BKCHCNBJ810    For and on behalf of

   BANK OF CHINA QINGDAO  SUNKUONG LIMITED

To:   ( SHANDONG BRANCH )  ( HSRO ) C. P. O. BOX 1780,

           SEOUL, KOREA.

          ( Signature )

# Chapter 8　Official Documents

**I . Make out a certificate of origin based on the particulars below：**

## ORIGINAL

| 1. Exporter<br><br>KKK TRADING CO. , LTD.<br>HUARONG MANSION RM2901 NO. 85 GUANJIAQIAO,<br>NANJING 210005, CHINA | Certificate No. |
|---|---|
| 2. Consignee<br><br>NEO GENERAL TRADING CO.<br>P. O.  BOX 99552, RIYADH 22766, KSA | **CERTIFICATE OF ORIGIN OF THE PEOPLE'S REPUBLIC OF CHINA** |

| 3. Means of transport and route<br><br>SHIPPED FROM SHANGHAI PORT, CHINA TO DAM-MAM PORT, SAUDI ARABIA<br>BY SEA | 5. For certifying authority use only |
|---|---|
| 4. Country / region of destination<br><br>SAUDI ARABIA | |

| 6. Marks and numbers | 7. Number and kind of packages;<br>description of goods | 8. H. S. Code | 9. Quantity | 10. Number and date<br>of invoices |
|---|---|---|---|---|
| ROSE BRAND<br>178/2023　（1750）<br>RIYADH<br>NOV. 8,2023 | ONE THOUSAND SEVEN HUN-DRED AND FIFTY CARTONS CANNED MUSHROOMS PIECES<br><br>AS PER L/C NO. 0011LC123756<br>L/C DATE：DEC. 02,2023 | 2024. 1011 | 1,750CATONS<br>\*\*\*\*\*\*\*\*\*\*\*\* | NEO20240116<br>\*\*\*\*\*\*\*\*\*\*\* |

| 11. Declaration by the exporter<br>The undersigned hereby declares that the above details and statements are correct, that all the goods were produced in China and that they comply with the Rules of Origin of the People's Republic of China.<br>　　　　KKK TRADING CO. , LTD.<br>　　　　　（signature）<br><br><br>NANJING,DEC. 24, 2023<br>----------------------------------------------------------<br>--------------<br>Place and date, signature and stamp of authorized signatory | 12. Certification<br>It is hereby certified that the declaration by the exporter is correct<br><br><br><br><br><br><br><br>------------------------------------------------------------<br>--------------<br>Place and date, signature and stamp of certifying authority |
|---|---|

**II.** Make out a customs declaration according to the sales contract and letter of credit in problem **I**, and the relevant information below.

中华人民共和国海关出口货物报关单

| 预录入编号： | | | | 海关编号： | | | |
|---|---|---|---|---|---|---|---|
| 出口口岸 | 上海海关 | 备案号 | | | | 出口日期 | 申报日期 |
| 经营单位 | KKK 国际贸易公司 | 运输方式 | 江海运输 | 运输工具名称 | 船舶 | | 提运单号 |
| 发货单位 | KKK 国际贸易公司 | 贸易方式 | 一般贸易 | 征免性质 | 一般征税 | | 结汇方式 信用证 |
| 许可证号 | | 运抵国(地区) 沙特阿拉伯 | | 指运港 达曼 | | | 境内货源地 |
| 批准文号 | | 成交方式 CIF | 运费 | 保费 | | | 杂费 |
| 合同协议号 | UY90 | 件数 1,700 | 包装种类 纸箱 | 毛重(公斤) 17,340. | | | 净重(公斤) 9,261.6 |
| 集装箱号 | | 随附单据 | | | | | 生产厂家 |

标记唛码及备注

ROSE BRAND
178/2024
RIYADH

| 项号 | 商品编号 | 商品名称、规格型号 | 数量及单位 | 最终目的国/地区 | 单价 | 总价 | 币制 | 征免 |
|---|---|---|---|---|---|---|---|---|
| 01 | 202410110 | 罐装蘑菇 | 1,700 箱 | 沙特阿拉伯 | 8.00 | 13,260.00 | 美元 | 照章征税 |

税费征收情况

| 录入员 | 录入单位 | 兹声明以上申报无讹并承担法律责任 | 海关审单批注及放行日期(签章) | |
|---|---|---|---|---|
| | | | 审单 | 审价 |
| 报关员 | | 申报单位(签章) | 征税 | 统计 |
| 单位地址 | | KKK 国际贸易公司 | 查验 | 放行 |
| 邮编 | 电话 | 填制日期 | 2024-04-06 | |

# Postscript(1st Edition)

According to the statistics of OECD, an average overseas transaction involves 35 kinds of documents with a total of 360 copies. Trade documentation and related procedures are an important component of international trade transactions and international trade facilitation system. It is thus of great necessity for international businessman to get familiar with international trade documentation; and for government agencies and international trade facilitation organizations to improve trade documents.

Although there is no substitute for practical experience, this book provides the reader with a solid foundation on which to build further knowledge of the documentary requirements of international trade. The book posses the following characteristics:

1. International

(1) It is written in English language. One of the reasons is that English is the working language of international trade. Mastering the knowledge of international trade documentation in English will help the students lay down a good foundation for their future work. Another reason is that universities in China are now encouraging their professors to teach specialty courses in English, and thus an appropriate text book written in English is expected.

(2) It is governed by international customs and practices, such as Incoterms® 2000, URC 522, UCP 600, ISBP for UCP 600, etc.

2. Comprehensive

(1) It covers all frequently used documents in international trade, including financial documents, commercial documents, official documents and etc. ; and it involves many sectors as banking, shipping, insurance, inspection, customs, etc.

(2) It integrates international trade theories and policies, international trade customs and practices, and international trade techniques and skills.

3. Professional

(1) It is based on information technology. All relevant documents can be transmitted and settled via international system for payment, taking SWIFT, etc. Students will have a proficient level of computer application, including Microsoft word, Excel and some specialized software for international trade documentation and payment.

(2) It produces strong background of international trade specialty. Specialized international trade knowledge is required for issuance and examination of trade documents, and for documents negotiation and payment.

4. Practical

(1) It involves all procedures of international trade practice, including goods delivery, shipping, insuring, inspecting, customs clearing, payment effecting, claim settling, and etc.

(2) It includes issuance, examination, amendment, and transmission of all frequently used documents.

Accordingly, this book may be an appropriate choice for the following potential users: ① Undergraduates majoring in International Trade, International Finance, International Business, and etc. And it might be particularly welcomed by teachers and students in universities encouraging teaching specialty courses in English, or bilingually in Chinese and English; ② People working in the field of international trade; ③ People interested in understanding international trade documentation.

This book covers 9 chapters. Chapters 1, 3, 4, 5, 7 are written by Zhang Ailing (from Beijing Language and Culture University), Chapter 2 is written by Zhang Qi (from Beijing Wuzi University), Chapter 8 is written by Zhang Luqing (from Capital Normal University), Chapter 6 and 9 are written by Jin Jing (from Beijing Language and Culture University).

In writing this book, we've referred to many literatures, which have been or might have not been listed in the references. Hereby, we would like to express our great thankfulness to all writers or editors of the literatures。

In retrospect, we would like to thank Prof. Liu Yuan from University of International Business and Economics (UIBE) and Dr. Luo Fei for their kind recommendation; thank Dr. Liang Huanlei and Qu Wei for providing us with many useful electronic specimens of trade documents; thank Prof. Yao Xinchao from UIBE for his professional answers to our various questions related to the writing of this book. Moreover, we would like to express our gratitude to Tian Yuchun and other editors from Capital University of Economics and Business Press, for their professional and helpful job.

Author

October 2009

# 第一版后记

经济合作与发展组织(OECD)的统计数据显示，每笔海外贸易平均需要使用35种共计360份单据,外贸制单及相关程序已成为决定国际贸易顺畅与否的重要因素。因此,从事国际贸易的商人需要熟悉外贸制单的方法和技巧,国家政府机构和国际性的贸易促进组织则需要完善贸易单据的制作方法,简化并加快其流转程序,提高其使用效率。

国际贸易的务实性决定了没有什么能够替代贸易实战经验,尽管如此,本书将尽可能为读者提供有关国际贸易制单的专业知识和方法技巧。该书的特点可概括为国际性、综合性、专业性、务实性四点。

一是国际性,体现为:

(1)本教材用英文编写。一方面,英语是国际贸易的通用工作语言,学生利用英语学习和掌握外贸制单的知识和技能,可以为将来的工作奠定良好的专业和英语基础。另一方面,近年来国内大学鼓励教师用英语或双语讲授专业课,迫切需要以英文撰写的合适的外贸制单教科书,但国内这方面的教材相对匮乏。

(2)教材编写以国际贸易惯例和规则为指导,无论是 Incoterms® 2000、URC 522, 还是 UCP 600、ISBP 821 等等,它们都是国际上广为接受的惯例与规则。

二是综合性,本书的综合性体现在:

(1)教材内容包括国际贸易中常用的单据,如商业单据、资金单据、官方单据等,涉及银行、运输、保险、商检、海关等多个部门。

(2)教材有机整合了国际贸易理论与政策、国际贸易实务操作技能、国际贸易法律、国际贸易惯例与规则等几部分的内容。

三是专业性,体现为:

(1)首先,外贸制单以信息技术为基础,各类单据通常以电子方式制作,并通过 SWIFT 等国际支付与结算系统进行传递和结算。因此,学生需要熟练掌握计算机文字处理和电子制表,具备专业电子制单软件的操作能力。

(2)其次,正确、完整、及时的外贸单证的制作依赖于扎实的国际贸易理论、政策、实务、法律、惯例与规则等方面的专业基础知识。

四是务实性,内容的务实体现为:

(1)教材内容涉及国际贸易实务中的发货、报验、报关、运输、保险、支付、索赔、理赔等操作环节。

(2)教材内容围绕各类常用单据的开立、审核、修改、流转等实际使用程序进行阐述。

因此,本书比较适合以下读者选用:国际贸易、外贸英语、国际金融、国际商务专业的本科生,特别是鼓励用英语或双语学习专业课的高等院校的学生;外贸从业人员;其他有兴趣学习外贸英文制单的有识之士。

本书共9章。其中,第1,3,4,5,7章由北京语言大学张爱玲博士编写,第2章由北京物资学院张琦教授编写,第8章由首都师范大学张鲁青博士编写,第6章、第9章由北京语言大学金晶博士编写。

在编写本书的过程中,我们参考和引用了许多文献资料,在此谨向已在书中列出或可能漏列的文献资料的作者致谢,正是你们的文献资料丰富了本书的内容。

感谢对外经济贸易大学的刘园教授和罗非博士的热心推荐,感谢梁焕磊博士和曲伟讲师提供单据样本的电子版本,感谢对外经济贸易大学姚新超教授对我们编写本书过程中遇到的各类问题的极富专业性的回答,最后,要特别感谢首都经贸大学出版社的田玉春等各位编辑,谢谢你们为本书出版所做出的辛勤细致的工作。

编者

2009年10月于满庭芳园

# Postscript( 2nd Edition)

Ever since its publication in 2010, the book "Foreign Trade Documentation" has been accepted by many relevant teachers, students and international business people. It is thus of possibility and feasibility for us to publish the 2nd edition of the book.

Firstly, the revision of Incoterms® 2010 and ISBP 745 during the past three years make it essential to update all related contents through the book; secondly, the changing demand from the teaching practice of international trade make it necessary to supplement with some new sections and improve some relevant contents. And all alterations and revisions are for readers' convenience in their comprehension and application of this 2nd edition.

Detailed revisions are as follows:

1. Add SUMMARY (in Chinese) at the beginning of each chapter;
2. Add EXERCISES at the end of each chapter (Chapter 9 excepted);
3. Add KEY TO EXERCISES at the end of the book;
4. Update all contents related to the revised usual customs and practices;
5. Revise relevant references.

The revision is completed by Associate Prof. Zhang Ailing from Beijing Language and Culture University (BLCU). The revision is also encouraged and supported by Prof. Yao Xinchao from University of International Business and Economics (UIBE), and Feng Xiaoyun from Shandong Women's University.

Moreover, we would like to extend our thanks to Editor Zhao Xia and Editor Tian Yuchun from Capital University of Economics and Business Press, for their professional help.

Author

26 August, 2013

# 第二版后记

本书自 2010 年 1 月出版以来,受到了广大教师和学生的认可,得以再版。在本书第一版出版后,国际商会又对 INCOTERMS® 2010,ISBP 745 等国际贸易惯例与规则进行了修订,因此,本书第二版首先围绕相关内容作了全面更新。同时,根据国际贸易教学实践的改革需要,对教材的写作框架和内容进行了增补与完善,从而更加方便读者的阅读、理解和应用。

本书第二版主要作了以下修改:

1. 在每章开始添加中文"内容提要";

2. 在每章(第 9 章除外)正文之后添加"作业练习";

3. 在全书参考文献之后添加"作业练习答案";

4. 更新与新修订的国际贸易惯例与规则有关的所有内容;

5. 补充更新参考文献。

本书第二版的修订,由北京语言大学张爱玲副教授负责完成。修订过程中得到了对外经济贸易大学的姚新超教授、山东女子学院的封肖云老师的鼓励和支持,在此表示衷心的感谢。

第二版的出版,要特别感谢首都经济贸易大学出版社的赵侠编辑和田玉春编辑,谢谢你们为本书再版所做的耐心细致的工作。

编者

2013 年 8 月 26 日

# Postscript (3rd Edition)

Ever since its publication in 2013, the book *Foreign Trade Documentation* (2nd Edition) has been accepted by relevant teachers, students and international business people. It is thus of possibility and feasibility for us to publish its 3rd edition.

In the 3rd edition, we completed our minor alterations to some detailed contents, and corrected few mistakes. In particular, we updated the part of customs declaration form, so as to meet the latest requirements of China's General Administration of Customs (CGAC), who made the Announcement No. (2016) 20 on March 24, 2016, and made it into effect on March 30, 2016.

The revision is completed by Associate Prof. Zhang Ailing from Beijing Language and Culture University (BLCU). The revision is also encouraged and supported by Prof. Yao Xinchao from University of International Business and Economics (UIBE), and Feng Yaopeng, Ph. D. from Beijing Language and Culture University.

Last but not least, we would like to extend our thanks to Editor Zhao Xia and Editor Tian Yuchun from Beijing Capital University of Economics and Business Press, for their professional help.

Author
September 2017

# 第三版后记

本书第二版自 2013 年 10 月出版以来,受到了广大教师和学生的认可,得以再版。

新版对教材的部分内容进行了一些调整,并改正了个别错误。本书重点更新了报关单部分的内容,以更好地适应中国海关报关单 2016 年版本的新要求。

本书第三版的修订由北京语言大学商学院的张爱玲副教授负责完成。修订过程中得到了对外经济贸易大学国际经贸学院的姚新超教授、北京语言大学商学院的冯耀鹏博士的支持和帮助,在此表示衷心感谢。

最后,要特别感谢北京首都经济贸易大学出版社的赵侠编辑和田玉春编辑,谢谢他们为本书再版所做的耐心细致的工作。

编者

2017 年 9 月

# Postscript ( 4th Edition)

Ever since its publication in 2018, the book *Foreign Trade Documentation* (3rd Edition) has been generally accepted by relevant professors, students, and international business professionals.

It is well known that the latest recent years have been experiencing great changes not seen in a century, which bringing severe challenges and risks to the development of international trade. However, the World Trade Report 2023 shows that trade has proved to be a source of security and peace, a driver of poverty reduction, and a critical tool for addressing climate change. And trade costs keep falling as digital technologies facilitate international transactions and economies continue to sign integration agreements.

China, as one of the most significant sourcing and destination country of traded goods and services, has been playing an important role in effectively responding to grave, intricate international trade developments and a series of immense risks and challenges. China has pursued a more proactive strategy of opening up. For instance, China has worked to build a globally oriented network of high-standard free trade areas and accelerated the development of pilot free trade zones and the Hainan Free Trade Port. As a collaborative endeavor, the Belt and Road Initiative has been welcomed by the international community both as a public good and a cooperation platform. China has become a major trading partner for more than 140 countries and regions, it leads the world in total volume of trade in goods, and it is a major destination for global investment and a leading country in outbound investment.

Considering the new changes in the climate of international and domestic trade and the corresponding adjustments in relevant laws, usual customs and practices, and related policies, the 4th edition of *Foreign Trade Documentation* has been revised and reprinted, so as to better serve the high-quality development of China's foreign trade practice, and to meet the teaching and learning needs of professors and students.

In the 4th edition, we completed our minor alterations to some detailed contents, and corrected few mistakes. In particular, we updated all contents related to Incoterms® 2020, ISBP 821, the emergence of RCEP Certificate of Origin, and the suspension of GSP Certificate of Origin, etc.

The revision is completed by Prof. Zhang Ailing from Beijing Language and Culture University(BLCU). During the revision process, we received financial support from the Beijing Language and Culture University Textbook Construction Special Fund (Project Approval No.

23JC05), The revision is also encouraged and supported by Prof. Yao Xinchao from University of International Business and Economics (UIBE), and Feng Yaopeng, Ph. D. from Beijing Language and Culture University.

Last but not least, we would like to extend our sincere thanks to editor Tian Yuchun from Beijing Capital University of Economics and Business Press, for his careful and professional assistance.

Author
January 2024

# 第四版后记

本书第三版自 2018 年 1 月出版以来,受到了广大师生和业界的认可,得以再版。

众所周知,当今世界正经历百年不遇之大变革,这给全球贸易发展带来严峻挑战和重大风险。然而,《世界贸易报告(2023)》显示,贸易依然是世界安全与和平的源泉、是脱贫减贫的驱动力和应对气候变化的关键工具。随着数字技术对国际交易促进的加强以及各经济体签署的一体化协议的继续增多,全球贸易成本不断下降,给全球贸易发展带来机遇。

作为最重要的商品和服务贸易来源国和目的地国之一,中国在有效应对国际贸易发展所面临的一系列严峻、复杂、巨大的风险和挑战方面都发挥了重要作用。比如,中国实行更加积极主动的开放战略,构建面向全球的高标准自由贸易区网络,加快推进自由贸易试验区、海南自由贸易港建设,共建"一带一路"成为深受欢迎的国际公共产品和国际合作平台,等等。目前,中国已成为世界上 140 多个国家和地区的主要贸易伙伴,货物贸易总额居世界第一,吸引外资和对外投资居世界前列,已形成更大范围、更宽领域、更深层次的对外开放格局。

考虑到国际国内贸易形势的新变化和相关法律、惯例、政策的相应调整,为了更好地服务中国高质量对外贸易发展实践,满足广大师生的教学需求,《外贸英文制单》得以修订再版。

新版对教材的部分内容进行了一些调整,并改正了个别错误。本书重点更新了《2020年版国际贸易术语解释通则》(Incoterms® 2020)、《关于审核跟单信用证项下单据的国际标准银行实务》(ISBP 821)、《区域全面经济伙伴关系协定》(RCEP)原产地证书,以及停止发放普惠制(GSP)原产地证书等相关内容。

本书第四版的修订由北京语言大学商学院的张爱玲教授负责完成。修订过程中受到了北京语言大学教材建设专项基金(项目批准号:23JC05)的支持,得到了对外经济贸易大学国际经贸学院的姚新超教授、北京语言大学商学院的冯耀鹏博士的支持和帮助,在此表示衷心感谢。

最后,要特别感谢首都经济贸易大学出版社的田玉春编辑,谢谢您为本书再版所做的耐心细致的工作。

编者
2024 年 1 月